The three field studies in this book provide a psychological and anthropological study of spirit possession in contemporary religious sects in the Caribbean and in Central and South America.

Although the results of the field studies differ, they share a common research plan for collecting and analyzing data. In each case, the following questions are asked:

- How is trance induced?
- What observable changes occur in the individual who becomes a spirit medium?
- How is the trance state sustained and terminated?
- What effect does the spirit message have on these sects and how does it relate to the larger heterogeneous society of which these sub-cultures are a part?

In addition, possession states are not viewed as disconnected performances in a type of religious theatre, but as socially accepted practices with deep cultural roots. For this reason, each study includes environmental, economic, political, and cultural data that are essential to an understanding of these religious sects.

Part One: Spirit-Possession Belief and Trance Behavior in Two Fundamentalist Groups in St. Vincent provides material on two hitherto unstudied religious groups: the Shakers and the Streams of Power Church. Each is described in terms of its organizational structure, beliefs and forms of worship. Shaker rituals of baptism and mourning are emphasized, the latter as a unique sensory deprivation experience.

Part Two: Umbanda Trance and Possession in São Paulo, Brazil offers the first detailed account of spirit possession in the interpersonal relations of the Umbandists. In describing the learning process involved in trance, a clear distinction is drawn between "spontaneous" and "controlled" modes of trance possession.

Part Three: Disturbances in the Apostolic Church: A Trance-Based Upheaval in Yucatán provides the first eyewitness account of the inception, evolution, and dissipation of a crisis cult of millenary orientation within the Pentecostal sect in a rural society of Latin America, focusing on the phenomenon of glossolalia (speaking in tongues) as practiced in this congregation.

Contemporary Religious Movements:
A Wiley-Interscience Series,
Edited by IRVING I. ZARETSKY

Felicitas D. Goodman
Jeannette H. Henney
Esther Pressel

Trance, Healing, and Hallucination

Three Field Studies in Religious Experience

A WILEY-INTERSCIENCE PUBLICATION

JOHN WILEY & SONS, New York • London • Sydney • Toronto

Library of Congress Cataloging in Publication Data:

Main entry under title:
Trance, healing, and hallucination.

(Contemporary religious movements)
"A Wiley-Interscience publication."
Each field study was originally presented as a thesis, Ohio State University.
CONTENTS: Henney, J. H.   Spirit-possession belief and trance behavior in two fundamentalist groups in St. Vincent.—Pressel, E.   Umbanda trance and possession in São Paulo, Brazil.—Goodman, F. D.   Disturbances in the Apostolic Church: a trance-based upheaval in Yucatan.—Bibliography
1. Trance.   2. Spirit possession.   3. Umbanda (Cultus)   4. Pentecostalism.   I. Henney, Jeannette H. Spirit possession belief and trance behavior in two fundamentalist groups in St. Vincent. 1974.   II. Pressel, Esther. Umbanda trance and possession in São Paulo, Brazil. 1974.   III. Goodman, Felicitas D. Disturbances in the Apostolic Church. 1974.

BV5090.T7   291.4′2   74-4159
ISBN 0-471-31390-4

Foreword

It is a particular pleasure for me to be able to present this volume by Felicitas D. Goodman, Jeannette H. Henney, and Esther Pressel. These three studies were first prepared as doctoral dissertations in the Department of Anthropology at the Ohio State University. As the authors' dissertation adviser and the director of a research project of which these studies were an outgrowth, I find their publication to be a matter of personal satisfaction to me. The research project was the Cross-Cultural Study of Dissociational States, supported in whole during the years 1963–1968 by a research grant (PHS MH-07463) from the National Institute of Mental Health; it provided the framework in which the field work was conducted and the findings analyzed. Since the context in which these investigations were carried out may help readers in their evaluation, it may be useful for me to sketch in their common basis in the work of the project and, indeed, the background of the project itself.

In 1962, in collaboration with a physical anthropologist, Dr. Louanna Pettay, now of Sacramento State University, and a psychiatrist, the late Dr. Adolf Haas, I proposed a cross-cultural comparative study of what we have come to call possession trance. My interest in this subject goes back to my own predoctoral field work in Haiti, where possession trance plays a key role in the Afro-Catholic religion known as *vodu*. My Haitian research had raised a number of issues and had made me aware of a significant dearth of comparative studies that might help to resolve them. Following Robert Lowie's dictum, it might have been said with reference to the phenomenon of possession trance that we do not understand ethnographic materials until we understand their distribution. Among the unresolved issues was that of the normalcy or pathology of the possession-trance state. For example, the Haitian physician J. C. Dorsainvil (1931) had seen such behavior as a sign of neurosis, hysteria, nervous instability. Professor M. J. Herskovits, the pioneer of anthropological research in Haiti, considered possession trance "normal" because it was clearly culturally learned. Within the context of Haitian culture it was appreciated and valued. Yet if it was learned, how was it learned? Such learning would appear to be different from that acquired consciously and intentionally.

Are only certain people capable of such learning? Surely something physiological must occur in an individual whose behavior and sense of personal identity are so radically transformed during a period of time. What is it that occurs, and what could we know about it?

In time, indeed, Haitian possession trance has come to acquire a certain notoriety in the anthropological literature. It has been compared with trance in Bali, which Belo (1960) and Gill and Brenman (1961) also compare with the behavior of hypnotic subjects. It has been compared with behavior in the zar cult of Ethiopia by Leiris (1958), who, as well as Metraux (1959), speaks of the histrionic, theatrical aspects of spirit-possession states.

Just what was one to make of this discussion? Is spirit-possession belief, linked to dissociational states (i.e., trance), a worldwide, unitary phenomenon, the same in Bali, in Ethiopia, and in Haiti?

The project, which eventually lasted five years, appeared to be an excellent means of clearing up some of these questions.

The goal of the Cross-Cultural Study of Dissociational States was outlined in our original grant application to the National Institute of Mental Health in the following terms (Bourguignon and Pettay, 1962): "The aim of the present study is the mapping, on a worldwide basis, of institutional types of dissociational states interpreted in native terminologies as due to possession by spirits. . . . The project plan involves the development of a scheme for analyzing institutionalized [dissociational] states along various parameters. . . ." The parameters to be included were biological, psychological, sociocultural, and historical. We saw the significance of this research as, among other things, providing "the basis for problem-oriented field work in this area" as well as "research training for graduate students in anthropological methods and techniques."

It should be remembered that our original proposal was written in 1962. Much has happened since then to place our research into a new, and at that time rather unanticipated, context. In 1962, we were able to say that "in Western societies, dissociational states are usually discussed in a pathological and clinical context; in many other societies, such states are both institutionalized, and culturally rewarded." And although we noted that in the preceding ten-year period psychiatrists, psychologists, and other behavioral scientists had become interested in the effects of drugs on behavior, in the therapeutic uses of hypnosis, in brainwashing and related phenomena, we did not anticipate the coming of the psychedelic revolution; the new charismatic movements in various sectors of Christianity, with their trance states and speaking in tongues; or the rapid growth of a new wave of religious sects derived from Hinduism, such as the Krishna Consciousness Movement or Transcendental Meditation. Nor did we anticipate the drug epidemic of the late 1960s and early 1970s. Yet the signs were all about us. There was then a brief period of experimentation with glossolalia in the Episcopal Church. Timothy Leary and his associates launched the International Federation for Internal Freedom (IFIF), which, in 1963, undertook to sponsor and publish the first issue of the short-lived *Psychedelic Review*. According to an advertisement in the latter, the main purpose of IFIF was asserted to be "to encourage, support and protect responsible investigation with psychedelic substances (e.g., LSD-25, psilocybin, etc.)." At the same time, the *Harvard Review* published a special issue on drugs and the mind, featuring Richard Alpert and Timothy Leary's article on the politics of consciousness expansion. Psychedelic substances were hailed as providing the basis for a new "internal freedom" for man.

In the approach of Leary and his group, synthetic versions of American Indian drugs were brought together with Tibetan and Hindu techniques of meditation in the context of our twentieth-century technological society. Their experimentations had been preceded by those of Aldous Huxley and Henri Michaux.

Much has happened in the intervening years, and what started for us as an attempt to bring order into the dispersed anthropological knowledge on certain types of "odd" beliefs and practices has become of direct relevance in the contemporary scene. As our research developed, as our collection of data increased, and as we began to take stock of our comparative knowledge, it also became clear that what we were dealing with had direct bearing on what was happening on the campus and in the world around us. The subjects of altered states of consciousness (a word barely in use in 1962) and of spirit possession appeared to be everywhere: in religious groups, in the popular books students were reading (e.g., those of Carlos Castaneda), in the movies, and in television programs. Students wanted to learn about drugs, about trance, about what they thought was the occult.

Our initial plan was a relatively small two-year study centering on a comparative review of the literature. This was followed by a more ambitious three-year project including several field studies. Three of these are reported in this volume. In the summer of 1962, while the research proposal was being developed, a graduate seminar in anthropology on the comparative study of trance and possession beliefs was held to explore some aspects of the cross-cultural literature. Esther Pressel was a member of that seminar group, which formulated some initial questions on the basis of a literature survey.

In 1963, when the project was funded, Jeannette H. Henney joined us as a graduate research associate and remained with the project for its duration. She was thus intimately associated with several aspects of our work, particularly the development of our outline (to be discussed) and the coding of a substantial portion of the cross-cultural literature. In a second phase of her work with the project she carried out field work in St. Vincent and analyzed her field data. These formed the basis of her dissertation and of the material presented here.

Esther Pressel formally joined the project as a graduate research associate in 1966, participating in some of the comparative research and familiarizing herself with our findings to prepare for field work in Brazil. Under the auspices of the project she carried out field work in São Paulo and returned to analyze her data.

Felicitas D. Goodman spent several short periods with the project in 1966, 1967, and again in 1968. She helped us first by translating source materials from various languages into English for our collection of comparative data. When Dr. Henney returned from the field with tapes of glossolalia she had recorded in the Streams of Power congregation in St. Vincent, I wondered whether Dr. Goodman might put her linguistic training to use to develop an approach to these materials. Her subsequent extensive work on glossolalia and her field work in Mexico in pursuit of this subject followed as an outcome of this initial attempt to work with materials acquired in the course of our research. Unfortunately, the project was no longer able to support Dr. Goodman's field work in Mexico. Nonetheless, it is a direct and organic outgrowth of our earlier work.

In starting our research in 1963, we began by an extensive review of the ethnographic literature, which eventually covered sources on over 1100 societies. Information on about one-third of the societies proved inadequate, but we amassed data on the presence and sometimes the absence of altered states of consciousness and possession beliefs for some 800 societies. Of these, 488 were societies for which coded data on various societal dimensions were available in Murdock's *Ethnographic Atlas*. Our statistical analyses were focused on this smaller group. (The major portion of the statistical data has been reported in Bourguignon, 1968a, 1973b.) In order to proceed with our survey of the literature, we developed the "Outline for the Cross-Cultural Study of Dissociational States (Trance) and Beliefs in Spirit Possession." This outline went through a number of versions before reaching the form in which it was included in the final report of the project (Bourguignon, 1968a). It was originally intended as a guide for coders of the literature and eventually as a checklist to be utilized in field studies. As such, it provided some common guidance, orientation, and structure to the studies presented here.

A few words about the outline may be in order here because of the influence it exerted on the field work by alerting observers to certain features of the elements under investigation and, perhaps, by stressing some concerns more than others. The formulation of the outline, it should be remembered, was the result of two principal sets of influences: the interests and qualifications of the project members who developed it and the type of data present—or, too frequently, absent—in the ethnographic literature. To begin with, then, our outline was divided into three sections: (1) general summary, (2) belief in possession by spirits, and (3) trance.

If we were to devise such a coding outline now, we would wish to distinguish in the section on belief in possession by spirits those beliefs that are manifested in altered states and those not so manifested, and, in the section on trance, those states and behaviors linked to a belief in spirits and those not so linked. Furthermore, since many societies have more than one possession-trance complex or more than one type of belief in possession by spirits—as well as also some form of trance not interpreted as spirit possession, which we came to call simply trance—the coding of more than one outline would be required per society. We did, however, in our general summary section distinguish between trance interpreted as spirit possession (possession trance) and trance not interpreted as spirit possession (trance). Furthermore, we separated spirit possession expressed in trance (possession trance) from that not expressed in trance (possession). In the literature, we found unfortunately all too often that trance was mentioned without specifying the accompanying beliefs. Similarly, spirit-possession belief might be mentioned, but the linked behavioral manifestations were not clearly specified. If the information could not be inferred from the descriptive materials, we had to exclude the society from our sample. Furthermore, we defined "trance" for ourselves in its overall sense as a general term comporting a variety of possible altered states of consciousness. We attempted to ascertain from the literature which of the following were in fact being reported on: dissociation, fugue, loss of consciousness, physiological collapse, obsessive ideas and/or compulsive actions, hallucinations (visions).

In the second section of our outline, we turned to possession beliefs, and here we wished to know what kind of behavior these beliefs purported to explain. Here we differentiated between "trance" (as subdivided in turn into the six categories noted above); such physical or mental reactions as physical illness, subnormal mental functioning, abnormal mental functioning, and misfortune; sleep phenomena, including somnambulism, sleep talking, and dreams; mediumistic behavior; and finally, impersonations in language, which we referred to as glossolalia.

In the case of mediumistic behavior we were interested in the sex of the medium, in whether or not the medium's message was interpreted by another person, and, if so, in the sex of the interpreter. These questions arose directly out of the various descriptive materials found in the literature. For example, the shaman among the Nuba as described by Nadel (1946) was a man; his message was not interpreted. The Delphic Pythia (Defradas, 1968) and the medium among the Hadjeraï (Fuchs, 1960; Pouillon, 1964) were women, and their messages were interpreted by men. We hoped to collect data on the political role of mediums and to learn which sex dominated this field either by being mediums or by, in effect, controlling the utterances of mediums.

The question of mediumistic impersonations led directly to a consideration of the utterances. Here we utilized the types proposed by May (1956) in his review of glossolalia and differentiated between the following eight categories: *phonations frustes* (mumbling, gurgling, groaning); pseudolanguage; verbal fabrication (neologisms); xenoglossia; spirit language; sacerdotal language; sleep talking; and vernacular speech. This is of course a purely formal, static labeling of possible forms of glossolalia. It does not deal with the subject of the vocal dynamics and psychological processes involved. However, for the analysis of data from written sources, it turned out to be frequently too re-fined to be effectively applicable.

We were, next, concerned with the time depth of possession theories as either traditional or recent in the culture under investigation. Assuming the presence of some manifestations of possession according to whatever the local theory required, we wanted to know whether there was a change over time in the frequency with which phenomena interpreted as possession were being reported. Were they said to be unchanging in frequency or, indeed, did the source simply contain a single case report? Having disposed in this manner of what might be considered the necessary background information, we wanted to know about the cultural context in which possession behavior occurred. Was it part of a diagnostic procedure? If so, who was possessed during this procedure: the diagnostician, the patient (or deviant, or sufferer), or both? Was it part of a therapeutic procedure? Or did it instead (or additionally) oc-cur in quite different ritual contexts: ancestor cult, spirit cult? Did it indeed occur in a nonritual context, that is, were certain sick people or deviants considered possessed, outside a ritual context? Or was spirit possession of some sort thought to be a matter of entertainment? An example of this, which might at first appear an unlikely category, is found in the animal-possession perfor-mances of Java, called *djaren kepang* (Darmadji and Pfeiffer, 1969).

Having located possession behaviors in their cultural context, we wanted to know who the possessed were: by roles, by sex and sex roles, by age—and for each of these categories we wanted to know the relative participation. By con-cerning ourselves with roles, we asked: Do the possessed act as medium-diviner-diagnostician-shaman? Prophet? Curer? Exorcist? Priest-cult leader? Patient-sufferer-deviant? Patient and potential shaman? Potential cult initiate? Initiate or member of a cult group? Visionary? With respect to sex, we wanted to know whether the possessed in a given society were men, women or transvestites; if of more than one sex, which predominated. We sought similar data on the participation of members of one or more age groups. Furthermore, what was the age of first possession? And then, who were the possessed by group status? Were they of high or low rank? Members of minorities or persons with special characteristics—physical, psychological, or moral—and were these attributes positive or negative—were they sinful or, on the contrary, pure?

Having attempted to identify the possessed persons, we sought to identify the possessing spirits: Were they human or animal? Could they inhabit objects other than human beings? Were the theories concerning possession by these spirits part of the total culture or of some subculture? We went to great length trying to identify the possessing spirits and differentiated a dozen categories of spirits of the dead by criteria of social organization, and another dozen of other spirits, including the creator god. We sought to categorize the intentions of the spirits (benevolent, malevolent, etc.), their individual characteristics, if any, their attributes, and their equipment.

The outline continues with a series of other headings concerning the relation between spirits and the persons they possess, behavior during possession, and so on. However, we may stop here for a moment for a few observations. It is clear, for example, how much these types of questions are influenced by familiarity with Afro-American and African, particularly West African, possession trance cults. The questions are relevant to Dr. Pressel's study of Umbanda, where, indeed, there are numerous spirits of the dead, with various characteristics and attributes, where a single person can be possessed by several spirits at varying times, and so on. Umbanda possessing spirits speak largely in the vernacular; they diagnose illness and give advice; they may perform therapeutic functions, but it is the spirit medium who is in possession trance, not necessarily (or ever?) the patient. On the other hand, most of these categories are quite irrelevant to the ecstatic Christian groups studied by Dr. Henney in St. Vincent and by Dr. Goodman in Yucatán. The possessing spririt is the Third Person of the Trinity, the Holy Spirit. A large number of persons are possessed by the same spirit simultaneously; there is no impersonation of the spirit. The Vincentian Shakers say that "the Spirit shakes you"; the Streams of Power adherents speak in tongues and then translate the message by stating, "Thus sayeth the Lord"; and the Yucatecan Pentecostals say that the Spirit "changes your language." Who are the possessed? Among the Christians, those of low status, but—and our categories do not provide for this—they acquire a new status within the groups they have joined or formed. In Brazil they are many different kinds of people—middle range in status, of many ethnic, racial, and even religious backgrounds.

And what are the special characteristics of those possessed? Here our outline appears to switch, or to be uncertain, as to whether we are looking for -emic or -etic categories—that is, categories of the participants or categories of the observers. Are the people who are possessed people of special psychological characteristics? Psychological bias suggests that they are likely to be. Of special physical characteristics? In these studies, there appears to be no clear-cut evidence on this point. Moral characteristics? The Christians say that possession is a sign from the Holy Spirit—a purification. However, conversion may come to the sinful as well as to the pure—or, best, to the repentant sinner. In Umbanda we read of previous lives and karmic illness, of the "need" to develop one's mediumship, but our categories do not seem to provide well for any of this.

I find, as I attempt to apply our categories to the data presented in this volume, that there are some difficulties in such a process of application. These difficulties, moreover, are of crucial importance and significance for anyone wishing to develop a guide for problem-oriented anthropological field work or a set of universally applicable coding categories for a sizable body of comparative materials. The more specific the categories, the more they are tied to the particular configurations of a specific culture or type of culture. Cultural variability and relativity rear their heads, and as we move into unfamiliar societies or unfamiliar aspects of known societies, we find ourselves with native categories and patterns of experience, which cut across those that we have derived from our own knowledge or from familiarity with the societies and cultures we have studied. In every ethnography there is always the new and the unexpected, and thus there is the danger that a set of preestablished categories will cause us to overlook what is before our eyes or will cause us to force the data, if we cannot escape discovering them, into the Procrustean bed of our comparative framework, our hypotheses, and our code sheets.

A good example of what I have in mind refers to certain aspects of our trance outline. Here there is much overlap with the possession outline, for we needed to know how trance was interpreted, who was involved in it, what the cultural context of trance was, and so on. Here it would have been better to separate trance and possession trance, for in the case of possession trance, as in the three studies before us, one finds oneself responding to the same questions under the heading of possession and the heading of trance. A new dimension is reached, however, when we wish to investigate the physical manifestations of trance: How is it induced? What observable changes occur in the individual? How is the trance state terminated? What sequels does it have, if any? Concerning the induction of trance, we did not find the use of drugs of any kind in our three studies. However, there were other processes at work, some of which we foresaw. For example, Dr. Pressel found that "whirling, spinning" was used to induce possession trance in Umbanda; she has described this in great detail and has linked it to the process of learning possession-trance behavior. Although we foresaw a variety of categories for observation, we remarkably neglected (the literature tells us little about this) a process of learning. Learning looms large, too, in the group studied by Dr. Goodman and, in a different manner, those investigated by Dr. Henney.

In listing another group of inducing factors, we recognized the possibility of sensory deprivation as a means of inducing an altered state, yet no further guide lines for observation and questioning are provided by our outline. Dr. Henney found that sensory deprivation was a significant factor in the induction of hallucinatory trance. Here we came to appreciate the difference between possession trance and hallucinatory trance glossed and conceptualized as a spiritual journey.

Our observers, then, were led to look for certain possibilities: sensory deprivation, which appears in one of the three studies; glossolalia, which appears in two of the three; "spinning and whirling," which appears in one. We were primarily looking for possession trance, yet hallucinatory (or visionary trance) occurs in all three contexts. The differences among them are instructive, and the outline prepared us only minimally for them. In St. Vincent, among the Shakers, Dr. Henney found a full-fledged visionary trance complex, termed "mourning," induced under conditions that are strikingly similar to those used in sensory-deprivation experiments.

The "mourning" ritual of the Shakers in St. Vincent has its rules and procedures, its dangers and its rewards. The visions are evaluated by the participant and by the leader, and are a basis for a change in status of the participant. Such a formal ritualization of hallucinatory or visionary trance does not exist either in the Yucatecan Apostolic Church or in Umbanda. Yet both Dr. Goodman and Dr. Pressel tell us about hallucinatory experiences among their people.

In Yucatán, at the height of the "upheaval," some people "saw" the Devil. These visions were not part of a ritual procedure, they surely were not sought, but the belief system of the church members had a place for such experiences; they could easily be integrated into the ongoing process of the "upheaval." Dr. Goodman links this phenomenon of hallucinatory trance to the great arousal of the glossolalia experience and of the religious movement in which the Apostolics were engaged. The experience came at a time of crisis for given individuals and for the group as a whole.

Dr. Pressel also tells us of visionary experiences. In Umbanda, visionary experiences are not part of ritual. Yet the informant who tells of having seen certain spirits in her kitchen reports the matter calmly. There was nothing "wrong" with seeing spirits—it was not a sign of psychopathology. It was, however, a sign that she needed to take certain steps, to join Umbanda. The sign came to her from the outside, from the world of spirits. It was a sign of helpfulness, not a symptom of personal disorganization, as such experiences might be interpreted in a psychiatric context.

Thus, although there is no visionary trance ritual in either Umbanda or among the Apostolics, in both instances there is an ideology, a set of sacred beliefs, into which the experiences are integrated. They are thus "ritualized" and "institutionalized," for they fall within the expected pattern, no matter how frequent or how rare they might be in actual statistical incidence.

In another sense, too, our outline did not prepare us for the findings. The literature, as well as my Haitian experience, had oriented us toward stable religious institutions, although we were aware that culture contact might lead to an increase in the incidence of altered states even in such stable institutions. This may well be the case for Umbanda. However, we had not been prepared for a religious upheaval like that encountered by Dr. Goodman. Indeed, only by visiting a particular group over a series of field seasons—and only by exceptional good luck—does one catch, as it were, a movement like this in statu nascendi. And only by extraordinary good fortune does one have the opportunity of observing such a movement run its full course from preconditions to full bloom to aftereffects. There are few cases in the literature of such a report on a complete cycle.

The studies reported here were influenced by the existence of our literature survey. The field workers were alerted to certain observations and to the asking of certain questions not only by familiarity with the ethnographic literature concerning their particular areas but also specifically by the outline, which served as a set of questions for which answers were sought. Some items could easily be answered, others easily dismissed as irrelevant, and still others could be pursued and, perhaps most importantly, could lead to the discovery of new and unanticipated questions.

The extent to which the resultant studies are different from one another is as important as the fact that they deal consistently with a basically common set of questions. The differences among them clearly reflect not only the individualities of the three anthropologists but also, perhaps more importantly, the differences in the three cultures. It is the cultural differences and the dynamics of the different situations that lead participant observers to consider certain questions, to follow up certain leads, to discover the unanticipated. The importance of serendipity, of alertness to research opportunities must ever be appreciated if anthropological research is to reveal other worlds of experiences and of "reality" to us. For we are not interested only in the specifics of behavior, which can be observed objectively. We must also be interested in the subjective aspects of behavior: What is its cultural meaning? How is it experienced by the individual?

Religion has frequently been discussed by anthroplogists as involving belief and behavior, mythology and ritual, or, in A. F. C. Wallace's terms, as ritual rationalized by mythology. It should be added that there is a third dimension—the dimension of experience, which validates mythology and ritual for the individual and the group, and without which both would remain dead letters.

The three studies before us show the diversity of possession trance in terms of the behavior exhibited, the beliefs to which it is linked, the subjective experiences involved, and the cultural and societal contexts in which it occurs. They also indicate some of the underlying unity of the phenomenon.

There is, for example, clear evidence in all three studies of the importance of learning in the acquisition of possession-trance behavior. Yet the specifics of the physiological processes are not as yet clearly understood. In the three examples at hand a variety of mechanisms of induction are used. There is in all some similarity to hypnosis, but the mechanisms of hypnosis, too, are not as yet clearly understood, so that reference to hypnosis in an explanation of possession trance is tantamount to attempting to explain one "unknown" by reference to another.

The people and groups described in this volume differ importantly from most of those that we used in our statistical sample: they all represent part societies, subcultures within larger complex and heterogeneous societies. Membership in the possession-trance groups is an option, an alternative, a personal decision open to Vincentians, Maya, and Brazilians. Indeed, the particular group they join in each case is only one of several that hold such options for them. In St. Vincent, Shakers and Streams of Power compete, to some extent, for membership. In Brazil, there are many syncretic religious groups with varying patterns of possession trance, including Pentecostalists. Even among the Maya, the Apostolic Church is only one of several that offer Baptism in the Spirit. With respect to such alternatives and to the complexity of their internal differentiations, these societies are quite similar to that of the United States, where a great variety of religious groups and movements of this type are currently available to the seeker of supernatural experiences. How does all of this compare to the rest of the world?

As I noted, our sample of 488 societies is taken from the *Ethnographic Atlas* and consists, for the most part, of simpler, less differentiated societies. And for the most part, too, we have attempted to focus on stable societies, not on religious movements. In this sample of societies, we found that 90 percent have one or more forms of institutionalized, ritualized altered states of consciousness, 74 percent have some belief in spirit possession, and 51 percent have possession trance. The societies described here are thus not at all atypical in having such beliefs, practices, and experiences. The "odd" societies apparently are not those that have patterned trance and/or possession trance. The "odd" societies appear to be those that have not.

These three studies by Drs. Goodman, Henney, and Pressel should make clear the variety of religious patterns and experiences in three developing countries, the forms they take, and the roles they play in the lives of individuals and societies. They add a significant dimension to our understanding of the place of religion in the total fabric of society; they highlight the uniqueness of each culture while pointing to the common human basis of these practices, beliefs, and experiences. They hold up the mirror of comparative explorations to the student of the contemporary American scene as well. Here, as in the three countries discussed in this volume, syncretic, ecstatic religions are flourishing. How similar is their appeal to Americans to the appeal of Umbanda to Brazilians? Of the Shakers and Streams of Power to the Vincentians? Of the Apostolics to the Maya? Can we, too, expect to see religious upheavals? To what extent and in what way do these religious beliefs and practices reveal the basic stresses in each of the societies under discussion?

This book contains some answers. It raises a good many more questions.

ERIKA BOURGUIGNON
The Ohio State University

Series Editor's Preface

The three monographic studies in this book deal with contemporary religious movements in the Caribbean and in Central and South America. These studies exemplify the kind of team research that anthropologists undertake. The researchers were members of a project that was organized and carried through over a number of years. They shared the preparatory work of defining the domain of investigation, surveyed and synthesized the existing literature to generate data-based hypotheses, and then individually pursued field research in three societies to test and develop the hypotheses.

The movements in St. Vincent's Island, the Yucatán peninsula, and Brazil represent the efforts of a collectivity of individuals to institutionalize altered states of consciousness within a social milieu. Spirit possession and trance behavior, manifested in religious rituals and performed by members of the group, are part of all three movements described here. These altered states of consciousness are accomplished by verbal and kinesic techniques and usually in the company of other group members. The institutionalization, ritualization, and stylization of the altered states are the foci of attention of the three studies.

The varieties of religious experience—particularly spirit mediumship, spirit possession, and trance behavior—have throughout this century been of interest to anthropologists working with social communities in non-Western societies.[1] The current spread and development of "religions of experience" in the United States and Europe have made it possible to add new data of ethnographic and theoretical import to our investigations. We are now in a position to undertake more rigorously cross-cultural comparative research on the culturally sensitive topic of altered states of consciousness.

Spirit possession and trance, not being neutral categories to most Western observers, have not always been studied rationally and dispassionately. Our cultural blindfolds have been most visible in the choice of labels, categories, and classification systems used in the analysis of such phenomena observed in Western, industrialized societies. Our professional and methodological difficulties have also been evident in the idiosyncratic approaches to our studies and in our failure to define the significant issues for field observation. Since the first reports of nineteenth-century European travelers in non-Western societies we have continued to demonstrate in part the Achilles' heel of our own socialization. Trance and possession states frequently signal to us our own intellectual ambivalence on such issues as control and loss of control; self-reliance and responsibility versus dependence on others, often on supernatural forces, and the shedding of responsibility; vacillation between being agents or agencies, actors or pawns. This cultural bias, coupled with a religious tradition that deemphasized trafficking with occult practices and the marginal status of ecstatic religion in our own society, virtually shut out this area from systematic professional research. Existing research extracted the material from its religious framework so as to deal with it more comfortably in psychiatric, technological, medical, or pharmacological terms. Though not always reductionism, this was a search for causal determinants of particular behavior. Only recently have we begun to examine such phenomena in their own terms and to reformulate and develop conceptual frameworks that would bridge worldviews in addition to our own and tap the cognitive reality of these practices. It is in that direction that this book may serve as a guidepost.

Although the three studies stem from the anthropologists' joint training and field preparation and their concern with like problems, there are differences among them. The overall framework is similar—possession states are viewed not as disconnected performances in a genre of religious theater, but as integral aspects of a social institution that is supported by a segment of a larger social unit and its cultural background. In all three societies there is a degree of acceptance by the traditional culture, and rules of performance are followed. The three studies differ along several dimensions. In terms of time, the Yucatán example of an "upheaval" is of shorter duration and reached a terminal point that was observed by the investigator. The Brazilian and St. Vincent movements are still extant. In terms of class stratification, the Umbandists (particularly leaders) in São Paulo are classified as urban upper lower and middle class, the Maya in Yucatán as peasants, and the members of the St. Vincent groups as lower-class wage earners. The movements differ in the degree of syncretism they display of indigenous and Christian traditions. The studies also differ in terms of the focus and methodology for field observation. In the case of the Yucatán congregation greater stress was placed on the linguistic correlates of possession—glossolalia— and on tape recording verbal utterances and submitting them to fine-grain analysis.

We need to keep in mind that while the overall research problem was similar, the investigated populations were not chosen for their shared social features to serve as constants that could be controlled and accounted for. Rather, the task that is fulfilled by these studies is a detailed analysis of altered states of consciousness based on explicit and shared definition of terms.

The material presented in this book has significance for comparative studies of similar religious movements in contemporary America. To the degree that we are interested in the institutionalization of altered states of consciousness around which new religious movements are developing, we might usefully look at the relationship between such movements and the relevant sociopolitical units of which they are a part. The significant questions are how developing movements accommodate themselves to secular and religious pressures by their surrounding society and how they maintain the flexibility needed to respond quickly and effectively to them. The Umbandists of São Paulo clearly resemble urban cults in America in terms of the church-and-state issue. The chartering of churches, the certification of ministers, and the securing of rights and privileges of *bona fide* religious bodies seem to be a recurring process addressed by many of these groups. We have only begun to systematically deal with such issues.[2]

Additional areas could be usefully explored. Among them are the socialization and initiation processes into altered states of consciousness and the relevant instruction in occult doctrines; the development and specialized use of language in possession cults; and the role of altered states of consciousness in bringing about social change and personal transformation. Research in these areas will clearly benefit from the studies presented in this book.

IRVING I. ZARETSKY

New Haven, Connecticut
December 1973

1. Irving I. Zaretsky, *Bibliography on Spirit Possession and Spirit Mediumship* (Evanston: Northwestern University Press, 1966).
2. Irving I. Zaretsky and Mark P. Leone, *Religious Movements in Contemporary America* (Princeton: Princeton University Press, 1974).

Contents

           SÃO PAULO, BRAZIL

           By ESTHER PRESSEL

           Preface   113

        1 Introduction   115

        2 Umbanda in the Brazilian Religious Milieu   121

        3 Umbanda in São Paulo   127

        4 Umbanda Centers: Belief and Ritual   134

        5 A Cult Leader   148

        6 The Clique: Cecília, the Leader   159

        7 The Clique: Two Children of Mamãe Oxum   171

        8 The Clique: Two Young Men   184

        9 Trance and Spirit Possession at the Individual Level 193

       10 Umbanda in the Brazilian Sociocultural Setting   207

       11 Conclusions   222

PART THREE   DISTURBANCES IN THE APOSTOLIC CHURCH:
             A TRANCE-BASED UPHEAVAL IN YUCATÁN

             By FELICITAS D. GOODMAN

             Preface   227

          1 Introduction   231

          2 Yucatán   241

          3 The Pentecostal Movement   248

          4 Speaking in Tongues   261

          5 Community and Congregation   269

Trance, Healing, and Hallucination

Part One: Jeannette H. Henney

Spirit-Possession Belief and Trance Behavior in Two Fundamentalist Groups in St. Vincent

PREFACE

The importance of serendipity in shaping a career cannot be overestimated. Who could have foreseen the chain of events that would follow the chance perusal of a university catalog almost twenty years ago? At that time, the full impact of the need for women's lives to be made more fulfilling had not yet hit us—Women's Liberation was unheard of, unconceived, unborn. For some of us, however, who found ourselves in that depressingly unfulfilling housewife-mother situation that occurs in our society when the youngest child has been waved off to nursery school, continuing education became the agency for supplemental life enrichment and enlivenment. As a result, and by a pure stroke

1

of luck, I discovered not only anthropology but also Dr. Erika Bourguignon—a fortuitous set of circumstances that eventually led to my association with the Cross-Cultural Study of Dissociational States and the opportunity to plan and carry out the field research that provided the empirical data for this study.

Many people have contributed, directly or indirectly, to my endeavor. I owe a great debt to Dr. Leo Estel for urging me to enter the field of anthropology, for his help in planning my trip to St. Vincent, one of his favorite islands, and for his interest in my work there.

I cannot begin to thank Dr. Bourguignon adequately for her continuing support and friendship, her always helpful and constructive criticism and suggestions, and her unfailing good humor and encouragement.

To all the Vincentians with whom I came in contact, I want to express my heartfelt thanks for making my visit to their beautiful island such a pleasure. Their courtesy and friendliness were indeed refreshing and welcome. I especially want to thank Miss Nesta Paynter for her interest in my study and for her part in its accomplishment. I also want to acknowledge the cooperation and kindness of Pointer Decausta Blucher of the Spiritual Baptist Church and Brother Henk Huisman of the Streams of Power Church. I offer a special thanks to the members of their congregations who were ever solicitous of my physical and spiritual welfare and who conveyed to me a warm feeling of belonging.

Families are so often called on to bear much of the brunt in undertakings like mine. My own wonderful family was no exception. To them I lovingly dedicate this effort.

1

Introduction

Although popular and scholarly interest in altered states of consciousness has increased tremendously in the past decade or so and although this general interest is being reflected in the amount of literature, both scientific and nonscientific, that is appearing on such states, the subject is far from being overstudied.

My own contribution is one of a "series of highly focused field studies" resulting from association with the Cross-Cultural Study of Dissociational States. I had a number of objectives in carrying out my research. In the first place, I wanted to add to the body of detailed observations of dissociational states. Although the scattered literature on this subject provides many descriptions of behavior during the altered state, few of them describe the phenomenon in much detail, few are based on more than a single occurrence, and many are of little value in making cross-cultural comparisons of such states. My purpose in studying possession trance was to provide a detailed description that was based on careful, systematic observation of many individuals on repeated occasions and would be useful for cross-cultural studies. Trance also occurs in the society that I dealt with, but it does not occur in a group context, and, although I also gathered data on it, the material was derived from informants.

My use of the terms "possession trance" and "trance" is in accordance with the usage developed for the Cross-Cultural Study of Dissociational States: "trance" refers to behavior that may be manifested in a variety of ways— hallucinations, compulsive actions, and the like; "possession" does not refer to behavior, but to theory or belief. In the special case in which a state of dissociation, or trance, is explained or interpreted to result from the entry of a spirit(s) or power into the affected person, we labeled the phenomenon "possession trance" (see also the Foreword to this volume).

Second, I wanted to contribute to the collection of data on Caribbean religion, especially Caribbean Protestantism. Syncretic religions have attracted considerable attention, but the area of nonsyncretic religion in the Caribbean has been somewhat neglected.

3

Furthermore, I wanted to gather information on a hitherto unstudied island in the Caribbean and thereby add to the fund of Caribbean ethnology. The Caribbean has been an area of interest for a number of scholars, but most of the work has concentrated on the larger islands. Many of the smaller islands represent virgin territory for the anthropologist.

Various approaches to the study of dissociational states have been developed over the years. My own material seemed to lend itself well to functional analysis on several levels: social, individual, and psychological.

On the social level, I utilized as an analytic tool Gluckman's (1954) concept of "rituals of rebellion"—the opportunities for ritualistic ventilation and releasing of tensions that pose no threat to the established order, but, on the contrary, contribute to its maintenance. Although Gluckman himself did not apply his concept to states of altered consciousness, others have found it profitable to do so. Grace Harris (1957) has viewed Teita altered states in this fashion. Gussler (1973) has applied the concept to spirit possession among the South African Nguni. I (Henney, 1966) found it useful for the analysis of Luo material. When applied to my data on the Caribbean, where possession trance is a phenomenon of the lower class, subordinated people who exhibit no aspirations in the direction of revolt, the concept helps to clarify the observed behavior.

Lewis (1966) has explored the relationship between states of altered consciousness and the status position of those involved. He argues that "depressed categories" of people may turn to spirit-possession cults, which he terms "deprivation cults." Later, in a more comprehensive study of spirit possession and trance, Lewis (1971: 31–32) develops the concept of amoral "peripheral cults," which may "embrace downtrodden categories of men who are subject to strong discrimination in rigidly stratified societies." Although my data do not wholly agree with Lewis's analysis, his concepts are nonetheless useful and contribute to an understanding of the Caribbean situation.

On the individual level, I have argued that possession trance functions as an "avenue to identity renewal" (Wallace, 1966: 140). In circumstances where individuals are treated as inferiors and are expected to remain subservient (and do), their self-image can obviously suffer. Given an appropriate belief system, possession trance can help to remedy a difficult situation that has few other possible solutions. I have followed Wallace and Fogelson's (1965: 380) paradigm in delineating the components of a possession trancer's identity and in analyzing the dynamics involved in the restoration of a supportable identity image through the mechanism of possession trance.

On the psychological level, I have suggested that possession trance serves a positive function by gratifying the prestige cravings of people who find little opportunity for such gratification in the larger society. Mischel (1958) has argued similarly for the Shangoists in Trinidad.

In analyzing my material I treated trance as an experience in sensory deprivation. This appeared to be a fruitful approach since the physical conditions in which the religious-trance experience occurs are so strikingly similar to those in which formal experiments in sensory deprivation are conducted. By comparing the results in the two situations, certain cultural influences can be identified and evaluated.

The results of these various analytical approaches are summarized in the final chapter.

In ordering my material I have first introduced myself, since all of what follows is filtered through me. Thus in Chapter 2 I give an account of some of my experiences in the field, some of the problems that plagued me, and the culture shock that I had been so sure I would escape. I also describe the methods and the equipment I used, how I was received, and what seemed to facilitate rapport. Next, in Chapter 3, I describe the setting for the study, including a brief historical sketch to provide a base for understanding contemporary patterns of social relations, as well as demographic information and data concerning current political and economic conditions—material necessary for understanding the position and problems of the members of the two religious cults to be examined. Chapter 4 zeroes in on the first of these, the Shakers: who they are, what they are, how they are organized, what their churches and meetings are like, and so on. In Chapter 5 I introduce the second religious group, Streams of Power, a fairly recent addition to St. Vincent. I describe their church, their worship service, and the possession-trance phenomenon as it occurs among them. Since both Streams of Power and the Shakers draw their membership from the lower class, I compare the two to expose the differences in their appeal. In Chapter 6 the two important Shaker rituals, baptism and mourning, are described in detail. Possession trance as it occurs in the Shaker church is treated in detail in Chapter 7, various levels being identified and described. In Chapter 8 Shaker trances, which occur in isolation, are analyzed as sensory-deprivation experiences. In Chapter 9 we look beyond the island to see what similar cults exist in the Caribbean and attempt to analyze some of the influences that have produced similarities and differences. Finally, in Chapter 10, after looking at what is happening elsewhere in the Caribbean, we return to examine the functions performed by Shakerism for the individual and for the society.

2

Field Work

My first impression of St. Vincent was of smiling, friendly, helpful people. I had read about this "friendliest island" in the Caribbean in travel literature, but had expected to find this an advertising overstatement. The initial impression persisted, however, and remained unchanged when I returned to the island several years later.

I had been working with the Cross-Cultural Study of Dissociational States, and when funds were made available for several field research projects, mine was one of them. The choice of locale depended on a number of considerations, among them the general interest in the Caribbean that prevailed among the anthropologists at Ohio State University, the lack of information on the smaller Caribbean islands that we were finding as we gathered data and mapped the distribution of dissociational states cross-culturally, and the fact that we were looking for an island that had not previously been studied, but that we knew had institutionalized dissociational states. St. Vincent seemed made to order: a small island in the Caribbean, offering the opportunity for pioneer work since it had not been studied by anthropologists, and having, as we knew from communication with a colleague, Bette Landman, a religious group that had only recently been given legal status and incorporated dissociational states into its system of beliefs and practices—the Shakers, or Spiritual Baptists.

In making preparations for leaving I corresponded with the proprietress of a recommended guest house located on the outskirts of the capital city of Kingstown and arranged for housing and meals. I also had some profitable correspondence with Professor Frances Henry of McGill University and Professor George Simpson of Oberlin College, who graciously provided me with a copy of a paper of his, then in preparation—"Baptismal, 'Mourning,' and 'Building' Ceremonies of the Shouters in Trinidad," which proved to be very useful in the field.[1] As I assumed that Trinidadian Shouters (also Spiritual Baptists) would bear a strong resemblance to St. Vincent Shakers, I packed copies of books and articles on the Shouters by G. E. Simpson as well as M. J. Herskovits and F. S. Herskovits. I also packed a copy of the outline devised by the personnel of the Cross-Cultural Study of Dissociational States

6

for facilitating the recording of observations on dissociational states. I bought a supply of film for my 35mm camera. I vacillated between taking and not taking a tape recorder and finally left it behind because it was bulky and heavy—a mistake, I soon discovered, but fortunately one that could be rectified. I saw my doctor, who gave me prescriptions for malaria pills, even though St. Vincent had no problem in this regard; a broad-spectrum anti-biotic, "just in case"; several other remedies for difficulties he thought might occur; and all the "shots" he considered appropriate. Finally, I bought several different kinds of insect repellent. I was uncertain about what to expect—my only prior visit to the Caribbean had been to Cuba, more than 25 years before.

From accounts by other anthropologists I have since discovered that many of my reactions and some of my experiences that seemed unique to me were not unique at all. Others also approached the undertaking with mixed feelings— eager and excited at the prospect of going, but, at the same time, apprehensive and anxious. I knew that there were Spiritual Baptists on the island and that they experienced dissociated states, but how would they accept me, if at all? I knew what kinds of information I wanted to collect, but how willing would they be to cooperate?

When I arrived in St. Vincent on a late Saturday afternoon in June 1966, I began working at once, asking questions and taking notes during the taxi ride from the airport to the guest house. In the evening, I had a long conversation with the proprietress of the guest house and found her to be intelligent, per-ceptive, and a veritable gold mine of information about the island and its people. Although her own prejudices were unconcealed—she was surprised that anyone would want to study the Shakers when there were so many other possible topics—she was able to rationalize my position to her satisfaction: since Shakerism is "part of what the people do, it should be studied and recorded." And the laundress for the guest house was a member of a Shaker congregation! At the end of my first day, I was full of optimism.

The next morning, I set out to become acquainted with Kingstown and its environs. However, on the way down the steep hill into the city, I slipped and fell, injuring my pride and self-confidence, and my foot. For the next couple of weeks I went to the hospital regularly to have the infected wound dressed, blessing my doctor for his foresight in giving me an antibiotic that was unavailable on the island, but worrying constantly about my work since I was relatively incapacitated. I became more and more depressed. Inconveniences that had seemed unimportant in my initial exuberance now assumed major proportions: the single bathtub for the total guest-house population; the extremely limited supply of water for bathing—and that, cold; the lack of pri-vacy—walls being mere partitions about 8 feet high with an open space at the top; the heat and humidity and rain; the insects; and so on. I, who could not remember ever having experienced it before, was homesick—desperately, miserably homesick.

I wrote to my children, parents, and friends, spending hours composing limericks to include in my letters, trying to express my woes humorously—but express them nonetheless. [Later I found that Hortense Powdermaker (1966: 105) had also written limericks in the field as an escape.] The day that brought mail from home was a red letter day, and I looked forward to it as a child looks forward to Christmas.

Slowly the situation improved. My injury was healing, and I was able to move about more comfortably. My whole outlook brightened, and as I took stock of what had seemed to be an interminably long and unproductive first two weeks, I was amazed at how much I had been able to accomplish. I had become well acquainted with the personable taxi driver who took me to and from the hospital. He belonged to the Streams of Power church, where glossolalia was an important feature of the worship service, and had already taken me to two of the Thursday evening services and one Sunday morning service. I had met some of the other members of the church and the evangelist, and was beginning to feel at home with them. I had had a number of fruitful conversations with guest-house personnel, especially the laundress, who had taken me to my first Shaker service in the church she attended at Lowmans, several miles from Kingstown.

This first encounter with the Shakers seemed to me, at the time, to be little less than a fiasco. My interest in the Shakers apparently had a contagious quality. The guest-house proprietress knew about the cult only through hearsay. When she was a child, her father, who was headmaster of a school, forbade his family to watch their then illegal services. So her curiosity had never been satisfied. Her employer (in addition to operating a hotel, she also had a part-time job in the city), an English woman, also became quite interested in the Shakers. When the time came for my first visit to the church, both women decided to accompany me. The confusion we caused that evening was equaled only by the havoc caused by the elements. When we arrived at the little church made of interlaced branches roofed with palm, the members scurried off to nearly houses to find suitable chairs for us to sit on, placing them near the altar facing the congregation. That our presence was a novelty was obvious from the stares we elicited and from the sermonizing in which we were referred to, for example, as "three angels," mention also being made of our "pink and white and beautiful faces."[2] The wind was high that evening and blew through the cracks in the walls, making it difficult for the worshipers to keep their candles (except for a small lantern, they were the only source of light) lit. The rain leaking through the roof caused further turmoil. The members kept moving our chairs, trying to find dry spots for us, so we finally put up our umbrellas. No one became dissociated during the service. Whether there was a sufficient deterrent in our presence, in the weather that kept everyone so busy, or in a combination of both, I have no way of knowing. However, at every other Shaker meeting I attended worshipers became dissociated.

My original plan had been to look for a Shaker church to study in Kingstown since transportation around the island is difficult and expensive. However, after my first visit to the church at Lowmans, I decided that, in spite of its distance from the city, I would concentrate my efforts on that particular congregation. I had been well received; I could expect my association with the laundress as informant to last throughout my stay in St. Vincent; and I was told by several interested non-Shakers that I was making a wise choice because the head of that congregation, Pointer[3] B., was one of the most respected and active Shaker pastors on the island. He had several other churches under his direction and seemed not only willing but eager to have me attend his services.

For the rest of the time that I was on the island, then, I attended almost all of the regular meetings of the Lowmans congregation. I also attended meetings of Pointer B.'s churches at Questelles and Chapmans Village, and meetings that were held by his various congregations for special purposes, such as blessing a house, celebrating a Forty Days Memorial, or laying a mourner "on the ground." A non-Shaker informant, Mr. S., an attorney who had risen from lower class beginnings, was instrumental in introducing me to the heads of two other Shaker churches. Word of my presence on the island and my specific interest in Shakerism had spread, and they were both eager to have me attend their services, which I did. Furthermore, on one occasion, in the course of a Sunday afternoon tour of the island, I happened upon a Shaker group holding a service in the middle of a road in a small village. I stayed to observe the meeting, and since it was held out of doors, I proceeded to take some pictures. When it was over, the pointer approached me, looking very serious, and I expected him to admonish me for photographing a religious service. However, he had a request to make. Would I take his picture with his open Bible and send him a copy? I was happy to comply and, after sending him the photograph, I received a thank-you letter from him.

During my first few visits to Shaker churches, I made no attempt to do more than observe as attentively as possible and take detailed notes. I was well acquainted with the literature describing dissociational states, many of which were violent and dramatic enough to be unmistakable; I had also witnessed a Macumba meeting in Brazil. However, when I first witnessed Shaker services, the dissociational states, in some cases and at a certain level (see Chapter 8), were so mild and controlled that I was uncertain as to whether or not the performers were, in fact, dissociated. Close and repeated observations were required to make me confident of my judgment.

After the novelty of my presence at the meetings had worn off and I was more or less taken for granted by the worshipers, I asked the pointer if he would object to my taking pictures during the meetings. I warned him that I would have to use flashbulbs, but he was quite pleased and assured me that I could photograph anything or anybody I wanted to. With his cooperation, I was able to record the facial expressions and postures of Shakers in both dissociated and normal states. Inadvertently, I discovered that a flash served as a test for levels of possession trance: a flash was sufficient to distract a person whose possession trance was not very deep, but it was unheeded by an individual at a deeper level.

More and more I regretted the lack of a tape recorder. Not much selection in tape recorders was available on the island, but I was able to find one that seemed suitable. As the pointer was more than willing to permit its use during services, I was able to record sermons, testimonials, songs, prayers, and, most important, the sounds of dissociation.

When I went to Shaker meetings, I followed some of their practices and observed some of their forms, but not all—I remained a participant observer, participating to a certain extent, but making no attempt to become an insider. I complied with their taboo against uncovered female heads. I bought a hat and was scrupulous about wearing it in their meetings, with one exception. On a rainy Sunday afternoon, I arrived at a meeting already in progress in a member's house. The tiny living room was crowded, so I entered by the back door, intending to stand with the other worshipers in the kitchen. I had taken off my rain coat and hat to shake them, when I was invited into the living room. A chair had been vacated for me next to the table serving as altar. I hurried to accept, trying to be inconspicuous as I squeezed past people and stumbled over their feet, completely forgetting that my head was not covered. I had been hardly seated when the pointer's wife pushed my hat down on my head with some force. From people who had always been courteous and respectful, the gesture was not only an eloquent reproof but also an indication of the importance of this particular norm to them and their consequent concern for me. When I apologized later for my oversight, the pointer's wife was flustered, but seemed relieved that I was not angry. I did not observe the taboo against wearing shoes in the meeting, but I was not alone—others also left their shoes on, and there were no repercussions.

When the worshipers stood for a hymn, I stood; when they sat down, I sat. When they performed their handshaking ritual, I accepted their handshakes, but I did not march around the church. When they knelt for a prayer, I remained seated with bowed head. I did not join in the responses nor in the hymns. I had not memorized the hymns as many of the Shakers had, I did not have a hymnal during my first visits to the church (nor did anyone offer me

one as members of the Streams of Power congregation were to do, and this led
me to believe that they did not expect me to participate in the singing), and I
was too busy watching, listening, and taking notes. When I did acquire a
hymnal and prayer book later, I had also burdened myself further with the
camera and the tape recorder.

I was aware that, willingly or unwillingly, witnesses to mass dissociational
states could be drawn into them,[4] and I had felt some apprehension that I, too,
might succumb. However, I never became dissociated, nor did I ever feel the
slightest urge to let myself go. [I have since enviously read Goodman's account
(1972a) of her experience and regret now that I cannot provide an account of
my personal subjective reactions as she does.] In informal moments, my
Shaker friends confided that they found the prospect of my "shaking" hilarious
and that they watched me in the meetings—hoping.

I have regretted that I did not have an assistant, but I did not have sufficient
time to select and train one. My technological devices seemed to be as much a
hindrance as a benefit. It always seemed that I was missing the best pictures
when I had to change flashbulbs. The tape always seemed to run out at the
very moment that the sounds of dissociation reached on optimum point.
Furthermore, I always seemed to miss taking notes I felt I should be taking because I was occupied with my other equipment. A sensitive, intelligent
assistant could have alleviated many of these problems.

An assistant might also have been helpful in decoding the language. English
is the language spoken on the island, no African dialect having ever been used
(Duncan, 1963: 29), but the Vincentians, and particularly the lower class Vincentians, speak English with a pronunciation, cadence, and choice of vocabu-
lary that make it sound very strange to someone accustomed to American
(Ohio) English and frequently unintelligible. For example, an informant told
me that when a person becomes a pointer, "the Holy Spirit give you a belt,
basin, towel, bell, Bible, and gong." For several weeks I watched attentively
for the gong and finally asked when I would see it. My informant said that the
pointer would wear his long, white *gown* at the baptism service. It had not occurred to me to question the word since I was unaware that I had misunderstood. I often did ask informants to repeat something more slowly or to explain
what they had said. However, at times, even after an explanation had been
given, I remained confused. On one occasion the pointer was talking about
"idolatries." The word did not seem to me to be appropriate, and noticing
that I was puzzled, he undertook to explain it. "Nobody in here knows
nothing about idolatries? When you see a sister have a book and you no have
it. You want it. You be corrupt. This is idolatries." I found sermons and
prayers in the church more difficult to understand than conversations with informants, partly, perhaps, because I was unable to see or watch their faces and

lips as closely and partly because I was more concerned with observing the worshipers in the church.

Pointer B. was very helpful in introducing me to the various members of his churches and in giving my presence and my actions his approbation and endorsement. Following his lead, the members were friendly, open, and receptive. I visited some of them in their homes to obtain interviews, and on occasion, they visited me. I also visited some of them at work. And I met and conversed with them on various casual occasions. Although I influenced the direction of the conversations to a certain extent, I did not work from a rigid schedule of questions—interviews of the open-ended variety seemed to me to be the most productive. The Shakers whom I interviewed were enthusiastic about their religion. They found my interest in it and in them curious, but gratifying, and they seemed to enjoy having an audience. I had introduced myself to them as a teacher who intended to write about their religion, and they were eager to contribute material.

On four occasions I hired a car for the day and arranged an excursion into the country, taking as many passengers as the car would hold. (I had no difficulty finding people to accompany me—they seemed to regard it as a privilege.) My expressed purpose was to visit other Shaker churches and meet other pointers, but I was also in a position to learn much from the informal conversations. I always carried the camera, and my guests enjoyed posing for informal snapshots (I later sent them copies of all their pictures); and I took the tape recorder so that they might hear the recordings I had made of the meetings. They thoroughly enjoyed the tapes, listened attentively, and joked about various individuals (including themselves) they were able to identify.

It was also my practice to hire a car to take me to the church meetings, and usually several church members asked to ride with me. Such trips lasted from about 20 minutes to as long as an hour one way, depending on the location of the meeting, and again provided an opportunity for me to "listen in" as well as to participate in the conversations.

In addition to my Shaker informants, I talked to other Vincentians who were not Shakers. They represented various socioeconomic and religious backgrounds, and from them I gained, among other things, some concept of the attitudes of the rest of the society toward Shakerism. I also visited non-Shaker churches; I attended services and special programs at the Anglican and Methodist churches in Kingstown. Furthermore, I attended a number of meetings of Streams of Power, a healing cult that had recently been introduced from Holland. Since the meeting times of the Streams of Power church rarely coincided with those of the Shakers, I tried to take full advantage of this unexpected bonus. As I had done with the Shaker pointer, I asked the Streams of Power evangelist for permission before taping services. I repeatedly observed the phenomenon of speaking in tongues as it occurred among the Streams of Power adherents and recorded numerous examples of it on tape. This material has been analyzed by Goodman (1968; 1972a,b). I also interviewed the evangelist and some of the members of his church.

After returning home, I was able to maintain contact with both the Shaker and Streams of Power churches through correspondence. I have been informed of important happenings, such as baptisms and the building of new churches. Several of my informants have advised me about personal events in their lives and have exchanged gifts and Christmas cards with me. When I returned to the island several years later for a short visit, it was gratifying to find that my friends had remembered me and to be so warmly welcomed.

As I look back over my total experience, certain factors stand out as having been particularly useful to me in establishing rapport with the various groups I encountered. The fact that I had lived in Brazil for several years was useful. My Protestant background was helpful: I was familiar with traditional forms and rituals, and in the Streams of Power church, Catholics are regarded with a certain amount of hostility. Being a woman, a widow, a mother, and a brand new grandmother gave me a number of advantages in the field. I was able to relate to women of many different ages and statuses, but, at the same time, I did not feel that my relationships with men were impaired. In some islands, being white in a predominantly nonwhite population might have created barriers, but in St. Vincent I met with no resentment because of my race. In some ways, I felt that my being white, and middle-class, and American was prestigious and advantageous. Certainly, these attributes conveyed prestige to the Shaker congregation I had chosen to associate with vis-à-vis other Shaker groups.

The Shakers themselves arrived at the clearest and most picturesque statement of our relationship. At first bewildered by my interest in them and unable to comprehend my continuing presence, one Shaker woman finally arrived at a solution that others accepted. She gave me an identification that made sense in terms of their beliefs, an identification that they could understand and that provided justification for my actions and their reactions: I was, she said, St. Veronica. This placed me in a class apart from them, yet explained my concern for them and demeanor toward them. I was one of them, yet not one of them—in other words, a participant observer?

NOTES

1. Later published in the *Journal of American Folklore* **79**: 537–550, 1966; and in *Religious Cults of the Caribbean: Trinidad, Jamaica, and Haiti,* Caribbean Monograph Series, No. 7, Institute of Caribbean Studies, University of Puerto Rico, 1970.

2. The proprietress of the guest house was not extremely dark, but not white either. See Lowenthal (1967) for the application by Vincentians of the term "white" to individuals who mix with whites.

3. "Pointer" is the title given to the head of a Shaker church.

4. See Maya Deren's account cited by Wallace (1966: 142–143) as well as accounts of the Kentucky Revival (e.g., Davenport, 1965: 205–210).

3

The Setting

The island of St. Vincent lies in the Caribbean Sea about 100 miles west of Barbados and 170 miles north of Trinidad. It is small—11 miles wide and 18 miles long—and mountainous. A volcano, Mt. Soufrière, presently considered semidormant (although it caused some anxious moments in the spring of 1972), is a prominent natural feature. Soil is quite fertile, and rainfall is adequate. A number of small rivers flow down the mountainsides. An average temperature of about 80° F prevails; only rarely does the temperature rise above 90° F (Duncan, 1963; Great Britain Colonial Office, 1966).

Columbus discovered and named St. Vincent in 1498, but many years passed before Europeans made any attempt at formal colonization.[1] Spain gave the islands of the Lesser Antilles little attention. They lacked riches. They were thickly forested, which prevented the Spaniards from raising cattle as they were able to do in, for example, Hispaniola. Moreover, they were occupied by the redoubtable Carib Indians, who were, according to Barbet in 1732 (Burns, 1954: 44–45),

> . . . bloody and inhuman man-eaters, and as such were dreaded by the inhabitants of the great islands of Cuba, Hispaniola and Jamaica, who were harmless people, and on whom they prey'd, coming over in piraguas or great canoes and carrying off many of them to devour.

The first English efforts at colonization in the Carribbean were made during the early years of the seventeenth century. In 1627, the English king granted to the Earl of Carlisle proprietary rights over the "Caribees Islands," which included St. Vincent. However, the French claimed the same islands on the basis of a grant made by Cardinal Richelieu in 1626 to d'Esnambuc, founder of the French colony on St. Kitts. A few French and English colonists settled on St. Vincent during this period. The French, who were more numerous than the English and more adept at establishing friendly relations with the Caribs, settled at the site of the present capital, Kingstown, and along the Leeward coast, where French place names have persisted to the present.

In 1660, the French Captain-General of St. Kitts made a treaty with the Caribs, giving them the rights to Dominica and St. Vincent in return for the repudiation of Carib claims to other islands. In 1668, several Carib chiefs on St. Vincent and St. Lucia agreed to a treaty acknowledging their allegiance to England. Meanwhile, the French and the British continued to dispute ownership of St. Vincent.

The first Negroes arrived on St. Vincent when slave ships were wrecked offshore in 1635 and again in 1672. Occasionally they were joined by escaped slaves who had been able to make their way from other islands in canoes or rafts (Bastide, 1972: 77). These Negroes, who had slipped out of European hands, intermingled with the Caribs, producing the hybrid offspring known as Black Caribs. The first Negroes with slave status arrived some years later, about 1720, when French planters from Martinique brought their slaves with them when they settled in St. Vincent (Duncan, 1963: 3). By 1764 there were 1300 French settlers and 3400 slaves on the island (Burns, 1954: 485 note).

Conflict involving the English and the French and/or the Spanish continued intermittently throughout the eighteenth century. The treaty of Aix-la-Chapelle in 1784 provided again for St. Vincent's neutrality, and the French and British were to evacuate their citizens and leave the island to the Caribs. But in 1763, the Treaty of Paris gave the island to the British. The French took St. Vincent during the American Revolution, but it was returned to the British by the Treaty of Versailles in 1783.

In an uprising in 1795, Caribs, with French help, took over most of the island. After putting down the rebellion, the British effectively eliminated the troublemakers: they deported 5080 Black Caribs to Roatan in the Bay of Honduras. The "Red" Caribs had not been involved in the fighting and were allowed to remain. Carib lands were sold or granted as rewards for service, and the remaining Caribs were sent to live in the extreme north of the island (Duncan, 1963: 23). By the 1920s only one pure Carib family was left in St. Vincent (Great Britain Colonial Office, 1966).

The nineteenth century was a period of peace and economic development. Sugar had been introduced to the Caribbean by Columbus and, by the end of the seventeenth century, had become the most important crop in many of the islands. But a sugar-based economy provided little room for a small-scale planter; for maximum profit, sugar had to be grown on large estates and manufactured on a large scale, which in turn required a large work force. Since immigration of white settlers and white indentured servants did not provide adequately for the increased labor requirements (Goveia, 1965: 105), the demand for African slaves increased rapidly. Concern then developed as a result of the ever-growing numbers of Africans in the islands and prompted the passage of "deficiency laws" requiring the maintenance of specified ratios of Caucasians to Blacks (Ragatz, 1928: 8).

Sugar growing, although attractive, was a hazardous and unpredictable undertaking, and "of those who engaged in the 'West Indian lottery' not one in fifty drew a prize" (Mathieson, 1926: 3). The crop was not only susceptible to an array of natural perils, but the capital needed for large-scale production was of such magnitude that operating on credit was an inevitable development, and economic depressions no less inevitable. St. Vincent was affected as much as, or more than, other West Indian islands (Carmichael, 1833, I: 63; Ragatz, 1928: 327).

The first Christian religious influence in St. Vincent had been introduced by Roman Catholic priests; one was working among the Caribs as early as 1700. With English rule, however, Catholic activities were restricted, and the Church of England became the established church. However, it catered only to the free, white, upper class, to which the clergy themselves frequently belonged (Goveia, 1965: 265–266), and in St. Vincent the slaves were not even permitted to enter the Anglican Church (Duncan, 1963: 37). Ragatz (1928: 21) has observed that "the Established Church in tropical America . . . failed sadly both as a religious and a cultural force due to the combination of inferior representatives and general indifference on the part of the planter class." Only with the coming of the Methodist missionaries was Christianity directed toward the slave population in St. Vincent—a situation very different from that prevailing in the Catholic islands.

The Methodist movement, begun by John Wesley, a Church of England clergyman, was dedicated to the attempt to recapture life according to the precepts of the Primitive Church through fasting, praying, meditating, and searching to know the Divine Will, and had been making rapid gains in Great Britain during the second quarter of the eighteenth century—"more people in the country took their religion seriously than at any previous period since the Reformation" (Bowen, 1937: 255). Wherever he preached, Wesley provoked unusual reactions in his listeners. As quoted by Bowen (1937: 249), he took note of scenes in which some of his audience.

> . . . began to call upon the Lord with strong cries and tears; some sank down and there remained no strength in them, others exceedingly trembled and quaked; some were torn with a kind of convulsive motion in every part of their bodies, and that so violently, that often four or five persons could not hold one of them. One woman greatly offended, being sure they might help it if they would; she also dropped down in as violent agony as the rest.

Methodism reached the West Indies in 1760 when Nathaniel Gilbert, the speaker in the House of Assembly in Antigua, began teaching the Gospel to the slaves. Influenced by Wesley when in England, he had been baptized together with ten of his slaves. He returned to Antigua "full of holy zeal"

(Thomas Jackson, 1839: 100; Ragatz, 1928: 29). The first Methodist missionaries from England under the direction of Dr. Thomas Coke arrived in the West Indies 27 years later; Dr. Coke placed one at Antigua, another at St. Vincent, and a third at St. Kitts. In contrast to the Anglican clergy, the Methodist missionaries were "men of no fixed status in the close-knit white community" (Goveia, 1965: 273), which made them peculiarly suitable for the task of promoting Methodism as "the religion of the blacks" in the West Indies (Garcia, 1965: 220).

Apparently the intense religious excitement that had distinguished the Methodist congregations in Great Britain was also likely to occur among the New World Methodist audiences. In St. Eustatius, a slave

> . . . who had been a member of the Methodist Society in America, had taken to exhorting in that island, and had been silenced by the governor, because the slaves were so affected at hearing him, that "many fell down as if they were dead, and some remained in a state of stupor during several hours." Sixteen persons had been thrown into these fits in one night. (Southey, 1925: 272.)

In Antigua, where converts to Methodism were increasing,

> . . . a symptom appeared of that enthusiasm of which it is so difficult for Methodism to clear itself, sanctioned as it had been by Wesley. At the baptism of some adults, one of them was so overcome by her feelings that she fell into a swoon; and Dr. Coke, instead of regarding this as a disorder, and impressing upon his disciples the duty of controlling their emotions, spoke of it as a memorable thing, and with evident satisfaction related that, as she lay entranced with an enraptured countenance, all she said for some time was, "Heaven! Heaven! Come! Come!" (Southey, 1925: 278-279.)

Methodism was reported to have been well received in St. Vincent, especially by the slaves. Some time after its introduction, however, the Methodist chapel was vandalized, the Bible was taken and hung from the public gallows. And in 1792, the Methodist missionary, Mr. Lumb, was imprisoned. A law had been passed pointedly aimed at discouraging missionary activities among the slaves. By its terms no one, except "the rectors of the parishes," was permitted to preach without obtaining a license from the legislature. To qualify for a license, however, an individual was required to have resided in St. Vincent for a year. This was a severe blow to Methodist aspirations and accomplishments in the island.

> Previously to the enacting of this law, no missionary could have been more respected than Mr. Lumb; and no society in the West Indies was in a more

flourishing condition than that of St. Vincent's. Nearly a thousand slaves had stretched out their hands to God: and throughout the island, the Negroes seemed everywhere ready to receive the Gospel. (Drew, 1818: 255.)

Complaints reached the British government, and, in 1793, a dispatch was sent to St. Vincent declaring that "His Majesty the King was graciously pleased to disannul the Act of the Assembly of St. Vincent" (Duncan, 1963: 10).

A conference of the Methodist Church in the West Indies was held in 1793, and it was reported that there were 6570 converts in all the Methodist societies in the West Indies and 30000 people regularly attending the services (Goveia, 1965: 293–294). In six years, the missionaries had done their work well.

The antislavery movement, begun in the last half of the eighteenth century in England, picked up momentum in the first part of the nineteenth. British sensitivities were awakened, the institution of slavery on which the single-crop economy of the West Indies had been dependent for so long was examined and found intolerable. The slave trade was abolished in 1807, and planters were forced to rely on natural increase or turn to illegal agencies to augment their slave supplies. Then in 1834, the slaves were emancipated. The British government provided compensation payments to slave owners; in St. Vincent, payments were made for 22,266 slaves (Burns, 1954: 629).

The wave of concern for human rights and the achievement of the goal of emancipation were accompanied by a logical breakdown of religious barriers and an expansion of religious activities. In St. Vincent, the Anglican Church altered its policy of limited focus and directed its appeal toward all classes of people. By 1830 restrictions against Roman Catholics had been lifted, thereby enabling the Catholic Church to operate as freely in the island as the Anglicans and the Methodists did (Duncan, 1963: 35).

The ramifications of emancipation were many. According to Ragatz (1928: 456),

> The overthrow of the traditional labor regime marked the final blow at the old-time prosperity of the West India islands . . . the shock of emancipation sent that magnificent structure, the old plantation system, tottering to the ground. Nor could it be rebuilt.

Slavery, however, had already left its indelible stains on the society and culture of every island.

After emancipation, the former slaves in the West Indies were not only reluctant to continue working as field hands but demanded wages that were unrealistic from the planters' point of view. Therefore cheaper sources of labor were tapped under an indentured labor system. In St. Vincent, beginning in 1846, Portuguese workers were imported from Madeira.[2] In 1848, free Africans were brought in from Sierra Leone,[3] and, beginning in 1861, East Indians arrived to augment the labor supply[4] (Burns, 1954: 662–663; Duncan, 1963: 36; Garcia, 1965: 247). In addition to the introduction of outside labor, the interisland movement of free labor that was established prior to emancipation continued. Workers emigrated from the smaller islands, where the economic opportunities were less attractive, to the south; for example, in Trinidad, they could "earn more than three times the wages for a nine-hour-day's work in St. Vincent or Grenada" (Garcia, 1965: 247). Although the mobile workers were offered allotments of land to entice them to stay, most of them eventually returned to their home islands where living costs were lower (Garcia, 1965: 247). Such mobility was an important factor in cultural exchanges.

During the last half of the nineteenth century and early in the twentieth, St. Vincent struggled continually against economic depression. The market prices of sugar declined, prompting some planters to turn to the less-profitable arrowroot. Natural disasters and disease intensified the desperateness of the situation. An epidemic of smallpox in 1849 was followed by an epidemic of yellow fever in 1852, and, in 1854, by cholera, which alone accounted for 2000 deaths. Several severe hurricanes took their toll in 1886 and 1898. Then in 1902 and 1903, Mt. Soufrière erupted, causing extensive damage and loss of life (Duncan, 1963: 38–46).

The dismal economic outlook continued to plague St. Vincent through the twentieth century. Sea Island cotton (introduced in 1903 in an attempt to boost the economy), sugar, and arrowroot have been important crops, but each has met with some misfortune. The Government Cotton Ginnery was burned down in 1959; the Mount Bentinck sugar factory was closed, not to reopen, by a strike in 1962; and the market for arrowroot has been diminishing. At the time of my study, bananas were the most important export crop. Canada had built a deep-water harbor for St. Vincent in 1964, which facilitated the loading and unloading of ships. Tourism, which has been a well-developed industry for some Caribbean islands, was relatively unimportant in St. Vincent in 1966, but by 1970 there were obvious signs of a growing interest in attracting North American visitors.

At mid-century, the political situation in St. Vincent was chaotic and confused. Universal adult suffrage became a reality in 1951, when a new constitution went into effect. In 1956, a ministerial system of government was introduced. Two years later, the ten English-speaking islands of the West Indies made an attempt at federation, but it collapsed in 1962. Independence, which had already been achieved by some of the West Indian islands and was fervently desired by the Vincentians, was postponed several times because of "unrest and tension in the territory" (*Caribbean Monthly Bulletin,* February

1967). Finally, in 1969, St. Vincent became an Associated State of the United Kingdom with control over its own internal affairs.

According to the 1960 census, the total population of the island was 79,948: 37,561 males and 42,387 females. The total population of Kingstown, the capital, was 4308: 2067 males, 2241 females. The census data show a preponderance of blacks for the island: 56,207 Negroes, 7361 mixed, 2444 East Indians, 1265 Carib Indians, 1840 whites. Primary education is free, but not compulsory, in St. Vincent and is available for children between five and fifteen years of age. About 83.6 percent of the males and 86.7 percent of the females fifteen years of age and over had finished a primary school education; about 8 percent of the males and 7.6 percent of the females fifteen years of age and over had had no schooling. In a total 15,511 women between 15 and 44 years of age, 3084 were married, 2985 were living under a common-law arrangement, 1993 were categorized as being part of a "visiting" union, 903 were single, for 6046 no union was reported, 498 were in some "other" type of union, and for 2 the type of union was not stated. Of a total 17,247 adult males fifteen years of age or older and not attending school, 5738 were married, widowed, divorced, or separated; 11,501 had never married. Male heads were reported for 8290 households. Almost as many—7423—had female heads. The extreme mobility of the West Indians is reflected in the statistics on immigration. In 1962 and 1963, the total number of immigrants was 17,707 and 19,345, respectively. For the same years, the total number of emigrants was 19,100 and 20,009. The report for St. Vincent (Great Britain Colonial Office, 1966: 36) offers the following breakdown for persons migrating to Britain in those years:

	1962	1963
Students	66	28
Seeking employment	599	483
Visitors	60	75
Total	725	586

The 1960 census data on religious affiliations indicated that 37,671 persons were Anglicans; 26,537 were Methodists; 8843 were Roman Catholics; 2195 belonged to the Presbyterian, Baptist, Seventh Day Adventist, Jehovah's Witnesses, or Pentecostal churches, none of which had over 1000 members. The category "other Christians" accounted for 3289; 398 either had no religious preference or it was unknown, and 10 were listed an non-Christian. It should be noted that Shakers, the subject of this study, have been confirmed, for the most part, in one or another of the established churches and hence would be counted as members of those churches in the census.

NOTES

1. Unless otherwise indicated, historical information has been obtained from Sir Alan Burns, *History of the British West Indies* (London: George Allen & Unwin Ltd., 1954).

2. Burns (1954: 662) states that 36,000 Madeiran Portuguese came to the West Indies between 1835 and 1882; more than 30,000 went to British Guiana, over 2000 to Antigua, about 900 to Trinidad, about 100 to Jamaica, and "a few" to Grenada, St. Vincent, St. Kitts, and Nevis.

3. More than 14,000 persons came from Africa to the West Indies at this time (Burns, 1954: 663).

4. Between 1862 and 1880, 2746 East Indian migrants arrived in St. Vincent (Garcia, 1965: 252).

4

The Shakers

"Shakers" is the popular name of a fundamentalist Protestant cult group in St. Vincent.[1] Vincentian Shakers are not, however, unique in being given that designation. Over the years, and in various places, the term "Shakers" has been applied to a number of unconnected religious groups. Probably the best known group to bear the name was the sect founded by Ann Lee ("Mother Ann") in England in the eighteenth century. The members of the sect were referred to as "Shakers" because of "their custom of dancing in a frenzy to express religious ecstasy" ("The Shakers," 1967:58). Mother Ann and some of her followers moved to the United States in 1774. Unlike Vincentian Shakers, they practiced communal living and celibacy, and although at one time they numbered 6000, by the middle of the twentieth century, very few remained. Near the end of the nineteenth century, a religion arose among the Indians of the Pacific Northwest that has continued to function with vigor to the present. Because dissociation, or "shaking," is an important feature of the religion, its adherents are also known as "Shakers" (Barnett, 1957).

Vincentian Shakers do not refer to themselves by that term, however. The proper, formal designation is "Spiritual Baptist," but they may also speak of themselves as "the converted people," "Christian pilgrims," or simply "Baptists."

Shaker informants say that John and Charles Wesley were the originators of their religion. Many of its elements do, indeed, point to a Methodist background or base, but this has been subjected to much elaboration and modification. Shaker beliefs and practices seem to be an eclectic blend of elements borrowed—perhaps with some adjustment—from Anglicanism, Catholicism, and Pentacostalism (which is not surprising considering that early socialization includes attendance at a non-Shaker church); traditional African elements that have been redesigned or retained; and unidentifiable elements, perhaps invented—all of which have been added to, and mingled with, the selected Methodist elements. One of the most outstanding features of the religion is that its adherents may experience mild states of dissociation, attributed to possession by the Holy Ghost.

23

The cult apparently had its origins in St. Vincent [2] and has been in operation there at least since the early years of this century. In 1912, it was outlawed. According to Mr. P.,[3] Inspector of Schools and a non-Shaker, "it was really a health measure more than a moral question; after shouting all night, Shakers were affected physically." But Mother O., a Shaker, declared: "From the time I was a child, the ministers of the other churches wanted a condemnation against this denomination." Vincentians offer a variety of reasons for the legal action: not only the putative physical and/or mental health impairment that resulted for the participants and the animosity of the organized churches but also the immoral practices reportedly engaged in by some of the members, the noisy meetings that lasted far into the night and disturbed others living in the vicinity, and so on. The ordinance that was passed "to render illegal the practices of 'Shakerism' as indulged in in the colony of St. Vincent" states (Rae, 1927: 1091).

> There has grown up a custom amongst a certain ignorant section of the in-
> habitants of the Colony of St. Vincent of attending or frequenting meetings
> from time to time at houses and places where practices are indulged in which
> tend to exercise a pernicious and demoralizing effect upon the said in-
> habitants, and which practices are commonly known as "Shakerism."

The Shakers went "underground" after 1912, but they were harried and persecuted by the police. Older members can recall meetings during that period when they were afraid "to shout," lest they be apprehended, brutally handled, and imprisoned. Beginning in the thirties, however, a more lenient policy toward the Shakers was adopted; according to Mother O., the last case against them was held circa 1932. Nonetheless, the cult remained illegal until 1965, when the law was repealed. Today, the pastor of a Shaker church, even as the head of any other recognized church, may christen babies, conduct funeral rites, and perform legal marriages provided the proper license has been obtained.

At present, Shakerism seems to be flourishing. According to a minister of one of the large denominational churches, this is not only because of the assured legal status of the religion but also because the government in power in 1965 and 1966 fostered and promoted it. He remarked that legalization of the Shakers had been a political move and that it was being alleged that the incumbent Chief Minister had been baptized as a Shaker. He added that the Chief Minister included Shakers in his processions and had even chosen Shaker pastors to lead prayers—all of which, he felt, had been responsible for the great upsurge in the number of Shaker converts.

Among Vincentians of higher classes, attitudes toward the Shakers range from hostility to acceptance. Mr. P., a dark-skinned, elderly man, expressed extreme concern because members of the organized religions, which he considered to be morally beneficial and uplifting were being attracted to Shakerism, which was morally degrading. He believed that the cult had its roots in Africa, which, for him, was sufficient reason to damn it. Other informants regarded it with tolerance, amused or apologetic; some mocked and poked fun at Shaker antics, others attempted to excuse them. However, they expressed satisfaction with St. Vincent's recently instituted "freedom of religion." Some Vincentians—especially the young, progressive, professional or business people—found pride in their own African ancestry and boasted about Shaker contributions to religion: the emotion and spirit, assumed to be African traits, that characterize a Shaker service and set it apart from the impersonal and impassive services of the Catholic and organized denominational churches. They also called attention to the "really nice little churches" that the Shakers are building on the island and expressed the opinion that the Shakers have adjusted their activities to some extent to make them more acceptable to the society as a whole.

Spiritual Baptists are also found in Trinidad, where they are known as "Shouters." The cult apparently spread there from St. Vincent[4] and has experienced similar legal hardships. Shouters activities were unlawful from 1917 to 1951, but more recently, even as in St. Vincent, the cult is reported to be flourishing (Simpson, 1966).

Shaker membership, as indicated, is predominantly drawn from the lower class segment of the Vincentian population. Hadley (1949:351) has enumerated and defined the components of the class structure in the West Indies generally, with particular reference to St. Vincent. He posits a three-way division of the society: (1) the "proletariat," which includes farm laborers, fishermen, and those workers to whom daily or weekly wages are paid, such as road-construction workers or dock hands; (2) the "unestablished, emergent or lower-middle class," which includes such salaried persons as elementary school teachers, business men in lesser positions, and civil service employees, as well as landed proprietors; and (3) the "established upper-middle class," composed of professional people, those serving in important capacities in business or the civil service, and entire families that have enjoyed such status for a generaton or more. Hadley (1949: 361) found "no aristocracy in any real sense of the word in the West Indies—there are merely people with more or less money."

Hadley used economic status, education, and occupation as the criteria for dividing St. Vincent society into classes. He did not include nuances of skin color as a factor contributing to class placement, although he recognized the antagonism existing between people of different skin color as a factor forming personality. Simpson (1962: 30) observed for the West Indies as a whole that "generally the poorest people are black and those with highest status are white or near-white." Lowenthal (1967: 597) averred that "race and color do not define West Indian classes. But class grievances are mainly expressed in terms of color." Skin-color differentiation and its importance are inextricably linked with the West Indian slave era when the slaves were almost without exception black. A white minority constituted the dominant class, and an inevitable hybrid group arose to form a free colored population. Over the years, however, color has become a "matter of culture. Whatever their actual appearance, middle-class folk tend to be considered and to view themselves as 'colored,' while lower-class folks are 'black' " (Lowenthal, 1967: 598).

St. Vincent is one of the West Indian islands that has a "poor white" population; they are "not part of the elite but are close in culture and status to the black peasantry", (Lowenthal, 1967: 593). With the exception of the poor whites, the poorest lower class people seem to have the darkest skin, but it cannot be said that the darkest people are necessarily the poorest and of the lowest class. It is not rare to find a dark individual in the lower middle, or even upper middle, class (using Hadley's terminology), but the reverse seems almost never true: except for the poor whites, light-skinned people are rarely found in the lower class. All of the Shakers observed were dark-skinned.

The particular congregation of Shakers studied was a group of about forty people. Most of them lived and worked in Kingstown, the capital and port city of the island, or in the surrounding areas. For individuals of their socioeconomic level, their opportunities for work, education, health and medical care, and the like differed somewhat from those available farther away from the city; for example, fewer men in the selected group of Shakers worked as agricultural laborers or fishermen than would probably have been the case with lower class people living deeper in the country or in the small villages along the coast. Instead, more men were working on road-building crews or as construction workers, part-time dock hands, delivery men, and so on. The women worked as household help, as laundresses, or as seamstresses. Some of them had part-time jobs as banana carriers. Some women held two jobs, loading bananas when a boat was in the harbor, and also working elsewhere in some other capacity. (For example, D. worked as a guest-house laundress, but carried bananas when a boat was loading.) Some women who were married or had formed stable, lasting attachments to men did not work. In several instances, the husbands were away from St. Vincent, working in England or Canada, or as sailors. They sent money back to their wives, apparently in such amounts that the women did not need to work. Some of the married women supplemented their resources by becoming entrepreneurs. One catered to school children with freshly roasted peanuts and candy. Another termed herself a "speculator"; when she "felt like it," she bought produce in wholesale lots and resold it in retail lots. On occasion, she attended markets in other islands. With her profits, she was ultimately able to buy a house.

Lower class Vincentian homes that I visited were usually small two-or three-room rectangular structures, built on one floor. In some, the kitchen was incorporated into the house; in others, the cooking was done in a shack away from the house. In any event, some cooking was done outdoors; for example, breadfruit was roasted over a fire built on the ground. The living rooms were usually furnished with a small sofa and one or two chairs with upholstered seats, a table and some straight chairs, and a small coffee table. The coffee table invariably held a vase of artificial flowers centered on a ruffled, crocheted doily, surrounded by what-nots. Curtains of flocked, pastel net usually adorned the windows. The walls were decorated with family pictures, highly colored religious pictures, postcards, calendars, and the like. Almost every home had a radio, and in several, treadle sewing machines were prominent. Most of the houses had electricity; none had a telephone. Around each house there was some land that provided space for a vegetable garden and a few fruit trees.

Most of the Shakers interviewed had received some formal education, but few had completed primary schooling. Most of them seemed to be able to read and write, however, although several required some prompting when attempting to read from the Bible. A non-Shaker informant commented that some Shakers cannot read, but have memorized long passages from the Bible and are consequently able to give the impression that they can read. On the other hand, the Shakers who have grown up near Kingstown probably have been exposed to better educational advantages than their country counterparts.

As children, most of the Shakers had received religious training and had been confirmed in one of the organized churches (perhaps a precautionary, as well as a practical, measure during the illegal period). They appear to find no incompatibility with their Shaker devotion and affiliation in maintaining an association, however inactive, with another church. The Shaker church does not provide the more complete range of religious services for all ages and situations that other churches may. Thus a couple desiring a marriage ceremony is told by the pointer to return to the church in which they had received infant baptism; although he may now perform a legal marriage, Pointer B. has never purchased the requisite license. Shaker parents may send their children to a church-operated school, as well as to the Sunday school and church services of a Protestant or Catholic church. The pattern of early socialization in a variety of other churches may have been a factor in the richness of the Shaker worship service.

Shaker churches are well scattered around St. Vincent. Known as "praise houses" or "prayer houses," they vary in physical aspects, but within certain limits. The differences are probably dictated as much by the funds available as by the tastes and desires of the individual congregation. The land on which a church stands may be owned or rented by the church. Rent for the land for one of Pointer B.'s churches was $5.00 BWI (about $3.00 in U.S. currency) per year. Alternatively, as in the case of the praise house at Lowmans, the land may belong to a member who donates its use to the church.

Praise houses are simply designed, rectangular buildings that can accommodate a gathering of between 50 and 75 people. The altar is at one end of the room. It may be very plain—a kitchen table converted for the purpose and covered with a plastic tablecloth—or it may be more elaborately embellished with a dais, altar rail, wooden candelabra, crosses, satin or velvet altar cloths, and so on. The floor may be concrete or packed earth. Some churches have whitewashed, plastered walls, galvanized-iron roofs, glass windows, and wooden doors. Others may be less prepossessing: the praise house at Lowmans was a simple structure of interlaced branches and a thatched roof, and only openings for windows and door. Pointer B. said that it was unfinished, and as soon as funds were available, the walls would be plastered, an iron roof would be added, and windows and doors put in. (Four years later, the work had not been started, and the church was still being used in its unfinished state.)

Religious pictures may hang on the walls. These may depict episodes in the life of Christ, or, in spite of the Protestant orientation of the group, they may portray Catholic saints. Banners may hang from the rafters, or the church may be bare. Unpainted wooden benches, usually without backs and arranged in various ways, provide seating, but they are often inadequate for the number of worshipers, and late-comers may have to stand. Some churches have electric lights and may be bright and well lit; others may depend for lighting on an oil lamp or two, candles, and the additional candles that all Shaker worshipers carry. Some churches have a center pole that is not necessarily of any structural function, but many do not. If there is a center pole, it serves as a secondary focal point with candles affixed to it and, perhaps, banners hung around it. Certain altar furnishings are seen in every Shaker church: a glass of water with flowers, a candle, a brass handbell, a Bible, and a saucer.

Churches may also be improvised. Meetings may be held at the intersection of two village streets (there is little traffic in the country), in which case a kitchen table will be used as an altar, and any chairs that happen to be available from homes nearby will be grouped around it. The bell, Bible, glass of water with flowers, candle, and saucer will grace the table as usual. Meetings may also be held in someone's house or yard. In the latter case, a tarpaulin may be borrowed from the Banana Association and erected to form a tent. The men arrange extension cords and bare lightbulbs to provide illumination and take a table and chairs from the house. When outdoor meetings are held in the city or a village, a crowd of bystanders will usually gather to watch the proceedings.

Ordinarily, each Spiritual Baptist church is independent and autonomous. Pointer B., however, had five churches (later, six) on the island under his direction—at Lowmans, Questelles, Chapmans Village, Brighton, and Spring Village. For each church he selected a leader, or in the case of the church at Chapmans Village, a pointer mother—his wife, to whom he delegated authority and responsibility for the church in his absence. When he was present, these persons assisted him in leading the worship service. If, in addition, leaders from other churches were visiting, the pointer and the several leaders sat in honored positions facing the congregation and each contributed to the service.

Several factors seem to influence Shakers in their choice of churches to attend regularly. Proximity is one consideration; all other things being equal, they seem to go to the nearest church. However, the personality of the pointer or leader can far outweigh the advantages of location. Several members of Pointer B.'s churches lived in Kingstown, where they had easier access to the praise houses of other Shaker pointers, but they spoke disparagingly of the leadership in those churches and compared it unfavorably with Pointer B.'s more able direction.

The congregations of Pointer B.'s various churches visited back and forth frequently, particularly between Lowmans and Questelles, which are not very far apart. When the distance was too far for walking, as is the case between Lowmans or Questelles and Chapmans Village or Brighton, a bus was hired to transport the congregation. Members of Pointer B.'s flock visited not only each other's churches but also the churches of other pointers on the island and invited them to visit and participate in their services. Occasionally, they were invited to hold thanksgiving or memorial services in the homes of members or nonmembers. They might also go to some of the small islands of the Grenadines—Union or Bequia—to hold services. Mischel (1958: 55) described a somewhat similar situation among the Shangoists of Trinidad. In St. Vincent, as she pointed out for Trinidad, a certain dedicated group of worshipers travel about, while others rarely, or never, do any visiting.

The freedom and autonomy that characterize each Shaker group *vis-à-vis* other Shaker groups contrast sharply with the hierarchical structure and positive emphasis on obedience and discipline existing within each group. "Obedience is the first step to Christ," and consequently each member is expected to obey those "elder to him" in the group. "Elder" as they use the word does not necessarily mean "older," but refers instead to those who have higher positions in the cult—positions that were supernaturally awarded to them during a period of retreat known as "mourning" and entitle them to deference from the lesser achievers. Mother A., for example, held a highly responsible position despite her 22 years. On the other hand, D. had been baptized but had never been to mourn and thus had not acquired an elevated position, and, although she was considerably older, she owed obedience to Mother A. In turn, those who comprise the group of elders owe help in the form of guidance and advice to those beneath them.

When a person goes to mourn, he is said to go on "a spirit journey" during which he acquires various "gifts": the right to a particular status in the church hierarchy, the right to wear certain colors, the right to carry certain equipment, and so on. Each time he repeats the ritual he stands to enhance his position.

The highest position in the church is that of pointer, and, according to informants from Pointer B.'s congregations, this apex position should be filled by a man. "A woman is not supposed to head a church. The leading instrument is supposed to be a man." Church leadership may be passed along in a family from father to son or perhaps from brother to brother. Pointer B.'s brother had been a Shaker pointer before Pointer B. even considered it. When Pointer B. received the call to accept baptism in the faith (see Chapter 6), his brother baptized him. Later, Pointer B. mourned under his brother, and worked with him as a leader in his church; he "carried on his church for him." When his brother died, Pointer B. again went "to renew the covenant," and the Lord commanded him to do the same work his brother had been doing. According to Mother E., during the spirit journey the Holy Spirit gives the person destined to become a pointer the symbols of his status: a belt, basin, towel, bell, Bible, and gown. Pointer B. informed me that he had a white gown, but during my entire stay in St. Vincent he never wore it.

The position of "leader" ranks below that of pointer and is in the nature of being an apprentice position. The leaders are men. They conduct meetings in the pointer's absence and read scripture, sermonize, lead hymns, and so on, when he is present. A leader is entitled to deference and has considerable responsibility. "The children should obey him in every point—he is rising." After receiving sufficient and proper "spiritual gifts," a leader, depending on the circumstances, may go elsewhere to become the pointer in a church of his own, or he may take over the church in which he has been working as a leader.

Men may hold other lesser positions in the church. For example, "captains" are men who "as a head of a ship, lead the whole crew in the spirit. They have a bar on the sleeve; sometimes a ribbon across the chest—these are king captains in the spirit." According to Pointer B., all the men have some office to fill, none of them being merely members or followers as many of the women are. This is interesting in view of the fact that some of the men had not gone to mourn; for example, J. had only been baptized, yet he served as "preacher" and sat with the pointer and leaders at the front of the church.

A number of statuses are open to women who go to mourn. The highest ranking position is that of "mother," with various grades existing within that category. The rights and duties of the different kinds of mothers seem to overlap considerably, and no clear statement of the prerogatives and responsibilities attached to each was forthcoming. A pointer mother, or assistance mother, is in the top grade and holds a position somewhat similar to that of leader for a man—the pointer's second-in-command, so to speak. She "assists the pointer in doing his work . . . and assists him when he have pilgrims to mourn or candidates to baptize. . . . She is mother of every little thing in the church and can do anything she sees that needs doing." Pointer B.'s wife was a pointer mother, and she served as head of one of his churches in his absence and took an important part in the meetings when he was present. However, as a woman, she also joined other mothers in performing certain tasks that no man was ever seen performing, such as washing the feet of persons going to mourn.

According to informants, a " 'mother matron' commands the children and assists the pointer. If someone does something wrong, she can go and speak to them over the wrong they did. She can give them a word of consolation." A " 'mother helper' works with the pilgrims. There is always someone in the mourning room with them. It is a higher office than 'nurse.' She washes their hands and feet, that's all, whether they mourn or baptize." A " 'queen mother' will also be a close nurse to the children and assist when they are in the room." In addition to the various mothers, a nurse also "works with candidates or pilgrims . . ., wipes their faces, gives them water, and prepares their meals," but, as indicated, the office of nurse is less prestigious than those in the mother category.

"Warriors" are also women, but their functions are different from those performed by mothers and nurses. During a meeting, "they sit near the pole and go around in adoption and see that everything is in order." Adoption, according to Mother A., is "when the power of God meets or touches one, they shake giving melodious sounds from their lips as that of music." The term is also used to mean hyperventilation by the Shouters in Trinidad (see Simpson, 1965: 114).

Although some duties may be handled by the holder of any one of several offices (for example, after immersion baptismal candidates may be assisted in changing their clothes by an assistance mother, a nurse, or a mother matron), it is not circumspect for a person to usurp privileges not rightfully hers. On one occasion, for example, D., emboldened by certain circumstances, arose from her seat and proceeded to remove the hot wax drippings from the hand of a candidate for baptism. This was outside her set of acceptable behaviors since she had never mourned and had no office in the church. The pointer noticed

her obtrusive actions, reprimanded her sharply, and sent her back to her seat.
A mother later finished the job that D. had begun.

As has been mentioned, Shakers who have gone to mourn and have been
awarded an office in the church are entitled to wear some insignia of that office
of some identifying uniform. For example, a queen mother is entitled to wear a
blue dress with a tight bodice, full skirt, short sleeves, and collarless square
neck, as well as a white apron with a bib. An assistance mother is entitled to
wear a mauve dress made in the same fashion with tight bodice, full skirt, and
short sleeves, as well as a white half-apron, a white tippet with white lace
around the edge, and a rope around her waist. A warrior can be identified by
the rosette on her dress. Whenever a group visits another church or has a special service like baptism, everyone wears the complete outfit to which he is
entitled, if he has it. It seems to be the responsibility of each person to provide
his own equipment, and acquisition of a uniform may be put off indefinitely,
presumably, depending on the person's resources. In the ordinary meetings,
most worshipers wear only part of their uniform, if they wear any of it. Sister
E., for instance, complained that she suffers from "pressure" and gets too hot
if she wears the tippet that belongs to the outfit she is entitled to wear. Mother
O. usually wore only the rope that was part of her outfit, tying it around the
waist of an ordinary dress.

Women who have mourned may also wear colored head ties, depending on
the gifts they had received. Women who hold no office in the church wear
white head ties. However, in compliance with the Biblical injunction, all
women do have their heads covered in church. Some women wear white wraps
even after mourning since they must wear "what the Spirit gives them."
Herskovits and Herskovits (1936: 8–9) report that the manner in which the
Negro women of Paramaribo tie their head ties can convey a variety of
meanings. Shaker women averred, however, that the manner in which they
tied the wraps around their heads had no significance. The important
consideration was to cover the head in church. In addition, most of the women
wear straw hats—even dressy ones with veiling, ribbons, and flowers—
perched on top of their head ties. Men do not have to cover their heads, and
many are bare-headed, but some wear a tie that covers only the forehead,
whereas others cover their entire heads as the women do. Shoes are supposed
to be removed in church, but although most worshipers do slip them off, some
do not.

Pointer B. maintains strict control over the conduct of the members of his
churches and seems to be feared and respected by them. He has several devices
at his command: he has a temper that flares suddenly; a raucous voice that he
uses advantageously for sharp, public reproof; and he carries a wide leather
strap. Ordinarily, he pounds the table, altar, or Bible with the edge of it for

emphasis or to mark the rhythm of a hymn. He uses it especially when he wants the tempo of a hymn quickened. On occasion, however, he will wield it against a group of inattentive or giggling women or against a specific individual. Discipline seems to be dispensed on two levels. The pointer may react impulsively and personally, apparently because his own sensibilities have been offended by the display of inappropriate behavior. He may also act as the instrument of the Holy Ghost, in which case the occasion becomes full of ritual.

During an outdoor meeting one evening, Pointer B. directed a lengthy ritual that reached its climax in the physical punishment of a woman. The performance took place in plain view of a sizable crowd of passersby who had gathered to watch the service. While the rest of the congregation was singing a hymn, the pointer led the woman, Mistress S., from her seat to the table serving as altar. Both of them became dissociated as he held her hands and swung her arms from side to side. They recovered only partly, and, while the pointer still held her by one hand, Mistress S. knelt and offered a chanted prayer. The pointer gave her three sips of water, then said, "I'm gonna give this Bible to this daughter." He put the Bible in her hands and she knelt with it. The pointer rang the bell at her three times, and Mistress S. performed a ritual known as "taking a prove," a divinatory method frequently resorted to among the Shakers, which consists of opening the Bible at random and noting the three verses indicated on each page by the thumbs; these passages are believed to carry a message for or about the performer. After Mistress S. had opened the Bible, a mother stepped forward and, carefully marking the relevant passages with her own thumbs, took it from her. Pointer B. announced, "The Bible is our teacher." Turning to the kneeling, agitated woman, he remarked, "Satan, he wait for you!" Then he addressed himself to the congregation, musingly, "I wonder if I charged this daughter wrongfully." The mother read the verses of the prove and the pointer appeared to be well satisfied. He proceeded to strike the woman's open palms with his strap several times. After hitting her, he held her head close to him for a moment, put the Bible on her head, raised her from her knees, put a lighted candle on her head, and then gave the candle to her. She returned to her seat and during the next hymn became more violently dissociated than was usual.

It seems that Mistress S. had been guilty of cursing several other women. The pointer's actions received approbation not only from the congregation but also from some of the bystanders, several of whom marveled at the singular fitness of the biblical passage of the prove. Discussing the matter later, one non-Shaker observer remarked with amazement, "The lady who disobey her honors to the Lawd got the part just to suit her complaint. That was just magnificent, I tell you that much, they got just the part they wanted!"

The pointer, then, may dispense discipline as an ordinary human being subject to human emotions. In his capacity as pointer of a church, responsible for his congregation, he acts in much the same way as an authoritarian father might be expected to behave in a family setting. The image of the pointer as father is reinforced by the reference to his congregation as "daughters" and "children." Certain disciplinary practices found in the Shaker church reflect disciplinary practices among lower class Vincentian families generally. Corporal punishment is an accepted manner of correcting children after they reach a certain age. Infants are indulged, fondled, picked up when they cry, but "when they get to two, you start to teach them. You flog them and put them on their knees." Herskovits (1958: 195–197) discussed the importance of whipping as a method of correction among New World and West African Negroes and suggested that a historical relationship to traditional methods obtains. Emphasis on corporal punishment may have received reinforcement from the physical punishment meted out to the slaves as well as from the prevailing British-derived educational methods.

In his role as a human being performing the job expected of him, the pointer may indulge in overt outbursts of righteous anger accompanied by corrective measures meted out directly and impulsively, without explanation, apology, or appeal to higher authority. He may lash out at a misbehaving woman with his strap, he may scowl and perhaps yell at her. Several times he threw kernels of corn from the altar-table at inattentive women. The infractions that invoke his displeasure are obvious to anyone who happens to be observing. Certain behavior is considered appropriate in the church context: being quiet and listening attentively, responding and singing at the proper times. Deviations from the standards of acceptable conduct are not difficult for the pointer, facing his audience, to spot.

When the pointer is acting as the agent of the supernatural, however, certain differences from the situations described above are apparent. The nature of the transgression seems to differ; it is regarded by the Shakers as being more serious than a simple lapse in deportment. The circumstances under which the transgression occurs seem to differ also. In the case of Mistress S., the act occurred outside the church and could, quite conceivably, have remained unknown to the pointer. Pointer B. said, however, that the Spirit reveals wrongdoing to him, so that he discovers the misdeed, not through his own perception, but by revelation from the supernatural. He subjects his information to further supernatural validation through the mechanism of the prove. He stated, "The Bible itself will take a prove. It will speak to you the same thing she [the wrongdoer] have done." The entire process of judgment and castigation on this level is carried out with dignity and ceremony, with a skillful buildup of tension and of an atmosphere of impending doom that is dissipated by the climax. Further postclimactic ritual reincorporates the miscreant into the group with reassurances of their acceptance of her and of her spiritual purification.

The attitude of the pointer throughout the ceremony is one of benevolence and love toward the culprit. He makes no display of anger. His behavior is consistent with the image of the supernatural as possibly punitive, but always compassionate. Since he is in a state of possession trance to a greater or lesser degree during the procedure, the pointer becomes more than the mere instrument of the Holy Ghost carrying out His instructions—he is possessed by "that Power" and impelled by it: "It is the Holy Spirit who give punishment to you." The pointer is under further compulsion to carry out the demands of the supernatural—he must do so in order to avoid possible penalty to himself: "If Pointer had not given Mistress S. the lashes, the Holy Spirit would have lashed him."

Conflict situations in Pointer B.'s churches seemed to be kept at a minimum by his firm leadership and severe methods of maintaining social control. For example, D. admitted that she tried to behave prudently because she feared a public exposition such as that Mistress S. had been subjected to. Not all Shaker churches on the island enjoyed the same relatively calm and peaceful state, however. In one church, it was said, a woman had usurped the position of leadership, which caused dissension and conflict within the group. I witnessed something of this on the occasion of a visit, together with several members of Pointer B.'s flock, to the church of another pointer. When we arrived, the congregation was embroiled in a loud and angry dispute. Two of the leaders walked out, obviously irate, and left. Although some of our group went in, they preferred that I remain outside, and after waiting for a while, hoping that the quarrel would abate, we also left. In both of these cases, trouble arose over a struggle for power. However, the individual Shaker who is in conflict with his pointer and is not in a position to challenge his power has little recourse but to leave and try to find a more satisfactory situation elsewhere, as Sister W. did when a pointer refused her the gifts she claimed from her mourning experience.

Shaker services are usually held on Wednesday, Friday, and Sunday nights, but this schedule is flexible. As members usually walk to the meetings, in inclement weather it is possible that no one will appear. If a boat is in the harbor on the usual meeting day, the services may be rescheduled for another evening or canceled to accommodate the members who work as dock hands or banana carriers. The Sunday meeting may be held in the afternoon if it is a street meeting or if someone opens his home to it. Additional meetings may be held if someone is being "put to mourn," or if the group is invited to conduct a memorial service. Meetings involving a given congregation may be held not only in its own church but also in other churches, in the homes of members or nonmembers, in the mourning room, or in the street.

The worshipers usually begin to arrive for an evening meeting at about 7:30 or 8:00 P.M. They do not arrive in any particular order. They kneel at the altar or center pole, cross themselves, and pray silently before taking a seat. They may drop a coin in the saucer on the altar. No collection is taken by passing a basket or plate through the congregation, nor is any reference made to the saucer or its contents during the meeting. Occcasionally, however, the pointer may devote a half-hour or so at the end of a meeting to a plea for pledges. (I was given several sheets of paper bearing the message "The Pointers, Mothers and The Spiritual Believers of the ST. BENEDICT SPIRITUAL BAPTIST CHURCH beg to solicit your kind contribution for assistance in rebuilding and renovating the said Church at Chapmans Village" and was asked to pass them around among my friends.) During the harvest festival, I was told, a musical program is produced to which tickets are sold for the purpose of raising funds.

While the worshipers are gathering, there may be some handshaking and quiet conversation, but soon someone will begin humming or singing a hymn, and the others will join in. There are no musical instruments or drums. Everyone carries a candle, which may be lit from the altar candles, from the candles on the center pole, or from a neighbor's candle. Many carry Bibles and hymnals.

The meeting begins, not according to the clock, but according to the number of people who have assembled. A hymn from the Methodist hymnal is announced by the leader and sung, with the congregation standing. Those who have hymn books follow the words in their copies; the others seem to have the words memorized. All stanzas are sung. Then the congregation is seated and the leader reads a Bible lesson. If present, the pointer frequently inserts comments, exclamatory repetitions of parts of the lesson being read, or such phrases as "Praise God!" The congregation may respond in an approving manner with an "Amen!" The pointer's comments, apparently intended to elucidate the biblical passage, are in turn frequently interspersed with hymns, which the pointer may introduce with an expression such as "Someone told me that. . . ." These are sung while the congregation remains seated.

Then another hymn, the signal for a particular ritual, is announced. Two individuals approach the altar. (Every time I witnessed this ritual in a praise house, the person who sprinkled the water was a woman, whereas the bell ringer, although usually a woman, was occasionally a man.) They kneel "to sanctify themselves first by praying to make themselves acceptable in His sight." One takes the glass of water with the flowers, which the leader previously prayed over, and goes to the east, west, north, and south corners of the room, to the doorways, the center pole, and the four corners of the altar. At each station, the person with the glass sprinkles water three times, "in the name of the Father, Son, and Holy Ghost," says a silent prayer, makes the sign of the cross with her lighted candle, and curtsies. The other person, who has taken the bell from the altar, follows her and rings the bell three times at each station. Standing before the altar, they each take a sip of water from the glass, replace the bell and the glass, shake hands—"to signify unity"—and return to their seats. This ritual was performed in somewhat modified fashion when the meeting was held outdoors. Lighted candles were placed in the center and at the four corners of the table serving as altar. After praying over the glass of water, the leader or pointer sprinkled the five candles and rang the bell over them.

The Apostles' Creed is recited with the congregation facing the center pole, if there is one, and holding their hands forward about waist high, palms open and up. Kneeling, they repeat the General Confession, the Lord's Prayer, and "O Lord, open Thou our eyes, and our lips shall show forth Thy praise." They stand to sing the Gloria Patri (the short hymn also known as the lesser doxology) in English and to repeat a psalm, chanting it with their eyes closed and hands raised as before. Then while another hymn is sung, everyone walks around in follow-the-leader fashion and shakes hands with everyone else, eventually returning to his seat.

The leader reads a psalm. Those who have brought their Bibles follow the reading. The pointer is again apt to interrupt to make some comment, often lengthy, on the text or to add emphasis with an "Amen!" or "Yes, man!" As before, comments may be interspersed with hymns. When the leader has finished, he states, "Here endeth the portion," and the congregation stands to sing the Gloria Patri. More or less the same routine is then followed for a biblical lesson taken from the New Testament.

After the lessons and the psalms, the pointer may sermonize at some length, interrupting himself periodically to insert a hymn. Various members of the congregation may offer lengthy prayers. The person leading the prayer kneels at the side of the altar and offers the prayer in a chanting fashion, with the congregation responding. Various members may also say a few "words of consolation" interspersed with hymns. These rarely last less than half an hour, usually longer.

Shakers insist that their chanted prayers and words of consolation are spontaneous and deny that they plan or prepare in advance. However, it is obvious that there is much repetition. Each speaker may repeat not only himself but also biblical and nonbiblical phrases that seem to be Shaker favorites and are used over and over by many who speak. One such phrase that may be heard several times in a single meeting, and at almost every meeting, is, "In my Father's house there are many mansions. If it were not so, I would have told you. He goes to prepare a place for us." In a chanted prayer, such phrases as "Loving God and my Redeemer" or "Jesus, guide them, if You please" seem to serve a double purpose. They provide the supplicant with a ready-made formula to use, and, since they may be repeated as a kind of refrain throughout the prayer, they set the rhythm scheme for the rest of the phrases. Thus, although the prayer or speech may be spontaneous, it is not necessarily original.

During the early part of the service, when the Methodist Order of Morning Worship is being so closely followed, possession trance rarely occurs, but the latter part of the service offers ample opportunity.

The service is closed with a benediction and again the Gloria Patri.

Other elements may be included in the service, depending on the purpose of the meeting or the whim of the pointer or leader, parts of the usual service may be omitted or the usual order may be somewhat altered. However, a high degree of consistency seems to prevail among the separate Shaker churches in spite of their lack of overall organization and in spite of the apparent opportunity for innovation. What variations do obtain between churches and pointers, as well as those within the same church, seem to be of a minor order.

Meetings held at the homes of members for the purpose of blessing or "christening" a house or part of it seem to be popular. They are termed "thanksgiving" meetings. The table serving as altar will have fruit, corn, and farina scattered over it, but the members do not recognize the foodstuffs as representing a sacrifice—"sacrifices were in the days before Jesus. . . . Jesus made Himself the sacrifice."

The usual Methodist Order of Morning Worship is observed. The sermonizing, words of consolation, and prayers, however, are concerned with the purpose of the meeting. The focal piece of ritual peculiar to this kind of service is carried out as follows: The pointer selects several people to assist him. He sends four with lighted candles to stand in the four corners of the room to be blessed. (If the whole dwelling is being blessed, he sends people with lighted candles into the other rooms as well.) A group of four then proceeds from corner to corner. The first person in the group carries the Bible and reads a psalm at each station. The pointer follows him, carrying a glass of brandy or wine and a lighted candle. He dips the unlit end of the candle in the brandy, prays, and makes three splashes of brandy in the corner "in the name of the Father, Son, and Holy Ghost." He marks a cross on the floor with the unlit end of the candle. The third person goes to the corner carrying a plate of broken pieces of bread, puts one on the rafter, and prays. The fourth carries the bell, prays, and rings the bell three times in each corner. In the last corner to be visited, the pointer also makes chalk designs on the wall. The four people perform the same rituals that they had performed at the corners at the doorway, and the pointer makes chalk designs on the floor before the door. A lighted candle is left standing on the floor in the doorway on top of the brandy that had been splashed there. The remaining brandy or wine is poured into glasses and passed to those in the congregation who want it, and it is immediately consumed. After the meeting, which is quickly brought to a close after the important ritual, "beer" (nonalcoholic ginger beer) and buns are brought out and a period of conviviality ensues.

Lower class individuals, I was told, even though they might not be members of a Shaker church, may invite a group of Shakers to their homes to conduct the traditional ceremonies after a death. These take place on the third night, the ninth night, and the fortieth night after the person has died. At the forty days memorial service that I attended, corn and farina were scattered on the improvised altar. The service was the familiar routine, the only deviations being in the subject matter of the sermonizing, prayers, words of consolation, and hymns chosen. These all dealt with the central theme of death, what a Christian might expect in the afterlife, and so on. After the service, "beer" and buns were offered as they seemed to be whenever a meeting took place at someone's house.

The composition of the group, of course, differed from the usual church congregation. It consisted of the immediate family of the deceased, his relatives and friends—none of whom might be Shakers—as well as members of the Shaker congregation that had been invited.

Thus, although it may not provide certain ceremonies and services that the organized churches offer, Shakerism does afford its adherents a rich and varied ritual life. However, other religious alternatives are available to the lower class Vincentian who is attracted neither by Catholicism, Anglicanism, or Methodism nor by Shakerism. One of these alternatives is the fairly new competitor in the area of religion in St. Vincent, Streams of Power, to which we not turn our attention.

NOTES

1. Whether the Shakers, or Spiritual Baptists, of St. Vincent should be designated as a cult or a sect is unimportant here. Herskovits and Herskovits (1947) and Herskovits (1958) refer to the Spiritual Baptists in Trinidad as a sect, and to Shango, a religion in Trinidad that has considerably more African retentions in its roster of beliefs and practices than the Spiritual Baptists of either St. Vincent or Trinidad, as a cult. Simpson (1965, 1966) refest to both Spiritual Baptists and Shango in Trinidad as cults. Obviously, usage varies.

    Yinger (1946:19) states that a sect "stresses acceptance of literal obedience to the Synoptic Gospels; it tends to be radical, with a small, voluntary membership that lacks continuity; it is usually associated with the lower classes. The sect stresses individual perfection and asceticism; it is either hostile or indifferent to the state, and opposes the ecclesiastical order. . . . The sect is lay religion, free from world authority. . . ." Later, he added (1957: 146) that "sect" refers to "any religious protest against a system in which attention to the various individual functions of religion has been obscured and made ineffective by the extreme emphasis on social and ecclesiastical order." The term "cult," according to Yinger (1957: 154) is applicable to a group that is "small, short-lived, often local, frequently built around a dominant leader (as compared with the greater tendency toward widespread lay participation in the sect). Both because its beliefs and rites deviate quite widely from those that are traditional in a society (there is less of a tendency to appeal to 'primitive Christianity,' for example) and because the problems of succession following the death of a charismatic leader are often difficult, the cult tends to be small, to break up easily, and is relatively unlikely to develop into an established sect or denomination. The cult is concerned almost wholly with problems of the individual, with little regard for questions of social order. . . . The cults are religious 'mutants,' extreme variations on the dominant themes by means of which men try to solve their problems." The Shakers seem to hover between being a sect and a cult as Yinger defines them. As in a sect, membership is small and voluntary, and associated with the lower class. Literal obedience and individual perfection are emphasized. Like a cult, on the other hand, the Shakers show little concern as a religious group for questions of social order and are preoccupied with the search for a mystical experience. Simpson (1956: 340–341) applies Yinger's categories to Jamaican religions and lists as cults those groups that are most similar to the Spiritual Baptists of Trinidad and St. Vincent.

The Shakers might be further described according to Clark's (1937:27) seven categories of sects (pessimistic, perfectionist, charismatic, communistic, legalistic, egocentric, esoteric). Again, they do not fit neatly into any one category. They have some of the features of the "perfectionist sects" in that they seek "personal perfection of life" and emphasize "strong emotional reactions." However, in addition, they incorporate into their worship glossolalia and dissociational states, which Clark classifies as "charismatic sect" features.

2.   Personal communication from Franklin Loveland, March 12, 1967. Smith (1962: 10) indicates that the Shakers of Grenada have an American Spiritual Baptist, or Shouters, provenience.

3.   Only initials will be used to protect the identity of informants.

        Wherever quotations of informants are cited, these are as nearly verbatim as I was able to take them down in my notes or transcribe from tapes. In the case of letters, the quotations are presented exactly as written.

4.   In the debates in the Legislative Council of Trinidad and Tobago, January–December 1917, Session of November 16, 1917, the following reference to the Shakers is made (Herskovits and Herskovits, 1947: 343): "Apparently the Shouters have had a somewhat stormy history from all I have been able to learn regarding them. They seem, if they did not arise there, to have flourished exceedingly in St. Vincent, and to have made themselves such an unmitigated nuisance that they had to be legislated out of existence. They then came to Trinidad and continual complaints have been received by the Government for some time past as to their practices."

5

Streams of Power—A Dutch Healing Cult

Streams of Power came to St. Vincent in February 1965. The movement was started in Holland about 1952 by an artist in fulfillment of a promise to preach God's word if he were cured of an illness. The blossoming of such religious movements is not unusual for Holland,[1] and this particular one has since spread to the Dutch West Indies and Dutch Guiana; to Trinidad, St. Lucia, Martinique, and St. Vincent; and to various parts of Europe and Africa.

The evangelist who introduced Streams of Power to St. Vincent conducted a highly successful crusade. He stated that as many as 14,000 people attended some of the sessions in the park in Kingstown. (A figure of 14,000 seems almost unbelievable, however, when the total population of St. Vincent, the total population of Kingstown, the problems posed by transportation, and the' physical aspects of the island are considered.) Many miraculous cures were reported. Several of the present members of the church who were suffering from various ailments, heart trouble, cancer, blindness, and so on, aver that they were healed at that time. As far as I know, none of these claims have been substantiated by the medical profession. However, a minister of one of the large organized churches stated that many who were allegedly healed had, in fact, not been healed.

The impact that Streams of Power made on the island was sufficient to pose a threat to the established churches, which took steps—even as drastic as excommunication—to restrain their members from attending Streams of Power meetings. A period of opposition and antagonism ensued, during which attempts were made by the larger churches to achieve the legal extinction of the new cult. The size of Streams of Power congregations declined sharply. According to several informants, the political climate of the island at that time, however, was such that the future of a religious group deriving its membership from the lower social strata was bright, if not assured. (It will be recalled that

41

the Spiritual Baptists attained legal status in the same general period.) The evangelist, recounting the tribulations of the first year, gave credit to the Chief Minister and his wife for the fact that, within a year's time, Streams of Power had been accorded full recognition and approval by the government. The cult seems to have settled into a period of relative calm; the hostility of the other churches is less evident. Its growth in St. Vincent, according to the evangelist in 1966 and again in 1970, though much less spectacular than in its introductory period, has remained steady and encouraging.

In 1966, the Streams of Power physical plant was very inviting. The words "Revival Hall" appeared on an arch over the driveway from the street. The big, rambling, white frame building that had once been the estate house of a plantation was perched picturesquely near the top of a steep hill overlooking Kingstown and the harbor. The former drawing room had been furnished with benches and would accommodate about 175 to 200 people. A stage had been built at one end of the room. A cross-shaped pulpit stood on the stage, a card table with a clean white drawn-work cloth and a vase of fresh flowers was at one side. A microphone indicated the presence of a public address system. A banner bearing the Streams of Power device—a white dove with a red cross on its chest against a bright-blue background—hung on the wall behind the stage. The evangelist explained that the blue background symbolizes heaven, freedom for man. The two wings of the dove represent the Old and New Testaments, "for we need both." The red cross is self-explanatory, since Christ died on the cross. An upright piano was at one side of the platform. (Instrumental music is important in Streams of Power services; various other instruments may be added—tambourines, guitars, bass—depending on their availability.) The rest of the house was used by the evangelist and his family for their living quarters and his office. Services were also held in other parts of the island, but they were either conducted along the road or in temporarily rented halls.

In 1970, Streams of Power was temporarily holding services in downtown Kingstown in a second-floor meeting room over a store. The Anglican Church had purchased the rented Revival Hall property, which made it necessary for Streams of Power to find another location. The size of the congregation seemed to have diminished over the years, but that might have been a transient response to the less attractive surroundings. A new church was in the process of being built, however, and was occupied later in the year.

Streams of Power meetings are held regularly on Sunday morning and Sunday evening, Monday evening, and Thursday evening. (The island's weekly newspaper listed Streams of Power with the other organized churches, giving the times and places of its various services, in 1966. By 1970, the practice had been discontinued.) The congregation is largely composed of women; about 20 percent are men and another 20 percent are children. The services begin on time and last for two hours. A period of singing that lasts about 40 minutes opens each service. The songs are either known to the congregation or are taken from an evangelistic hymnal, *Redemption Songs*. The singing is loud and fast, and there is much clapping of hands, stamping of feet, and gesturing. There are some songs with "gimmicks" in which some of the words are omitted the second time the song is sung and gestures are substituted. The piano and instrumental accompaniment is also loud and not necessarily accurate.

The period of singing is followed by the "service of adoration," during which glossolalia, or "speaking in tongues," is the prominent feature. The evangelist, with his head elevated and his eyes tightly closed, begins whispering repeatedly into the microphone such phrases as "Thank You, Jesus," "Halleluiah," or "Praise the Lord," setting the pattern for the congregation, who do the same. Periodically, someone in the congregation breaks in with a series of unintelligible words or syllables. According to informants, the Holy Spirit chooses one person at a time, indicating to him when to speak; two or more people do not speak in tongues at the same time. (I was present at several meetings when two people did begin to speak at the same time, notwithstanding; the louder one seemed to be the one who continued, the other person stopped.) The speaker then continues, after his glossolalic utterance, with a sentence such as "So speaks the Lord," and proceeds to offer a bit of counsel in English. About seven or eight people of both sexes may make contributions of this nature. The evangelist may also do so, but he does not speak in tongues routinely. The evangelist then closes the service of adoration with a prayer.

No singing or music, hand clapping or drumming, accompanies the service of adoration. It is a period of quiet reverence, in distinct contrast to the noisy singing period preceding it.

On Sunday, after the service of adoration, the evangelist preaches a sermon; on Thursday night he devotes the remaining time to Bible teaching and on Monday evening, to a prayer meeting. The Thursday night Bible teaching is organized to develop a certain theme or topic. The evangelist refers to a specific passage, giving those who have brought their Bibles with them (almost everyone) an opportunity to find the reference, then reads the passage with gusto, making appropriate comments, and with occasional attempts at humor that the congregation seems to appreciate. Many bring pencils and paper with them and write down each reference, apparently for further study.

Several more hymns are sung. During one of them an offering is taken in a soft hat, but no appeal is made for generosity. A prayer and a benediction end the meeting.

When someone is speaking in tongues, the Streams of Power adherents believe that the Spirit is giving a message in a foreign tongue, the essence of which is subsequently repeated in the vernacular. The unknown tongue is believed to be a legitimate foreign language that could be understood by persons familiar with it.[2] The words spoken afterward in English presumably interpret the glossolalic message, which is said to be intended for some person or persons in the congregation. Interpretation thus rests not with the performer, nor with an interpreter, but with the Spirit. According to the evangelist, the person who is speaking "doesn't even know what he is saying; the Holy Spirit is within the person and uses the person to speak through."

Speaking in tongues is regarded as a highly desirable "gift of the Spirit" that is accessible to anyone who is a "child of God" (in other words, to anyone who has repented). The evangelist emphasized that speaking in tongues makes a believer strong and guarantees that he will not backslide. The members who speak in tongues state that they feel "uplifted" or "exalted" at the time. They say that they remember speaking in tongues, but do not remember what they say. The trances manifested in glossolalia are of short duration: from about 30 seconds to about a minute. Most of those who performed showed no more excitement than most people might who are speaking in public. They kept their eyes closed. Only occasionally was trembling or shaking noted, and then it was minimal. Excitement was discernible in some of the voices and in the somewhat more rapid breathing of some of the speakers; for example, one woman, who performed several times, spoke somewhat louder and more dramatically than most speakers and shook her shoulder and right arm up and down. None of the performers became so engrossed that they continued beyond a short period of time, however. Recovery was always very rapid, almost instantaneous.

I witnessed a healing session one evening after the service. The evangelist invited those who were ailing and desirous of ritual treatment to come forward. Several people sat down on the front benches. The evangelist approached each individual in turn, asked the nature of the complaint, put his hands on the affected person's shoulders, raised his eyes heavenward, and in a loud voice called on Jesus to cure the person. There was no trembling or excitement evident on the part of either the evangelist or the patient.

Several informants explained that the laying on of hands was not the curing agent. It was "believing in God. But you can't just *say* you believe. God knows, and nothing would happen." According to them, God does not make a person sick: "It is the Devil, and these are evil spirits in you making you sick. Healing is driving out these evil spirits." Certain catergories of illness or malfunctioning, such as fever or deafness, are believed to be the work of the Devil.

Curing may also be carried out for a person *in absentia.* I heard of a case involving an old woman who was blind. The woman's daughter took her mother's handkerchief to be blessed by the evangelist. She returned home, placed the handkerchief over her mother's eyes, and the old woman was cured.

In many ways Streams of Power and Shakerism are very similar. Both preach a fundamentalist approach to Protestant Christianity; they quote biblical passages to support their beliefs and practices, and accept the Bible literally and its infallibility unquestioningly. That they both may cite the same passage to justify differing beliefs and practices does not seem to concern either group. (Both the Shakers and the adherents of Streams of Power refer to Acts 2: 4—"they were all filled with the Holy Ghost, and began to speak with other tongues"—to justify their belief in possession by the Holy Ghost. For the Shakers, however, dissociation manifested by shaking is evidence of such possession. Streams of Power members, on the other hand, frown on shaking behavior and, by emphasizing the importance of speaking in tongues, interpret the passage to justify their own particular brand of glossolalia.) Nor do members of either group seem perturbed by the fact that they are selective in the passages they use for guidance—accepting some, but ignoring others. Both groups appeal to the lower economic and less educated classes. They require baptism by immersion and preach that man is a sinful creature, repentance being an absolute necessity. They emphasize the desirability and worth of individual, personal communication and interaction with the supernatural. In the services of both groups, there is much audience participation and involvement. Each person joins in the singing of the hymns and songs, providing music is not assigned to a choir. Individuals may respond or exclaim during prayers or sermons. Furthermore, both groups believe that a person may be entered by the Holy Spirit and caused to behave in an unusual fashion during meetings.

The dissimilarities are, however, more significant. The Streams of Power branch in St. Vincent is only one outpost of an organization that is obviously able to support a rather elaborate operation. The evangelist indicated that the collections and gifts obtained from his congregation were supplemented by funds from Holland. Each Shaker church, on the other hand, is autonomous. Pointer B.'s churches appear to be the only exception. The Shaker membership is small and poor. The saucer on the altar rarely contains more than a few pennies. There is no superorganization to come to the aid of the Shakers.

The leadership of the two churches is strikingly different. The evangelist's household is representative of a comfortably situated, middle-class Dutch family. The evangelist and his wife give the impression of having been fairly well educated. They dress fashionably. They have a nursemaid for their children, who usually look well scrubbed. Moreover, they are white. The Pointer, however, seems even less affluent than some of his parishioners. He rents a room in a small house in Kingstown. His wife and children live in the country, where his wife takes charge of one of his churches. He receives no salary for his work as pointer; it is said, "He will get a crown of righteousness as his reward." He is a part-time dock hand when a boat is in the harbor. He said that he has unsuccessfully tried to get steady work or a better job to maintain his family more adequately. His home in the country is small and poor. He has twelve children, nine of whom are at home. They are not very clean, and their clothing is ragged. Pointer B. is a part of the very group to which he ministers. His education, economic position, and racial background are similar. His problems are much the same. The evangelist, on the other hand, appears to come from a higher class than most of his flock and is a foreigner. He does not share the social and economic pressures, the educational inadequacies, nor any childhood recollections of St. Vincent with his people. He does not speak their language in his home. He is not even of their color.

Streams of Power meetings seem very simple and scheduled in comparison to Shaker meetings. They are devoid of familiar Protestant litany; none of the responses, creeds, prayers, and so on, that are common to the Shaker and Methodist services are used. The songs are simple and easy to sing. Many of them repeat the same, or nearly the same, phrases over and over, so that learning is minimal and fairly effortless. The sermons are also simple and direct, full of down-to-earth examples and stereotypes that are easy to understand. For example, one evening the evangelist recounted the difficulties a brother evangelist was having on a predominantly Catholic island. The government had closed the hall in which he held meetings, yet "the people there didn't even know they could buy a Bible for $1.00 until Brother C. sold them, telling them to read the word of God for themselves." The sermons are often designed to hold up to ridicule or inspection certain human frailties; for example, in developing the topic that everyone, whether he knows it or not, has a god he worships, the evangelist remarked that "the drunk has alcohol for his god, the cigarette smoker worships cigarettes, the American worships the dollar." Streams of Power meetings are predictable. They last two hours, each part of the service is timed, and one part follows another in the established sequence; opening songs, service of adoration or blessing, sermon or Bible study, closing songs, closing prayers.

By contrast, Shaker services are more complex and less scheduled. Although the Shakers use some of the same songs that are used in the Streams of Power church, most of the Shaker hymns are taken from the Methodist hymnal and are considerably more complicated both in words and music. Shaker meetings are much longer, but the length is indefinite. They are more involved with ritual, which is also more elaborate: the Methodist Order of Morning Worship, the consecration of the corners, the ritual handshaking, the lengthy chanted antiphonic prayers, and so on. Shaker services are further embellished with uniforms and other insignia of office, head ties, kneeling, making the sign of the cross, removing shoes in the praise house, carrying candles, and so on.

Shaker sermonizing draws heavily on the Bible for examples, rarely on ordinary present-day life and happenings. Preaching is performed with a solemn mien and is obviously not intended to be amusing—the relationship with the supernatural and the biblical references are very serious and important, and are never treated lightly. Sermonizing is not directed toward drinking, smoking, politics, or any other contemporary problems, but is concerned with the promises made by God, as indicated in the Bible, for those who follow His precepts, as well as the penalties to be incurred by those who do not.

The attitudes of the leaders in the two churches differ radically. The Streams of Power evangelist projects a "Pollyanna" type of image. He tries to convince his congregation that others are worse off than they are and that they are fortunate to have so much to be thankful for. He is usually smiling broadly, full of enthusiasm, eager to amuse, constantly trying to promote goodwill, and apparently trying to demonstrate that religion can be palatable, attractive, and not too difficult. The Shaker pointer, on the other hand, influenced by his own different background of experiences, admits to his congregation that the way is hard. He makes no effort to make his meetings gay and pleasant—quite the opposite, he is authoritarian, strict, and prone to using his strap against those who misbehave, which would be unheard of in a Streams of Power church. Where the evangelist cajoles, pleasantly ridicules, and gently urges his flock, the pointer commands, rebukes, and punishes his.

Although both churches draw their members from the lower class, even a cursory examination of the two groups reveals that a distinction can be made between the socioeconomic status of the Streams of Power devotees and that of the Shakers. Despite the fact that the evangelist, probably under the influence of his own status, describes his congregation as "very poor" and of the "lowest class," many of his people do not fit this category. Some of the Streams' of Power women work as cashiers in department stores, some as nurses in the local hospital, some as teachers; some of the men are taxi drivers. None of the Shaker women have professional jobs, and most of the men are manual laborers. Streams of Power women wear neat modish dresses (albeit inexpensive), high-heeled shoes, and dressy hats to church. The men usually wear white shirts, jackets, and ties. Shaker women, on the other hand, wear flat-heeled shoes, usually sandals that can be easily slipped off and on, blouses and full skirts or full-skirted dresses (which may be torn and fastened with safety pins), and head ties. The men wear their shirts open at the neck and often no jacket.

The total atmosphere is different in the two churches. An observer does not gather the impression during a Shaker service that the worshipers are enjoying themselves. By contrast, a Streams of Power meeting is quite friendly and gay, the evangelist is constantly striving for a laugh from his audience, conviviality and camaraderie characterize the meetings. If refreshments are served after a service, the Shakers become jovial, even silly, but during a meeting they are very sedate. They clap their hands and tap their feet, but with unsmiling seriousness. They keep their eyes closed much of the time. Even the ritual handshaking is performed deliberately, without a smile and without apparent recognition of the person whose hand is being shaken. When a Shaker leader has finished sermonizing, it is customary for several members to shake his hand and speak to him while the rest of the congregation is singing. But the leader never seems to pay any attention to the person speaking to him; he looks away from the speaker and sings, although continuing to shake hands. In short, there seems to be a greater emphasis among the Shakers on individual seeking and individual involvement: each person's main concern is his own relationship with the deity and his eventual fate. With Streams of Power, these are important considerations also, but a stronger emphasis seems to be placed on the current situations of its worshipers and on fostering good relations among men.

NOTES

1. Personal communication from G. A. Banck, December 8, 1966.
2. An example is given in a Streams of Power pamphlet *(Life and Life More Abundant,* p. 10):

> "Some years ago, Tommy Hicks was in Russia. Suddenly, his interpreter did not want to translate for him any longer; she spat in his face and said: I do not want to translate this nonsense any more, and went away. There he stood, without interpreter, in a foreign country, before multitudes of people. Then he began to speak in tongues, and the Holy Spirit gave him the language of the people to whom he was speaking, that means the Russian language. The crowd was moved to tears, and many surrendered themselves to Jesus. It happened many times that a message in tongues was understood by somebody who was a guest in the meeting, so that the Lord spoke to someone in his mother-tongue. This is wonderful! This is not only a special blessing for the one who was spoken to by the Holy Spirit in this way, but also again, a proof to all of us that the strange words which we speak really form a language which is understood and spoken somewhere in the world."

6

Shaker Rituals

In order to become a Shaker, an individual must undergo baptism. The Shakers believe, however, that God will send a sign in the form of a dream, vision, or any experience or occurrence that can be interpreted as a supernatural sign to a person whom He wants to accept baptism. Not everyone in a congregation, therefore, will have been baptized.

The divine call does not appear to be very difficult to achieve. Vincentians, generally, regard dreams with awe and respect—not only their own dreams but also those that other people may have concerning them. A 25-year-old Methodist communicant who attended the Methodist services regularly and ridiculed the Shakers unmercifully admitted that she would obey a summons to join them if she were to have a dream that could be interpreted as an invitation or a command to accept baptism—or if someone else were to have such a dream about her. One Shaker woman spoke of being quite perturbed because she had had several dreams indicating that her adult daughter should be baptized, but she had been unable to convince the girl to accept baptism as yet.

Several members revealed that they had been great scoffers of the religion before they had received the supernatural directive that brought them into it. Not many obeyed the first summons—baptism is acknowledged to be somewhat of an ordeal—and most informants admitted that they had procrastinated. Mother E. waited eleven years. Another woman had three dreams before making her decision. The pointer heard a voice one day when he was in the mountains, but he waited until he had a vision some time later before he sought baptism.

The significant dreams and visions included certain repetitive elements: a white gentleman dressed in white, water and bodies of water, stones falling from heaven but not hitting or harming the dreamer, being in strange surroundings, hearing specific hymns, perhaps not previously known. One woman described a typical dream: "I dreamt that I was traveling and found myself looking out on the sea. I saw a ship and a clock and a gun. I saw a gentleman with his hand open and below him was marked, 'This is my good shepherd. I lay down my life for my sheep.' He wore a gown and was looking

young to me. I ax a question and the answer came back to me—as soon as the
gun fired and the clock strike twelve, the world is going to end. And I found
myself singing, 'Take my life and let it be consecrated, Lord, to Thee.' " One
informant reported a different kind of experience. One evening, when she was
attending a service, she felt an impulse to go forward and kneel at the altar,
which she interpreted as the sign to seek baptism. Frequently, another member
of the family was already a Shaker, but informants were insistent that this was
not a factor in their own acceptance of the faith.

Illness seems to plague those who ignore the divine bid. One woman said,
"Since I was twelve years, I find I did get a different vision to go and baptize.
But I didn't go until I was 23. I was ill all that time, but still I did not go."
Another woman declared, "You don't feel good until you accept baptism."

Children may attend Shaker services, and young children, seven or eight
years old or younger, frequently do accompany their mothers. (It was
interesting to note the relative absence of older children who were presumably
old enough to be left at home to care for themselves or, perhaps, for younger
children.) The pointer can christen children by sprinkling, but they must undergo baptism later if they want to be Shakers. The earliest age for baptism is
twelve. Shakers send their children to other churches for religious instruction
since the Shaker church does not provide formal religious education. For
example, Mother E.'s daughter attends the Catholic school and church, and is
almost ready to make her First Communion. Despite the apparent conflict
with the firmly held notion that a person does not become a Shaker because a
member of his family is one, Mother E. said that, when she is old enough, her
daughter intends to accept baptism and the Shaker religion as her mother had
done.

The decision to accept baptism is the starting point for a series of rituals
focusing on the baptismal candidate. In a ceremony known as "bowing,"[1]
which takes place during the course of a regular meeting, the aspirant is
separated from the congregation and introduced as a candidate. The bowing
ceremony I witnessed was divided between two meetings. The pointer was
absent on the first evening, and the two leaders and the mother who were offi-
ciating in his stead were not qualified to conduct all parts of the ritual. Several evenings later, the pointer completed the ceremony. At the first meeting,
except for a lengthy comment on baptism by Leader M., the early part of the
service followed the usual pattern. Leader M. then extended an invitation to
"anyone who wants to give his heart to Christ Jesus" to "come now and
bow." A man and a young woman went forward and knelt on the ground
before him. The congregation stood and sang while Leader M. exhorted
everyone to come to Jesus. A woman arranged the kneeling candidates, placing
their hands in the positions they would be required to hold for the duration of
each meeting attended before baptism: each held a lighted candle in the right

hand, the left hand being held open with the palm up. Both hands were extended, waist high, at right angles to the body. The candidates kept their eyes closed and were instructed to meditate constantly on their sins.

Leader P. addressed some remarks particularly to "those of you who are about to ax Jesus to give you some of that water." Mother A. spoke next. She put the Bible, with her lighted candle held on top of it, on the head of first one and then the other of the candidates, while praying over them. Holding the Bible and candle balanced on the man's head with one hand, she took the woman candidate's candle in her other hand, held it on the woman's head, prayed, marked the sign of the cross over the woman's head with the candle, and finally handed the candle back to her. She put the Bible on the head of each again and rang the bell over them. Taking the candle of each in turn, she then marked a cross with it before them. She helped them to rise from their knees, explaining that she had not yet had everything revealed to her, so she would leave the rest to the elder (Pointer B.). Before leaving them, however, she said, "Not only are you going to sit there with your hands open but you are going to repent every one of your sins. He is going to make of you a better child."

Pointer B. continued the rites at the next meeting. It was held at another church (Questelles; the first part had taken place at Lowmans), but the composition of the congregation was about the same. The man who had bowed was not present, but the pointer said that, even so, it was his duty to introduce the woman candidate to the Christ Jesus. During one of the early hymns, he used a piece of chalk to mark a circle on the floor around the center pole. He made four straight lines out from the pole to the circle and within the quadrants thus formed proceeded to draw designs.[2] Mother A. had put a lighted candle on the floor by the pole. He moved it to a place on one of the lines drawn out from the pole. Taking a glass of water and another candle, he dipped the unlighted end of the candle in the water and sprinkled his drawing with it. He then rang the bell in each of the four quadrants.

After the routine part of the service was over, Pointer B. gave a prayer book to Mother A. He directed the candidate to kneel on a pillow before him (this was a more elaborately furnished church than the other). With his hand on the woman's head, he prayed aloud asking the Holy Spirit to abide in her. While the seated congregation sang a hymn, Pointer B. put on the kneeling woman's head a lighted candle and then the Bible with the candle on top of it. He rang the bell beside her. The mother read the questions for a candidate for baptism from the prayer book, and the woman responded. The congregation sang another hymn while the pointer marked a cross on her head with the lighted candle and gave her three sips of water. He marked a cross on her forehead and her palms with chalk.

The pointer announced that he was going to "take a prove." Mother A.

made a cross on the woman's chest with the edge of the Bible and handed it to her. The candidate held it with both hands, the edges pointed toward her, and made the sign of the cross with it. After she opened it, Mother A. carefully noted where her thumbs touched the pages and took the book from her. Mother A. then read the three verses indicated by her thumbs on each page, and the pointer interpreted the message to the congregation.

The bowing ritual required several hours. The pointer, leaders, and Mother A. were frequently in various stages of dissociation, which, though seemingly hampering and retarding their activities considerably, at the same time seemed to augment the excitement and importance of the proceedings.

A period of preparation lasting from several weeks to several months follows for the candidates. The pointer decides when they are ready for the final baptism rite, but it is likely that he is influenced as much by the number of candidates he has been able to gather as he is by their state of preparedness—it is gratifying to be able to point to a goodly number of "children."[3] According to Mother E., "the leader will give them [the candidates] the 51st psalm to read," to learn and be able to repeat back to him, and "they have to learn plenty other things." Mother O. stated that "when they are in the mercy seat,[4] the leader and mothers teach them where to walk and how to speak in the way leading to the Lord—they [candidates] read and learn things from the Bible—and [they, i.e., leader and mothers] teach them the way to baptism." At the meetings, the candidates sit on the front bench, "the bench of repentance," and they "have their hand open, beggin' and askin' God to forgive them for all their sins while they are on the mercy seat."

The night before the baptism ceremony, the candidates remain in the church, praying, listening to words of consolation, and undergoing a shortened version of mourning. After white blindfolds are tied over their eyes, the candidates are laid on the ground—symbolizing death and eventual rebirth in baptism. Mother A. wrote her description of one baptism as follows:

> Pointer have had the baptism on the 28th August, and it was a very fine one. . . . The baptism was done at Lowmans. On Saturday night, there was a vast amount of members turned out. The bands [blindfolds] for the candidates were thus signed by Pointer. Pointer have had a long lecturing to his seven Candidates (as you know, when he begins he does not want to stop). Passages of scripture had been read and explained. Candidates were thus question from a certain book. Many other heart touching consolations were given by others (Leaders, Mothers and who had thus gained opportunity). During the meeting, Candidates were ordered to kneel, whilst bands were placed on their hands and shoulders and afterwards tied on head by Pointer with the aid of myself and other Mothers; after which Pointer prayed. After a short period of singing and demonstrating, the meeting was thus brought to

an end. That was about 1:50 A.M. The candidates were thus lain to have a rest with the company of some of the members.

On Sunday morning, members from various parts gathered in the church (though it was raining a lot). A short meeting was held, after which we all journeyed to the river. After reaching the river, the meeting were commenced, Baptism lesson were read and meeting carried on. One or two persons prayed, hymns were sung, then Pointer taking the cross from cross bearer, pushed his way through water. (Before Pointer go in river the water was consecrated.) He prayed, sung a hymn, then beckoned the cross bearer to come to him. The cross bearer was placed in an opposite direction, so that Candidates can be plunged just to the foot of the cross. A hymn was sung then Candidates were beckon to be brought (one by one). Each Candidate were spoken to before being plunged . . . they were taken to and taken from Pointer by two mothers. At intervals, the Candidates as they go in water were taken to a sheltered place where they were undressed by myself and other Mothers. Even too Mother B., Mother R., Pointer and I replaced fresh bands. After which we all marched from there singing back to church. For a short time in church, meeting was held, then lunch were required. After lunch, meeting was called in. Many sweet sermons were unfurled, by leaders, pointers, mothers and other elders who gained opportunity. Then washing and anointing was done (during service) by myself, Mother B., Mother R. and Pointer B. At intervals candidates were put to prayer and then testified.

Dissociation, more violent then usual for Shakers, is reported to be common for baptismal candidates. One mother described them as shaking so uncontrollably that it was necessary to support them lest they fall back into the water. Shakers obviously enjoy the baptismal ceremony. They describe fondly the beauty of the candidates garbed in white and proudly display their processional banners and the cross under which the candidates are plunged. One woman, however, admitted that it was difficult to be a candidate.

"Mourning" is another Shaker rite, one of great importance both for those who undergo its rigors and for those who do not. The former are in a position to benefit from its blessings; the latter do not acquire the resulting advantages and consequently remain ordinary members of the church. Unlike baptism, mourning can be repeated, with the possibility of deriving further benefits. After the initial experience, however, the rite is more accurately referred to as "building." Baptism, mourning, and building are rites that intensify division and increase specialization. Baptism separates the converted from the nonconverted. Mourning divides the Shaker in-group into those who have mourned and hence have some position in the church from mere members. Furthermore, since not all of those who mourn receive the same gifts, mourning initiates the separation into various capacities that is furthered by building, the more exclusive in-group of mourners being divided into various

classes of elders. Thus, for any given Shaker, there are those who are elder to
him in the church and, if he has been to mourn, there are also those to whom
he is elder.

Mourning in the Shaker sense has the special meaning of mourning for
one's sins, not grieving for the dead. Synonymous expressions are "taking a
spiritual journey" or "taking a pilgrim journey" and "going to the secret
room." Justification for the rite is found in the Bible. Brother J. gave the
following (minimally edited) explanation:

> Then was Jesus led up in the wilderness to be tempted by the devil and there
> he fasted 40 days and 40 nights. And there he was until the tempter came and
> after Satan had finished tempting him, Angels came and ministered unto him.
> So you will see that is how we goes to the room by ourself to pray. And Mat-
> thew 5:4 says "Blessed are they that mourn for they shall be comforted." The
> bands on our forehead represent the thorn Jesus had on his forehead.

A sign from the Holy Spirit is required before mourning is undertaken, even
as it is for baptism. Again, since this can be as indefinite as the interpretation
of someone else's dream, it is unlikely that a supernatural sign would be difficult to obtain.

Since mourning involves a continuous period of isolation lasting from 6 to
14 days or more, the Shaker who decides to undertake it may have to do some
prior planning and preparing. Brother J. decided to spend his vacation going
to mourn. Sister W. and A., a male member of the congregation, planned to
seek short-term employment in order to earn the money needed to buy the
bands and food for the mourning period. Sister W. did not regard this as an
unsurmountable difficulty. The Chief Minister at that time had not only been
her teacher in school but had also been instrumental in legalizing Shakerism,
and she intended to apply to him for work. She said that she and A. would
each need about $5 or $6 BWI.[5] From his job on road construction A. received
$1.60 per day.

Sister W., A., and a man, whom I did not know, from another part of the
island were put to mourn at the same time. Sister W., a large, powerfully built
woman, had mourned once before, but not under Pointer B. She complained
that her previous pointer had "robbed" her. During her spiritual journey, she
had seen the queen remove her crown and place it on her (Sister W.'s) head,
which indicated that she was entitled to a ritual known as "being crowned,"
but the pointer had not crowned her. When she took her grievance to Pointer
B., he had told her that he could do nothing to rectify the injustice and that
she would have to repeat the ritual. The mourning experience was also familiar to A., a short, slight man who lived with Sister W. and her husband,
and had once been a choir boy in the Methodist church. He had already
mourned five times and had been filling the office of prover for Pointer B.

At the regular Wednesday evening service, held the night before the trio were put to mourn, the sermons, prayers, and words of consolation centered on mourning. The leader and other speakers expounded at length on its hardships and difficulties, stressing the fact that not all who aspired to mourn were able to complete the task—some fell by the wayside. The hope was repeatedly expressed that those embarking on the undertaking would be able to persevere to the end.

The tiny mourning room near Pointer B.'s house at Chapmans Village in the country was the setting for the opening ceremony of the mourning ritual the next evening. As Sister W. had anticipated ("all the girls who want to will come to see us put to mourn"), the room was crowded. Some worshipers were standing outside looking in the open door. A circle had been made on the floor with chalk. A lighted candle was standing in the middle of the circle, with four other candles placed around it, and a variety of designs had been drawn within the circle. According to informants, the chalk design would serve as a "map" for the mourners on their spiritual journey (see Appendix). The usual Methodist Order of Morning Worship was followed, and the consecration of the corners was performed. Meanwhile, the three mourners, or "pilgrims," stood or knelt together at one side of the room. They kept their hands in the receptive or begging attitude that the baptismal candidates had maintained, with palms open and up. Several leaders and mothers led hymns or knelt to offer the typically chanted prayers, which were accompanied by fairly general dissociation.

At Pointer B.'s behest, several women prepared a basin of water with green leaves and a lighted candle in it, to "wash the feet of the pilgrims." Pointer B. said a prayer over the basin, the candle was removed, and the mourners' faces, hands, and feet were washed.

Proves were taken for each mourner, to the apparent satisfaction of the pointer. He then wrapped the Bible in the bands, which were of various colors—white, blue, mauve—and resembled wide neckties or ascots. Designs (circles, crosses, etc.) had been made on them with chalk and dripped candle wax. The pointer placed the bands across the heads, outstretched hands, and shoulders of the mourners. At this point, in response to the pointer's question, Sister W. confessed that she had been guilty of calling someone a fool, so the pointer lit a candle, held it over her head, and prayed. Turning his attention again to the bands, he lifted and removed Sister W.'s head tie, marked three crosses on her forehead, and tied the bands, one at a time, across her eyes. Mother B. followed him and replaced Sister W.'s head tie, covering the top of her head and the bands, and knotting it loosely around her neck. Moving on to the men, the pointer and mother repeated the procedure.

The pointer gave each blindfolded mourner three sips of water and marked a cross on each of their upturned palms before slapping it three times with his

leather strap. Mother B. lit six candles, each mourner being given one to hold
in each hand. After delivering a lengthy chanted prayer, the pointer brought
the service to a close.

The room was then readied for the mourners' occupancy. Several mothers
arranged burlap pallets, each with a pillow, on the floor and hung cloths over
a rope stretched across the room to form two sections: one for Sister W., the
other for the men. Still holding their lighted candles, the mourners waited for
the preparations to be completed and the room cleared so that they might be
"laid on the ground." They lie either on their right sides or on their backs because they believe that "you can't get nothin' on the left."

Although the mourners' diet is limited, Shaker informants insist that it is
adequate.[6] For breakfast and the evening meal, the mourners are given "bush
tea," made of guinea pepper and mint, with or without milk, and bread. At
lunch they are given rice and codfish, but no fresh fish or potatoes. However,
individuals with dietary problems would not be excluded from mourning on
that account because the Spirit could intervene and make known that they
were to have foods other than those generally provided. The kitchen in which
the mourners' food is prepared must be near the mourning room so that meals
can be carried directly and quickly to them, and the food must be carefully
covered to keep Satan from contaminating it and gaining access to the vulnerable mourners.

Shakers compare going to mourn with going to school: there is more to be
learned each time you go back. Apropos of speaking in tongues, it was said,
"In one class, you may get one unknown tongue, and the next time you go to
mourn, you may get another." According to the pointer, when you go to
mourn you "regenerate. Then you have the true zeal of the Spirit. You go for
a deeper knowledge of God." During the period of confinement, the pointer
instructs the mourners in how to live according to the Bible, the other sisters
and brothers may "pray and offer words of consolation" to the mourners, but
what is most important is that the Holy Spirit is believed to be in contact with
them, teaching them. They expect to travel, and in the course of their spiritual
journey they expect to discover what their work in the church is to be. Such
gifts are revealed symbolically; for example, if a mourner were to see a book, it
would mean that he was to preach.

For certain individuals—those who have committed evil deeds, such as
murder or abortion, those who bear malice toward others, those who have insufficient faith—it is useless, if not dangerous, to mourn. The pointer is
responsible for culling out such misfits and releasing them. Otherwise, they
might become insane. According to Mother E., about eight of the persons who
have mourned under Pointer B. have been so affected. There have been eleven
souls, she said, that he has rejected.

Mourners may hope that by praying very fervently and diligently they will be able to achieve a satisfactory journey quickly and be ready to leave the secret room. Dismissal is in the pointer's hands. He questions each mourner about his travel experiences, and only if they meet his expectations is the mourner discharged.

When all the mourners have ended the period of confinement, they are given an opportunity to "shout," or describe in detail their visions and travel experiences to the rest of the congregation. Again, as they were during the beginning ceremony of mourning before being "laid on the ground," they are the center of attention and the objects of specific rituals.

I attended one session at which two mourners "shouted." Each one regaled the congregation with a rambling, detailed account of his spiritual journey. They frequently interrupted their recitals to interpose hymns which had been featured on their journeys ("I hear a song . . ." or "I heard someone singing . . .") and which the congregation then joined in singing. One mourner had apparently experienced some anxious moments before the desired visions appeared: "I prayed four days—four solid days! I don't see nothing. When I prayed, I started, 'My God! What have I done? You turn Your back against me. I don't kill nobody!'" In recounting their experiences the mourners indicated that many of the visions represented familiar and ordinary experiences, such as walking down the road to the next village, meeting and conversing with one of the mothers of the church, going to church, having an ache or pain. Some of the visions were more exotic and out of the ordinary for them, but still within the range of possibility: "I find myself into an office and I have to sign. I take a pen. I have to sign." Others were, however, extraordinary: "I heard a voice speak to me. It said it would send Peter and Gabriel to visit me. Hear what I said, people? The voice I heard sent Gabriel and Peter."

The mourner who has had the appropriate vision is entitled to be the recipient of the very impressive and highly desired ritual of "crowning," in which the Bible is placed on the mourner's head and a number of lighted candles are held around it. However, as was evident from Sister W.'s experience, the pointer must attest to any gift claimed by the mourner; otherwise it will not be granted. In addition to the gifts of church status and the right to be crowned, a pilgrim, in the course of his journey, may also be given the color for a head tie and other directives about wearing apparel and ritual paraphernalia. Those who have been to mourn will usually wear colored head ties; those who have not wear white. However, the Spirit will occasionally decree that a mourner should continue to wear white. Pointer B. took much pride in wearing only "what I get from the Spirit" and spoke disdainfully of another pointer who "enlarges himself and wears other things to increase his importance."

The values of mourning for a Shaker are obvious. A successful spiritual journey becomes his key for admittance into the Shaker elite.

NOTES

1. Note the similarity to the "vowing" service of the Jamaican revivalist churches (Simpson, 1956: 369–370).

2. An example of a chalk design is shown in the Appendix. The one described in text was much less elaborate.

3. Pointer B. reported that he had baptized a total of 584 "children" and, at that time, had nine candidates preparing for baptism. Apparently two withdrew (or, perhaps, were indeed unprepared) before the baptism ceremony, since Mother A. reported in the letter quoted in text that seven candidates finally accepted the rite.

4. The bench on which the candidates for baptism sit—used here to mean the period between bowing and baptism.

5. At that time, one British West Indian dollar was worth about 60 cents in United States currency.

6. This is not, however, the opinion of some non-Shakers. One Vincentian doctor declared that mourners are intentionally starved and given insufficient liquids to make them more disposed to delusions.

7

Possession Trance

Among the Shakers, possession by the Holy Spirit is manifested by a state of dissociation, a common occurrence during their meetings. Although the Shakers conceptualize this trance as resulting from the entry of the Spirit into the body of the worshiper, the details of the concept seem to be somewhat vague and confused. According to Pointer B., the "Power is a breeze descended that comes as a rushing wind into the heart. When It leaves, you feel something leaving you." Mother A. mentioned having the feeling "that you were in the spirit" and said that the Spirit might "manifest on someone and bring something in the person's heart." Sister E. gave the clearest statement: "That Power sincerely be inside you."

The same ambiguity can be found in the discussion of spirit possession among the Spiritual Baptists of Trinidad by Herskovits and Herskovits. They state that the " 'Spirit' actually touches the worshipper with an unseen hand, and a shiver electrifies his body causing him first to stiffen, then to begin to shake. The 'Spirit' fills him with joy, causing him to dance, to speak in tongues, to prophesy, to 'see.' " Although it is not clear whether or not the Spirit is believed to actually enter the person, Herskovits and Herskovits (1947: 192–193) seem to be satisfied that this is an example of possession: "The phenomenon of possession by the 'Spirit,' the physical manifestations of such possession in the shaking, the dancing, the speaking in tongues, the bringing back of spiritual gifts are all at the core of the Shouters worship everywhere."

In his discussion of the Trinidadian Spiritual Baptists, Simpson (1966) also leaves an uncertain impression. He states that the "spirit may come to" a person or that a person may "get the spirit" and speaks of the "manifestations of the spirit on the pilgrims." He also seems to regard this phenomenon as spirit possession (1966: 541).

Dissociation rarely occurs during the early part of the service. At that time, worshipers are occupied with giving the proper responses, following the Bible lessons in their own Bibles, singing hymns from their hymnals, kneeling, sitting, standing, shaking hands, and the like, so that states of dissociation apparently have little opportunity to develop. The infrequent worshiper who does begin to slip into possession trance, as evinced by a sob, a yell, or a shudder, very quickly recovers.

As the service proceeds beyond the early period in which the conventional, prescribed forms are read or recited from memory, the opportunity for more originality and improvisation occurs. The leaders, for the most part, have been assuming the responsibility for the program, but at this point a member of the congregation may take an important solo part by offering "a few words" or a prayer. When the speaker takes his position to give the words of consolation, he stands while the congregation remains seated. He usually begins by singing the first few words of a hymn, and the congregation quickly joins in. While he preaches, he walks back and forth. As he becomes more deeply engrossed in his subject, he may wave his arms and appear more excited. Periodically, after the initial hymn, he interrupts his sermonizing with the favorite device of Shaker speakers by saying, "I t'ink I heard someone say . . ." or some other appropriate phrase to lead into a hymn, which again everyone sings. While the speaker is performing, the congregation usually maintains a steady, monotonous background of low singing or humming, which often becomes louder and more persistent. When a worshiper offers a prayer, he takes his position at the corner or side of the altar and kneels before the seated congregation; he chants or sings the prayer, the congregation chanting a response at the end of each rhythmic verse. Dissociation is most likely to occur—in fact, can be expected—during activities of this nature.

The worshipers sit with their eyes closed or half-closed on the narrow, backless benches. Often holding up their heads, yawning perhaps, and appearing to be half asleep, they give the impression that they are lost in their own reflections and have withdrawn from what is transpiring around them.[1] This impression becomes even stronger when they sing while someone is preaching. However, though they seem less than interested in the sermon, they do not appear to be any more interested in their own singing—it is done in an absent-minded manner; they have something else on their minds.

When the worshipers stand for a hymn, they keep time with bodily motions: they sway from side to side; swing about in a semicircle, pivoting first on one foot and then on the other; clap their hands or slap themselves lightly with a branch of sago palm or a book; or pound their Bibles or prayer books with the end of their candles. When seated for a hymn, they also mark the beat in some way: by rocking back and forth, by twisting from side to side at the waist, by tapping their bare feet, by clapping their hands, or by some arm–hand or head movement. They do not cross their legs.[2]

Possession trance occurs as a single-individual phenomenon, a phenomenon involving several individuals each of whom acts as a soloist, or as a group phenomenon, in which case it takes on choral aspects. At any time (although, as noted, it is less likely in the early part of the service) a person may exhibit symptoms of developing possession trance. He may be the sole person in the church to be so affected at the time, or there may be several individuals scattered through the congregation. He may be the person who has been performing—preaching or praying—or he may have been a member of the more or less passive audience. If he had been a listener, he was sitting with his eyes closed or nearly closed, humming, singing, making the proper responses, and marking the rhythm established by the singing or praying in some manner. The first external sign of dissociation may be a convulsive jerk of one or both arms, of one or both shoulders, or of the head. It may be a shudder, shiver, or trembling; a sudden shout, sob, hiss, or series of unintelligible sounds; or any combination of such movements or vocalizations (or both), indicating a departure from the person's earlier apathetic behavior. He may even stand up suddenly and dance. These observable signs of the diminution of internal control appear to be spontaneous and have a random quality lacking rhythmic patterning. If several persons are affected at the same time, their motions and sounds are not standardized; each will exhibit a different set of symptoms. At this phase of possession trance, the symptoms, viewed either for an individual or for several persons scattered through the church, are random and unpatterned. However, patterning of a different kind can be discerned: each person in possession trance develops his own peculiar style, and from one session to another the movements and sounds of a particular individual can often be predicted and identified at this level. For example, Mother O.'s head would always droop as though she were dozing, then suddenly jerk back. She would move her arm forward and up, with the fist tightly clenched. Her usual shout accompanying these movements was "Hi! Yi!" Sister W. would shake her shoulders and jerk both arms forward and up; she would frequently sob.

The first indication of developing possession trance in a person who has been performing may be a quaver in his voice. He may jerk spasmodically, tremble and shake, and occasionally break into his own prayer or preaching with a yell. If he is on his feet, as he becomes increasingly excited, he will pace back and forth ever more rapidly. He will, however, maintain sufficient control to be able to continue his sermon or prayer intelligibly. When Mother R. was addressing the congregation, she would become breathless and excited, her voice would develop a noticeable quaver, and she would interrupt her sermonizing periodically with a loud "Holy Ghost!"

Possession trance might not advance beyond this first level. The manifestations might more or less quickly abate—or they might continue, with the possession trance being maintained at this level for some time. There might also be repeated returns to this level after periods of normalcy.

Possession trance might, however, develop further into the next level. When this occurs, it often involves more than a single person and becomes a group phenomenon. As more and more individuals throughout the church become involved in the random symptoms of the first level of possession trance, a subtle change to behavior characteristic of the second level takes place. Not every person in possession trance makes the change at the same time, nor is there a definite break and shift in behavior. Each person will have established a pattern of movements that he now repeats over and over, very rapidly. Perhaps only the arms or head will be involved, perhaps more of the body. If the person is standing, the feet may be included in the action pattern, but he will not move far from his own circumscribed area. At this level of possession trance, most persons bend forward from the waist, with the knees slightly bent if they are standing. When Leader M. was on his knees praying and had achieved this level of possession trance, he would bend forward and put his knuckles on the ground, almost touch his head to the ground, and jerk back up again. He repeated this over and over with remarkable speed, gasping as he jerked back. Leader R. would almost touch his head to his knees when he was seated, then jerk it up and back, bubbling his lips on the way down, and audibly gulping air on the way up.

Idiosyncratic movements and sounds, and breathing peculiarities become less conspicuous because of the concerted attention persons in possession trance give to the same rhythm pattern. Whatever the prior activity had been—prayer, sermon, or hymn—is immaterial; in each case, a rhythmic beat has been provided through the singing, humming, or chanting for the worshipers to cling to. The pointer or leader frequently quickens the pace by beating out a faster tempo on the altar with his book or strap, or by singing louder and more raucously in faster time, and the congregation readily accepts and adapts to such changes. When a hymn is begun, the words that are sung are distinct and intelligible. As the singing continues and possession trance begins to appear, the words slowly degenerate into repeated syllables. When the second level of trance is reached, the syllables, in turn, change to mere grunts and gasps—but these are emitted in unison, with each possessed person contributing to the maintenance of the established beat.

That the Shakers themselves are aware of differences in possession-trance levels came to my attention when I played for them some of the tapes I had made. They identified individuals at the first possession-trance level (with evident enjoyment and even some amusement) from their distinctive sounds.

They were, however, unable to do this at the second level; sounds are too well blended, intelligible speech is no longer produced, nor are idiosyncratic shouts.

At the second level of possession trance, several persons rolled their eyes back so that only the whites could be seen. Others kept their eyes closed. Some showed signs of profuse sweating, which might not seem unusual in the hot, humid climate and in view of the physical exertion, but others engaged in the same activities did not. Some sprayed saliva, but there was no frothing. There was no yelling or shouting at this level. In several instances, a possession trancer was seen to brush a lighted candle without reacting. It is interesting that, in spite of the number of lighted candles and the apparent inattention of the dissociated individuals, nothing ever caught fire.

When possessed persons are crowded together, the standardization and depersonalization of their motion patterns becomes conspicuous. Each individual, as if in a dance line, then produces much the same movements. This phenomenon was observed several times when the group was standing in a cluster: all of the dissociated individuals were bent over at the waist, knees flexed, jerking up and down, in precise time. This appears to be very similar to the "trumping and laboring" described by Moore (1965: 64) for several Jamaican revival cults: "a shuffling two-step dance done to 2/2 rhythm, bending forward and up in rhythmic sequence, while sucking the breath into the body and releasing it with a grunting sound."

Sooner or later, the second level of possession trance changes. The smoothly patterned phenomenon in which each individual submits to the group-impressed rhythmic beat is disrupted as the dissociated persons emit loud sighs and yells, and breathe with complete disregard for the previous regular timing. Where they had been crowded together, some move out of the cluster, obliterating the chorus-line appearance. All movements and sounds again become individualistic.

Occasionally, the second level ends abruptly. At other times, the end is approached gradually, with some possession trancers continuing to exhibit second-level behavior while others no longer do so. In some cases, the decision to disregard the second-level rhythmic precision seems to be generated within the group of possession trancers themselves, but at other times, there seems to be an external signal—someone may begin singing a new hymn with a different tempo or the bell may be rung.

In the ensuing period, at the third level, the movements and sounds, having degenerated from the smooth rhythmic performance of the preceding level, are again random, patternless, and spasmodic even as they were in the first level. However, the sounds are unlike those of the first level in that they are not occasional shouts and noises superimposed on a musical background. In the third level, possession trancers are not humming or singing. They behave as if bewildered and appear to be breathless (perhaps from exertion); they gasp and groan, sigh and shout in noisy confusion. No outside assistance is needed to return them to normal.

Some individuals are highly dependable possession trancers and achieve dissociational states at almost every meeting, but other worshipers never exhibit the diagnostic symptoms. Shakers explain this apparent lack by saying that the Holy Spirit, in fact, enters those persons also, but only shakes them within. However, it would appear that externally manifested shaking is valued more since Shakers also say that individuals who shake more have greater "zeal." The nonshaking worshipers continue the background singing or humming during the periods of group dissociation when the possession trancers are presumably no longer able, or interested in doing so.

Possession trance as described so far might be labeled the typical Shaker possession trance. It is extremely well controlled. No violence is done to one's self or to others. There is very little movement away from the general location in the church occupied by the worshiper. Occasionally, however, the trance may not conform to this usual pattern. The possession trancer—more often a woman than a man—may exhibit much more boisterous behavior than is common and may even become so unsteady as to be on the verge of falling. Each time this was witnessed, several people near the affected person were ready to support her and to help her kneel lest she be hurt. In one instance, the woman involved had, that evening, become a candidate for baptism and had been the central figure in a long, possibly stressful, ceremony. Another time, the aberrant possession trancer was a woman whom the pointer had just taken to task for a misdeed and had punished as the climax to a long, obviously stressful, ritual to establish her guilt. On becoming violently dissociated, although not in danger of falling, being seated, she waved her arms about wildly, striking the persons seated around her. Several times, the pointer also appeared to be less controlled than usual. Reeling and staggering as if intoxicated, he was prevented from falling by nearby worshipers who put out their hands to support and steady him. It was reported that persons being baptized might also display more extreme symptoms of dissociation: they might shake so much that it is necessary to hold them to prevent their falling back into the water. It would seem that instances of less controlled possession-trance behavior are more likely to occur in situations replete with unusual emotional overtones and stress for the individual, and may be regarded as atypical.[3]

Shakers say that they know when possession trance is imminent. They claim to experience an inner trembling prior to the external manifestations. They report a selective amnesia for possession trance: they remember their personal, private interaction with the Spirit, but nothing else. After the departure of the Spirit, they claim to have a feeling of well-being, strength, and relaxation.

The worshipers emphatically deny using any devices to induce the Spirit to possess them—other than fulfilling the fundamental requirement of being "pure in heart." The decision to enter or not to enter a particular worshiper is entirely in the hands of the Spirit. Moore (1965: 64) reports that Jamaican revival cultists achieve possession trance by hyperventilating. When the Shakers were confronted with this information and questioned about their own practices, they vehemently denied that they hyperventilated in order to induce a state of dissociation—such breathing occurred after the Spirit had manifested Itself and was shaking them. This was corroborated by observation. Among the Shakers, breathing anomalies do not occur in the early period of dissociation nor as a preparatory device; rather they seem to be indicative of the greatest distance from reality and normality that was witnessed. According to informants, possession trancers can fall into a state of unconsciousness, but no

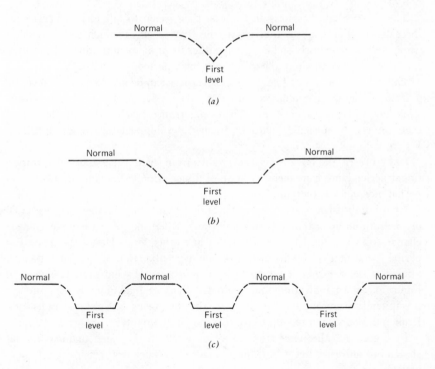

Figure 1. First-level possession trances: (a) brief duration; (b) extended duration; (c) repetitive.

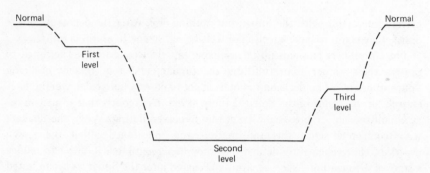

Figure 2.   Progress of possession trance reaching second level and returning to normal. The relative lengths of lines are not intended to be an accurate indication of the duration of the level or transition in question.

instance occurred during the period of observation, nor were any specific anecdotes recounted to substantiate the report.

The usual Shaker possession trances, then, seem to fall rather nicely into three levels. For a given individual, the first level, at which the possession trance seems to be fairly shallow, may either be of momentary duration or may continue at approximately the same level for a period of time, perhaps as long as half an hour or more. The possession trancer can be diverted at this level by a flash of light, the pointer's voice, or other external stimuli. The various situations in which a person in possession trance reaches the first level and then returns to normalcy without further development are diagrammed in Figure 1.

In Figure 1a, the possession trancer slips from the normal state, via a transitional period, into a momentary state of dissociation. After another transition period, normalcy is reestablished.

I have designated as a period of transition that time, whether inappreciable or measurable by ordinary means and units, when the subject is undergoing a change from any level in the scheme to any other level. Hence the transition period is not marked by distinctive behavior peculiar to it alone, but rather by a meld of the behaviors characteristic of the stages adjacent to it. It is used in Figure 1 as an indication and reminder that an individual rarely plunges precipitately from one level to another, the shift being blurred and indistinct. Broken lines are used to emphasize this indefinite quality.

In Figure 1b, the possession trance develops in the same manner as that shown in Figure 1a, but it lasts for a longer period before the transition to normalcy occurs.

In some cases, as shown in Figure 1c, the achievement of the shallow, first-level possession trance and the subsequent attainment of normalcy may occur repeatedly without a deeper possession trance being reached in the interim.

In some cases, possession trance becomes perceptibly deeper than in the first level, and environmental distractions are no longer heeded.[4] The second-level possession trance develops from the first level and eventually shifts to a third level, characterized by confusion and apparent bewilderment as well as random movements and sounds. The third level is usually brief, and, after a transition period, the subject may again return to normalcy. This situation is shown in Figure 2.

The third level is diagrammed as being less deep than the second level but deeper than the first because it was my impression that the third level shared with the second a more restricted awareness of distractions, yet no longer partook of the greater losing of one's self in rhythm that was characteristic of the second level.

During the course of an evening, the diagram of an individual's possession-trance activities, his trance "map" so to speak, may present a series of ups and downs from one level to another, without any break in which the person returns to normalcy during the total period of dissociation. This situation is diagrammed in Figure 3.

If the possession-trance maps of all affected persons were superimposed on one another, we would have a picture of the group possession-trance pattern for a meeting. The transition periods of all the individuals would not coincide, of course, nor would the lengths of time each individual remained at a certain level, but, where the individual possession-trance maps would agree during the second-level possession trances, the resultant reinforcement would produce the

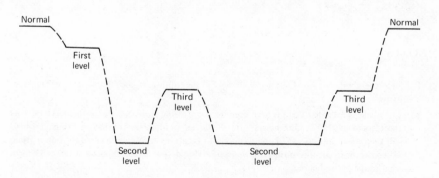

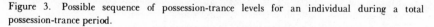

Figure 3. Possible sequence of possession-trance levels for an individual during a total possession-trance period.

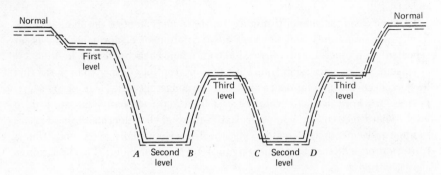

Figure 4. Possession-trance maps for several individuals superimposed to show fields of reinforcement.

choral phenomenon described above and shown in Figure 4. At points *A* and
C, most of the possession trancers are engaging in the same rhythmic pattern.
At points *B* and *D*, they are beginning to return to more individualized
rhythms (or nonrhythm) and actions. From *A* to *B* and *C* to *D*, however, the
choral aspects are prominent.

A fourth level might have been included to cover the situation in which a
possession trancer has apparently withdrawn farther than is ordinarily the
case, has lost his ability to interact in a coordinated manner with his surroundings, and is in danger of falling or colliding with others. However, as has
been stated, this is not the usual case.

On the whole, Shaker possession trances seem to be relatively simple and
uncomplicated, a source of satisfaction and probable benefit to the participants.[5]

NOTES

1. Note the similarities to Field's (1960: 56–57) description of the "possession fit" in West
    Africa.

2. The Shakers aver that there is no reason for not crossing their legs. According to Herskovits
    and Herskovits (1947: 336), however, the Trinidadian Shouters say that "anything 'crossed'
    will keep the 'saints' away." Lending support to that, Sister W. volunteered the information,
    "If you want to cut the spirit, cross yourself and fold your hands. You see it cease. You can
    see it in the praise house."

3. Mischel and Mischel (1958: 252) mention crises such as "serious marital or other interper-
    sonal problems . . . difficult decisions . . . involvement in court cases, or . . . other severely
    frustrating or conflict-producing events" as situations stimulating the induction of possession
    trance among Shangoists in Trinidad. Although the Shakers did not seem to require extraor-

dinary stimulus for their typical possession trances, such stimulus did appear to be a factor in the production of the atypical phenomenon.

4. The distractions that occurred at the services witnessed, however, were of low magnitude; perhaps more demanding stimuli might be able to penetrate the barrier against certain aspects of the environment.

5. I have also investigated the relationship between Shaker possession trance and sex in a paper presented at the 1972 Meeting of the American Anthropological Association in Toronto (Henney, 1972).

8

Trance among the Shakers

Trance unaccompanied by a belief in spirit possession occurs among the Shakers during the period of seclusion referred to as mourning. The mourner is expected to go on a "spiritual journey" and see various signs indicating his future work in the cult. Although the mourning experience, as Simpson (1970: 150) indicates for the Shouters in Trinidad, may include dream states and imaginative thinking, as well as dissociational states, it is likely that much of the experience is derived from hallucination and that the mourner "sees" and "hears" what he later reports. Investigators of the effects of sensory deprivation on humans have placed their subjects in conditions so strikingly similar to those in which mourners are placed that it is not surprising to find certain parallels in the outcomes. Where the results of sensory-deprivation experiments and the mourning-room experiences differ, psychological and cultural differences in the structuring of the experience and in the makeup of the subjects undergoing it are probable influential factors.

Dr. D. O. Hebb and his associates at McGill University began a series of experiments in 1951 to determine the effects of sensory deprivation on human beings. Their subjects were male college students, who were paid 20 dollars a day to participate in the study. They were instructed to lie on a bed in a lighted 8 × 6 × 4-foot room for as long as they were willing, usually three or four days. They wore cotton gloves and cardboard cuffs to lessen tactual perception and translucent goggles that admitted light but precluded patterned vision. The room was partially soundproof. Auditory perception was further limited by a foam-rubber pillow and the masking sounds of an air conditioner and an intercommunication system. The latter connected the subject and the experimenter, who was always stationed outside the room, but communication was kept at a minimum. The subjects were taken to the toilet and given food when they requested it (Bexton, Heron, and Scott, 1954; Heron, Doane, and Scott, 1956; Heron, 1961; Scott et al., 1959; Doane et al., 1959).

Hallucinations were reported by some of the subjects. In one experiment, all fourteen subjects described imagery of a simple nature, eleven reported more complex forms, seven reported figures or objects without backgrounds, and three described full-blown scenes (Bexton et al., 1954: 74). The three McGill experimenters who utilized themselves as subjects all experienced hallucinations after the first day. They likened their experiences to those reported "after administration of certain drugs (such as mescal and lysergic acid) and after certain types of brain damage" (Heron et al., 1956: 14–18).

The translucent goggles worn by the subjects were changed to opaque ones in order to discover the effect of light on hallucinating. For the first two hours after the goggles were changed, hallucinatory activity increased, but then stopped or decreased sharply. A return to translucent goggles brought a corresponding return to hallucinating. Doane et al. (1959: 214) suggested that "unpatterned sensory stimulation increases the probability of hallucinatory activity."

Bexton et al. (1954: 75) found that "there was some control over content; by 'trying' the subject might see certain objects suggested by the experimenter, but not always as he intended." Heron (1961: 18), however, in a study involving 29 subjects, 25 of whom reported hallucinations, found that the subjects were unable to exert much control over the content, activation, or cessation of the phenomenon.

The effect of propaganda presented to the subjects during isolation was tested and compared with the effect on a control group. "Both groups showed a significant change of attitude after listening to the propaganda, but the change was much greater for the experimental subject than it was for the controls" (Scott et al., 1959: 205).

Vernon and associates, experimenting later at Princeton University, placed their subjects in a 4 × 6-foot cubicle with a 15 × 9-foot "floating room" especially constructed for maximum soundproofing and lightproofing. The subjects, who wore earplugs and cardboard cuffs, were instructed to remain as quiet as possible. The cubicle was equipped with a bed and a chair. The subjects were blindfolded when led to toilet facilities and, in some experiments, to meals outside the room. A hidden microphone permitted the researchers to monitor the subjects. A "panic button" was within easy reach if a subject wished to terminate his stay before the experiment was completed. For some studies a 48-hour confinement period was used; for others, a 72-hour period (Vernon and Hoffman, 1956; Vernon, McGill, and Schiffman, 1958; Vernon and McGill, 1957; Vernon, 1963).

In the first Princeton study, a red light was used to illuminate the experimental chamber during meals. No hallucinations were reported. After the red light was extinguished and meals were taken without illumination, six of the nine subjects reported hallucinations. Conditions were further changed so that the subjects no longer needed to leave the dark room for toilet necessities. An increase in hallucinations was expected because the conditions were more severe. However, only one subject reported a hallucination, and it was considered doubtful. Vernon et al. (1958: 34) reasoned that a minimum of hallucinations was produced by conditions in which all visual stimulation was eliminated, some hallucinations resulted from conditions permitting a small amount of light stimulation, but "confinement permitting a great deal of visual stimulation, but not pattern vision, produces . . . not only the greatest number but also the greatest variety of hallucinations."

In experiments at the University of Manitoba, Zubek and associates (Zubek, Sansom, and Prysianzniuk, 1960; Zubek et al., 1961) used conditions of silence and darkness similar to those used at Princeton, but with a confinement period of one week. The subjects did not usually begin to hallucinate until the third day of confinement. At Duke Univeristy, however, after only two hours in a partially soundproof, completely dark room, seven of ten experimental subjects, chosen at random without regard to sex, occupation, education, or economic status, reported visual phenomena ranging from flashes of light to fairly complex illusions or hallucinations (Cohen et al., 1961; Silverman et al., 1962).

Freedman, Grunebaum, and Greenblatt (1961) summarized the results of eight sensory-deprivation studies by various investigators and found that hallucinations occurred in all studies (four) in which the light conditions eliminated normal perception, but only in half the cases in which a complete blackout was maintained. In all cases in which motility was restricted, however, hallucinations were reported. More important than activity might be the position of the subject: Zuckerman (1969a: 116) found that subjects confined in chairs seem to experience visual sensations much less frequently than those lying on their backs.

Freedman and associates (1961: 62) suggested that although "some one sensory occlusion may be necessary to produce 'sensory deprivation' effects, the sufficient condition may prove to be a combination of different atypical conditions." At the University of Miami, Arnhoff, Leon, and Brownfield (1962: 900) used the McGill sensory-deprivation conditions for a group of twelve subjects and received no reports of hallucinations. They concluded that "major disruptive psychological effects . . . are the product of a complex interaction of personality, anxiety, expectation, situational structuring, and amount and patterning of external sensory input."

C. W. Jackson and Kelly (1962), working at the University of Michigan, investigated the effect that the expectations of the subject might have on the results of sensory-deprivation experiments. Fourteen male college students were placed in isolation conditions of the McGill type for one hour. Each was informed of bizarre cognitive and perceptual results that might occur and given a pill, professedly a hallucinogenic drug, but actually a placebo, purportedly for reinforcing the sensory deprivation effects and increasing the possibility of imagery, odd sensations and ideas, and so on. All subjects reported auditory and kinesthetic phenomena, and twelve reported emotional experiences. The investigators concluded that certain factors in sensory-deprivation experiments have not been given sufficient attention although they are of considerable significance. These include the anticipations and expectations of the subject, whether or not he is motivated to "experience and report," and the utilization of "continuous free associative reporting" (C. W. Jackson and Pollard, 1962: 340).

The "matrix of social cues," or "demand characteristics," is also a salient feature of the sensory-deprivation situation that contributes to the resulting effects, according to Orne and Scheibe (1964: 3), who point out that cues within the experimental procedure, such as the panic button used in the Princeton investigations, can provide the subject with "eloquent instructions."

In some studies, external stimulation has been limited by the use of more exotic devices that bear less resemblance to the Shaker mourning-room practices. Shurley (1962) attempted to keep all sensory input to a nearly absolute minimum by submerging his subjects in a water tank. A group of Harvard investigators placed their subjects in a tank-type respirator (Solomon and Mendelson, 1962; Mendelson et al., 1961). Hallucinations were reported by some subjects in both experiments.

Shaker mourning-room practices and the reported subjective experiences of the mourners are in many respects similar to sensory-deprivation experiments. Experimental subjects in the McGill studies were placed in conditions that strongly resemble mourning-room conditions. In both situations the subjects are confined to a small area where they remain in a supine position. Interference with visual perception is maintained: the mourner's bands and the sensory-deprivation subject's goggles serve to limit pattern vision effectively while admitting some light. The individuals undergoing the experience in both cases are not only taken from their usual environments, separated from their ordinary social contacts, and deprived of their normal schedule of activities but also placed in positions of dependency. Mourners are under the supervision and care of the mourning-room attendants; research subjects are dependent on the investigation personnel. Both encounter stimulation that is extraordinary in its monotony and very reduced scope. The length of the confinement period is an unknown for the subjects in both situations. Sensory-deprivation subjects are further hampered by mechanical devices that restrict their mobility. Mourners are not subjected to similar physical restraints, but their belief system exerts a similar effect: unless they lie on their backs or right sides, they cannot attain the highly desirable trip. As would be expected, mourners, experiencing conditions similar to those imposed on subjects participating in sensory-deprivation experiments, report similar visual and auditory phenomena.

Sensory-deprivation studies carried out after 1959 report fewer hallucinations than had been reported earlier, partly because of increased precision in the definition of hallucinations. According to Zubek (1964: 39), "more attention is now being paid to differentiating among such phenomena as hallucinations, delusions, fantasies, hypnagogic states, etc. . . ." At the end of the 1960s, however, Zuckerman (1969a: 86–94) was using the inclusive terms "reported visual sensations" and "reported auditory sensations," distinctions among the various specific reactions being too difficult to make since they "must depend on the way the subject verbalizes his reactions," and the average subject is unsophisticated in this area.

Precise distinctions are equally impossible for the Shaker material. Wallace (1959: 59) has suggested that it is desirable for the anthropologist to define hallucination broadly as "pseudoperception" occurring in the absence of appropriate stimulation but being as vivid as if the stimulation had, in fact, been applied. Wallace includes in his definition "dreams, the waking 'hallucinations' of psychiatric terminology, and hypnagogic imagery," which would be suitable for Shaker data. However, he excludes "the fainter audiovisual imagery of reflective thought," which would be difficult for the Shakers since they do not seem to make any such distinctions. Mourners undoubtedly experience a wide range of visual and auditory sensations that can be attributed to hallucination, dreaming, wishful thinking, hypnagogic and hypnopompic transitional states, and the like. They are probably abnormally alert to all of them and to their content because of the particular mental set engendered by their belief system. The Shouters in Trinidad also seem to experience a range of phenomena from simple daydreams to complex hallucinations. Simpson[1] writes of the Shouter mourners:

> . . . My impression is the visions seen by the Pilgrims on such occasions included the three phenomena . . . dreams, the results of imaginative thinking, and visions in which dissociation is actually involved. However, they all believe they have had the visions or at least they call whatever experience they have had during their spiritual "travel," visions.

Like the subjects in some sensory-deprivation experiments, the mourners know what behavior is considered probable and suitable for the mourning-room period. Some are returning to "build" on a prior experience, and they are fully aware of what to anticipate and what others anticipate for them. When the period of isolation is finished, each mourner describes his experiences in great detail during a church service, affording those who have not yet undertaken the rite an opportunity to establish expectations. The topic is also freely discussed in ordinary conversation.[2] Furthermore, all candidates for baptism are subjected to an attenuated sample of mourning during the pre-baptism might, when they are "banded" and "put on the ground" for several hours. Hence it is unlikely that even new, inexperienced mourners approach the rite in ignorance.

Further cues to expected behavior and achievement are provided for the aspiring mourner during the service in the mourning room. The mourners stand apart from the rest of the worshipers and are given special attention: their feet are washed, they confess their sins, "proves" are taken for them, they are blessed, and so on. These actions demonstrate the sacred significance not only of their undertaking but also of the mourners themselves. A chalk design, drawn and referred to by the pointer as a "map," is prominently displayed on the floor, serving, in the words of Orne and Scheibe, as "eloquent instructions" of what is expected of them. That their friends are concerned and realize the importance of the trying experience before them is obvious from the number who appear as well as the prevailing sympathetic and supportive attitude. In the particular service I attended, the presence of a number of worshipers was all the more impressive because the location of the mourning room some miles out in the country posed transportation problems for many of them.

Smythies (1956: 338–339) suggests that the way people regard their own hallucinations and the attitude displayed toward persons who experience hallucinations are significant factors in their production. Shakers are eagerly receptive to their own hallucinations and regard those who experience visions as being especially favored. Since hallucinations and trances are positively valued by the Shaker subculture, the motivation for mourners to " experience and report" is strong. Achieving a satisfactory spiritual journey brings numerous benefits to the pilgrim: approbation from the pointer, felicitations from friends, increased prestige in the church, and an opportunity to share the joys and tribulations of his journey with the assembled worshipers when he "shouts."

The subjects in many sensory-deprivation experiments were college students, who, at the time this research was most popular, were not likely to regard hallucinations as desirable religious experiences (although they might today). They may have been cooperative and enthusiastic subjects, but even so they would not have been induced to experience and report by the same kinds of rewards that motivate the Shakers so strongly. The rewards to be derived from a successful spiritual journey are not only highly desirable but even crucial for people who have little opportunity to satisfy their prestige cravings.

C. W. Jackson and Pollard (1962) mention continuous reporting as an experimental device that is apt to promote sensory-deprivation phenomena. Zuckerman (1969a: 125) suggests further that "sensitizing the subject to the phenomena by requiring some reports during isolation will tend to produce more complex reports after isolation." Shakers make use of the same technique. Throughout their journeys, the mourners keep the pointer informed of their progress, and he advises and guides them. When he is satisfied with the reports of their trips, he terminates the period of isolation. The reports made after isolation by the "shouting" mourners support Zuckerman's statement.

Conditions of sensory deprivation are characterized by stress and anxiety, which may aid in generating perceptual disturbances. It may be argued that both mourners and experimental subjects are liable to the same stresses due to restricted motility and visual perception, confinement, isolation, and dependency. Nonetheless, it seems more likely that the mourners would find the physical conditions themselves less stressful because of their familiarity with the procedure and knowledge of what to expect, their relationship with the mourning-room personnel and the pointer, their beliefs, and the goals they are seeking. Most important is the fact that they are not experimental subjects in a scientific investigation but children of God embarking on a difficult but exciting adventure destined to bring them into closer rapport with the divine. This should guarantee them a quite different outlook.

Of course, the mourners may derive anxiety and stress from other sources. The hoped-for visions might not materialize; even if they do, the pointer might not confirm the gifts the mourner believes he is entitled to. Knowing that the pointer will reject or release a mourner whom he deems unworthy or unfit could also cause anxiety for the aspiring pilgrim. It is common knowledge that some mourners have gone mad and have been sent to the mental hospital.[3] A mourner might regard the constant presence of the mourning-room attendants with feelings of ambivalence: their presence might be a comfort, but, on the other hand, it might generate stress, calling attention as it does to his position of dependency and the concern others have for his welfare.

The McGill studies indicated that subjects under conditions of sensory deprivation are more susceptible to suggestion than would normally be the case. Moreover, attitudes acquired under such conditions tend to persist. Increased susceptibility to suggestion is undoubtedly operative in the case of the mourners. Positive attitudes toward Shakerism must surely be established before Shakers submit to the mourning ritual. However, it is highly probable that implicit or explicit suggestions are given during the confinement period. Although they would not reverse the pilgrims' attitudes, these suggestions would intensify, reinforce, and strengthen them. Shakers who had undergone the mourning experience were apt to become dissociated at almost every meeting. The mourning-room experience might well have affected their attitude toward dissociation as well as their aptitude for it. (I was told that "teaching" took place during mourning, but no mention was made of any direct instruction in becoming dissociated. However, even presuming a lack of specific instruction, conditions of sensory deprivation combined with the non-deprivational factors of the mourning-room situation might generate dissociational states repeatedly, thereby establishing a facility in becoming dissociated that would carry over into the postmourning period. Repeated hypnosis seems to render subjects increasingly susceptible.) Also, those who had mourned were never seen as objects of the pointer's wrath or correctional measures during a meeting. Their acceptable deportment might have been influenced by indoctrination during mourning. Furthermore, believing as they do that a "good life" and "purity of heart" are prerequisites for a satisfactory mourning experience, the successful mourners, having accomplished the ordeal, might well feel superior to nonmourners and might feel encouraged to display their dedication.

Sensory-deprivation investigators have been interested in the content of their subjects' hallucinations principally as an indication of their complexity. Several of them have reported on the ability or lack of ability of their subjects to exercise control over the content. Shakers seem to be able to control the content of their hallucinations fairly well, although they would ascribe such control to the supernatural. The content of their reported visions seems to be restricted to culturally prescribed topics or to material that lends itself to culturally biased interpretations Their hallucinations also seem to be quite complex.

Wallace (1959: 63) has remarked on the variations in hallucinations produced by mescaline intoxication among American Indians and whites. In the latter, the content of hallucinations is predominantly "idiosyncratic," whereas the content of Indian hallucinations conforms to their "doctrinal" patterns. Wallace attributes these differences in hallucination content as well as other variations in feelings and behavior to two factors: the milieu in which the drug is administered and the "psychological meaning" assigned to the effects of the drug by each group. White individuals normally take the drug "once or twice, in a clinical research setting, with definite knowledge of an experimental or a clinical purpose in the investigation, and without any commitment to or interest in peyote, or to mescaline in any form, as a personal religion. . . ." Indians, on the other hand, take the drug "repeatedly, in a solemn religious setting to the accompaniment of serious ritual, with a definite knowledge of a religious purpose in the usage and, often, with hope for personal salvation, of which the vision is the evidence" (Wallace, 1959: 64).

Much the same variation in factors obtains between the settings for sensory-deprivation experiments and Shaker rituals. Although details of the structuring of the situation for the experimental subjects are not always included in the published reports, it can be assumed, when not definitely stated, that the subjects were informed or were aware that a scientific experiment was being conducted, whether its full and exact purpose was explained to them or not. The Shakers, on the other hand, like the Indians, are engaging in an important religious ritual. For the experimental subject, the experience would probably be an isolated occurrence, whereas the mourner might, and probably would, repeat it. Subjects for sensory-deprivation studies would have no more "commitment to" nor "interest in" the research than subjects for drug investigations would. They were often paid for their time and presence, which would tend to make their participation just another job, giving them no special satisfactions nor any unusual personal rewards. In studies utilizing unpaid volunteers or the researchers as subjects, commitment and interest were probably greater, but still of a different affective quality than that operative in the case of the mourners. Researchers would not regard the experience as an end in itself, but as a mere device for gaining understanding and knowledge. For the mourners, however, the experience is worthwhile in itself; it has tremendous religious significance, is personally and culturally valued, and confers lasting benefits on those who successfully complete it.

Weinstein (1962: 237) gathered information on the content of hallucinations among psychiatric patients in the American Virgin Islands and found that the hallucinations and delusions described "are not bizarre or exotic phenomena but rather are very much a part of the fabric of the society in which they occur." The content of Shaker hallucinations is also greatly affected by the cultural milieu. Mourners may report journeys to exotic places and encounters with exotic personages, but the material from which these accounts are woven is derived from their folklore, the Bible, sacred pictures, and hymns—with which they are well acquainted. Moreover, much of the content is concerned with the very ordinary—people, places, and pursuits with which they are quite familiar.

Certain resulting phenomena appear to be fairly common and predictable for all situations in which the human organism is confronted with reduced sensory stimuli. Kracke (1967: 18) sums these up as follows: "a deep regression; signs of stress, at least for a certain period; emotional lability; disorganization of sensory and intellectual co-ordination; free flow of fantasy, with some inability to direct or focus thoughts; and hallucination." In his investigation of the implications of sensory-deprivation studies for psychoanalytic ego psychology, Kracke (1967: 27, 17) suggests that "there is evidence of built-in sensory needs," and when these needs are unfulfilled, the ensuing "apparent disintegration of ego structures . . . may itself be part of a mechanism for the preservation of these structures."

In addition to these underlying commonalities, variation also obtains. For example, the content of hallucinations varies considerably and appears to be largely dependent on cultural sources. The "psychological meaning" attached to the experience, the expectations and pressures—internal and external, personal and societal—to experience or not to experience, to take note of or not to take note of,to report or not to report, all derive from the cultural milieu, and all are forces that cannot be ignored.

It seems obvious, as Zuckerman (1969b: 432) has observed, that "a single variable approach to the study of the phenomena is not likely to yield much understanding. . . ." In addition to the physiological effects of sensory deprivation on the human organism, psychological and cultural factors appear to contribute quite significantly to the total phenomenon.

NOTES

1. Personal communication to the author, October 13, 1966.

2. Little information is provided in the published accounts of sensory-deprivation experiments to indicate whether or not any communication was taking place among their subjects or what relationship, if any, existed among them. Vernon did imply that the subjects for the Princeton studies were apt to be friends and that the researchers cautioned them not to discuss their experiences lest they reveal information that might influence a possible subject. He states that this "worked very well," but does not say how he knows that the directions were, in fact, followed. Unfortunately he did not run an experiment in which intersubject communication was permitted. As already mentioned, in some studies the investigators outlined to the subjects the kinds of reactions that might occur under conditions of sensory deprivation or the reactions they expected or hoped for, but none of the studies was designed to utilize past subjects as models and indoctrinators in the manner of the Shakers.

3. According to the Public Health doctor, the occurrence of insanity during mourning is less common today than in the past.

9

Comparison of the Shakers and Similar Religious Groups in the Caribbean

Religious groups in which elements of Christianity and African religions are intermingled are an outstanding feature of the Caribbean islands. These hybrid religions range from the "very African" religion of the Haitian peasants (Herskovits, 1947: 615) to the Shaker religion of St. Vincent, which has retained very few Africanisms. Herskovits (1958: 214) has observed that "the most striking and recognizable survivals of African religion are in those behavioristic aspects that, given overt expression, are susceptible of reinterpretation in terms of a new theology while retaining their older established forms."

Herskovits and Herskovits (1947: 305–309) have discussed the Africanisms they found among the Shouters of Trinidad. Some of the features that they consider African are also found among the Shakers: the importance of the center pole, the removal of shoes during worship, chalk markings on the floor, sprinkling the corners and center pole three times with water, "talking in tongues," the wearing of white dresses by women initiates, the "mourning" period of seclusion, hand clapping and foot tapping as rhythmic accompaniment, and the rhythms of the hymns. The most important aspect of Shaker worship, possession trance, resembles the Herskovits' description of African possession trance in several ways. The Shaker phenomenon also occurs in the presence of others, and stimulus as well as rhythmic background is provided by singing, foot tapping, and hands clapping. However, Shaker possession trances differ in one important respect: the concept of *becoming* the possessing spirit is absent. A Shaker does not "perform after the fashion of the spirit who has taken possession of him" (Herskovits, 1958: 245). Shakers conceptualize the worshiper experiencing possession trance as being seized and shaken by the Holy Spirit, but without impersonation.

The variation in the degree of retention of African traits in the Caribbean has provoked questions that have troubled students of Caribbean religion for some time. With reference to St. Vincent, we might ask why the island lacks the spirit cults that are so prominent on some of the other islands. Why is there no religion in St. Vincent with more conspicuous African elements than those of the Shaker cult? How can we explain the development or acceptance of a religion that includes so few African traits? How does St. Vincent differ today, and how did it differ in the past, from those islands that have religions of a more African nature? In short, how does St. Vincent compare with other islands in which we find religions that are similar in many ways to Shakerism but exhibit a stronger African influence?

Because of their Vincentian derivation, the Shouters, or Spiritual Baptists, of Trinidad would be expected to bear a close resemblance to the Shakers of St. Vincent. They appeared in Trinidad, presumably, with the same belief system and practices that the Spiritual Baptists of St. Vincent had at the time of migration. The two groups have since had more than 50 years to operate separately in markedly different milieus, although with some intercommunication. The nature of the inevitable changes and the differences in environmental influences might suggest answers for some of our questions. Furthermore, the Revivalists of Jamaica have been reported (Simpson, 1961: 2) as being similar to the Spiritual Baptists of Trinidad, yet the Jamaican environment differs in some ways from Trinidad or St. Vincent. By inspecting the different milieus that nurtured these religions, we may find clues to the differential retention of Africanisms.

After becoming established in St. Vincent, the Spiritual Baptists, as already mentioned, spread to Trinidad, where they found fertile ground for growth and where they were considered sufficiently problematic for the legislators to outlaw them in 1917. The prohibition against them was lifted in 1951. The line of communication between the Shouters in Trinidad and the Shakers in St. Vincent seems to have remained active through the years. Pointer B. stated: "Most of the Trinidadians come to St. Vincent to take their spiritual work and then go back."[1] His own brother, also a pointer, had gone to Trinidad, where he carried on "this work" until his death.

In spite of the absence of a unifying administrative body and in spite of the different influences to which each insular "branch" of the Spiritual Baptists has been exposed, the Shouters and the Shakers are remarkably similar in practices and beliefs. The Shouters also draw their membership from the lesser privileged lower class. Obedience and discipline are important in the Shouters church too, and a variety of offices in the church are available to those devotees who undergo the mourning ritual. The rites of baptism and mourning are much the same in Trinidad and in St. Vincent. The bell, candles, Bible, and flowers in water on the altar are common to both. The Shouter ritual for consecrating corners and doorways, described by Herskovits and Herskovits (1947: 218–219), is very similar to the ritual witnessed in St. Vincent. In the Trinidadian Spiritual Baptist services, the worshipers also chant "the rambling prayers characteristic of these meetings, punctuated with song in which the members" join (Herskovits and Herskovits, 1947: 220). The description of a "prayer by a lad who knelt and held a candle as he half-chanted his rhythmic and almost metered plea" (Herskovits and Herskovits, 1947: 214) would fit the St. Vincent Shakers equally well.

Hymns seem to be "jazzed" in much the same way by both groups. Herskovits and Herskovits (1947: 220) describe the "jazzing" of a hymn at a Shouters service they attended:

> . . . The people were carrying the melodic line sung slightly faster, while the song-leader and a few others ornamented it with harmonized 'ram-bam-bam, bam, bam, ram-a-bam,' simulating drums and making the song irresistible to patting feet, and handclapping.

Although I am not prepared to make as fine an analysis of the singing, the change of words to syllables, the quickening of the tempo, and the importance of the rhythm that I observed among the Shakers seem to be quite similar.

Nonetheless, there are some conspicuous differences between the Trinidad and St. Vincent Spiritual Baptists. Some seem to be superficial, but others are not. There is no mention of the Methodist prayer book and hymnal, so important in St. Vincent, being used by the Shouters. (The Shouters are reported to use the Sankey hymnal, and the Shakers also sing some Sankey hymns—there is overlap in the two collections. But the Shakers carry the combined Methodist hymnal-prayer book and use it frequently during services.) The Shouters use oil to anoint the hands and feet of baptismal canadidates and mourners, which the Shakers did not mention. Although they both use chalk designs, they do not use the same ones, nor are the designs mutually understood. Thus Pointer B., when confronted with samples of the chalk designs that Simpson (1966, *passim*) had collected among the Shouters, was nonplussed and unable to decipher them. When I explained some of the symbols to him, he countered by giving examples of symbols that *he* used and their meanings, and he explained that every pointer has "his own alphabet."

The ritual handshake occurs in both groups. According to Herskovits and Herskovits (1947: 218), in Trinidad the handshake is "exchanged with everyone present, three downward shakes of the right hand, then the hands elevated above the head, the touching of the left breast of first one and then the other party to the handshake, and a final downward shake." In St. Vincent, the handshake is strong, definite, and emphatic; some persons preface it with a gesture that is almost a salute, but there is no further embellishment.

Shaker informants state that they do not offer sacrifices as their Trinidadian counterparts are apt to do,[2] neither "fruits or vegetables into the sea, nor goats or chickens." They support their rejection of bloody sacrifices with biblical references. Various foods were placed on the table that served as an altar at the thanksgiving services held in the homes, but the food was not disposed of by throwing it into the sea or river, nor by burning it, but was distributed among the worshipers after the service and consumed or taken home.

Simpson (1965: 115) makes the following comment:

> When a Spiritual Baptist is possessed by the Holy Spirit in a church he is likely to fall on his knees, sit down, pick up the large brass handbell, spin the "chariot wheel," pick up the "lota" (an East Indian cup) and throw water into every corner of the church, or run for the shepherd's crook. When a person is possessed by an orisha power in a Shouters church, he is likely to call for and look for the implement of the god manifesting on him, e.g., a *shay-shay*, a sword, a whip, an axe, etc.

In St. Vincent, a Shaker might be helped to his knees if he were more violently dissociated than usual, but I never saw anyone fall on his knees. And he might have rung the handbell when dissociated, but the shepherd's crook, "chariot wheel," and "lota" were not seen in any Shaker church I visited. The Vincentian Spiritual Baptists are aware that there are differences between their version of the religion and what they know, have heard, or perhaps suspect about the religion in Trindad. They regard their version as being right and true, and tend to speak disparagingly of the Shouters. Pointer B. remarked, "In Trinidad, they use the Spirit; it is not the Spirit using them. Some is jus' practice their own understanding, some use books,[3] but this is not the Holy Spirit."

Simpson (1965: 114–115) states that he "saw no 'groaning' or 'grunting' (hyperventilating or overbreathing) at *shango* ceremonies, but this method of facilitating spirit possession, called 'adoption' in Trinidad, is followed by some devotees in some Shouters groups." The Shouters, however, insist that they do not "groan" to bring the Spirit. One Trinidadian said (Simpson, 1966: 542):

> "Adoption" (groaning) is seeing things and speaking in the unknown tongue.
> If you do that before the spirit manifests, you are "mocking." The spirit causes you to do that. You don't do that to invite the spirit.

A similar, but somewhat stronger, statement was offered by Vincentian informants. They seemed to feel that they *could* do nothing to invite the spirit, which controlled absolutely the choice of when and on whom to manifest. They gave the impression that they thought it was presumptuous of a mere human to think that he could influence the supernatural in such a situation, but they also insisted that the spirit manifested on worshipers who were "pure." Like the Shouters, they maintained that the abnormal breathing was caused by the Spirit during manifestation and did not occur prior to it.

St. Vincent Shaker informants further maintain that a person cannot be possessed by a saint nor, they declare most emphatically, by any African powers—"only by the Holy Ghost." In Trinidad, however, Simpson (1965: 115n.) made the following observation:

> It is not unusual for a *shango* power to manifest on a worshiper at a Spiritual Baptist ceremony. This is a slightly embarrassing situation, but when it happens nothing can be done about it. Since many people attend both *shango* and Shouters ceremonies, it is not surprising that occasionally a spirit appears in the wrong place.

Some of the differences apparent between the Vincentian and Trinidadian versions of Spiritual Baptism can certainly be attributed to the presence of, and interaction with, Shango in Trinidad. Shango is a syncretic religion that combines "religious and magical practices . . . derived from the Yoruba traditions of southwestern Nigeria and from Catholicism" (Simpson, 1961: 1). Shango is not practiced in St. Vincent, and the Shakers have therefore been exempt from its direct influence.

The African elements in Shango include dancing, drumming, hand clapping, spirit possession, animal sacrifice, and the offering of food to the gods, as well as the belief that the gods will reveal remedies for sickness or misfortune (Simpson, 1961: 3). Shangoists identify African gods with Catholic saints and may become possessed by a wide variety of spirits. Shango has adopted other Catholic practices and implements: prayers, rosaries, crucifixes, candles, the occasional reading of biblical passages, and the sign of the cross. The wide use of charms and the ritualistic uses of water seem to be "African–Christian syncretisms" (Simpson, 1961: 3).

Simpson (1964: 26) states that in Trinidad both Shango and Shouters elements are mixed to some extent in the same service. He mentions the possibility of Shango leaders providing opportunities for Shangoists to participate in the Spiritual Baptist rites of baptism, mourning, and building, which are not offered by the Shango cult. Such cooperation is not universal, however: some Spiritual Baptist leaders disdain Shango elements in their services; some Shango leaders, in spite of being dependent on them for the rites mentioned, scorn the Spiritual Baptists. Nevertheless, according to Simpson (1961: 3), "spirit possession in Spiritual Baptist ceremonies is seldom, if ever, limited to manifestations of the Holy Spirit. Sooner or later one or more devotees become possessed by one of the Shango powers."

African spirit cults other than Shango have also appeared in Trinidad. For example, an African immigrant who had been a diviner and healer in his native land established a Rada community in Trinidad in 1868. Their religion is a blend of Christian and Dahomean religious traditions in which the African deities were identified with Christian saints. Characteristic practices include spirit possession, drumming, dancing, and sacrificing (Carr, 1953).

Simpson (1961: 2) has reported that the Trinidadian Spiritual Baptists and the Revival Zionists of Jamaica are fairly similar. Jamaica has several varieties of revivalism; Moore (1965) described three groups known as Revival, Zionists, and Pocomania. Among the differences he found in the groups was "the method of trumping, since spirit possession in Revival and Poco groups comes with the breath released in a downward motion, while the Zionists labor and trump releasing their breath with an upward beat." Poco groups use strong liquor or marihuana, Zionists and Revival groups do not; Poco is more concerned with the working of evil, even using a ground altar "because of the evil forces that lurk there." Moore also stated (1965: 64) that "the violence of Poco (devil worship) possession cannot be matched in any of the other cults." According to Simpson (1956: 342), preaching and explaining the Bible are less important in Pocomania than in Revival Zion. More important are singing, "spiritual dancing," and witchcraft; healing techniques are "more extreme," and the leaders are probably less stable emotionally. However, he found it difficult to distinguish sharply among the various kinds of revivalism.

Like the St. Vincent Shakers and the Trinidadian Shouters, the Jamaican Revivalists derive their followers from low-income, low-status groups. Dissociational states believed to indicate possession by supernatural entities are also a prominent feature. The physical aspects of Revivalist churches are much the same as those of the Spiritual Baptist churches in Trinidad and St. Vincent, and some of the ritual equipment is the same: the large wooden cross used in baptism, the banners with inscriptions that are carried in processions, containers of water with flowers, special robes and insignia of position, candles, the Bible, and so on. Many of the same elements are included in their services: Bible reading, hymn singing, praying, impromptu sermonizing, giving testimony, and the like.

The Revivalists, however, have certain paraphernalia that are never seen in a Vincentian Shaker church. They may wave a red flag at the beginning of a service to "'cut down' all evil spirits" (Simpson, 1956: 362), or use swords and machetes for the same purpose; they blow a whistle to stop the singing, restore order, or inform the spirit that the service is going to begin. Their ritualistic implements include sacred stones, keys, shepherd's crooks, colored candles, de Laurence books, a central altar. One of the most striking differences is the use of drums or other musical instruments, which is not found among the Spiritual Baptists of Trinidad or St. Vincent.

The Revivalists believe in the existence of, and possible possession by, a great variety of spirits. Moore (1965: 68–69) found that many peasants in Jamaica believe that

> Oto, the top sky god of Cumina, still is present in Revival and Revival Zion, but his Western name is God the Father, God the Son and God the Holy Ghost. . . . African sky gods and earthbound gods are generally replaced in name by the great saints and celestial spirits of the Old and New Testaments, with particular reference to Revelation in the New Testament.

Simpson, however, working in West Kingston, found that the "Pocomanians and Revival Zionists do not worship old African gods"; they do not even recognize the names of West African deities. One informant said that the names of African gods might be used in private ceremonies (Simpson, 1956: 435–436).

Like Shangoists and some Trinidadian Shouters, Revivalists may perform bloody sacrifices and are more preoccupied with healing than was found to be the case in St. Vincent. Little use is made of chalk designs, and no mention was made of any specific denominational liturgy or ritual procedures. Baptism is an important rite among the Revivalists, but mourning in Jamaica is a "memorial service for a dead member of a family" rather than the period of seculsion so named by the Vincentian and Trinidadian Spiritual Baptists. However, a revivalist ritual exists that seems to bear some resemblance to the Spiritual Baptist mourning ritual: to atone for his sins, a Revivalist may spend three days or a week fasting and praying, then give testimony in church and perhaps a "table" (a combined religious service and feast). No increase in rank accrues to such a person as it does among the Spiritual Baptists, nor is there any report of visions, taking a spiritual journey, and the like.

Possession trance among the Revivalists appears to be a more violent affair than it is among the Shakers. "The possessed person may scream, whirl, leap, moan, tremble, cling to other worshippers, run, crawl, fall to the ground, or roll on the ground" (Simpson, 1956: 352). Even as the worshipers are subject to possession by a variety of spirits, so they may exhibit a variety of behaviors, depending on the possessing spirit. However, Simpson (1956: 353) suggests that "a possession is identifiable mainly because those present know whom a given person follows or because that person shouts the name of his spirit or quotes him." As already mentioned, although possession is a desirable state for the St. Vincent Shakers, consistent with their professed belief that the Spirit controls the choice of who is to be possessed and when, they make no overt move to invite possession. The Jamaican revivalists, on the other hand, have several admitted ways of inducing possession: "divine concentration," spinning a worshiper around, striking him with a rod, and "labouring in the spirit." Simpson (1956: 354) explains the last method as consisting of "trumping" ("stamping hard with the right foot while the body is bent forward from the waist and breath is expelled") and "sounding," the groaning that occurs when they overbreathe "on the up-swing" ("stamping more lightly with the left foot as the body straightens up and as the maximum amount of air is breathed in").

Moore (1965: 64–65) describes the possession-trance phenomenon in some detail. During the singing of a hymn, the words and the tune "give way to trumping and laboring." While dancing in a counterclockwise direction around the altar, the worshipers change from a "mild swaying motion" to a "deep bend from the waist." They suck in each breath loudly, then release it when they bend, "making a kind of grunting sound." As the dancing continues and becomes more intense, some worshipers become dissociated, possessed by the Holy Ghost or the spirits of the saints of former members who are now deceased. Possession trancers are assisted by other worshipers until their movements stabilize, then they continue dancing alone even though they appear to be unconscious. "The words and even the music of the original Sankey hymn have vanished and the rhythmic sound is now spirit-possession music." The degeneration of the words and music as described would seem to be much the same phenomenon among the Revivalists and the St. Vincent Spiritual Baptists.

Cults retaining more African characteristics than revivalism exhibits are also found in Jamaica. Moore and Simpson (1957: 983–984) have rated the Jamaican religious groups (other than the major conventional denominations) from "quite Christian-European to non-Christian–non-European" on the basis of "the use of the Bible at services; prayers to God the Father, Son, and Holy Ghost; the use of Christian hymns; the absence of spirits other than God at services; and the use of the English language exclusively during services." They arranged the groups from the Church of God and Pentecostal Holiness Zion Tabernacles through Revival and Revival Zion to Pocomania, and, finally, to African Cumina or Maroon Dance.

Hogg (1960) has since reported on the Convince cult, which has retained more African elements than any other Jamaican cult except Cumina. In Cumina, the possessing spirits are sky gods, earth gods, and ancestral zombies; in Convince, they are the ghosts of former cult members. Cumina members are usually born into the cult, which is "primarily a family religion" (Moore and Simpson, 1958: 74), linking the living with the dead, the New World with Africa. Members of Convince are chosen by the spirits through visions or by possession. There seems to be less interaction between the more African cults and revivalism in Jamaica than is true of the more African Shango and the more Christian Shouters in Trinidad.

In both Trinidad and Jamaica, obeah, described in the laws of Trinidad and Tobago as "every pretended assumption of supernatural power or knowledge whatever for fraudulent or illicit purposes or for gain or for injury to any person" (Herskovits and Herskovits, 1947: 346), seems to play a more important role in the religious practices of the Shouters and the Revivalists than it does among the Shakers in St. Vincent. To the Shakers (or so they reported), obeah is an evil practice that occurs on some of "the other islands" or, perhaps, in the country. It was practiced to a considerable extent in the past, "but now you have a lot of lights."[4] Healing, by the same token, seems to be a far less important religious responsibility to the Shakers than it is to the Shouters of Trinidad or the Jamaican Revivalists. Informants said that the pointer *might* be given knowledge in a dream of a herbal cure for some ill, but no one knew of any specific instance. The pointer might also go to the bedside of someone who was ailing and pray over him, but not, they stated emphatically, to cure him. Shakers who were ill seemed quite willing to avail themselves of the local hospital facilities. (It should be remembered that these Shakers lived in or near the capital city; those living in the less accessible areas might possibly react differently.)

We turn now to a consideration of some of the mechanisms that seem to have been involved in the development of the various kinds of Afro-Christian religions in the West Indies, particularly those blending Protestantism and African traditions, and particularly for the island of St. Vincent.

In a situation of culture contact as exemplified by the West Indies, where a slave population and a dominant population were interacting, some accommodations could be expected to occur. Certain African traits might be preserved in an unaltered state; these are referred to as retentions. Other traits, however, might undergo varying amounts and kinds of change. Such traits have been termed reinterpretations and, in special cases, syncretisms (Herskovits, 1947: 553–558; also see Bourguignon, 1954). According to Herskovits (1947: 553–554), "reinterpretation marks all aspects of cultural change. . . . Syncretism is one form of reinterpretation." Syncretism, Herskovits and Herskovits (1947: 330) elaborate, is a phenomenon

> . . . observed and reported upon especially from many parts of the New
> World, where Africans have translated their aboriginal religious structure

into the patterns of worship of their new environment. Such renderings of belief and worship have proved both simplest and most felicitous when the accommodation was made to a pattern of Catholicism, since its multiplicity of saints made feasible parallelisms to a multiplicity of nature deities.

Where the dominant religious influence was Protestantism, however, "reinterpretations of necessity were of a less direct and more subtle character" (Herskovits and Herskovits, 1947: 304). Thus Shakerism's African traits that have been strained through Methodism are reinterpretations, but Shakerism, lacking as it does the identification of African deities with Christian saints, would not be considered a syncretic cult.[5]

Bourguignon (1967: 7–8) suggests further that

> . . . whereas Catholicism provided an opportunity for reinterpretation and syncretism at the perceptual and cognitive level—in the cult of saints and in some aspects of its ritualism—it did not provide such an opportunity within its organizational structure. . . . The structure of the church . . . was both rigid and integrated—taking the African in, but allowing no room for innovation in dogma, ritual or Church organization. Protestantism, in many ways, appears to have represented the very opposite: it did not integrate the African into its own rigid forms, but, particularly with the coming of Methodism, allowed for separate structures, in which both innovation and reinterpretation were possible. This was true in particular with regard to biblical interpretation and ritual, including enthusiastic services and initiation practices (baptism, "mourning," and "building").

The role of the Bible and its interpretation in the hands of untaught leaders and congregations should not be overlooked, not only as a possible active force in the development of belief and ritual but also as a rationalizing agency for possibly reinterpreted practices and beliefs that have become part of the various Afro-Protestant religions. Moore (1965: 67–68) points out that the Africans were confronted with "Epistles and Gospel or lesson from the Bible, read but not explained. . . . Careful instruction as to the nature of the sacraments in cultural terms they could understand was lacking." Mrs. Carmichael (1833: 237), writing about St. Vincent in the early nineteenth century, reported that, although the white and colored people in the Methodist congregation were able to understand the sermon, "the slave population comprehended almost nothing of it. . . . It was evident that they had not one rational or distinct idea upon the subject, although many of them had attended [church services] for years." Reading the Bible or hearing it read without the traditional understanding or explanation provided undoutedly contributed to idiosyncratic interpretations.[6] For example, Vincentian Spiritual Baptists state that the Bible tells them to go to mourn: "It says in the Bible, 'Blessed are they that mourn.'" Herskovits (1958: 223) mentions that the Bible is used to support the custom of removing shoes in church among the Trinidadian Shouters. The Shakers cite the same authority for the same custom.

Spirit possession evinced by dissociation, one of the most conspicuous features of the Afro-Protestant religions and our major concern, also finds its *raison d'être* in biblical text. Attempts to find the source of the possession-trance phenomenon in a particular culture have produced disagreements. Smith (1960: 36) objects to regarding possession trance an an African element because many West African tribes do not practice it while some Europeans do. Simpson and Hammond (1960: 48) spell out the differences between the typical West African possession trance and the European type, and argue that it seems to be "mainly" a West African trait. We cannot overlook the fact, however, that in the eighteenth century such new European religious groups as the Quakers, Moravians, and Methodists found their way to the West Indies—groups that were noted for their enthusiastic, and even ecstatic, approach to religion. Although the Methodist missionaries may not have engaged in direct teaching of excitement, it seems obvious that, on encountering such behavior in their black congregations, they, having been inured to demonstrative reactions in the English congregations, accepted it and did not attempt to halt it. In Jamaica, the Baptists tolerated the "infiltration of African religious practices . . . requiring special dreams, and seizure by 'the spirit,' as a qualification for baptism . . ." (Curtain, 1955: 164–165). Thus, although Simpson and Hammond (1960: 48–49) indicate that the motor behavior and the positive value attached to possession trance were African traits, the apparent ready acceptance of the phenomenon by some of the religious sects operating in the area also contributed to the firm establishment of possession trance as part of the developing religions.

Klein (1966) compared the differing policies toward the slaves that guided the Catholic Church in Cuba and the Church of England in Virginia. He demonstrated that the Catholic Church, by assuming a paternalistic attitude toward the slaves, by admitting them to the Church, and by various other means, was instrumental in encouraging religious syncretism and in facilitating the assimilation of the African into Cuban society. The Church of England, on the other hand, did not enjoy the same powerful position. In Virginia, the church was subordinate to the local planters, and the religious destinies of the slaves depended on the wishes of their owners. The general atmosphere for the slaves was repressive, and those who were converted were in the minority. Klein (1966: 321) claims that there was "absolutely no syncretization of Christian belief with folk religion of African origin. . . ." The planters were no more eager for their slaves to be influenced by the nonconformist preachers who began to arrive in the mid-eighteenth century than they had been for them to be proselytized by the Church of England clergy earlier.

The situation in the British West Indies was much as described by Klein for Virginia. The Church of England was the established church in the British islands, and it was concerned with the white population, not the slaves. The planters were "unanimously opposed to any action [on the part of the clergy] likely to arouse discontent in the minds of their slaves" (Ragatz, 1928: 28). In St. Vincent, the slaves were not allowed to enter the Anglican church, and when the Methodist missionaries arrived, attempts were made to interfere with their activities. In 1800, the Methodists were charged with contributing to "insubordination and discontent" among the slaves (Ragatz, 1928: 28).

Goveia (1966), however, observed that Klein, in attempting to explain the varying features of slavery that characterize it in different parts of the New World, has emphasized the influence of religion to the exclusion of other factors. She suggests that the ratio of Negro slaves to whites was also a significant factor. Klein reported a slave population approximately equal to the white population in Santiago de Cuba for the years 1752–1755. The situation in the British West Indies was quite different. In Jamaica in 1788, there were about 18,000 whites to about 226,000 slaves; on Dominica in 1804, about 1600 whites to about 22,000 slaves (Ragatz, 1928: 30). Mrs. Carmichael (1833: 56) wrote that a small estate on St. Vincent would have about 100 slaves and at most two white men in addition to the planter. In islands where the number of slaves was so disproportionate, the white people were constantly fearful of a slave revolt. Requiring a set ratio of whites to blacks was attempted through deficiency laws, white militias were organized, and martial law was usually declared when large gatherings of slaves were anticipated (Ragatz, 1928: 31). In such a climate of uneasiness, a planter's hostility to attempts to convert and teach Chritianty to his slaves, and to gather them together for religious meetings can be better understood.

The form of government in the various Caribbean islands and the accompanying complacency, or lack of it, of the people in complying with its decrees must also be considered. Mathieson (1926: 43) has noted that "slavery is always more tolerable under arbitrary than under constitutional rule; for in a free state not only do the slave-owners make or help to make the laws, but, being unaccustomed to the interference of the Government, they are more likely to resent it when exerted in restraint of their authority."

Slavery in autocratic Spanish Cuba, then, was characterized by a fairly equal distribution of whites and Negroes, by careful supervision of the rights and religion of the slaves by the ubiquitous Catholic Church, and by religious syncretism. Slavery in the more democratic British West Indies was characterized by an overwhelming preponderance of Negroes; tension on the part of the minority whites, which was translated into further repression of the slaves; an established Protestant church that reflected the attitudes and will of the planters by ignoring the religious life of the slaves; and the later introduction of nonconformist religions that catered to the slaves. As in Virginia, no religious syncretism took place in St. Vincent, and Methodism became the religion of the slaves.

When we look at Jamaica, however, this neat formula breaks down. In Jamaica, where the same general conditions prevailed, religious syncretism did take place. Why would syncretism occur in Jamaica but not in St. Vincent?

Aside from the general historical background shared by the various islands of the British West Indies, each island has a unique history that has contributed to the religious character as it appears today. For example, some islands were exposed to denominations that were not introduced into other islands: Mrs. Carmichael (1833: 238) decried the absence in St. Vincent of Moravian missionaries, who were active in Antigua; and Carriacou seems to have been exempt from any direct denominational influences (Smith, 1962). Some islands have been affected by individual innovators; this was the case in Jamaica with Bedward and in Grenada with Norman Paul.[7] Some were influenced by Negroes emigrating from the United States or Africa: the Native Baptist Church was introduced into Jamaica by American blacks, the introduction of the Rada religion was due to the presence of a free African immigrant in Trinidad, and Shango in Grenada was the religion of several communities of free Africans who arrived in 1849. (Grenada had originally been colonized by the French, whose Catholic influence has remained even though Grenada became a British colony the same year that St. Vincent did. Like Trinidad and St. Vincent, Grenada also has Spiritual Baptists.)

Interisland mobility and communication are other factors whose importance cannot be discounted. From the time of discovery (and before) there seems to have been considerable movement between islands. The possibility of ideas, innovations and news of innovations, cult members, and, of course, cults, moving from one island to another must therefore be considered. Unfortunately, we do not have the necessary historical data to fill in the details of all the various religious influences that may have helped to shape the present situation.

Smith (1965: 22) points to the "importance of group cohesion for the persistence and survival of a trait or complex of traits," illustrating his statement with the example of Grenadian Shango that developed in three closed Yoruba communities. M. Leiris (quoted by Bourguignon, 1968: 7) observed that escaped slaves were also able to form communities that served as repositories for African traditions in some islands. This was the case with the

Maroons in Jamaica. In St. Vincent, although escaped slaves formed a society separate from the slave society, they lived among the Carib Indians, and, instead of preserving their African traditions in a more or less pure form, they adopted many Indian customs (Coelho, 1948: 1). The racial composition of the group was also eventually altered. Since the mixed African–Carib population disturbed the peace of the island, they were deported soon after St. Vincent was officially open for colonization and hence had little, if any, effect on the Vincentian religious situation. Further, the "cultural heterogeneity" of the slaves on the island, an important factor in their lack of group cohesion and probably in the gradual extinction of traditional African religious traits, "was apparently reinforced by plantation practices, since attempts were made to prevent any substantial numbers of slaves of a common tribal background from being concentrated on the same plantation" (Mintz, 1966: 921).

The size of an island may also be significant in the development of its present religious character. It was probably a consideration in the past in assigning clergy and missionaries. Even today, some of the small islands lack a resident church and are dependent for religious leadership and ritual events on occasional visits by religious groups from the larger islands. The larger islands, by the same token, are more likely to show the effects of the onslaughts of a variety of religious forces, as Jamaica does. Size, however, is not the whole answer either; for example, Grenada, is hardly larger than St. Vincent, yet it contains a variety of religious groups.

It becomes increasingly obvious that there is no adequate theory of religious syncretism in the Caribbean. Bourguignon (1967: 14–15) discusses the subject at length and suggests that "we need more, and anthropologically better informed, historical work" in the area. She also suggests that answers to the following questions should be sought:

> What were the teachings of the churches, and to whom were they available? And in addition to the formal teachings, what were the folk beliefs and practices brought by European settlers? In fact, what was the nature of these settlers and of the types of contacts established by them with the Africans?
>
> What were the policies in the field of religion, of the churches in the colonies . . . and how were these policies mediated, and, indeed, by what forces were these policies influenced?
>
> What was the sequence of events: Sequence of colonial administrations; sequence of religious movements . . . continuation—or cessation—of contacts between the colony, or ex-colony, and the metropolis on the one hand, and with West Africa on the other?
>
> What was the social organization within the various Caribbean countries at various points of their histories, and what do we know of the inter-island contacts, which appear to weigh so heavily at present?

To this list we might add several more questions. In addition to the policies of the established churches in the various colonies, we might also inquire about the policies of the various missions and the various missionaries involved. We know, for example, that the Baptists in Jamaica were able to capitalize on the previous work of the Native Baptists, that they permitted the inclusion of Africanisms, and that they experienced a rapid increase in membership from 1831 to 1845. However, as the missionary churches began attacking their morals, the Negroes developed a distrust of the missionaries. The Baptists then began training native ministers, but this measure did not restore the earlier position of the Baptists, because the newly trained ministers left the church and started new cults (Curtin, 1955: 169). Thus, in Jamaica, the policies of the missionary churches drove the Negroes to the Afro-Christian cults whose beliefs were in harmony with the Negro value systems and to the African cults.

It might also be fruitful to examine contacts between various subsocieties *within* the islands. We have such an example in Trinidad in the case of the interaction between Shango cultists and the Spiritual Baptists. It might also be productive to obtain more information concerning the contacts that have been made, and perhaps are being made, between the United States and the islands. For example, Smith cites the American Spiritual Baptists as the provenience for the Spiritual Baptists of Grenada. It would be useful to know more about the American Spiritual Baptists, when they appeared in Grenada, where they came from in the United States, what the conditions of their introduction into Grenada might have been, what connection, if any, they might have had with the Spiritual Baptists of Trinidad and St. Vincent, and so on.

With such historical information, we might be able to explain religious syncretism more satisfactorily.

NOTES

1. Training outside Trinidad is not mentioned by Herskovits and Herskovits nor by Simpson.

2. Simpson (1964: 25–26) observed a Shouters service in 1960 in which food, oil, and candles were thrown into a fire and two pigeons were killed. Later a tray full of fruit, flowers, and a glass of water was dumped into the sea—offerings for saints. This passage was discussed with several Shakers, who were vehement in their disapproval.

3. Probably the de Laurence books. Herskovits and Herskovits (1947: 228–229) report that "... great interest was expressed in the books of de Laurence who furnished tracts on healing, and magic formulae of various kinds. 'The work that de Laurence does is a correct Baptist work. They are taught in the spirit. . . .'"

4. It was obvious, however, that the Shakers had not rejected all magic; for example, some babies with Shaker mothers wore black shoes strings around their waists to ward off evil. Such practices are not connected with Shakerism, however, but are part of the lore of the general

population. Streams of Power adherents were just as likely to observe such precautions, "just in case" there might be some truth in them.

5. The term "syncretism" does not appear to mean the same thing to all people. Moore (1965), for example, wrote at some length on "religous syncretism in Jamaica," yet Smith (1965: 12) declares that "where Protestantism has been historically dominant, as in Jamaica, Barbados, St. Kitts, St. Vincent, and Antigua, aesthetically rich religious syncretisms such as Shango are absent; and Revivalism or Shakerism (Shouting Baptist) is the characteristic folk ritual form."

6. See LaBarre (1962: 11-12) for another example of this phenomenon.

7. Bedward was a religious leader and healer who attracted a large following between 1891 and 1921. He was arrested and sent to the insane asylum when he claimed that he was Jesus Christ and that he was going to ascend into Heaven, taking his awaiting followers with him. Nevertheless, he had a great influence on the revivalist movement in Jamaica (Simpson, 1956: 337).

Norman Paul was a Grenadian "healer, diviner, and seer who practiced a highly individual form of cult" that blended Shakerism, Shango, and Seventh Day Adventism (Smith, 1963: 7).

10

Functions of Shakerism

When we consider the value of Shakerism for its participants, we find that many of the same functions that have been noted for similar cults in other societies (see, for example, Simpson, 1956, 1965; Hogg, 1960), are applicable here.

Shakerism provides its devotees with an inexpensive and time-consuming form of diversion, a leisure-time activity that is entertaining for spectators and worshipers alike.[1] The trips the group takes to various parts of the island for memorial services, thanksgiving services, and visits to other churches, as well as the trips that are taken to other islands, are high points in the lives of the Shakers. They look forward to them eagerly and enjoy the bus or boat ride, a special treat for them, often passing the time en route singing hymns.

The church also affords its members some outlet for aesthetic yearnings. As slaves, the blacks were probably not in a position to continue any of their traditional art forms or to develop new ones. Even today, Vincentians do not seem to be producing crafts or art of any particular note (with the possible exception of some "primitive" paintings). An altar table decorated for a thanksgiving service gives pleasure to those who adorn it and those who observe it. In one case, for example, I saw kernels of corn and flower blossoms arranged in groups of three at intervals around the table, which was also decorated with saucers of farina and corn, and piles of fruit. When questioned about the significance of the food and the arrangement of the corn and flowers in groups of three, informants stated that no sacrifice was involved, nor was there any reason for grouping in threes. The only reason for the food and the arrangement was an aesthetic one—to make the table "look nice." The Shakers also appreciate an attractive church. They comment on the colors and richness of altar cloths, on the beauty of other furnishings—candelabra, banners, religious pictures. Singing is an obvious source of enjoyment, and an annual program of choral music is produced for which tickets are sold. Furthermore, although they may be unaware of its aesthetic qualities and although some upper class Vincentians regard it as a disgraceful Africanism, the Shakers have developed a rhythmic creation of no little beauty in their possession-trance phenomenon. The bodily motions and metered breathing of the possessed worshipers, considered individually or in the choral context, and the singing and humming of the other members of the congregation in the background, form an impressive and well-integrated production.

Although I am unable to attest to specific therapeutic values in the dissociational states achieved by the Shakers, I did not notice any obvious detrimental effects. Like the Africans portrayed in the Jean Rouch film *Les Maîtres Fous*, and contrary to the opinion of Simey (1947: 38) as well as some non-Shaker, upper class Vincentians that "the energies of the devotees are sapped," the Shakers were apparently relaxed and normal after a trance, and they seemed to be quite able to work, suffering no ill effects the following day. Informants declare that they feel uplifted by the experience: "You feel happy after; the joy is unspeakable." The tension-releasing and anxiety-reducing aspects of dissociation have been noted by many observers (e.g., Mischel and Mischel, 1958; Sargant, 1959; Simpson, 1965). As a device for such release, Shakerism serves a positive purpose.

Furthermore, Shakerism, like Shango (Mischel, 1958), affords its worshipers an opportunity to achieve a prestige denied them by the larger society. Not only is prestige available through the mechanism of spirit possession, but the offices in the cult are accessible to those who mourn (and, apparently, to men whether they mourn or not). This is not to suggest that there are no forces at work in the attainment of these positions other than the worshiper's desire to achieve one. Undoubtedly other factors are also involved, such as the personal feelings of the pointer for the aspirant or the relationship of the aspirant to other cult members. Nevertheless, positions are open to cult members, and those who do attain them can find prestige in holding them.

The feeling of security that comes from belonging to a group may also attract lower class Vincentians to Shakerism. Sermons in Shaker meetings frequently emphasize the thought that "everyone of you have a servant. Going down the road, if you need something, you can ask a sister or a brother."

Shakerism has no ostensible political function other than as its members represent potential votes. There is no concern with politics at the cult level nor in the cult context, although the Shakers are interested in political developments as members of a social class and as Vincentians.

I have argued elsewhere (Henney, 1973) that possession trance offers the Shakers a means of establishing a tolerable position for themselves in a society that provides them with few secular channels to prestige and a comfortable identity image. Wallace and Fogelson (1965) conceptualize a person's total identity as being made up of a number of component parts: his real identity, his claimed identity, his feared identity, and his ideal identity. Wallace and

Fogelson (1965: 382) go on to say that, since an individual

> ... strives to keep his real identity reasonably close to the ideal, and
> reasonably far away from the feared identity, by definition the ideal identity
> is relatively more positive, and the feared identity more negative, in affective
> value than the real identity. Thus, there is generally a motivation, more or
> less pressing . . . to increase the distance between the real and the feared
> identity. . . . To the extent that real, ideal, and feared identities are interna-
> lizations of the implicit or explicit commentaries and values of others, they
> are built upon, and require, repeated validation in social communication.

For a lower class individual, however, the identity component that receives
the most frequent validation in interaction with the larger society is his feared
identity. Members of the upper classes[2] openly regard those of the lower class
with disdain, characterizing them as lazy, stupid, unreliable, and generally inferior. If a lower class person is also a Shaker, his situation may be aggravated
since Shakerism, in and of itself, is viewed negatively by many upper class
members.

A lower class person is also frustrated by his inability to—or, at least, the
improbability of his being able to—overcome the barriers to his occupational,
educational, and financial improvement. Thus, as a result of communication
with certain others, which validates his feared identity rather than his ideal
identity, and as a result of his own self-evaluation, the lower class Vincentian
may experience a "profound sense of dissatisfaction with [his] secular
identity" (Wallace, 1966: 152).

Shakerism provides the lower class individual one possible pathway for the
relief of an identity image that has been impaired by the reinforcement of its
feared identity component and for the validation of its ideal identity
component. Since the Spirit is believed to shake only those who are pure,
possession trance is a public demonstration of worthiness and righteousness.
Shaker devotees have usually had religious training in a denominational or
Catholic church and are aware that the kind of involvement with the Holy
Spirit that the Shakers enjoy is lacking in those churches. Quite obviously,
Shakers are special people in the eyes of God. For Shakers who do not
experience dissociation, their belief system provides the comforting thought
that the Spirit may possess a worshiper and shake him internally.

A worshiper's identity image may be further enhanced by other elements in
Shaker worship. The content of biblical texts, hymns, prayers, and sermons is
significant and emphasizes for the congregation that they are the chosen people
of God. Frequently repeated are such texts as "He has gone to prepare a place
for you" and references to the coming of Christ and the Judgment Day when,
it is implied, the Shakers will come into their own: "I hear Christ is coming

with a crown. He will soon appear to gather His chosen ones home. One morning, we are going to receive our blessing." Occasionally, reference to the congregation is more explicit: "I know Jesus choose me. I know the Lord choose many here."

In their sermons, Shakers stress that the sufferings of Jesus and other biblical characters far exceeded the tribulations of the Shakers. The implication is made that the Shakers, being favored by God even as the biblical examples, should expect—even welcome—suffering since it brings them into closer affiliation with that heavenly group. For example, in one sermon the pointer asked, "As Christ came with the heavy cross, must He bear it alone? No! There is one for you and me. . . . We know the Christian pathway is not a bed of roses. We know we are not toiling in vain, for one morning we will get our reward. Everyone of us would want to meet on that beautiful shore. Jesus will welcome us there."

In addition to the possibility of being possessed by the Holy Spirit, their baptismal ritual sets Shakers apart from the upper classes. "The man Christ Jesus was baptized in the River Jordan, for unless man is baptized, he cannot enter the Kingdom of God. We have to be born again to enter into that Eternal Life." For the Shakers, a river or the sea represents the River Jordan, and they, like Jesus, are baptized by immersion in the River and are therefore eligible for salvation.

Wallace (1966: 140) has suggested that "some kind of identification with an admired model of the human personality, and differentiation from a despised model" is associated with restoration of identity.[3] Shakers turn to the Bible for their admired models; those who disparage and deride them and their beliefs provide despised models. Worldly conditions that are difficult for the Shakers to escape are extolled as virtues; people who possess what the Shakers cannot attain are held in contempt. Being unable to acquire material wealth and a satisfactory present, they emphasize spiritual wealth and a more satisfactory future. Hence, through the mechanism of their religion, they build for themselves a more comfortable identity that is validated by "social communication" with the Holy Spirit through possession trance and is widely separated from the feared identity component.

The goals and satisfaction to be derived from the cult, however, differ slightly for the two sexes. Both seem to be motivated by the general desire for an improved identity image, but the achievements possible for each in the larger society differ, and therefore the compensations sought are of a somewhat different nature. Women in the lower class seem to have more work opportunities open to them than men do. With a small amount of capital, they can set themselves up in businesses of their own,[4] and as entrepreneurs, they are in a position to find gratification for prestige yearnings. Some women do not need to work at all since their husbands provide for them adequately—a situation that seems to carry feelings of superiority with it. For the men, on the other hand, job opportunities seem to be less plentiful—unless (or so they believe) they emigrate. The hope of emigration, which was the dream of most males I interviewed, is a tantalizing prospect that tends to keep the men dissatisfied with the present and uncertain about the future. The kinds of jobs that are available to men in the local community do not fulfill their desires, so that there are frequent complaints and expressed wishes of finding better jobs with better pay.

In the cult, men can find certain mechanisms to counterbalance their inability to achieve prestigious positions in the larger society. They all hold offices, which may be a necessary ploy to attract them to the cult: since men are avid for job betterment, they may be more sensitive than women to the disadvantages of being affiliated with a stigmatized group.

The women find pleasure in the social contacts provided by the cult. Furthermore, the cult organization and the strict discipline dispensed by a male authority figure may afford certain satisfactions for women who are heads of households. During a social period after a meeting, one woman was observed teasing the pointer until she succeeded in provoking him into lashing her with his strap. Then, although in tears, she was apparently satisfied and was smiling. I would suggest that this kind of compulsion may play a part in the satisfactions sought and obtained in the cult by some women.

Identity renewal among the Shakers might be regarded as a "ritual of rebellion," Gluckman (1954: 3), in developing the concept of rituals of rebellion, stated

> ... Whatever the ostensible purpose of the ceremonies, a most striking feature of their organization is the way in which they openly express social tensions: women have to assert license and dominance as against their formal subordination to men, princes have to behave to the king as if they covet the throne, and subjects openly state their resentment of authority.

Similarly, the Shakers have to behave as if they were superior to those to whom they are normally subordinate. This they accomplish by building an ideal identity representing themselves as chosen by God, proof of which is obviously and dramatically provided by the Holy Spirit when It selects Shaker worshipers as Its hosts. Thus it might be argued that a renewal of identity is an accompanying feature of such ritualized expressions of social tensions.

However, Gluckman goes on to say, "these ritual rebellions proceed within an established and sacred traditional system, in which there is dispute about particular distributions of power, and not about the structure of the system itself." The Shakers operate within the system: they may be unhappy with their position and find tension release in their practices, but they are not attempting to overturn the established structure.

Lewis (1966: 318), addressing directly the phenomenon of possession trance, has observed that "women and other depressed categories" often turn to possession trance as a means of applying "mystical pressures upon their superiors in circumstances of deprivation and frustration when few other sanctions are available to them." The women who would be attracted to Shakerism are not any more "depressed" as a category than the men—(perhaps less so), but the Shakers as a whole would qualify. However, they do not exert on their superiors pressures that are acknowledged or, in fact, perceived by either group. Shaker possession trance differs from Lewis's examples in that it is a worthwhile experience, highly valued for its own sake, that brings pleasure and a feeling of well-being, rather than an affliction requiring treatment and the attention of those being pressured. Nonetheless, we would certainly agree with Lewis (1971: 35) that "the circumstances which encourage the ecstatic response are precisely those where men feel themselves constantly threatened by exacting pressures which they do not know how to combat or control, except through those heroic flights of ecstasy by which they seek to demonstrate that they are the equals of the gods."

It is interesting to note that in its early days, Methodism (on which the Shaker religion is based) allowed for "instituted protest" (Gluckman, 1954: 3) against the imperfections in the established order and, by so doing, maintained the order and "helped to steady the country during the French Revolution, and prevented similar upheaval from taking place in England (Bowen, 1937: viii). As Sargant (1959: 201) remarked, "Wesley had taught the masses to be less concerned with their miserable life on earth, as victims of the Industrial Revolution, than with the life to come; they could now put up with almost anything." Simpson (1965: 127) has noted for the Shangoists in Trinidad that

> . . . the time, thought, energy, and resources which are invested in *shango* are not available as a means to an alternate end, i.e., trying to bring about social, economic, and political changes. Also, the emotional release from accumulated frustration obtained from *shango* activity reduces the amount of fervor available for political activity. In terms of the perpetuation of the *status quo* this consequence is positive.

Theoretically, a religion like Shakerism, which features divine inspiration, "is always open to dramatic new revelations, to novel messages from the gods" (Lewis, 1971: 174) and hence could be a significant agency for social change. In practice, however, Shakerism, like Shango and early Methodism, monopolizes the time and energies of its devotees and curtails resources that might otherwise be channeled into the instigation of change. Although not all lower class Vincentians are uninterested in active sociopolitical involvement, the Shaker group during the time of my study seemed to fit Leacock and Leacock's (1972: 324) characterization of Batuque members in Belem as a segment of a society "in which the lower class knows its place and keeps to it."

Hence, as it operates at present, Shakerism fails to generate disturbances of the established system. It provides its members with a ritual context within which to demonstrate their putative superiority, to improve their identity image, and to discharge built-up frustrations in religious activities. By so doing, it is instrumental in the maintenance of the status quo.

NOTES

1. St. Vincent offers little in the way of recreation for lower class individuals. Every house I visited did have a radio. The island has a weekly newspaper, but the Shakers I knew did not seem to read it. There is no television, nor are there many telephones even among the more privileged people. Kingstown has two movie theaters, but none of the Shakers that I interviewed mentioned attending. Political rallies were popular when I was there, but seemed to have little appeal for the Shakers with whom I was acquainted. Although they all intended to take advantage of their franchise and had decided opinions about the candidates for election, they seemed to be interested in political developments more as spectators than as participants. Carnival season apparently offers an exciting respite to routine living, but only for a limited time.

2. I am applying the label "upper class" to all non-lower class persons, or nonproletarians. This would include Hadley's (1949) "lower-middle" and "upper-middle" categories.

3. Finding an acceptable personality with which to identify oneself seems to require simultaneous identification of others in some consistent manner. See Chapter 2 for the Shaker identification of me.

4. Women with small amounts of capital who set themselves up as vendors are not unusual for the Caribbean. See Mintz (1960; 1964) for discussions of economic activities among Haitian and Jamaican women similar to those among women in St. Vincent.

11

Conclusions

States of dissociation are salient features of worship in two religious groups, the Shakers and Streams of Power, that operate in the West Indian Island of St. Vincent. Devotees of each religion may experience dissociation in a group context during church services, but although both groups offer the same explanation for the experience—entry of the Holy Spirit into the affected person—and although we use the same label, "possession trance," to cover both situations, the outward, visible manifestations of the experience differ greatly from one group to the other. Among the Streams of Power adherents the emphasis in possession trance is on speaking in tongues, and the performance is of short duration. Among the Shakers, the emphasis is on bodily motion and sound, with the possibility of progression to a deeper level in which hyperventilation and subordination to group-imposed rhythm are conspicuous; the performance may require considerably more time than do the Streams of Power possession trances. Furthermore, Streams of Power has institutionalized only one form of dissociational state, possession trance; Shakers have also institutionalized trance. Trance occurs during periods of ritual isolation known as "mourning," when it takes the form of hallucinations and is interpreted as a "spiritual journey" during which the entranced person's spirit is believed to travel away from his corporeal body. Trance may also occur in the form of visions outside the ritual context, in which case it is interpreted as a sign from God to accept baptism or mourning; however, "culture pattern dreams" (Bourguignon, 1972: 416, quoting Lincoln) may also fulfill this function.

Mischel and Mischel (1958: 253) noted levels of possession trance among the Shangoists of Trinidad:

> The level of possession (the depth, involvement, loss of control and consciousness, and intensity of behavior) is by no means constant, either among individuals or at different times with the same person. At times it appears to consist merely of a brief "overshadowing" or momentary loss of control, dizziness, and a partial and temporary loss of consciousness. On other occasions, it involves an almost total and prolonged loss of consciousness, and of many

controls over motor behavior. . . . It should be emphasized that possession
does not appear to be an all-or-none process, utterly separated from the individual's usual state. Rather, an extension and distortion of everyday behavior
seems to be involved, and possession behavior cannot be rigidly dichotomized
from the person's secular roles. It would appear more useful to deal with different levels of involvement in possession behavior rather than "possession"
versus "normality."

However, they made no attempt to develop the concept further.

It has been observed that the Shaker possession trances are mild; though apparently simple, they are of sufficient complexity to enable one to discern, on
the basis of overt behavioral changes, different levels through which the
possession trances progress. The usual possession trances for the Shakers fall
rather precisely into three divisions, according to certain relevant criteria, with
intervening transitional periods of short duration. Typical possession trances
have been diagrammed, and it has been shown that, by superimposing an individual's possession-trance pattern over those of other possession trancers, the
diagrams indicate reinforcement at certain points, explaining the choruslike
aspects of the possession-trance group taken as a whole.

The concept of levels of possession trance as it has been expanded here
would seem to have some usefulness and meaning cross-culturally. Darmadji
and Pfeiffer (1969: 9) reported their findings on Kuda-kepang in Java and
commented:

> . . . Das Verhalten vor, während und nach dem Trancezustand weist eine
> Reihe von Zügen auf, die sich bei solchen Zustanden in aller Welt wie-
> derholen. So kam J. Henney auf Grund ihrer Beobachtungen bei den Shakers
> auf St. Vincent zu einer ähnlichen Stadieneinteilung wie wir.[1]

Dissociation during mourning is not interpreted as spirit possession. In
many ways, the conditions under which mourning is fulfilled are very similar
to those used in sensory-deprivation experiments: the mourner is confined, his
visual perception is limited by a blindfold, his motility is restricted since he is
required to lie on the ground in a specified position, he is fed a limited diet, he
is isolated from his ordinary contacts and activities, and he is in a situation of
dependency. Under such conditions, both mourners and subjects in sensory-
deprivation experiments report hallucinations. However, certain aspects of the
hallucinatory experience reported by the mourners differ from those reported
by the experimental subjects. These variations lead us to conclude that, insofar
as the results of similar sensory-deprivation experiences are the same for different groups of people, they are dependent on "biological commonalities," but
in the areas where they are different, we are dealing with results that have

been influenced by variations in culture. Thus it would seem that the capacity for hallucinating under certain conditions is a biological possibility common to humans, but the probability of hallucinating and the content of the hallucinations will vary with the expectations of the people involved, their belief system and other similar factors.

Shakerism has been considered from the standpoint of its value for its participants. It has been argued that it serves a positive function by providing lower class Vincentians caught in an apparently unresolvable socioeconomic plight, aggravated by racial prejudices rooted in the bridgeless chasm between slave and planter, and by unequal educational and vocational opportunities, an image with which to identify—an image demonstrating that superiority and worth lie in the very qualities with which the Shakers are most generously endowed: poverty, rejection, persecution, and the like. Furthermore, by withdrawing and seeking identification with a biblical hero or even with Christ Himself, the Shakers are, in reality, however unconsciously, staging a ritual of rebellion. They indicate their scorn for the treasures of the other classes, which they may covet but are unable to obtain, by regarding them as sinful and less worthy and desirable as goals than the Kingdom of Heaven. By expressing their disdain through identification with Christian martyrs and heroes, they reassure themselves of their superiority over the group that is ordinarily superior to them. Yet, consistent with the concept of rituals of rebellion, their rebellion against the classes that dominate them remains in ritual form and does not become open revolt, but actually serves to maintain the established system. By directing the worshipers' aspirations toward the afterlife, by concentrating their resources on becoming eligible for its rewards, and by soothing and relieving their envious desires with a satisfying belief that they, not the upper class—the "despised" model—are the chosen of God, Shakerism supports the status quo.

Shakerism has been compared with similar cults in the Caribbean—in particular, the Shouters of Trinidad and the Revivalists of Jamaica—in an effort to isolate the forces operating, first of all, in the development of such groups, and second, in their acceptance and persistence—often in the face of opposition. Although several influences appear to have a larger or smaller role in the development and reception of syncretic religions in the Caribbean, no one factor nor any one group of factors can be singled out as the necessary precursor or concomitant. Catholicism, where it was the dominant religion, encouraged the acceptance of Christianity by the slaves and provided a slate of saints with which native African deities and spirits could be matched and merged; *vodun* in Catholic Haiti and Shango in Catholic Trinidad exemplify such syncretization. Where the Anglican Church was the established church, admission of the slaves to Christianity was discouraged and syncretization of

Christian and African elements less likely to occur. Nor is it found in some islands that are and have been predominantly Anglican—for example, St.
Vincent. However, in Jamaica, Moore (1965) reported that African spirits
were identified with Old and New Testament personalities. Additional factors
contributing to religious syncretism appear to include the size of the island,
colonizing country, interisland movements, individual innovators, specific
missionary influences, size of the slave population, economy of the island, fortuitous immigration, and, in general, historical accidents. The problem of
explaining religious syncretism in the Caribbean, however, remains unsolved.

Looking now at Streams of Power, the possession-trance phenomenon
manifested in glossolalia did not lend itself to the same kind of observational
analysis that Shaker possession trance did. Goodman, however, working with
my tapes, discovered a recurring pattern: "a threshold of onset, a rising
gradient of intensity, a peak, and a rapid drop or decay" (1968: 14). She compared this glossolalia pattern with the sequences of levels of Shaker possession
trances and found them to be very similar. She concluded that the "pattern,
reflected in the glossolalia in the phonological, accent, and intonational structure, can be shown to exist also in other artifacts of trance, such as . . . kinetic
behavior. . . ."

The possession-trance phenomenon in the two churches seems to reflect the
simple–complex dichotomy prevalent in other aspects of their worship. Among
the Shakers, possession trance can be a lengthy and impressive phenomenon of
some beauty, involving regularity of rhythm and a certain grace of movement.
In the Streams of Power church, possession trance is not very dramatic, is over
quickly, and seems much less forceful by comparison. The Shakers also believe
that they may speak in tongues, but it forms only one small part of their
possession-trance behavior complex and is unlike the Streams of Power variety. For the Shakers, speaking in tongues is a benefit that may be acquired
by those who mourn and is said to be like having a telephone line to God. No
interpretation is made in the vernacular, nor is speaking in tongues a matter in
most cases of the supernatural using the person as a medium through whom
His message passes on its way to another.

The presence of two religious bodies that use possession trance in their
services and drawing their members from the same general class reservoir
brings up the question of what differential benefits they confer. Why are some
people who are seeking a religious base attracted to one instead of the other?
Streams of Power stresses the present, healing is important, possession trance
is relatively unimportant. It seems to appeal to certain Vincentians who have
been able to achieve a modicum of prestige satisfaction in the larger society
and are not wholly (or nearly so) dependent on the church for such satisfaction, yet have not reached a sufficiently high social and economic level to

feel as comfortable in one of the organized churches as they do in a church where the members are more on a par. They seem to need more emotional involvement than that provided by the colder, more detached services of the organized churches. Yet, partly because of the position they have reached in the community, they disdain a religion that has the reputation of being "African." Since Streams of Power is an introduced religion, a packaged product so to speak, its particular brand of possession trance escapes being so labeled. Streams of Power offers its worshipers the opportunity to identify with a group led by a dynamic, personable young man, who—coming as he does from across the sea, driving a car, having a telephone, and living in some luxury—may serve as a symbol of the promise and opportunities believed by many Vincentians to exist in the world outside the island. He also offers them a religion that serves as an inexpensive diversion; does not require too much time, energy, or intellect; makes vices of such pleasures as smoking and drinking, which they can ill afford in their economic circumstances; and teaches virtues (e.g., legal marriage) advantageous to a group engaged in the competitive struggle for upward mobility. In short, Streams of Power seems to embody many of the values of the Protestant ethic (Weber, 1958), especially the belief in the possibility of upward movement with hard work and avoidance of evil habits and conduct.

The Shaker church, on the other hand, is different in orientation and goals. It appeals to those Vincentians who have "few realistically available means for the attainment of prestige in the larger society" (Mischel, 1958: 169). With its hierarchy of offices, Shakerism provides opportunities for its adherents to satisfy their prestige cravings. They may achieve not only positions of authority, marked by such tangible evidence as insignia of office, within the cult but also the highly gratifying experience of being chosen by the deity to serve as its host. Possession trance affords the opportunity to be important—very important—since God as the Holy Ghost become involved individually in their lives, which He does not even do with the most economically advantaged Vincentians. Although possession trance is also available to Streams of Power worshipers, it is probably acceptable to them only because the manifestations are brief and shallow; Shaker manifestations are rejected as "having too much flesh" in them, which would make them inconsistent with the Streams of Power set of virtues.

Bourguignon (1972: 428) suggests that various forms of altered states of consciousness—dreams, trance, and possession trance—"expand the field of experience and of action of the self." Shakerism offers a wider range of contact possibilities with the supernatural through states of dissociation than does Streams of Power. Perhaps expansion of the field of experience and of action of the self are more important for the Shakers since they are more deprived of prestige opportunities, they are a more "depressed category," and fewer secular channels are open to them.

The investigation of the variety of belief systems applied to dissociational states by the Shakers and Streams of Power demonstrates the importance of culturally patterned cognitive factors for dissociational behavior and experience.

NOTES

1. "The behavior before, during, and after the trance condition shows a number of traits which in such states repeat themselves all over the world. On the basis of her observations with the Shakers on St. Vincent, J. Henney arrived at a similar organization of stages as we did." (Translated by Dr. Felicitas Goodman.)

APPENDIX

A Chalk Design Made for a Shaker Mourning Ritual

Pointer B. made a copy of the chalk design that he had drawn on the mourning-room floor before the service at which three pilgrims were "laid on the ground." He presented it to me and offered the following meanings for some of the symbols used in the drawing shown on p. 111:

Charter

Compass

Nazareth

Pilgrim

Signal of the city. Every city you enter have a signal.

Canaan

Ladder to Heaven

Sago palm. The significance of sago; faithful unto death, palms of victory, the prize (?) is in view.

$\oplus E$

Emanuel

Bell

Christian had lost his course. Evangelist spin him and gave him three lashes. Sign of the pointer who point Christian to that celestial shore Mr. Wooly Wiseman met him and told him that he would get rid of the burden on his back. He went to the hill; he journeyed many days and nights and he couldn't get rid of the hill. A storm came. There was no way he could escape. He began to pray. Evangelist knew then that Christian was off line. He promised not to turn back but go toward the true God.

L

Love. If you have no love in Christ, you are a dead symbol. God so loved the world.

T

Travel

Baptism. Became soldier born.

Jericho

Zion. You hit all the cities around.

If I rebuke these people the very stones will shout for joy. Sweeping Jerusalem, my happy home. The symbol shows the mystery of the Lord going to Jerusalem. Christ mourned (wept) in Jerusalem.

Pointer B. explained: "When you go to the Throne of Grace, you meet these things. When David was in the spirit, he saw the ladder Jacob climbed. We must be making steps to Christ. Obedience is the first step to Christ.

"Five candles is five-pointed stars. These are the five cities. You have to travel to them first. Canaan, Calvary, Victory, Jericho, and Zion—these are five schools.

"Each pointer has a different alphabet. A working mother in the spirit can point souls, that is, can make chalk marks on the floor; not all will know it. But she can't make everything."

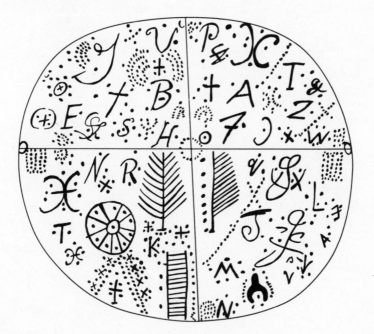

Part Two: Esther Pressel

Umbanda Trance and Possession in São Paulo, Brazil

PREFACE

Although North American anthropologists are more than aware that the terms "race" and "culture" are not synonymous, there has been a tendency to regard Afro-Brazilian culture as something that is practiced by Afro-Brazilians. This is perhaps due to the legacy of Afro-American studies left by Herskovits, who was concerned with finding the most pure African cultural elements retained through the processes of "syncretism" and "reinterpretation" (Herskovits, 1937b, 1948). The Brazilian research of Herskovits (1943, 1959, 1966) was conducted primarily on the Candomblé spirit-possession cult in Bahia, where one of the largest Afro-Brazilian populations still lives. As a result, we are only today coming to realize that other parts of Brazil, with far fewer persons of African descent, have accepted African religious beliefs and have adapted them to their particular needs. It is to be hoped that this particular study about Umbanda—a religion with some African elements but widely accepted by Euro-Brazilians in São Paulo—will dispel any further impressions that Afro-Brazilian cultural elements are associated primarily with persons of African ancestry.

The work reported in this study was done during an eleven-month period in 1967. It was part of a larger research project supported by the National Institute of Mental Health of the U.S. Public Health Service. The project, entitled Cross-Cultural Study of Dissociational States, was under the direction of Dr. Erika Bourguignon, of the Department of Anthropology, the Ohio State University. I especially wish to thank Professor Erika Bourguignon, whose comments and suggestions in her letters to me in the field were extremely helpful. I also express my appreciation to Professors H. S. Morris, Gene Poirier, and Thomas R. Williams for their comments on this study in its dissertational form.

Dr. Irving Zaretsky offered valuable suggestions for revising an earlier draft of the manuscript. Mr. Eric Valentine bravely coordinated this part of the book with the studies of Drs. Goodman and Henney. The manuscript benefited greatly from Mrs. Valda Aldzeris' editorial supervision and Mrs. Ausra Richards' copy editing. The final responsibility for the contents of this part of the book, however, is my own.

Research in cultural anthropology cannot be accomplished without the friendship of the individuals one studies. Due to the intimate nature of some of the information these people provided, I shall not mention their specific names. However, their particular personalities are a major part of the data in this study, and lacking their generous cooperation, I could not have done my research. A debt of gratitude is also due to Therezinha Guimarães Mathias, who was my friend, major field assistant, and typist in São Paulo. Without her gifted insight into the nature of Brazilian society and national character, many observations might have slipped by me.

Three other personal notes of thanks are inevitable: one to my parents, who usually suggested that I do whatever I felt was best for me; the second to Urso Prêto—my Kiowa-Apache "guardian spirit," who finally decided to reveal himself to me in Brazil, where he thought I might be more inclined to accept spirits; and the third to Mrs. Fran Roberts for her admirable patience in typing various drafts of this study.

Since I sometimes use Portuguese words to describe Umbanda beliefs, a few comments on the pronounciation of this language are in order. The Portuguese orthography is generally phonetic and is similar to Spanish in pronounciation. There are, however, certain deviations. The Portuguese x is pronounced like the English sh; therefore, exu and orixá become "eshu" and "orisha." Vowels may be nasalized, and this is indicated in Portuguese by a tilde (e.g., mãe). Also, an m following a vowel at the end of a word (e.g., -am, -em, -im, -om and -um) indicates that the preceding vowel is nasalized. The m in these cases is not a bilabial sound and is not pronounced. The -lh- sound cluster in the middle of a word indicates palatalization, so that trabalho becomes "trabalYo." The Portuguese j is pronounced like the s in "pleasure."

1

Introduction

This study is concerned principally with the description and analysis of trance and spirit possession in a rapidly expanding Brazilian religion known as Umbanda. Although certain Brazilian spirit-possession religions of African origin have been described,[1] there is practically no published information on how spirit possession behavior is learned or in what ways spirits are related to the more ordinary everyday activities of a spirit medium. Moreover, the anthropological literature on Afro-Brazilian religions provides relatively little information concerning the psychological motivations for becoming a vehicle for spirits. Descriptions of the biological trance that accompanies spirit possession are also limited. Previous work on Brazilian possession religions has been focused primarily on the shared beliefs and rituals that are a part of the social system, one notable exception being a single life history of a medium in the Brazilian Batuque religion in Belém, provided in appendix form by Leacock and Leacock (1972). In contrast to these earlier works, the present study deliberately attempts to emphasize the behavior of individuals who are spirit mediums.

Brazil was an ideal site for my particular purposes and needs. Trance and possession are very common in this country, and strangers are usually welcomed to public sessions. Furthermore, as I began making friends with mediums, it was not at all difficult to be invited to private sessions, which provided a great deal of my data. As I was a novice in anthropological field work and had only a year in which to gather data, the openness of the spirit sessions and of the mediums themselves was especially helpful in obtaining the data on individuals heretofore overlooked in the literature on Brazil.

From my preparatory reading, I learned that Umbanda is not the only spiritualist religion in Brazil today. Trance and spirit possession are practiced among the indigenous Indians of Brazil; in the traditional lower class Afro-Brazilian cults like Candomblé; in Protestant sects, such as the Pentecostalists; and in Kardecismo, a form of French spiritualism introduced to Brazil in the nineteenth century. Out of these varied possibilities, I selected Umbanda for three reasons. First, at the time of this research in 1967, nearly all previous work on possession cults in Brazil had been focused on the older syncretized religions, such as Candomblé in northeastern Brazil. A study of Umbanda would introduce new data on a religion that (a) has national, rather than regional, appeal; (b) is apparently linked with modern, rather than traditional, Brazilian culture; (c) is not limited to the African- and Indian-derived populations in Brazil, but has wide appeal to persons of European descent as well; and (d) is oriented more toward the middle, rather than lower, classes in São Paulo. Second, at the time of my research very little had been published on Umbanda. One notable exception was Camargo's (1961) study in Portuguese of the spiritual continuum between Umbanda and Kardecismo in São Paulo. Renshaw (1966) provided a very brief descriptive account of Umbanda in Campinas. McGregor (1967) had written a personal journalistic account. Levy (1968) studied Umbanda in São Paulo and wrote her M.A. thesis on this subject. Third, very little research has been done on the learning processes involved in trance states. Since Umbanda leaders hold sessions in which mediumistic abilities are developed, I felt that this learning situation could be easily studied.

Nearly all of my field research was conducted in the city of São Paulo. I made brief side trips of Belo Horizonte, Rio de Janeiro, Pôrto Alegre, Santos, and to the small interior city of Bauru, where I was able to locate *centros* (centers, i.e., places of worship) of Umbanda. In traveling, one of the first things I would do on checking into a hotel was to go to a beauty salon. While having my hair and nails done, I invariably heard the other customers gossiping about spirits. One beautician even kept her Umbanda manual beside the hair rollers and studied it when not occupied. Needless to say, I had no difficulty in locating Umbanda centers when visiting a strange town. In addition to my trips outside São Paulo, I collected data about the national spread of Umbanda from the popular press as well as from books, magazines, and newspapers published by the Umbandists themselves. In São Paulo I was able to visit twelve centers to become acquainted with the tremendous variety of ritual and belief found in what Camargo (1961) has called "a continuum of spiritualism in São Paulo." At one pole of Carmargo's continuum are the more African forms of Umbanda, heavily influenced by Candomblé and Macumba. At the other is the European spiritualism of Allen Kardec. The wide middle band includes just about every type of mixture of African and European spiritualism as well as admixtures with Catholic and indigenous Indian elements.

From the twelve centers I visited in São Paulo, I selected two for further research. In terms of ritual songs and dances, these two centers tended to fall culturally toward the African end of the continuum. However, the underlying beliefs and spirit theories of these two groups are those of the familiar spirits of Kardecismo, and not those of the spirits of African gods that one finds in the conservative cults of Candomblé. The active membership in the one center was about 20 and in the other, about 40. Using the racial categories of the United States,[2] I estimate that the proportion of whites in the former was about 60 percent and in the latter, about 20 percent. It is difficult to state percentages and numbers precisely because roughly 30 percent of the total number of 60 changed during the year of field work. Mediums left for other centers, and new participants arrived on the scene. Indeed, the centers seemed to revolve about the cult leader and a few close assistants. Clearly, in no instance was the group as a whole in charge, as in some Protestant congregations in the United States, which may hire and fire their spiritual leader.

In addition to these national and local observations, I did an intensive study of the importance of spirits in the personal lives of nine people. Five of them formed a friendship clique that conducted private sessions in the homes of "clients." These sessions provided me with an opportunity to converse more freely with the spirits than is normally possible in the public sessions at the centers. The members of this clique participated in the sessions of the two centers I finally selected for study. I did in-depth open-ended interviews based on the Ohio State group's "Cross-Cultural Outline for the Study of Dissociational States" with these nine individuals. The interviews were taped and typed up verbatim. When ideas from these interviews seemed significant, I checked them out in conversations with Umbandists from other centers and other social scientists who have studied Umbanda; in addition, I consulted books and newspapers published by Umbandists. I taped some spirit sessions and took photographs of spirits at the request of the mediums I studied.

In doing this research a number of methodological problems arose. I chose to follow the traditional anthropological approach of participation-observation and found it extremely difficult to be in all places at one time. The metropolitan nature of São Paulo simply did not permit this. I lived only half a block from my major informant and could visit her frequently with little difficulty. However, I was sometimes forced to rely on personal, and probably biased, accounts from my other informants as to what had occurred to them during working hours in factories and offices, and in their homes. Members of a particular Umbanda center tend not to live very close to each other. This meant that I often had to travel over a rather wide area of São Paulo to see informants in their homes. Furthermore, when I visited them, there was always the possibility that they would be watching television after a long day of work. Some of the best data were perhaps gathered in restaurants where my major informants went for pizza and drinks after attending a public or private spiritual session.

In collecting data the anthropologist who works in a small village obviously has certain advantages I did not have. Nevertheless, for the purposes of this study I believe that the data recorded in my notes are superior to those I might have obtained from impersonal questionnaires. In spite of urbanization, Brazilians are still largely personal in psychological orientation. It is highly doubtful that they would have provided the intimate information I was able to obtain if standardized questionnaires had been utilized. One Brazilian social scientist advised me at the beginning of the year, "You will find that Brazilians either will like you as a person and will do everything to help you with your studies, or they will not like you and will be of no use whatsoever." Throughout the year of field work, I found little to contradict this prediction.

As a participant, I attended Umbanda public sessions in the role of a client, seated with other nonmediums who had come to seek supernatural assistance from the spirits. I consulted with Umbanda spirits about any special ailments or personal problems I had at the time. Very early in the year I came to recognize the usefulness of spirits for my own work. One of my older informants, Cecília, took me to the apartment of two young men, insisting that they would be of great use in my work, since they "knew" English. Stepping out of the bus in front of their building, she assured me that I could visit them at any time. I responded that a Brazilian friend in the United States had forewarned me about gossip that would result from going alone to the apartments of men. As we rode up the elevator, Cecília told me not to worry about this. In about an hour, I learned what she had meant. Cecília's Indian spirit possessed her in an impromptu session. When the major item of spiritual business had been completed, the Indian spirit turned to the men and asked who I was. They introduced me to Cecília's possessing spirit and explained why I had come to Brazil. The Indian gave his personal blessing to my work and told the others in the room that they should aid my research in any way they could. Furthermore, I was to visit the men, who were instructed to treat me as a sister and that "nothing" was to happen. Sometime later in the year, when other friends of Cecília's commented on my visits to the apartment of these men, Cecília very quickly assured them that her Indian spirit had made the appropriate arrangements for these very proper meetings. What might have turned into malicious gossip was stopped at that point.

At first, I went to private spirit meetings primarily as an observer. As I became more knowledgeable about the ritual activities and behavior of spirits, I began to assist in small ways, such as helping a spirit light his cigar or pipe. I sometimes provided money for special foods the spirits liked or other ritual paraphernalia. Some close Brazilian friends were obviously curious about my own capacities for mediumship, urging me to take a more active "participant" role. Strongly suspecting that an anthropologist in a trance state would not be able to do much observing, I begged off by noting that in only half-learning to become a medium I might run the risk of "spiritual disorders" on my return home, where there would be no Umbanda centers to help me. Toward the end of the year I did agree to participate in a limited way. My informants, however, could never come to an agreement as to whether a spirit had actually possessed me or whether a spirit was just nearby, influencing my behavior a bit. Since cultural reality is in large measure socially determined, I cannot explain what had possessed me to do such a thing.

My participation and observation were not limited to religious sessions. Indeed, one of the major purposes of my investigation was to learn the part spirits play in the everyday life of a person and to determine whether certain stressful events in an individual's daily life would influence the behavior of his spirits. The amount of time I spent every week with each of the nine persons studied in depth varied. I saw three of them on a somewhat irregular and limited basis. I attempted to visit the other six informants at least once, and sometimes twice, a week in their homes. I also met regularly with the five informants comprising the friendship clique described in this study. We spent several hours together after public sessions each week.

Although I did not have any letters of introduction to Umbandists, there was never any difficulty in making contacts. For example, during my first day in São Paulo, I wandered into a downtown restaurant owned by a middle-aged man of Italian descent who had traveled throughout Brazil and South America. I mentioned that I was a university student from the United States and was planning to study Umbanda, my research being part of a larger comparative study of spiritualist religions throughout the world. This explanation of my presence I offered to all acquaintances formally or informally made throughout the year. My statement of purpose was enough to induce the restaurant owner, as well as nearly everyone else, to begin talking about his personal experiences with Umbanda. As a rule, the better educated individual was more cautious in divulging his belief in spirits and would usually first ask about mine. I usually responded with my personal belief, namely, that all religions are but roads to the same "God." When pressed to state whether I *really* did believe in spirits, I simply replied that I had not had the opportunity to be brought up in a spiritualist religion and felt it only fair to withhold judgment until learning more about Umbanda. These answers seemed to satisfy the people I met and worked with and, I believe, helped to maintain the "observer" part of my status.

Although my central interest in studying Umbanda was at the level of the individual, an understanding of behavior is impossible without some knowledge of the larger social context. Therefore the next two chapters set the scene, giving the reader some idea of the general Brazilian religious milieu and of the urban environment in which one finds Umbanda. Chapter 4 is a discussion of Umbanda beliefs and rituals that help channel the behavior of individuals. With this background, I next describe the life histories of six individuals I studied, especially the events that led to their decisions to develop mediumistic capacities, and the relations between their spirits and everyday behavior. From the total of nine persons studied intensively, I selected the six individuals described in Chapters 5 through 8 because I had obtained the most complete data on them. Moreover, since five of them were close friends, holding private sessions for themselves and for clients, a greater amount of social interaction among these five could be examined. At the end of each of these case-history chapters I have included a very brief analysis that will help the reader understand the functioning of spirit possession in each of the mediums described. Chapter 9 is a summary and discussion of Umbandist possession-trance phenomena in terms of learning these behavioral forms; the nature of trance states, as well as the behavior before and after trance; the interpersonal relations associated with spirit possession; and the reasons for continuing in the role of medium over an extended period.

Finally, in doing this study of Umbanda in São Paulo I was struck by two questions that are somewhat more related to the nature of the Brazilian sociocultural milieu than to the level of the individual. First, it seemed unusual to me that the cultural concept of spirit possession should continue to have such widespread acceptance in a modern industrial setting. Second, I was intrigued by the apparent diffusion of Umbanda to nearly all parts of Brazil, and into the middle class, in contrast to other Brazilian spirit-possession religions that failed to expand. Therefore, in Chapter 10 I discuss the hypothesis that Umbanda represents a religious innovation that is related to socioeconomic changes in Brazil during the last 50 years.

NOTES

1. Roger Bastide (1960) provides an excellent summary of the literature on Afro-Brazilian religions.
2. Racial categories in Brazil are far more complex than those in the United States. See Marvin Harris (1970) for a better understanding of the cultural concept of race in Brazil.

2

Umbanda in the Brazilian Religious Milieu

Brazil is the most Catholic country in the world in terms of the numbers of persons who are baptized in the Catholic Church. Over 90 percent of Brazil's 90 million people are officially Catholic. Spiritualism, however, is an extremely powerful force in this country. Just how strong the various spiritualist religions are in Brazil is anybody's guess. In a recent publication[1] of the Catholic Church in the United States, it was estimated that 90 percent of Brazilians were spiritualists! I regard this figure as somewhat high, but would not hesitate in the least to use the figure of 50 percent and upward. This estimate includes spirit mediums as well as ordinary persons who have attended sessions at one time or another to obtain spiritual assistance. Umbanda membership, of course, represents only a portion of the total number of spiritualists in Brazil. Since many Umbandists are listed as Catholics in the national census, no accurate data are available.

It was not at all unusual to observe babies being baptized in both Catholic and Umbanda rituals. Marriage ceremonies are also performed by both religions. I especially remember one couple who, having gone through both Catholic and civil ceremonies, had come in the late afternoon to an Umbanda center to be married a third time by an Umbanda Indian spirit wearing an elaborate feathered headdress. The bride wore a lovely traditional long white gown, and the groom was decked out in a morning coat. The middle-aged *padrinho* and *madrinha* (godparents) of the couple were good middle-class Italian-Brazilian Catholics who saw little personal conflict in the multiplicity of ceremonies. As the evening's party wore on, they joked about the priest and how he would be having convulsions if he were to know about the Umbanda wedding ceremony.

The dual religious commitment to Catholicism and Umbanda is neither a recent phenomenon nor a trait limited to Brazil. It is rooted in the history of Afro-Brazilian culture extending back into the sixteenth century, when African

121

slaves were brought across the Atlantic to man the sugar plantations in the northeastern part of the country. Afro-Americans in Brazil as well as in other parts of the larger Caribbean "plantation America" region retained impressive segments of their religious culture. On the special days of the saints observed by Catholic plantation owners, Africans celebrated the worship of their own deities. Gradually, Catholic saints and African gods were syncretized (Herskovits, 1937b). An example of this process is the West African Yoruba *orixá* Ogum, who was god of iron and patron of blacksmiths forging iron tools and weapons. In some regions of Brazil, Africans equated Ogum with St. George, who is frequently depicted on a white charger, slaying the dragon with a long iron sword. The syncretism proceeded along two lines. First, the material cultural item of iron weapons links Ogum and St. George. Second, the Yoruba *orixás* and Catholic saints were structural intermediaries between a high and remote Olorun, or God, and ordinary men on earth. This rapprochement of African and European religious culture has continued down to the present. Umbandists of Italian and German descent in São Paulo claim that the *orixás* and saints represent the same entities and that the differences in names became apparent when Africans and Europeans finally met in Brazil.

During the latter part of the era of Brazilian slavery, and after emancipation in 1888, Afro-Brazilians began to practice their religion more openly in urban cult houses. These religions were known under various names: in São Luís, Tambor das Minas was strongly influenced by Dahomean beliefs; Xangô in Recife and Candomblé in Salvador were primarily of Yoruba origin; Batuque in Belém and Candomblé de Caboclo in Salvador added Amerindian cultural elements to the Afro-Catholic blend; and in the more southern states of Minas Gerais, Guanabara (Rio de Jáneiro), and São Paulo, the Afro-Brazilian religion known as Macumba combined Yoruba *orixás* with cultural elements from the Congolese and Angolan areas in Africa. Bastide (1960) provides an excellent survey of the literature describing these and other Afro-Brazilian religions.

Of the religious cults mentioned here, Macumba is of special interest as the immediate predecessor of Umbanda. Little is known about the cults that antedate Macumba in the region just south of the old plantation northeast. When these earlier groups were first studied, they were in a state of transformation into Macumba. According to Bastide (1960: 411), Macumba was partly an outgrowth of the introduction of the Yoruba *orixás* into the earlier "Bantu" cult known as Cabula. Some Congolese and Angolan influences in this region of Brazil continue to exist in Umbanda; for example, the high god is given the name Zambe, instead of the Yoruba name Olorun. It is interesting to note that the Suku of the southwestern Congo still refer to their creator god as Nzambi (Kopytoff, 1965: 467).

The literature cited by Bastide (1960) indicates that Macumba differed from the more traditional Yoruba Candomblé in at least five other important ways:

1. Macumba featured possession by spirits of the dead, including dead Afro-Brazilians and Amerindians, whereas the most respected Candomblé cult houses in Bahia admitted only possession by the *orixá* deities.
2. Men were permitted to be mediums in Macumba, but not in the older versions of Candomblé.
3. The group solidarity found in Candomblé cult houses of the northeast was not present in Macumba. This perhaps can be attributed to the fragmentary nature of the more highly urbanized and industrialized southern cities of São Paulo and Rio de Janeiro at the time.
4. Whether actually true or not, Macumba developed a reputation for heavy dealings in the black magic of the *exu* spirits. In contrast, the Yoruba trickster *exu* deity was not given as much attention in Candomblé as he seemed to enjoy in Macumba.
5. The religious beliefs of Allen Kardec, a French spiritualist—or spiritist, as the Kardecists prefer to be called—began to filter into Macumba, but not into traditional Candomblé.

These cumulative religious shifts, coupled with the social, economic, and political changes discussed in Chapter 10, provided the setting for the early development of Umbanda in the 1920s and 1930s.

Today Umbanda has pretty much supplanted Macumba; however, the term "Macumba" remains. It is frequently used by the detractors of Umbanda as a derogatory and generalized term for Umbanda and other religions of Afro-Brazilian origin. Unfortunately, the United Stated news media have picked up this term, constantly misusing it in their usually sensationalized reports of Umbanda. In Brazil, a sense of carefulness is associated with the much maligned "Macumba." The prevalent attitude of many Brazilians, who, while proclaiming disbelief, do not care to take unnecessary chances, is perhaps epitomized in a cartoon that appeared in *O Cruzeiro* shortly before I arrived in Brazil. A Euro-Brazilian man and his girlfriend are driving in a large fancy car through an urban street intersection. A package—no doubt of magical origin—is in the middle of the intersection. The young man has turned to his girlfriend and is telling her that he, of course, does not "believe in these superstitions." At the same time he is swerving the automobile to avoid hitting the package. The cultural elements in this cartoon are straight out of Yoruba religious beliefs about the deity Exu, whose domain is the roads. Packages from Exu "works" are left at intersections to be picked up by this spirit.

The descendants of the old practitioners of Macumba black magic (*magia negra*) are today found in a cult known as Quimbanda. Quimbandists specialize in working with spirits of Exu said to be the spirits of dead people who had lived especially wicked lives. They are believed to send black magic against a business competitor. Quimbanda magic may also be used in love affairs. The more spiritually evolved *exus* in Umbanda utilize white magic (*magia branca*) to counteract the influences of the disreputable Quimbanda *exus*—or so the theory goes. In reality, there is something of a continuum between Quimbanda and Umbanda. Some Umbanda *exus* are just as capable of performing antisocial magic as their counterparts in Quimbanda. It seems to depend on one's particular viewpoint as to whether *exu* magic is "good" or "evil." Although Umbandists claim that they have purged Macumba of its "more primitive and debasing" features associated with black magic, they continue to refer to themselves as *macumbeiros* (Macumbists) as a sign of a friendly bond in a joking situation. They do not, however, care to have that label and its not fully accurate connotations utilized by outsiders such as the Catholic Church.

The established Catholic Church is perhaps less concerned about the traditional and lower class Afro-Brazilian religions like Batuque and Candomblé. These spiritualists religions seem to have their place as a part of the "superstition of the ignorant poor." What really worries the church, however, are the growing numbers of people in the upwardly mobile and educated middle class who actively participate in spirit-possession religions. The major competition comes from Umbanda and two other spiritualist religions, Kardecismo and Pentacostalism. Willems (1966) believes that the existence of these three religious movements constitutes evidence of a major change in the traditional Brazilian social structure. They are alike in three ways: (1) all are concerned with spirit possession; (2) all recruit the bulk of their membership from the upwardly mobile; and (3) all perform similar functions. Healing is emphasized in these groups, whose members cannot always afford adequate medical services. Each group attempts to reconstruct the personal community for its members, who have often left the security of their families as well as their traditional religion in rural villages. Finally, in rejecting the paternalistic tutelage of the traditional upper class of Brazil, these three groups emphasize a certain amount of social equality among their members (Willems, 1966: 221–230).

Pentacostalists believe that they may be possessed by the Holy Spirit through the act of *tomada* (seizure). Pentacostalism is probably of least concern to the Catholic hierarchy, which still officially baptizes over 90 percent of the nation's people. Kardecismo focuses its ritual on possession by the spirits of dead doctors, lawyers, professors, and even kings. If a "suffering soul" should possess a medium, it is frequently the spirit of a dead priest! Kardecist spirit sessions are usually rather quiet and sedate. The mediums sit around a table (*sessão da mesa*), and the spirits may hold lengthy intellectual discussions with themselves and members of the audience. Kardecismo was brought to Brazil from France in the nineteenth century. The Brazilian sociologist Camargo (1961) recognizes a "continuum of spiritualism" between Umbanda and Kardecismo. At one end, in Kardecismo, are the more "elevated" spirits with an intellectual bent. At the other end, one finds the Umbanda spirits of Afro-Brazilian slaves and Amerindians whose works are said to be "more of the heart." What links the two religions is their common belief in spirits of the dead that possess mediums as well as their shared belief in spiritual fluids (*fluidos*). Fluids account for one's spiritual well-being. While the concept of spiritual fluids seems to have been borrowed from Kardecismo, I am inclined to think that the idea of spirits of the dead did not come entirely from this European-derived religion. The notion of spirits of the dead that can possess was present in the more southern African areas such as Congo and Angola, and it is not improbable that this earlier African belief was later reinforced by Kardecismo in Brazil. The Umbanda centers that are more African in their cultural orientation tend to utilize colored clothing, loud drumming, and occasional animal sacrifices in their rituals. The Umbanda centers that are closer to Kardecismo are more sedate and do not drum or use animal sacrifices. Nor do they make use of the "table" or of the usual type of Kardecist spirits.

Of the three modern religious movements, Umbanda is probably of the greatest concern to the Catholic Church. There are several reasons for this. For one thing, Umbanda is an outgrowth of the earlier lower class "fetish" religions. The old Afro-Brazilian and Amerindian religious elements did not die out as lower class peasants moved into the educated middle class. Furthermore, European immigrants to Brazil have strongly embraced Umbanda. In São Paulo, approximately 50 percent of Umbanda members are Euro-Brazilian. Finally, Brazilians have generally been extremely tolerant of religions other than their official Catholic faith. As a result, when Umbandists make their annual coastal pilgrimage to pay their respects to Iemanjá, the West African Yoruba goddess of the oceans, they get extensive and usually favorable press coverage. During every month I was in Brazil, there were articles about Umbanda in one or another of the major newspapers or magazines. Umbanda music is played on the radio, and cult leaders are interviewed on television. Since returning home, I have learned from a Brazilian student that an Umbanda spirit session was nationally televised.

Candomblé, Batuque, and several other cults continue to exist in certain regions of Brazil. Umbandists tend to regard these cults as more "folkloric" in nature. They recognize their own roots in these religions, and many Umbandists feel that these earlier religious forms, especially Candomblé, were more supernaturally powerful than Umbanda. They believe this to be especially true of the magical aspects of their religion. Other Umbandists, more in tune with Kardecismo, regard the animal sacrifices of the earlier religious forms as more "primitive." What are regarded today as folkloric aspects are sometimes played up commercially. A few cult leaders utilize their mediums to give special public productions that tourists and curious Brazilians pay to see. In some instances theatrical productions of "Macumba" are staged in night clubs and theaters in São Paulo and, I would assume, in Rio de Janeiro. I found some Umbandists who disagreed with, and others who approved of, these theatrical activities. Only a very tiny minority of Umbandists participate in these money-making productions. Special rituals are held for them to ensure that they will not experience possession trance during the performance. Interestingly, the preventive rituals are not always effective.

By far the large majority of Umbandists take their religion quite seriously. They are impressed with the spiritual works which help individuals who are sick and with personal problems. Umbandists look with pride on their faith as a truly Brazilian religion—one with a cultural heritage from the three continents of South America, Africa, and Europe.

NOTE

1.   "Macumba: Brazil's Devil Worshippers," *Our Sunday Visitor,* March 12, 1972, pp. 8–9. Huntington, Ind.: Our Sunday Visitor, Inc.

3

Umbanda in São Paulo

The metropolis of São Paulo is the industrial and financial heart of Brazil. Brazilians say that the quality of life there differs from that found in the rest of the country. The tempo of life is faster. One senses the difference as five million bodies spill into the streets of the city each morning. Perhaps the difference is partly due to the city's location. Other major Brazilian cities— Recife, Salvador, Rio de Janeiro—are situated along the coast, where their inhabitants can easily visit, and enjoy the leisure of, the beaches. São Paulo is located on an inland plateau. For relaxation *paulistas* must journey several hours down a steep escarpment over the winding rail and auto roads that finally lead to the small port city of Santos. The rainy season in June, July, and August seems cold and damp without central heating. A thick industrial smog sets in at this time of year. To combat the heaviness of this sunless atmosphere one feels almost forced to exert the energy of one's body in work until the bright sunny skies of January, February, and March once again appear.

Concrete and steel buildings, and bridges and roads sprawl out over the landscape. Skyscrapers reach upward on either side of narrow and winding dark streets through which throngs of humanity pour, rushing to destinations unknown to the passerby. Hundreds of lumbering buses and thousands of impatient taxis and private cars struggle through the congested streets. The absence of an underground transit system compounds the traffic problem. During the long rush hours it may take as much as an hour to travel the short distance of a mile, and even the proverbial patience and good nature of Brazilians wear thin at times.

A ring of several dozens of largely middle-class *bairros* (districts, quarters) surround the central downtown area. One or two major throughfares in each *bairro* link it to the central city. They are always filled with noisy buses and automobiles. The hundreds of residential streets are empty by comparison. The main arteries are lined with small shops of all kinds, restaurants, and bars where one can purchase a tiny cup of thick Brazilian coffee half-filled with sugar or a small glass of *pinga* (Brazilian sugar-cane alcohol). Each middle-class *bairro* has its own business district in which its inhabitants may

127

purchase much of the merchandise found in the center city: medicines, clothing, furniture, electrical appliances, and the like. There is usually an open market area where food and flowers are sold. The diet is varied, but fresh beef, rice, beans, Italian pasta, and fresh fruits are the most important items. A few air-conditioned supermarkets sell food at slightly higher prices than those prevailing in the markets. Each *bairro* usually has at least one Catholic church, schools, small parks, and several movie theaters, though they are not quite as grand as those in the center city. Brazilians are avid moviegoers who seem to prefer films from Italy and the United States to those produced in their own country.

The middle-class *bairro* is usually filled with a variety of housing. Most prevalent are two-story single-family houses enclosed by an outside wall for privacy. The façades are usually tile and stucco painted in muted pastel colors. One also finds many older three- and four-story apartment buildings. Some private houses are now being replaced by ten- to fifteen-story apartment buildings in gleaming white. There are servants' quarters in nearly all middle-class homes since domestic help is still relatively cheap. Private houses and apartments have terraces and balconies on which sit potted plants, flowers, and palms. They provide a small measure of serenity in this busy city. Some of the older and larger private homes have been turned into *pensões,* which furnish room and board to students and people without families. A few of the large houses have shamefully been transformed into slum dwellings in which a family of five lives in one room, sharing lavatory facilities with as many as ten other families.

One occasionally finds pockets of *favelas* (slums) interspersed among the middle-class *bairros.* On the whole, however, the shacks of the impoverished migrants are situated on the perimeter of São Paulo. The reader who is interested in learning about the life of the *favelado* should turn to *Child of the Dark,*[1] the personal diary of Carolina Maria de Jesus, who lived in one of the tin and rough-lumber shacks.

The city's population is a conglomerate of first- and second-generation Germans, Japanese, Italians, Poles, Portuguese, Spanish, and Syrians who intermingle with the native *paulistas* and with the thousands of other Brazilians who leave their rural homelands each year to seek new and better lives in the city. The Latin immigrants soon blend into the Brazilian culture since they have the least difficulty in learning to speak Portuguese. The particular accents and slightly different patterns of behavior of the *estrangeiros* (foreigners) sometimes become the focus of good-natured joking.

People who come to live in the city from other regions of Brazil are also recognized by their slightly different usage of a few words, their speech patterns, and their stereotyped personalities as described by Wagley (1971: 23):

The *paulista* from the state of São Paulo is an energetic, efficient businessman. The *gaúcho* from Rio Grande do Sul is a crude cowboy. The *carioca*, the inhabitant of Rio de Janeiro, is sly, urbane, talkative, and funloving. The *cearense* from the northeastern state of Ceará is a keen commercial man and a wandering exile driven by drought from his beloved homeland like the proverbial Jew. The *mineiro* from Minas Gerais is political and highly traditional, with a dry sense of humor, and the *bahiano* from Bahia is eloquent and superficially brilliant. "Bahiano burro nasce morto" (The stupid Bahian is a still birth), as the saying goes.

Differences among ethnic and regional peoples are noticeable and are frequently focal points of conversation.

Another type of difference found in São Paulo is that of social class. Observers of the modern Brazilian scene agree that the class structure today is in a rapid flux and that social and economic mobility is definitely present. Formerly, the Brazilian class structure was essentially a two-part system consisting of a power-holding elite class of European origin and a lower class of peasants and urban poor whose lives were directed by the elite. A very tiny middle class filled bureaucratic posts, but it identified with the upper elite. Together, the elite and the middle class shared the written tradition inherited from Europe, or what Redfield has called the Great Tradition. An upper class person from the northeast had essentially the same cultural expectations and behavior as his counterpart several thousand miles away in the southern part of the country. On the other hand, the culture of the peasants varied greatly throughout the different regions of Brazil. Until recently Brazil had a highly stable class structure in which upward mobility such as we find in Umbanda did not exist. Wagley (1971: 93–94) perceives four new classes emerging in Brazil today: (1) a new factory-in-the-field proletariat; (2) a rapidly expanding metropolitan lower class; (3) a new middle class; and (4) a metropolitan upper class. What follows is, in part, a summary of Wagley's (1971: 103–121) observations on the emerging class structure.

In the rural areas a field proletariat has emerged as small family plantations and farms have been reorganized into the national marketing system. As farming becomes big business and agriculture is mechanized, increasing numbers of illiterate persons from the traditional peasant class migrate to urban areas to seek employment. They form the rapidly expanding metropolitan lower class, which also includes industrial workers. The migrants usually live in shacks located in the outlying *favelas* mentioned earlier. Running water, sewage systems, and electricity are not always available in these areas. The first generation is usually rural in outlook and culture, but the second generation rapidly acquires new tastes for material possessions. Education in these areas is not good or nonexistent. Although upward class mobility is possible, it is extremely difficult to achieve with an inadequate education and increasing competition as more migrants arrive on the scene. Once the migrants are able to enter the industrial working force, they are usually better off. Houses are better constructed and have more modern conveniences. It is not too unusual to find a television set in the homes of factory workers. As a result, they become more tuned into national issues. These people are in the upper part of the lower class, aspiring for upward mobility into the middle class. Many are hoping to achieve it through education and hard work. A large number of Umbandists in São Paulo come from the upper-lower class.

Until recently the middle class was not significant in either size or power. As industry and commerce have rapidly expanded, many new jobs have become available in offices and stores. The new middle class differs from its traditional predecessor in having increased expectations of material possessions, which include a privately owned apartment or house, a car, and all the gadgets and conveniences one finds in a modern home. Whenever possible, middle-class people send their children to private schools, which, they believe, provide a better education than do the overcrowded public schools. Spiralling inflation is the worst enemy of the new middle class. These people attend Umbanda sessions for help in getting better jobs and improving their small business operations, as well as for reducing the anxiety and tension associated with their economic difficulties.

The traditional upper class in Brazil was a land-owning aristocracy. A new metropolitan upper class is taking the place of the old elite. People in this class are the owners of modern industries and large commercial enterprises. Marriage, in many cases, welds together the traditional elite and the *arrivistas* from the middle class. The new upper class remains open, at least for the present, to those who can manipulate their way up through a combination of education, money, professional competence, and political influence. By and large, this class, when associated with spiritualism, will attend sessions of Kardecismo.

Social change is accompanied by new life styles, modern role expectations, and changing values. In this milieu of cultural transformation, in which the extended family is dissolving and close personal relations between employer and employee have ceased to exist, many people turn to Umbanda for help in coping with new problems in their daily lives. It is not so surprising, then, that individuals should reach for assistance to a religion that offers a more personalized touch with its ministerings than does the tradition-oriented Catholic Church.

Umbanda is strongest in the larger cities, and it diffuses to smaller Brazilian towns as they become linked to the developing national socioeconomic structure. It is difficult to know with any certainty just how many Umbandists there are in São Paulo or in the whole of Brazil. Unfortunately, the national census does not make a distinction between the spiritualists of Kardecismo and of Umbanda. This does not make much difference, since many spiritualists still list themselves as Catholics in the census. Umbandists tend to exaggerate their membership figures into "millions and millions of faithful." Camargo (1961: 53–54) found that in the city of São Paulo the Federação Espírita de Umbanda claimed 260 affiliated centers, followed by the União Espírita de Umbanda and the Igreja Cristã de Umbanda, which controlled 100 centers each. Other minor federations had 30 to 50 cult groups in them. According to Levy (1968: 35),

> The number of *centros* in the city has been calculated by the two inspectors[2] as being about 4000. I am confident that this is not an exaggeration.

The long lists of centers and meeting times found in Umbanda newspapers indicate that the figure of 4000 centers may be fairly accurate. Some other indices of the popularity of Umbanda are the elections in recent years of several Umbandist state deputies in Guanabara (Rio de Janeiro) and Rio Grande do Sul. Atilla Nunes campaigned by daily playing over the radio two hours of Umbanda music and chants interspersed with "news of what goes on in the world of Umbanda both here and in the 'Aruanda' (the spiritual dwelling of Indian and Neĝro spirit guides)" (McGregor, 1967: 179).

The second Umbanda Congress in 1961 was held in Rio de Janeiro's Maracanazinho stadium (McGregor, 1967: 178). This suggests national strength. What was conspicuously absent at the time of this study was national structure. The authors of Umbanda books and writers in Umbanda newspapers, some of which are published by the Umbanda federations, agree that the movement should be unified. However, when one takes into account Brazilian individuality, nobody can agree just how it should be done. Even in the city of São Paulo there were at least fourteen very loosely federated bodies with which the centers may become affiliated. About the only thing that each of the larger federations appears to manage is an annual meeting. The centers of a particular federation attend en masse in ritual garments to listen to the leaders of the federation extoll the virtues and growth of Umbanda. Then most of the several thousand mediums gathered there go simultaneously into trance and are possessed by their spirits. In addition to experiencing this annual display of esprit de corps, the individual cult centers seem to find federation membership useful for one other reason. The certificate of membership in a federation apparently helps to keep the police from looking into "illegal practicing of medicine."

The relative lack of structure in Umbanda is noted by Camargo (1961: 53), who points out that attempts to unify the movement are *"fracos, senão negativos"* (weak, or else negative). He observes that there is much animosity among cult leaders, who attack each other's doctrines and rituals, going so far as to claim that the religious practices of their competitors completely lack authenticity (Camargo, 1961: 53). I found this to be true time and again during the year of field work. It seems that this lack of unity at the lower level of Umbanda structure (i.e., the cult house and leader) is reflected in the overall absence of unity at the level of the federations.

The real functioning units of structure in Umbanda are the individual centers. The observer can find centers in all parts of the city, rich and poor. Usually, they are located the middle-class and working-class districts. Some are above stores and in abandoned garages. Most either rent or own their own building near the main business districts as well as in ordinary residential neighborhoods. The head of a Umbanda center is called a *mãe de santo* or *pai de santo* (mother-in-sainthood or father-in-sainthood). The cult leader usually has charismatic qualities, which are used to attract and direct the mediums who practice at the center. The mediums are referred to as *filhos* (sons and daughters). *Cambonos* are persons (male or female) who are either in the early stages of developing their mediumship or they are people who prefer not to be mediums. Their major function is to assist the mediums who are possessed by spirits. Another type of participant in Umbanda centers is the drummer. There are usually two or three drummers, and they are nearly always men.

The cult leader makes the final decision on which mediums, assistants, and drummers will be allowed to participate in the center's ritual activities. Theoretically, the cult leader also makes the final decisions in all matters pertaining to ritual, behavior of the *filhos* while in the center, and finances. Some of these matters may be delegated to the center's board of directors or to a *mãe pequeno* or *pai pequeno* (little mother or little father), who is the cult leader's closest assistant. The board of directors may include between two and five persons, nearly always men. They tend to be selected by the cult leader on the basis of what they can contribute to the center. They are frequently individuals who can help provide financial aid by paying the rent for a center. They may have a car that can be placed at the disposal of the cult leader on special occasions. The directors may help to keep records on membership dues and contributions. Being solidly middle class, they lend a certain amount of prestige to the center, and in return they derive a feeling of prestige from acting out their role. They usually believe that they receive good advice and magical assistance in their personal business affairs from the cult leader's spirits. In some instances I observed, it appeared that the directors enjoyed the opportunity to meet in a somewhat structured situation the single women who were mediums.

Although Umbanda centers include persons from every socioeconomic group, individuals from the upper-lower and middle classes make up the bulk of the membership in São Paulo. In the twelve Umbanda centers I visited in São Paulo, women accounted for 60 to 75 percent of the spirit mediums. As I have just pointed out, men do participate in other ways. They act as drummers for Umbanda music and perform important functions as members of the boards of directors of Umbanda centers. The majority of Umbandists are in their twenties or thirties. A lesser number are 40 years or older. About 50 percent of the Umbandists in São Paulo are of European descent. Most of the others are racially mixed, and a few are Japanese-Brazilians.

It is difficult to estimate the prestige of Umbanda within the context of the larger Brazilian society. The size of the membership is one indicator. The election of Umbandists to state legislatures is another. Popular magazines read by the middle and upper classes very frequently include articles on, and photographs of, Umbanda activities. These reports are sometimes straightforward and sometimes somewhat sensational in nature. I would say that, on the whole, Brazilians are very accepting of spiritualist religions. Some people, however, tend to think of Umbanda as being "lower class" and therefore less prestigious than Kardecismo, which emphasizes intellectual understanding of doctrine and intellectual discussions among their spirits and members of the audience. Umbandists on the whole are not as intellectually oriented and say that their religion is "one of the heart, and not of the mind."

NOTES

1. Carolina Maria de Jesus, *Child of the Dark,* translated by David St. Clair (New York: E. P. Dutton & Co., Inc., 1962).

2. Levy is referring to men of the *delegacia de costumes,* or special police, who deal with "moral" affairs. In the case of Umbanda centers, they look into complaints stemming from loud drumming into the night.

4

Umbanda Centers: Belief and Ritual

Umbanda *centros* are extremely varied in terms of their external forms, rituals, and beliefs. Yet, in visiting various Umbanda centers, I found certain features to be relatively constant. Everywhere the major ritual activity involves dissociation, or trance, which Umbandists interpret as possession by spirits of the dead. The spiritual entities diagnose and treat illnesses, and help solve a myriad of personal problems for the believers, who may come to the two weekly public sessions in search of spiritual assistance.

In this chapter, I first describe the two principal sets of religious beliefs found in Umbanda. One set of beliefs has to do with five major types of spirit. The second involves a theory of spiritual "fluids," which Umbandists have apparently borrowed from Kardecismo. After outlining Umbanda beliefs, I describe the physical setting of the centers and the typical ritual activities conducted in them.

The data presented in this chapter come from four sources: (1) my own observations in twelve Umbanda centers in São Paulo; (2) the views of informants, some of whom were mediums in centers other than those I had visited; (3) books written by Umbandists; and (4) the observations of social scientists, such as Camargo (1961) and Levy (1968). Both Camargo and Levy have commented on the tremendous variation in Umbanda belief and ritual, and I agree with their observation. Therefore, in reading this chapter, one should be aware that each medium has his or her own highly individual interpretation of what is "right" and that a visit to any given Umbanda center is bound to yield some beliefs and rituals that will differ somewhat from the description given here.

THE MAJOR SPIRIT TYPES

There are five major types of spirit in Umbanda. As we shall see, four of the types are fairly common and appear with regularity at Umbanda centers.

134

These spirits can be either male or female. Both male and female mediums may be possessed by spirits of either sex, and each medium is possessed by all four spirits. I shall outline the general characteristics of each spirit type, but it should be noted that each individual spirit has its own particular personality. The more general role of each of these four spirit types is learned by every Umbanda medium. The more specific personality traits of each spirit seem to stem from the medium and his interaction with others.

Caboclos. The *caboclo* spirits possess the mediums once each week. The particular night they arrive is regular for each center; however, one center will feature *caboclos* on Monday, whereas another may have these spirits come on Thursday nights. They are said to be the spirits of dead Brazilian Indians.

While possessed by a *caboclo*, a medium will display protruded lips, furrowed brows, and eyes that slowly open and close, staring into space. A few may beat their chests, and jump into the air, landing in a position ready to shoot an imaginary arrow. *Caboclos* like to puff on a cigar. They also prefer to drink beer, although this is not always permitted in public sessions. These spirits project a personality that is somewhat stern and aloof. If an individual should argue with an Indian spirit, the *caboclo* would quickly reprimand him. *Caboclo* spirits are appreciated for their advice in situations requiring quick and decisive action, such as obtaining or maintaining a job.

Prêtos Velhos. The *prêtos vehlos* possess mediums at the second weekly session. Regarded as spirits of dead Afro-Brazilian slaves, they are stooped and bent over from many years of hard labor and tremble from old age. The *prêtos velhos* speak with slow and quivering voices as they smoke their pipes. These spirits like to sip red wine.

The *prêtos velhos* are very gentle and easy to approach. Seated on their low stools and conversing with someone who has come for help, they are almost grandfatherly in manner. The *prêtos velhos* seem to have apparently infinite patience. They are adept at handling long and drawn-out intricate personal problems, such as familial difficulties or love affairs. Furthermore, their extensive knowledge of herbal remedies is useful in treating illnesses. Umbanda stores that carry special herbs and other ritual paraphernalia are found throughout São Paulo. However, it is just as probable that a *prêto velho* will send a client to a pharmacy to purchase a modern drug for his illness.

Crianças. The *criança* is the third type of spirit. These are spirits of children who died between three and five year of age. Spirits of this type usually appear only once each month. The playful and innocent child spirit is more accessible than the other spirits. It skips, rolls, and tumbles throughout the entire Umbanda center, approaching members of the audience to ask for sweets and soft drinks. Even a 50-year-old medium possessed by *criança* is high-spirited. Everyone present loves this extroverted creature.

Unlike the *caboclo* and the *prêto velho,* the *criança* spirit is not so stringently defined by race and culture. If one asks for the child's ethnic origins, the *criança* spirit will usually describe them. Ordinarily, however, the child is thought to be Brazilian, that is, without a specific ethnic identity. One can apparently ask the child spirit to help with any illness or personal problem. It does not seem to specialize as the other spirits do.

Exus and Pombagiras.   The fourth type of spirit is the *exu* and his feminine counterpart, the *pombagira.* These are spirits of people who led especially wicked lives. *Exus* are frequently foreigners, and I personally encountered *exus* with such diverse backgrounds as French, Mexican, and Japanese. In addition to these, my informants indicated that they knew of *exus* who were German, Italian, and Portuguese. I also found some *exus* who were Brazilian, but with special regional backgrounds.

The *exu* spirits are antisocial characters who seem to enjoy exhibiting their base nature through cursing, off-color stories and songs, and bad manners in general. The more wicked *exus* may specialize in performing antisocial acts, such as breaking up marriages and crushing business competitors. Other "good" *exus,* said to be more spiritually evolved, may be used to counteract the evil magic of the "bad" *exus. Exu* spirits are usually present in Umbanda centers one night each month.

Three of these four spirit types—the *caboclo, prêto velho,* and *criança*—had led rather good lives and at death passed on into the *aruanda* (heaven). Therefore, they are thought to be with a spiritual, or heavenly, "light." The *exus,* in contrast, had led especially wicked lives. Since they failed to make it to heaven, they are usually said to be without "light." The spirits of persons who commit suicide automatically become *exus.* The *exus* spend much of their time in cemeteries, which are regarded as particularly dangerous places for mediums with undeveloped spiritual abilities.

Because of the somewhat negative connotations associated with *exus,* some Umbandists claim that they do not work with this type of spirit. Furthermore, some Umbanda centers do not hold public *exu* sessions. A closer inspection of the situation, however, revealed that these centers do conduct smaller, private *exu* spirit meetings, and all Umbandists I met eventually admitted that they did indeed have an *exu* spirit.

Most Umbandists like to make a distinction between the more spiritually evolved *exus* they practice with and the more base *exus* found in Quimbanda. To move into a higher spiritual plane and be regarded as a "good" Umbanda *exu,* the spirit has had to perform a number of good works to counteract the *magia negra* (black magic) of the Quimbanda *exus*. Since what is regarded as white magic by one person may be thought of as being black magic by another individual, the matter of good versus bad *exus* is resolved more in terms of personal inclination. It is for this reason that there is a continuum of sorts between Quimbanda and Umbanda.

Exus differ from the other spirit types in another important way. They usually demand some sort of payment, either in money or· material goods, before performing a service for a client. A bottle of rum will nearly always please an *exu*. The *pombagira*, or female *exu*, loves expensive perfume. In contrast, the other spirit types do not insist on prepayment for services performed. The emphasis in these cases is on *caridade* (charity). However, if a client is satisfied with the assistance he has received from a *caboclo* or *prêto velho,* it is quite proper to offer a small gift, such as flowers, candles, tobacco, or any other ritual paraphernalia used by Umbandists.

Orixás. The preceding four spirit types represent the more ordinary spirits that possess Umbanda mediums. They are the spirits that usually diagnose and help cure illnesses and other personal difficulties that clients may bring to a center. The fifth spirit type, the *orixá,* is thought to come from a more elevated realm. In the West African Yoruba religion, the *orixás* were spirits of deities that possessed humans. During the period of Brazilian slavery the *orixás* were syncretized with Catholic saints; for example, Oxum, goddess of calm fresh waters, became identified and equated in some regions of Brazil with the Virgin Mary. Even today the saint's name and that of the *orixá* are regarded as two terms for the same entity. As Umbanda evolved from such earlier syncretic cults as Candomblé, the *orixás* became more remote from man on earth.

Umbandists believe these deities to be so powerful that a medium would explode if possession were to occur. It is for this reason that the *orixás* send spiritual envoys to possess Umbandists. These envoys are very highly evolved spirits of the dead—almost next to the saints or deities themselves. The *orixás* or, more accurately, their envoys do not directly communicate with clients. Instead, they may offer a blessing through very limited gestures. These spirits very rarely appear in Umbanda centers. When they do possess a medium, they are regarded with awe.

Orixás are important as guardian spirits. Each Umbandist is a *filho(a)* (son, daughter) of a specific deity. After paying a fee to a cult leader for the necessary divination, an individual can learn which *orixá* protects him. However, this does not always occur, and friends of the medium speculate about the matter. This is entirely possible because it is believed that an *orixá* exercises a certain amount of influence over the personality of his *filho(a)*. For example, if a medium (male or female) behaves in a suave, very feminine manner, his friends may guess that he is protected by the goddess Oxum.

The *orixás* are important in the larger Umbanda belief system in that they head the seven major *linhas* (lines) of the spiritual hierarchy. Umbandists loosely organize all of their spirits under these seven *linhas*, each of which is subdivided into seven *falanges* (phalanxes). In turn, each *falange* is further subdivided into seven *legiões* (legions) of spirits.

There is much disagreement over which spirits belong in the specific parts of the hierarchy. Even the seven major *orixás* at the head of the hierarchy may vary from one Umbanda center to another. Umbandists, attempting to codify their religious beliefs in books, disagree among themselves as to which *linhas* should be included. Furthermore, an *orixá* is not always syncretized with the same saint by different Umbanda authors; for example, Iemanjá is sometimes thought to be Saint Barbara and sometimes the Virgin Mary. An arrangement of the *linhas* found to be common in São Paulo by Camargo (1961: 38) follows:

1. Linha do Oxalá—Jesus Cristo.
2. Linha de Iemanjá—Virgem Maria.
3. Linha do Oriente—São João Batista.
4. Linha de Oxóce—São Sebastião.
5. Linha de Xangô—São Jerônimo.
6. Linha de Ogum—São Jorge.
7. Linha Africana—São Cipriano.

In this particular arrangement, two of the major divisions—Linha do Oriente and Linha Africana—are not commanded by *orixás*. Some Umbandists would argue against including the Linha do Oriente. The Linha Africana, however, is very popular, and most of the *prêto velho* spirits are included in this subdivision. Although the *caboclo* spirits are found in various parts of the spiritual organization, they are most frequently thought of as belonging to the hunter, Oxóce. As a *santo*, Oxóce is Saint Sebastian, who is pictured with arrows piercing his body! Some Umbandists believe that the saints Cosmas and Damian head one of the seven major divisions; the *criança* spirits are linked to this *linha*.

THEORY OF SUPERNATURAL FLUIDS

As already mentioned, spirits less evolved than the *orixás* (i.e., the *caboclos, prêtos velhos, crianças* and *exus*) are the ones individuals commonly consult when personal difficulties arise. The consultation is based on a theory of special supernatural fluids. Apparently this theory is borrowed from Kardecismo and provides the major cultural link between these two spirit-possession religions in Brazil. Although Umbandists place a great deal of emphasis on a theory of supernatural fluids, they have not developed a well-codified cosmology that goes beyond describing the relationship between supernatural fluids and the behavior and well-being of an individual. The rank and file of Kardecismo, who tend to be more intellectually oriented than Umbandists, seem to have a better sense of how the theory of fluids fits into their cosmology.

Supernatural fluids, according to both religions, are spiritual emanations that surround one's body and affect one's well-being. They are believed to emanate from three sources: (1) one's own innate spirit; (2) the spirits of the dead which are freely floating about; and (3) spirits of living persons who are close by. Bad fluids are often associated with the *exus*. An individual surrounded by bad fluids is sickly and trouble-ridden. A healthy individual free from anxiety is said to have good fluids. Illnesses are classified etiologically by Umbandists. Camargo (1961: 100–102) has drawn up a list of five commonly recognized causes of illnesses, to which I have added the sixth, the "evil eye."

1. *Sickness as a consequence of religious negligence or ignorance.* When a medium fails to perform certain *obrigações* (obligations) he owes to his *orixá* or other, lesser, spirits, sickness or other personal problems may occur. The specific duty usually includes leaving some food or drink in a particular place for the spirit.

2. *Magical etiology of illness.* A *coisa feita* (thing done) refers to an *exu* work of black magic performed in Quimbanda. It frequently involves blocking the paths of the client's competitors in business or love. Bringing illness is one means of accomplishing this aim.

3. *Perturbations provoked by spirits.* An unhappy disincarnate spirit may agitate the "fluids" in an individual, bringing illness or various kinds of personal problems. In some cases, a spirit may come to disturb an individual to get revenge for actions committed in a previous incarnation. In other instances, the spirit is merely perverse and/or ignorant, thus disturbing the life of an innocent victim. The latter type of spirit needs to be enlightened in an Umbanda center as to its proper behavior.

4. *Karmic illnesses.* In a previous incarnation a spirit may have led a somewhat wicked life. Death and subsequent reincarnation in another individual may bring trials in the forms of illnesses and other disorders to this person. It is believed that these difficulties may serve to redeem sins committed in the former life. The concept of Karmic illnesses is found in Kardecismo, whence it was probably borrowed by Umbandists.

5. *Illnesses resulting from undeveloped mediumship.* This category

represents a general catchall and tends to overlap any of the other causes in this list. When no other easily discernible cause can be determined, undeveloped mediumship may be cited. Through developing his mediumship, an individual learns how to interpret spiritual realities as well as to defend himself against these realities.

6. *Illnesses caused by the "evil eye."* As in other parts of the world where this folk concept exists, children are especially defenseless against the evil eye. Umbandists also believe that adults with strong innate mediumistic tendencies are very receptive to the influences of the evil eye. Therefore, such persons should develop their mediumship as a precautionary measure to resist bad fluids passed along through the evil-eye mechanism.

Although the preceding list tends to be focused on illnesses, I found that Umbanists lump together personal difficulties and illnesses under the term "spiritual disorders." I believe that they are successful in treating clients because their system of causes takes into account the link between psychological problems and physical illness. Umbandists, however, view the common underlying cause as spiritual, and not as psychological or biological. They also recognize purely mental and physical illnesses, but normally do not attempt to cure them. The following summary will clarify for the reader the Umbanda concepts of illness:

	Mental Illness	Physical Illness	Spiritual Disorders
Causes:	Psychological	Biological	Spiritual
Examples:	Depression	Headaches	Depression and/or headaches
Cured by:	Psychologists, psychiatrists	Medical doctors	Umbanda spirits

The preceding summary shows that spiritual problems and illnesses may mimic the more common psychological and biological difficulties. Thus a person suffering from headaches, on failing to obtain relief from a medical doctor, may turn to an Umbanda spirit for supernatural assistance. Umbandists also enjoy citing examples of individuals who were dismissed as incurable by psychologists and later were cured by spiritual means. The classification of a patient's disorder as spiritual, instead of mental or physical, seems to depend on finding a spiritual cause and ascertaining that the patient can once again be an adequately functioning member of his society.

In assigning one of the six causes Umbandists generally regard headaches or other physical symptoms as secondary. The reason for this is that the same symptom may appear in all six categories. Instead, what is usually taken into account is the behavior of the patient or of persons with whom he has social relations. This is especially true when assigning causes 1, 2, 3, and 6. If such behavioral signs are absent or unknown to the diagnostician, category 5 (i.e., undeveloped mediumship) is designated as the cause of the client's spiritual disorders. Even after the patient's mediumistic abilities have been successfully developed, personal difficulties and illnesses may remain. In such instances, category 4 (i.e., Karmic causes) may be used to explain these more chronic states of poor health and problems.

THE PHYSICAL SETTING OF UMBANDA CENTERS

Most consultations with spirits occur within the context of public Umbanda sessions. Umbanda centers are usually located in the middle-class and working-class districts in São Paulo. As noted in Chapter 3, some are housed above stores or in abandoned garages; however, most either rent or own their own building near the business district or in an ordinary residential neighborhood.

Over the entrance of each center hangs a sign, such as "Tenda Espiritual São Jorge"; "Terreiro Espiritual Umbanda Pai Joaquim de Aruanda"; "Templo Espiritual Umbanda Inhacã e Iemanjá"; "Tenda Espiritual Umbanda Pai José de Angola." These names refer to the saint, or *orixá*, or to the spirits of dead slaves and Indians who are the major protectors and guides of the center's cult leader. The words "*tenda*" and "*terreiro*" refer to open structures used in the warmer climates of Bahia, which is considered to be the spiritual home of African culture in Brazil. The cooler physical and social climate of São Paulo precludes the use of open structures.

Outside the main entrance of many centers is a small, inconspicuously placed "altar" dedicated to the *exu* spirits. Before entering the center, an individual may pause briefly to pay homage at the *exu* altar. With fingers interlaced and palms extended downward, the individual softly repeats the word "*exu*" several times. The altar is inside a small box in which offerings of food and drink are placed to satisfy the demands of these spirits. Hopefully this will permit spiritual sessions in the center to proceed without the interference of the potentially maleficent *exus*.

On entering the center, one usually finds it illuminated by glaring electric lights. There is often a table at the door where several men sit. These are the "directors" of the center, who have been selected by the cult leader and who look after the more mundane aspects of running the center. Sometimes, the Candomblé term "*ogan*" is used to refer to a director. Their functions vary, but they primarily look after the financial affairs. At the table they collect the monthly dues of the associates if they care to pay. They may also see to it that each person who enters signs his name in a guest book. Somewhere near the entrance there may be a bulletin board on which various items have been posted: a notice of a fund-raising picnic, a reminder that women are not permitted to wear slacks in the center, and perhaps a few photographs of members possessed by their spirits, taken at a religious *festa* (celebration, i.e., special ritual event held in honor of an *orixá*).

Umbanda centers are divided into two major parts by a railing. Those who have come to ask for spiritual assistance sit in the rear half on wooden benches arranged in two rows. The two sexes, about equal in number, sit on opposite sides of the room. Depending on the size of the center, there may be as few as 30, and as many as 300, persons who have come for the session. There is frequently a sign on the wall reminding that "silence is a prayer," but it is ignored as friends from opposite sides of the city gossip about their daily affairs. A few people may hold bouquets of roses, carnations, or gladioli which they will present to a favorite spirit. They may also bring cigars for *caboclo* spirits and pipe tobacco for the *prêto velho* spirits.

The front half of the center is devoted to the ritual activities of the spirits. The major piece of furniture in this part of the center is the *congá* (altar), which is covered by a white drape. Statues of the *orixás, caboclos,* and *prêto velhos* are found on the altar. The *orixás,* or saints, nearly always present on the altar are the blessing Christ with open arms, the Virgin Mary, and St. George on a white charger. Usually there are statues of the saints Cosmas and Damian, who represent the *criança* spirits in Umbanda. The large altar also holds flowers, candles, and a glass of water. The water is considered to be a necessity since it is supposed to aid in drawing off evil spiritual fluids from any *exu* spirits that may appear in the center. Two or three *atebaques* (drums), which "call" the spirits to possess the mediums, are off to the side of the altar. Men normally play the drums, but in a few centers a woman may also participate as a drummer.

TYPICAL RITUAL ACTIVITIES

On the night of a public session one can observe the mediums entering the dressing rooms of a center from about 7:30 P.M. on. There they change from street clothing into their ritual garments. They have prepared for the session by avoiding heavy foods and alcohol during the day. Before coming to the center they took an ordinary bath followed by a ritual bath of seven herbs in their homes. As the rear half of the center fills up with those who have come to seek assistance, the mediums gradually begin to wander into the front part of the center. Men and women stand at opposite sides of the altar, women accounting for 60 to 75 percent of the total number of mediums.

The ritual garb of the mediums is nearly always white, but colored clothing may be seen in a few centers that are more African in cultural orientation. Women wear blouses with a simple round or square neckline and billowing skirts of midcalf length. Underneath are as many as five stiffly starched petticoats, which partially cover ankle-length pantalettes. A small triangular kerchief is tied behind the head. Yards of lace have been sewed through all the items. The men wear white trousers and shirts. Both sexes wear white tennis shoes, and everyone carries a white hand towel embroidered with the symbol of the center and edged with lace; it is used to wipe off perspiration and on occasion to help control a wild spirit that may appear. Some cult leaders require mediums in their centers to wear a ribbon diagonally across the chest or around the waist. It is usually the symbolic color of the leader's *orixá*. The most important single items of the ritual costume are the *guias*, or strands of beads, which represent the spirits of each medium. The number of strings of beads is limited only by what the medium is able to afford and the number of spirits that possess him.

At about 8:30 P.M., when a sufficient number of mediums have assembled in front of the altar, the cult leader opens the *gira* (turn-around, i.e., the session). The drummers begin to beat the *atebaques* as the mediums sway or dance counterclockwise to the rhythm. The audience joins in the singing of songs, or *pontos,* to various *orixas* and to the other, lesser, spiritual entities. An assistant brings in a silver censer suspended from a long chain. It contains smoldering perfuming herbs and is used for the *defumação* (perfuming and purification). The assistant carriers it to the altar, to the drums, to each of the mediums, and finally to the members of the audience. A wave of the hand brings the fumes closer to purify the body and to offer protection against evil fluids brought to the center. Then each medium goes to *saravá* (salute, i.e., prostrate himself) the altar as the cult leader blesses him and extends a hand to be kissed. In some centers it is customary to pay homage to, then send away through songs, any *exus* that may be lurking around.

After more drumming and singing, an assistant may take up a collection from the audience. The cult leader or an assistant may then give a brief sermon in which the mediums are reminded of the Christian virtues of love and charity, and of the superiority of the works of Umbanda—small today, but grand tomorrow. The faults in the ritual behavior of the mediums may be called to attention. Prayers are offered to Oxalá (Jesus Christ) and to other spiritual entities for the sick and troubled, and then permission is asked to open the *trabalho* (work, i.e., session of spirits who will "work" that night).

Without drum accompaniment, the mediums and the audience join together in singing

Eu abro a minha "gira,"
Com Deus e Nossa Senhora. . . .
I open my session,
With God and Our Lady. . . .

When this song is ended, the drums are once more beaten furiously, and while everyone sings, the mediums being to call their spirits. *Pontos* may be sung to call specific spirits, such as *Caboclo Sete Flechas* (Indian of Seven Arrows):

Caboclo das Sete Flechas
Quando vem, lá de Aruanda,
Trazendo arco e flechas,
Para salvar, filhas de Umbanda
Êle é caboclo, éle é flecheiro,
Êle é caboclo matador de feiticeiro.

When the Indian of Seven Arrows
Comes, there from Heaven,
Bringing a bow and arrows,
To save, children of Umbanda,
He is an Indian, he is an archer,
He is the Indian who kills the black magician.

Some mediums begin to spin around rapidly, and as their heads and chests jerk back and forth in opposing directions, the spirits *baixam* (lower) themselves into their *cavalos* (horses, i.e., mediums). The hair of some female mediums becomes disarrayed. Since it is the night of the Indian spirits, the facial expressions of what had been smiling mediums are transformed into the stern countenance of the *caboclo* spirits. Some of the Indians may move about as if they were shooting an imaginary arrow. They shout in the *lingua* (tongue) of their "nation." The spirits may dance for a few minutes, greeting each other by touching each other's right and then left forearms. When the drumming stops, they find their places and wait for members of the audience to come for the *consultas* (consultations) during which requests for help are made. The hands of the mediums rest behind their bodies, palms outward and fingers snapping impatiently.

An assistant known as a *cambono* watches over each spirit. He (or she) is frequently a medium still at the elementary levels of spiritual development. In some instances, the *cambono* may be a developed medium who for one reason or another does not choose to participate by receiving spirits. The assistant makes certain that the spirit does not cause a medium to fall while in trance and sees to the general needs of the incorporated spirit. For example, he lights the cigar of an Indian spirit, or, when a spirit causes its medium to perspire heavily, he takes the embroidered towel from the medium's waist and wipes the face and neck.

Before the members of the audience can enter the front area of the center where the spirits stand, they must remove their shoes. Some Umbandists believe that this allows for better contact with the ground, thus permitting the "fluid charges" to become more activated; however, since most Umbanda centers have hardwood or concrete floors, this practice may simply be a retention of a similar one found in Candomblé. Others say that removing one's shoes is merely a sign of respect to the spirits. A more practical explanation lies in the fact that part of the ritual sometimes involves spinning an individual and that high heels could be dangerous.

On entering the sacred front area, a person is directed to one of the spirits by an assistant. If an individual wishes to speak with a specific spirit, he must wait his turn in line. The cult leader's spirit may be quite popular, and it may be necessary for a person to pick up a numbered tag at the entrance door. This encourages people to come early so they can get a low number and not need to wait until eleven or twelve o'clock for their consultation.

The *consulta* may cover any illness or personal problem that one could imagine—*qualquer coisa* (anything) as my informants put it. There are the usual aches and pains, nervous tension, fatigue, as well as "heart" and "liver" ailment. When people wish to emphasize the spectacular, they cite cases of cancer cured by the spirits or refer to the several centers that specialize in spiritual "operations." There is always the problem of getting and/or keeping a job. However, it is not just the working people who bring their problems. Some businessmen also feel in need of some assistance from the "good" Umbanda *exus,* who can break a spell cast on them by some practitioner of black magic. Family quarrels, difficulties in love affairs, and even poor scholastic grades are brought to Umbanda centers.

Each personal problem or illness requires and receives individual attention from a spirit. In addition to giving advice for the specific difficulty, a spirit may tell one to purchase from an Umbanda store herbs for special baths at home or candles to burn while praying to an *orixá.* Before taking leave of a spirit, the person is rid of his bad fluids, which are giving him difficulty. This ritual is known as *passes.* The spirit passes his right hand over the person's body, pulling out the bad fluids. With each downward stroke the spirit flicks his wrist and with a snap of his fingers disposes of the fluids. Before sending the person away, the spirit may ritually blow smoke over him for added protection from evil fluids. After a final embrace from the spirit, the person returns to his seat.

Drumming and singing continue off and on during the consultation period. A spirit may occasionally possess a member of the audience, causing the individual to shriek and shake violently. The cult leader or an assistant will walk back to the possessed and gently quiet him. If the uninvited spirit should insist on remaining, he will be led to the front part of the *centro*. The cult leader tells the spirit that his *cavalo* needs to attend sessions regularly to develop his mediumistic capacities. After the spirit has left, the individual himself is told that he must return for further spiritual development.

As the crowd gradually begins to thin out, a few spirits not occupied with consultations begin to converse with each other. Others may dance a bit, as long as they do not disturb the session. Several *caboclos* may decide to leave early and hand their unfinished cigars to an assistant.

To avoid leaving his medium *carregado* (loaded, charged) with evil fluids accumulated during the "passes," the spirit shakes the clothing of his medium and makes passes with his hand over the body. Particular attention is paid to the head. As the spirit begins jerking the head and chest of its medium with opposing motions back and forth, a *cambono* steps near to assist the medium if necessary.

Some mediums fall backward into the arms of the assistant as the spirit leaves. They squint their eyes as if not accustomed to the bright light, wipe away perspiration, and may accept a glass of water. Disoriented, they may put a hand over their eyes.

As the lines shorten in front of some of the more respected and developed spirits, the assistants and those mediums whose spirits have already left may go to consult with a *caboclo*. The sessions usually last three hours. As the few who remain in the rear begin to yawn, an assistant moves among the spirits, quietly letting them know that the end of the session is near. The remaining spirits leave together as a special song is sung. The spirits may be dancing at this point. While everyone joins in singing the closing song, each medium again prostrates himself in front of the altar, and the cult leader gives him a final blessing.

The mediums return to the dressing rooms. After changing into street clothing, they leave with friends or relatives who have remained until the end. Later in the week the mediums return to the center for another night of spiritual "works." However, instead of the *caboclos*, it is the *prêtos velhos* who possess them. Usually, the *criança* spirits and the *exus* appear at an Umbanda center once a month.

In addition to the regular public sessions, cult leaders hold special *festas* for various *orixás* throughout the year. The most popular are those for Oxóce (St. Sebastian) and for Ogum (St. George). People bring special foods and frequently liquor to these festive occasions. There may also be a *festa* for the *prêtos velhos* on May 13 to celebrate the liberation of Brazilian slaves. In December, the entire center may journey to the seashore in rented buses to honor the *orixá*, Iemanjá, who is the goddess of the sea. There may be special Easter sessions, and at Christmas gifts are brought for the poor. A cult leader's spirit may baptize babies and perform marriage ceremonies, although these are not recognized as legally binding. All of these activities are highly idiosyncratic. The ritual is always changing with the fluctuating whims of a cult leader and/or his spirits.

5

A Cult Leader

The special characteristics of belief and ritual of each Umbanda center are a reflection of the individuality of its cult leader. No two centers are alike, just as no two cult leaders can ever be the same. As Camargo (1961: 33) has put it,

> Umbanda is a religious aspiration in search of a form. Really, what is seen in São Paulo are various interchanges between religious organizations, without unity of doctrine or of ritual. Each *terreiro* has its system, and each cult leader thinks that he monopolizes the most complete truth.[1]

Cult leaders and their spirits draw mediums and a following of people with spiritual problems on a personal level. Whenever there is conflict between a medium and a cult leader, it is the former who withdraws from the center and seeks to practice spiritualism in another center. A cult leader is referred to as *mãe de santo* or *pai de santo* (mother-in-sainthood or father-in-sainthood). The more formal and traditional Yoruba terms of *ialorixá* (female) and *babalaô* (male) are used in Umbanda newspapers. There appear to be more women who become cult leaders than men. Out of 150 *centros* listed in the December 1966 edition of the *Tribuna Umbandista,* 93 were headed by *ialorixás* and 57 by *babalões*.

During the period of field work I frequented sessions at two centers headed by *mães de santo.* Both centers were linked to larger Umbanda federations in São Paulo. The one cult leader, Badia,[2] a dark Afro-Brazilian about 50 years old, had a rather simple but very active center in which about 40 mediums practiced. Most of her *filhos* (i.e., mediums) were between 20 and 30 years old and were not too well developed spiritually. The public sessions were frequently disorderly, causing some of the older mediums and directors of the center to comment on Badia's unwillingness to assert her authority. The relative absence of developed mediums in this center meant that Badia's own spirits had to handle a large number of people who came for help, and she frequently was busy with private sessions both afternoons and evenings throughout the entire week.

The second cult leader, Nair, was less occupied with the activities of her center. She permitted me to interview her at some length in her home. The data provide some insight into the reasons for becoming a medium. They also illustrate how spirits become involved in interpersonal relations.

Nair was born in São Paulo in 1907. Her mother had come from Italy to Brazil when she was two years old. Nair's father was the son of a Portuguese and had been an officer in the Brazilian army. There was enough money to send Nair to primary school and later to the *ginásio*. She did well in school and went on to normal school, becoming a primary school teacher. Nair believed that she had experienced spiritual problems as a child in school, but that her mother and father were unable to recognize the difficulties as such. In school she could do arithmetic problems in her head, but when called to the blackboard, she would feel her mind go blank and become nervous and tense. When told by the teacher to paint a particular form, she would follow instructions, but always with some modification of her own. She now attributes these problems and special traits to spirits that affected her behavior.

When she married, Nair gave up her position as a primary school teacher and her difficulties began. She had six children, but only two lived. There were frequent illnesses that doctors could not cure. Her husband earned very little. There was much intrafamilial bickering until her husband left her temporarily. Finally a friend suggested to her husband that he should attend a spiritual session of Kardecismo. He liked it and wanted Nair to attend with him. She did not care to change her religion from Catholicism to Kardecismo and did not go with him.

Nair's husband returned to live with her and eventually persuaded her to attend a session. When they arrived at the meeting, the president of the session told her to sit at the table with the mediums. She was reluctant, saying that she knew nothing about this religion and had come only as a visitor. The leader responded that she would sit at the table, for she had mediumship. He said that she was the cause of her family problems and explained that her capacity for mediumship was like a lightning rod. Having not developed this particular ability, she attracted only bad spiritual fluids. Nair was told that she would have to develop her mediumship in order to become a focal point for good fluids, which would help improve the situation at home.

Nair agreed to join the *corrente*[3] of mediums, but felt nothing the first, second, and third sessions she attended. After some time, the session's presiding officer instructed Nair to take a pencil in her hand. She was to rest her hand on the table, but with the arm off the surface. He asked her to pray about anything for five minutes. Nair said that the pencil began to move and that she wrote page after page, stopping only for the president to tear off the filled sheets. The message that the spirit gave at this time was that she needed to practice charity, that the troubles in her life were due to her great capacity for mediumship, and that she needed to develop her spiritual abilities. The spirit continued to give her messages, which Nair said she had typed and made into a "book." She was about 35 years old at the time.

Nair and her husband continued to attend spiritualist sessions. Eventually they were conducting sessions in their own home. Nair began to receive (*receber*, i.e., be possessed) a *caboclo* spirit whose name was Águia Branca (White Eagle). A *prêto velho* with the name of Pai Candú (Father Candú) also began to possess her. Although they were still practicing "at the table," Nair's possessing spirits would leave the table to make strange and unknown marks, or *pontos risquados*, on the floor.

It was obvious to everyone that Nair's spirits belonged to Umbanda, and not to the more refined, dignified, and intellectual table of Kardec spirits of dead doctors, lawyers, and teachers. Nair's husband regarded her spirits as uneducated and stupid. Finally, a friend suggested that Nair attend a session of Umbanda. She followed this advice, and one night while she was seated in the audience the *pai de santo* called her to the front. A *caboclo* spirit possessed her, jumped about, and did a number of other things until the cult leader told her that she needed to practice spiritualism in Umbanda. When Nair told her husband this, he became quite angry. Their arguments increased as her *caboclo* and *prêto velho* spirits continued to possess her during the Kardecismo sessions in their home. The altercations became so bad that Nair's husband decided the marriage was not workable and left his home and wife for the second time, going to live with their married daughter. Nair was about 42 years old at the time; her seven-year-old son remained with her.

Nair continued to hold sessions in her home. One day Pai Candú, a *prêto velho* who was possessing Nair, told the group gathered for a session that Nair's husband had left because her spirits had sent him away. He explained that the spirits had known that Nair had to develop her mediumship in Umbanda; that her husband would not accept her Umbanda spirits; and that the spirits had separated the couple to enable Nair to develop spiritually. Pai Candú added that Nair was to have patience because she would suffer even more, but that later she would be compensated for her present difficulties.

During this time Nair and her spirits helped many individuals with spiritual problems. She practiced Umbanda for eight years in another cult leader's center. Satisfied with the assistance they received, Nair's followers brought gifts, such as statues of Catholic saints (*orixás*) for the altar in her home. Mediums began to practice with Nair in her home. Eventually, her following was large enough and the necessary ritual paraphernalia sufficient for Nair to open an Umbanda center of her own.

Before she opened her center, Nair decided to be formally initiated (*fazer o santo*) by Joãozinho da Goméia in Rio de Janeiro. He is one of the major cult leaders in Brazilian Candomblé according to an elaborate article in *O Cruzeiro* (September 23, 1967). Nair underwent the 21-day period of seclusion as a *filha da Iemanjá*. The usual shaving of the hair of the head was performed. When she emerged from isolation, Nair was possessed by an elevated spiritual envoy of Iemanjá. In one rare moment of speech the envoy announced that her name was Iatagum and that she was an Afro-Brazilian. Nair could have become a *mãe de santo* through the less rigorous rituals of Umbanda in which a three-day seclusion period is acceptable and the head is not shaved. There is, however, a certain mystique and feeling of awe about Candomblé. People believe that it represents something more pure and knowledgeable and difficult than Umbanda. After her initiation, Nair went to Bahia to tour the famous centers of Candomblé.

Returning to São Paulo in 1956, Nair opened her center with the help of one of her major followers, Ildicir, who provided space for Nair's center rent-free and paid all taxes and utilities. Nair called it the Terreiro de Iatagum to honor the envoy of her *orixá*, Iemanjá. This *orixá* is the goddess of sea waters and is turbulent like the ocean. Nair wears the symbol of Iemanjá—a silver fish hung from a chain about her neck. Imprinted fish symbols are on the curtain separating the front and back portions of Nair's center. Each year on the anniversary of her initiation, Nair holds a special celebration in honor of Iemanjá and dresses in the ritual costume of her *orixá*.

Some time after Nair had opened her center, both her *prêto velho*, Pai Candú, and her second *caboclo*, Pena Verde (Green Feather), announced that there would be a great change in her life within four months. Nair's reaction on learning this news was, "My God, is it possible that I shall suffer still more?" Within the four months Nair's married daughter came to tell her that Nair's husband was desperately ill with asthmatic bronchitis. She asked her mother to visit him. Nair went and found him in such poor condition that he did not recognize her at first. She stayed with him for two days, during which he seemed to improve somewhat. Three days later Nair had a special *festa* at her center, and Ildicir invited Nair's husband to attend. Having come and, according to Nair, liked it, he decided to live with her after fifteen years of separation. Nair pointed out that she did not ask him to return home, saying that it was the spirits who decided that he should return. She also believed that the spirits began to help him better understand her form of spiritualism. His physical condition also began to improve.

Nair believes that spiritual and physical illnesses display identical symptoms. She believes that many people mistakenly go to doctors for what appears to be a physical illness. When medicine brings no improvement, they often seek a spiritual cause and cure. Headaches are the most common illness, but they do not make spectacular stories to tell a curious anthropologist. The cases Nair described as having been cured by Pena Verde are perhaps not representative, but they do give some indication of the spiritual illnesses mediums deals with. I shall let Nair describe three of these cases in her own words.

There was a little girl who lived here on Christiano Viana in an apartment. She was five years old and did not walk. *She did not walk!* The servant brought her here in her arms. She said that she could not bring the girl again because her employer, the girl's mother, did not believe in our religion. So I took the name of the girl and her address. We held a session "at a distance" for her here in the house. One month later the servant returned with the girl walking beside her. The mother learned about the cure later and invited me to her home to thank me.

Some days later a woman whose father was the owner of this apartment came to me. The superintendent of the apartment building knew about my curing the little girl's legs and told her about me. She brought me her infant, whose skin was dry and who had the face of a monkey. When I looked at the infant, I was badly frightened. It was truly a monkey, understand? The flesh was dried on top of its bones; only skin and bones. So I said to her, "I cannot cure this." She said, "Oh, I was told that you bless." I replied, "I never bless." And at this point my spirit said to me, "Put the infant on the bed and go do what I tell you." So I carried the child to the bed and the spirit asked for good oil and some cotton. He told me to remove all the child's clothing. I took off its clothes and began to grease it, starting with the head, then under the arms—everything. I said a prayer which I don't remember anymore because it was in that hour that the spirit gave it to me. I did this and the woman even brought me a can of oil. I told her it was necessary to come seven times. And she said, "Yes, *senhora*. Tomorrow I shall come." The child vomited, did not eat, was dying. On the seventh day, she told me that the child was already sucking and no longer ill. After four or five months, she brought the child to me, fat, much fatter. I was so pleased that I felt giddy. Then she said to me, "O *Dona* Nair, if it had not been for you, I would have lost my son." I felt giddy because I had never done such a thing before. I do things my spirits tell me, but I myself do not know how to perform them.

There was another case. The man was president of a Lions Club just outside São Paulo. The director of my *terreiro* brought him. He met him in a bar, and noticing that this man was limping he asked, "What is it that you have?" And he spoke, "I have an illness that doctors cannot cure." So he brought him to the *terreiro*. He entered, just crying to speak with Pena Verde and he could hardly walk. So Pena Verde said, "You come tomorrow to the house of my horse, and she is going to do something for you." And me, myself, saying,

"Oh, whatever am I going to do? I don't know how to cure this." The next day I got some sheep's wool, washed it, disinfected it with alcohol, and put it in a bottle. He came just as I had finished dinner with my son, Antônio. I had told the man to bring oil, and now I asked him to pull up the leg of his trousers. God forgive me, but when I saw the man's leg, I was so upset that I wanted to vomit. I had just finished dinner, understand? I really felt bad. I said to Antônio, "I'll return in a minute." And I went out and vomited. Those scabs. Bloody, With that pus. And I said, "Whatever shall I do with this leg?" And then I went to my bedroom and Antônio said to me, "Mother, concentrate on this. Who knows? The spirits may help." At this, the spirit came and went to clean the man's leg with oil. Next the sheep's skin was pasted on the scabs and then ripped off. Everything was raw flesh. I remember a little piece of the prayer, but not all of it. I know it went something like this:

Peter and Paul went to Rome.
Peter and Paul returned from Rome.
Jesus Christ questioned, "Peter and Paul,
Why did you return from Rome?"
And then they replied, "We went to Rome
With erysipelas and returned without it."

After seven days the man's leg was better, but still delicate. The skin had a rosy color. Pena Verde spoke, "Now, you need to take care. Don't bruise it. And avoid exerting yourself because the skin is very delicate yet." He was completely cured. Now, later when I went to make this same prayer on other persons, nothing happened because I wasn't with Pena Verde. Understand? There are these things, no?

These three examples, I believe, were probably among the more spectacular cases Nair had dealt with during her years of practice. They are similar to exciting cases other mediums enjoy repeating, perhaps because they illustrate the superiority of spiritualism over medicine. However, during my year of research I saw no miraculous cures. What did appear with great frequency in my notes were cases of sociopsychological adjustment. The spirits seemed quite capable of handling these problems. For example, in December 1966, Nair and her spirits began working with the problems of Virgínia, who was 35 years old. Virgínia was of Italian and Portuguese ancestry. The family evidently had done well. Her brother had studied science in the university, and Virgínia had been graduated from normal school. She had married and had had three sons, the eldest being twelve years old. The family had been in contact with Umbanda three or four times before Virgínia began attending Nair's sessions regularly. They felt other centers were dirty, the spirits drank too much liquor and were sometimes crude, and they rarely found any mediums who were as educated as they.[4] Nair's center was without most of these faults, and Virgínia found it compatible. Some of the mediums at Nair's center told me that Virgínia's husband had left her and that Nair had held a private session of *exu* to help bring him back. As far as I know, he did not return during the year of field work.

Meantime Virgínia had difficulties in disciplining her sons. The eldest, according to Nair, told lies, was very nervous, and refused to study his school lessons. To counteract the bad fluids that were troubling him, Nair held a private session for him. For five days he took an ordinary bath each day after school. Then he was sent over to Nair's home, where one of Nair's assistants gave him a ritual bath filled with special herbs to help purify him. He later joined his mother in the group of mediums at Nair's center. Whenever Virgínia was unable to discipline him, she telephoned Nair. At the next public session Nair's *caboclo*, Pena Verde, would reprimand the boy. This mother believed that her son's behavior improved. Virgínia's second son later joined his brother and mother in the group of mediums. Nair said that she did not care to take such young children into her center. However, the second son was jealous of the attention given his brother, and Nair let him in to reduce these difficulties.

Virgínia's sister Luisa was a Catholic who faithfully attended mass each week. She came to Nair's sessions only to keep her sister company and perhaps out of curiosity. She had finished her secondary schooling and had been preparing for two years to take the entrance exams of the medical school at the University of São Paulo. When she took these in January of 1967, she was quite ill with the grippe. As a result, she failed the exams and felt depressed for several months. She did not quite believe in spiritualism and said that she would not join the mediums. But Pena Verde turned her in a circle one evening until she felt weightless, as if being lifted into the air. As she left the center that night, she could not keep from crying. Within a week she received a notice from the university stating that there were openings in the veterinary medical school, where the first year of classes is identical with that for medicine. She began to feel less depressed and wondered whether her good fortune was perhaps due to Pena Verde's help. She made plans to take the medical school entrance exams the following year.

The activities at Nair's center did not occupy all of her time. At sixty, she was a very active woman who looked ten to fifteen years younger. She liked to take short courses in art and music, and had at one time even taken a course in breeding chickens. While her husband was away for fifteen years she had operated a dressmaking establishment on the fashionable Rua Augusta. Even after closing the shop she continued to knit dresses on special machines in her home. She had had a small shop where she sold special herbs, candles, images, and other Umbanda paraphernalia. She closed this store sometime after she decided to change the ritual of her center from Umbanda to Candomblé. The incident that precipitated this decision is described in the next paragraph.

Before my arrival, Nair had held weekly Umbanda sessions for the *prêtos velhos* and *caboclos*. The mediums each held their own consultations at these sessions. One night a spirit of one of the mediums told Nair's special assistant and close friend that she had heart disease and was soon going to die. The supposedly afflicted woman put the center into turmoil, complaining and crying to Pena Verde. Pena Verde announced that the mediums could no longer hold consultations with clients. Henceforth, only Pena Verde would conduct consultations. More than half of Nair's *filhos* left her for other Umbanda centers. Those who remained performed ritual dances during which their *caboclos* possessed them. People who came for spiritual assistance were asked to think about their problems and wishes while the *caboclos* danced. After the spirits left, Pena Verde possessed Nair and individuals could speak only with him. If it appeared that a longer consultation was needed, the individual was invited to Nair's home for special attention.

Attendance rapidly dropped off at Nair's center. The first night that I attended a session Pena Verde announced that henceforth there would be only one session per week. During the year I often heard some complaints in the neighborhood and from Nair's *filhos* that she was moving toward the folkloric aspects of Umbanda and was interested only in making money. Nair held three of what she termed "folkloric demonstrations of Candomblé" during my year of research—two in the center and the third at a radio station. The demonstrations were obviously intended to be shows, and tickets were sold for one of these productions. There was a specific program, but no dramatic script was written. The mediums were supposed to dance for their *orixás*, but were not to be possessed by them. However, most mediums did become possessed, and I believe this might have been due to the pressure they were put under as "amateur actors" by Nair.

As the year of field work progressed, I found Nair demanding that the *orixás* of her *filhos* appear at regular sessions. These elevated spirits were often followed by child spirits, which she referred to as *ere*, the term used in Candomblé. Pena Verde continually emphasized that his *cavalo* was a genuine *mãe de santo*, having undergone the arduous initiation of Candomblé, which made her a "slave to her saint" (i.e., to Iemanjá). Furthermore, Pena Verde continued one night to explain to the audience that this meant his *cavalo* was no longer permitted to have sexual relations. The spirit turned to Nair's husband for confirmation, but he was already fleeing from the center. Pena Verde explained that this did not mean his *cavalo* was a refrigerator. He only wanted to emphasize the privations of becoming a true cult leader. That evening, Nair had some difficulty in coming out of trance. Although her husband did return to help bring her out of trance, he stayed away from the sessions for several months. When he did return, he sat in the rear of the center with the audience, rather than in the special section in the front reserved for guests of honor as he had previously done. Nair's *filhos* discussed the impropriety of Pena Verde's behavior. Some even went so far as to question whether it had, indeed, been Pena Verde speaking. Everyone agreed that it was a most strange happening.

This was not the only occasion of questioning within the center. It had been rumored that a new director of the center had offered Nair another location for her center. Soon after this, Pena Verde talked with Ildicir, the owner of the present location, at a public session. Pena Verde told Ildicir that the *orixás* were no longer with her and that she would be surrounded by *exu* spirits. Pena Verde asked Ildicir to hand over the deed of the center to Nair. After some discussion, Ildicir told Pena Verde that she was going to say something to him in her thoughts. If her thoughts were incorrect, then Pena Verde was to correct her verbally. He was to remain silent if Ildicir were correct. Ildicir then mentally "talked" to Pena Verde:

> This building is currently in the hands of myself and my husband. The building was originally given to our daughter by her grandparents, and it is illegal to sell or give away the building without our daughter's permission. If I attempt to get permission to give away this building, it will only create a great deal of trouble in our family. I have already been very generous to allow your *cavalo* to use the building rent-free for as long as she wants it.[5]

Pena Verde responded, but on a totally different subject. Ildicir concluded that Pena Verde was not really present and that it had been Nair who was speaking. During the remainder of my field research Ildicir did not return to Nair's center. Instead, she attended Badia's sessions, which she felt were disorderly, but at least honest.

ANALYSIS

A streak of independence seems to show through Nair's life history. During her childhood she preferred to add individual interpretations to her school art. As a daughter of the middle class, she would have had no financial need to attend normal school or to assume a teaching occupation. During the period of separation from her husband, she continued to take short courses and to work. Although one might argue that she earned money to support herself during these later years, I believe Nair genuinely enjoyed being an active woman. In fact, it was after she married, had children, and stopped teaching that her spiritual problems began. All of these data suggest that Nair apparently had difficulty in assuming the more usual Brazilian feminine role as a relatively passive woman.

The interesting thing concerning the diagnosis of Nair's problems is the locus of cause. She was viewed as an individual with strong inborn mediumistic tendencies, which once again set her apart from the more ordinary person. Being like a lightning rod that attracted bad fluids explained why so much upheaval occurred in her family's life. The blame was not laid directly on Nair herself, but on her undeveloped mediumship. Furthermore, one of her spirits explained that her spirits, and not Nair, had sent away her husband so that her spiritual development in Umbanda could proceed effectively. Once again the medium was relieved of personal fault and possible subsequent guilt.

It would be a mistake, however, to conclude that spirits are totally self-serving, helping the medium to get off the hook. A certain modicum of control is a part of the system. The decision to develop her mediumship belonged to Nair, and was not an act of her spirit. Furthermore, once development had occurred, the spirits were expected to assume acceptable forms of behavior just as people are. When Nair's spirits overstepped the bounds of propriety, it became a matter of public opinion as to whether it was Nair or her spirit that was actually speaking. For a spirit to discuss his medium's sexual behavior in public was highly questionable, although I am certain that this would have been deemed acceptable within the context of a more intimate private session. Common sense and a few tests provided a measure for evaluating the legitimacy of a spirit. Ildicir weighed her own family's happiness against Nair's felt needs for her own *centro*; tested Pena Verde through silent conversation; and concluded that it had been merely Nair's wishes, and not those of Nair's spirit, that were being expressed.

The data in this chapter illustrate the dynamic quality of a cult center and its activities. Nair's center could be placed somewhere toward the African end of the continuum of Umbanda and Kardecismo in São Paulo. This placement is not based on belief, but primarily on the use of ritual clothing, which was colored, instead of white, and on the absence of consultations, except for Pena Verde, in the public ritual of this center. Nair was a proud woman, an authoritarian who maintained full control of discipline in her center. She did not permit the spirits of her mediums to express themselves. So it was said that the spirits told their *cavalos* to seek new *mães de santo*. Some of Nair's *filhos* remained and new *filhos* joined. Five of Nair's mediums formed a special friendship clique. It was this group of friends who were my major informants. I describe their backgrounds and reasons for becoming mediums, as well as some of their activities I observed, in the next three chapters.

NOTES

1. The excerpt cited was translated by me.

2. All names in this and the following chapters are fictitious. I mention racial and/or ethnic identities to emphasize the point that Umbanda—unlike traditional Candomblé, which was primarily Afro-Brazilian—is not a folk religion limited to a specific racial or ethnic group.

3. In Kardecismo,*corrente* refers to the chain formed when mediums join hands to concentrate on spirits. In Umbanda, *corrente* is used synonymously with *linha*, speaking of a *corrente dos espíritos*.

4. However, practically all of the mediums in Nair's center were not as educated as Nair or Virgínia's family. The family related better to Nair and a few of the more formally educated individuals in her center.

5. I obtained this material indirectly, from my major informant, Cecília, whom I describe in Chapter 6. Ildicir had given Cecília this information.

6

The Clique: Cecília, the Leader

Cult leaders usually do not want their mediums to practice outside the public sessions held at centers. They state that most mediums are not sufficiently developed spiritually to handle private sessions. The *mediums*, however, argue that the cult leaders are jealous of their mediumship and of the private sessions outside their centers. The five mediums who practiced in the clique believed that their spirits needed to express themselves. Since this was not possible in Nair's center, they held private sessions behind her back. The small group included João, a 33-year-old light mulatto male who cooked lunch for the employees in an exclusive beauty salon and served coffee to the customers; Juvenir, a 25-year-old white male who was an accounting clerk in the offices of a major Brazilian airline; Thales, a 21-year-old white male who had just gotten out of the army and was a servant for a wealthy family; Maria, a 37-year-old mulatto female who operated a beauty salon; and Cecília, a 52-year-old mulatto female who was the wife of a taxi driver.

These five individuals represent a segment of the rural-to-urban migration that is a part of the industrialization of Brazil. João's family had come to São Paulo from the far northern arid lands of the state of Alagoas. Thales had left his home in the temperate southern zone of Brazil, which is devoted to small mixed farming. Juvenir, Cecília, and Maria had been brought up in the more remote parts of the state of São Paulo. All of them had left their extended families, and only João had come to São Paulo with his natal nuclear family. Considering their original backgrounds, all five had done reasonably well in their adopted city. In each instance, however, there was a feeling that material life might be even better, and each hoped for further improvements. As a group they performed private sessions for their friends and for themselves. They were thus able to conform to Nair's particular demand that spirits ought not to speak in her center. The private sessions seemed to allow an opportunity for their spirits to express themselves.

Cecília, the oldest and most experienced medium, was the focal point of this group. She was born in 1915 in a small town in the interior of the state of São Paulo. Her father had been the head cook on a *fazenda* (large farm). Her mother was a seamstress. Cecília's formal education was limited to two years of primary schooling. She said that her first experience relating to the spiritual world occurred when she was eight years old. She saw an image of a woman from the waist up in a pool of water. Her mother told her that it was only her eyes playing tricks on her as the children were romping about in the water. Cecília today believes the image might have been her *orixá*, Nanã. When she was several years older, Cecília began to think seriously about the nature of spiritual forces. Her mother had been nervous and quite ill, losing consciousness and breaking out into a cold sweat for periods of ten to fifteen minutes. The family called in a Syrian to bless the sick woman. He told Cecília that, whenever her mother became nervous and ill, she should pray because she had the right forces to help her mother. Cecília turned the man's words over in her head. It must not be physical force he was talking about, for she could not possibly lift her heavy mother. She decided that the Syrian was talking about some sort of spiritual force she had. She said she used this inner strength several times when her mother attempted suicide. Later in her life Cecília came to believe that her mother's difficulty had been due to undeveloped mediumship. There had been no Umbanda center in their small town to which her mother might have been taken. Cecília did not learn about such places until she was fourteen, when her family went to visit relatives in Rio de Janeiro.

When she was seventeen, Cecília moved to São Paulo, where she worked as a cook in a wealthy home—the same occupation as her father's, she added. She remembers the great fun she had going to the *bailes prêtos* (dances for blacks) at that time. Cecília married when she was 20 years old. Her husband had a pushcart from which he sold ice cream and gradually worked his way up until he was operating a bar. They had three children—a girl when Cecília was 25 and mixed twins the following year.

Then a series of events occurred to upset their secure family life. Her husband began acting strangely. He fought with and fired his employees, and soon lost his bar. The older girl died when Cecília was 28, and the boy was killed by an automobile the following year. A friend suggested that Cecília go to a center for spiritual help. There a spirit advised that she needed to think seriously about her mediumship, for her dead mother had a mission to fulfill through her. This news made her sad because she had never wanted to become involved with spiritualism. Cecília left temporarily for the nearby port city of Santos, to bathe in the ocean waters. She believed this helped to prepare her spiritually. After returning she attended a session that was a mixture of Kardecismo and Umbanda. At the table of mediums, she was possessed by her mother's spirit. Cecília learned that her mother's suffering in life had been due to undeveloped mediumship. The spirit could evolve, however, through

Cecília's own spiritual development. The group of mediums then passed to another room in which they received Umbanda spirits. A *caboclo* whose name was Sete Forquilha (Seven Fork) possessed Cecília. At a later session she was possessed by Pai Augostinho, a *prêto velho*.

There was never any doubt in Cecília's mind that spirits existed, but she was reluctant to become a medium. Still, several strange events seemed to push her in this direction. One night she dreamed that she and her husband were fleeing through a wooded area. Pursuing them was her Indian spirit, carrying a spear. After catching up with them, the *caboclo* attempted to seize her from her husband for the purpose of sexual relations. There were some other unusual events, which she related as follows:

One day I was cooking beans, and I took a little bit of meal and mixed it with the beans and fried it together with some meat I had drying in the house. I took some in my hand and sat down on the floor to eat it. It was so good! When I finished eating, I looked at the corner in the kitchen and I saw this face and neck, sweating! Oh, how the sweat rolled off his face. His hair was falling. Loose! With sideburns. Beard. I said, "Our Lady! What can this be?" I wasn't troubled by his presence. He didn't want to incorporate.[1] I was alone in the house with my daughter. She was still small. And I wasn't even troubled by him.

Several days later when day broke and I awakened, I had a head the size of a clothes closet. I tried to go outside, but I just ran into the door. I vomited. I vomited what I didn't even have in my stomach. I hadn't even eaten, yet! I had only taken some coffee. That coffee had turned into something like you find in a chamber pot in my stomach. So, I went running, feeling terrible, running to the house of my *mãe de santo*. And I told her, "Look mother, for the love of God, help me! I don't know what has taken hold of me today, but I can't stand it. I'm really sick. Help me!" And she said to me, "Well, good for you! You deserve what you've got. I'm not going to hurry just for this. First, I'm going to take my bath, and then I'm going to take my ritual bath with herbs. And only then will I see you." Then I begged her, "For the love of God, see me *now*, for I can't stand this any longer." And that which I felt in my stomach, my head—such heaviness—left me. But my face stayed fixed in a strange manner and my arms were open. At that point she became more calm. She knew what it was.[2] She also knew that I didn't like it! That I wanted none of this. So she had been tormenting me.

As she started talking with me, I received a Japanese[3] spirit. He said that every time I didn't want to go to the center, he was going to come and strike me with these things. And then he told the story of his life. That he had been a prisoner of war. He had hid children in a tunnel so they wouldn't get killed. He was discovered and put into solitary confinement. A room so small he could only stand up in it. They threw hot water on his head until he was forced to tell what he knew at times. He then said that all of the symptoms I felt were his. And that he was going to stay by my side. That he was one more light that would be at my side while I practiced spiritualism. He bid the *mãe* goodbye and left. And then I received the *boiadeiro* (cowboy).[4] When he left, I received an old boyfriend who had died in an accident.

He said that he wanted to possess me, because he also needed to evolve spiritually. But that he wasn't going to stay with me. He had come only this one time. He said that while he was still alive he had wanted me very much, but now he was staying only to protect me; that he was going to open the road for me so I would have some luck; that I had found someone who would care for me just as he would have done if alive; that he had come only to ask for a pardon for certain things. He had courted me but had liked another girl. He did wrong by the other girl. I knew it and separated myself from him. He didn't want me to leave. Thought that I should marry him, even with things as they were. But I said to him, "Why should I make the other girl unhappy? I don't have to. I'm free. I'm still young. Marry the other girl." I didn't want him anymore. Then he tried to attack me but even at this I still told him that I didn't want him anymore. I *really* didn't want him. Even now I like him less because he wanted to come against me. He followed me around to all the places I went. Where I'd go, he'd follow. So his spirit had come this time to ask for pardon. That he was wrong. And after he left, my uncle's spirit came. All of this in one day!

In additon to these rather strange spiritual events in Cecília's life at about age 30, her husband was believed to be experiencing the effects of a bad *exu* spirit. He had had a mistress who had become dissatisfied with him. She supposedly had paid an *exu* spirit to bring harm to him. Cecília claimed that as a result he had gone berserk, selling his possessions, smashing his car with his bare fists. (By this time he was a taxi driver.) Her neighbors told her that she should urge him to go to a center for help. When he refused to go for a spiritual consultation, Cecília went herself. The cult leader told her that she would have to develop her mediumistic abilities to help her husband overcome his spiritual problems. Cecília had been reluctant to do this, but the fate of several spirits of the dead and the solution of her family problems seemed to rest with her willingness to become a medium. She believed that it was the will of God and that she no longer could ignore her destiny.

The first center in which she practiced was a mixture of Kardecismo and Umbanda. When it closed several years later, she moved to an Umbanda center that had both a male and a female cult leader. She felt she had learned a great deal from the *pai de santo*. She left this center voluntarily, explaining to me that there had been too many conflicts between the *pai de santo* and his wife, who was the *mãe de santo*. The two cult leaders could not agree on the procedures to be followed in their center. This made Cecília feel insecure in practicing her mediumship. She then joined Nair's center. When Nair moved more toward Candomblé, Cecília stayed but also began practicing at Badia's center on a part-time basis. Badia did not have very many developed mediums and welcomed Cecília's presence. Cecília said that Badia had asked her to become her *mãe pequena* (little mother, i.e., major assistant). She had turned down the generous offer, privately telling her friends that she would like to be fully initiated into Candomblé before assuming such an important role in the religion. She also felt that her daughter and grandchildren needed her. For this reason, she said, she must remain at home.

Cida, her 26-year-old daughter, her husband, and their three youngsters lived with Cecília and her husband in a two-bedroom apartment. Cecília looked after the children while their parents worked. The eldest, a boy, was five, the next boy was three, and a baby girl was born on February 9, 1967. I mention this date as the starting point for a number of stressful events that seemed to induce unusual behavior in Cecília's spirits in the following weeks. The baby had a cleft lip; it was repaired, but the family worried a great deal about it. About the time of the baby's birth, Cecília's teenage niece moved into the household, in order to attend school in São Paulo. The two new additions to the household produced more work for Cecília and were a financial strain as well. It is interesting that a new *caboclo* spirit began to possess her at this time.

Although Cecília rarely mentioned her desire to become a cult leader, the new *caboclo* spirit, Pena Branca (White Feather), began to act and speak on behalf of his medium. One week after the birth of her granddaughter, I took the following notes on Cecília's very unusual behavior in Nair's center:

During the preliminary dances, Cecília frequently wipes perspiration from her brow. Later, when the *caboclos* come, her spirit does not dance in the counterclockwise circle with the others. Instead, she[5] wanders around the front of the center, stopping, looking as if she is lost, dropping her head slightly forward, shutting her eyes, and then wandering off in another direction. At one point she comes over to where I am sitting in the front row. Nair, who is not possessed, has been observing Cecília. Cecília's spirit looks as if he wants to speak to me and, to avoid possible trouble,[6] I turn my head away, ignoring Cecília. She stays in the corner in front of me for about half a minute, wandering around. Then she suddenly lowers her head and begins half vaulting, half falling across the rear of the center's front half, toward an open door. Behind this door is a closet in which Nair keeps the elaborate feathered costume of Pena Verde, used for special occasions. She sticks the upper part of her body past the door, and by this time the assistants are trying to help her back into the front of the center. Cecília flails her arms around as she moves to the wall next to the door. She does not seem to want any assistance. For a few seconds she pounds her head on the wall beside the door. Then her eyes seem to be aware of what is going on in the room, she

164   UMBANDA TRANCE AND POSSESSION IN SAO PAULO, BRAZIL

loses her balance for a second, swaying, and goes back into trance. During the rest of the dances of the *caboclos*, Cecília dances in the circle with the other *caboclos*, but occasionally wanders out of the circle, again looking as if lost.

The reason for this very unusual behavior became clearer the following night, when the clique held a private session for one of their friends. The *exu* spirits of Cecília, Maria, and João had come, had performed the major item of business for their friend, and had left. A few minutes later Cecília was possessed by Pena Branca, who is not her regular *caboclo* spirit. The incident is described in my notes as follows:

Pena Branca speaks in a very loud voice, the facial expression being one of great anger. He says that he is not happy with his horse because she did not want him to come to earth. He announces that he will cut in half each year that his horse has yet to live, (i.e., Cecília's life will be cut in half) if she does not let Pena Branca possess her. Pena Branca says that he does not like Nair's *terreiro* because the *caboclos* there have to put their heads between their legs (i.e., be humble and obedient). He emphasizes this point several times by throwing Cecília's hand between her thighs, and then between the thighs of João and Juvenir, who are not at this time possessed. The *caboclos* are not permitted to talk, smoke, or drink at the *terreiro*, and Pena Branca says he does not like this. He says he is going to make his horse urinate in front of everybody at Nair's. Then Pena Branca shouts that he is a chief, that he wants to be the head of his own *terreiro*. At this point Pena Branca violently throws down his glass of beer, smashing it on the floor. Immediately, Pena Branca leaves, and Cecília collapses on the floor, stretched out. But she is still in trance. Juvenir starts cleaning up the shattered glass, and João is bent over Cecília, saying "Dona Cecília" several times. João and my landlady, who is at the session, manage to lift Cecília to a sitting position on the floor. Her eyes are open and staring straight ahead. It is something like a catatonic state. No movements of the others can attract her attention. She remains like this for three minutes. Then she returns to normal, gets up clutching her abdomen, and drinks some water.

On the day after this outpouring by Pena Branca, I talked with Cecília, who spoke of aching a great deal because Pena Branca had been extremely rough with her. She had put hot compresses on her arms and shoulders. Cecília confessed to being ashamed of the things Pena Branca had said the night before and expressed a strong preference for Sete Forquilha. She explained that it had been Pena Branca who had possessed her two nights before at Nair's center. She speculated that Pena Branca who wants to be the head of a cult center, was jealous of Pena Verde and had gone to the open closet looking for Pena Verde's green feathered costume. That day Cecília asked me for a small loan of money for food and for school books for her niece, who had just come to live with her. It was the first and only time she requested financial aid from me.

During the following weeks Cecília began to complain to friends about her ne'er-do-well son-in-law. This intensified when he was out drinking with friends instead of baby-sitting on the nights Cecília wanted to attend sessions at Nair's center. (At this time his wife, Cida, was working the 3 to 11 P.M. shift as a nurse's aid.)

Cecília never linked Pena Branca's appearances to the family problems and financial difficulties she was having. It does seem evident, however, that her unconscious desire for power to control her personal life was expressed in the symbolic form of Pena Branca.

Pena Branca appeared a third time, much later during the year of my field work. By this time Cecília was beginning to admit to close friends that she would like to be a cult leader. She would always add that her husband wanted a wife, and not a *mãe de santo*. At this point she would laugh about Pena Verde's comment that Nair no longer had sexual relations since her initiation into Candomblé. Cecília said she had explained this situation to Pena Branca, hoping that he would understand. When he did possess Cecília again, Pena Branca was considerably more subdued and gave her no difficulty. Moreover, he did not appear to behave in a manner significantly different from that of her regular *caboclo*, Sete Forquilha.

The exact reason for Pena Branca's third appearance is still uncertain to me, but three things are suggestive. First, the private session held by the clique that day was for an important local man, the operator of a small Italian pasta factory. The owner of the building had ordered the man to pay more rent or move out. Pena Branca boasted to this man of being the head of a *linha*[7] of spirits. Perhaps, then, the difficult spiritual task at hand had required a spirit more evolved and more powerful than Sete Forquilha.

Second, the session was held on a Sunday afternoon because Cecília's husband had temporarily "grounded" her late-nighttime activities at private sessions. He was a very understanding husband who never complained about Cecília's being away until 2:00 or 3:00 A.M., but she always had to inform him of her activities and whereabouts before leaving the house. As she had forgotten to do this, he had taken her house key for three weeks. She did not overtly blame him, but seemed more annoyed with herself at having forgotten to tell him. The session was therefore held on a Sunday afternoon, and possibly Pena Branca appeared as a symbol of domestic power.

Third, Nair was having an elaborate ritual goat sacrifice on the following Tuesday for her special *festa* of Iemanjá the following Thursday. Perhaps

Cecília's covert jealousy of Nair was symbolized in Pena Branca's appearance. Cecília said that she did not understand Pena Branca's reason for possessing her this third time. She was happy because he seemed to accept her familial obligations and inability to immediately become a cult leader, and because he was no longer giving her so much trouble.

During the year of field work, I observed Cecília possessed by eleven different spirits. Pena Branca was the only spirit who seemed to give her personal difficulty. His presence was apparently linked to Cecília's familial and financial problems, and with her desire to become a cult leader. Besides the two *caboclos* Sete Forquilha and Pena Branca, Cecília called and was possessed by an envoy of the female *orixá* Nanã, two male and one female *prêtos velhos*, a male child spirit, a male *boiadeiro* (cowboy), a male *caipoeiro* (a "hick" from the interior of São Paulo), and two male *exus*. Moreover, Cecília and her friends told about a variety of other spirits that had possessed her before my arrival, including a *pombagira* and a Chinese. Each spirit could be distinguished by its behavioral attributes. With the single exception of Nanã, all of them could entertain their audience for hours with jokes, funmaking, and an occasional story about their lives on earth. An example of a special service performed by the *caboclo*, Sete Forquilha is described next.

Cecília invited me to attend a private session for some friends in a nearby *bairro* where she had lived for a number of years. The couple, about 40 years old, had three daughters aged fourteen, ten, and seven. The husband was a carpenter in charge of maintenance at one of the local schools. The family lived in a six-room house with spacious rooms and had an American car of late 1940 or early 1950 vintage. The wife was of Italian descent.

The husband's mother, who had come from Hungary and had been very poor, had managed to work her way up the ladder financially and had purchased a house in which she lived with her son's family until her death a year earlier. She also had two daughters, but they had not cared for her in her old age as her son and his wife had. The old woman had wanted the house to remain in the family. After she died, her two daughters wanted their two-thirds of the inheritance. Since their brother was unable to raise the cash necessary to pay them off immediately, they wanted him to sell the house. The man's eldest daughter was especially sentimental about her grandmother's wish for the house to remain in the family. Her father felt he had no alternative except to sell it. Her mother, a good friend of Cecília's, had asked that Sete Forquilha offer some advice.

On arrival, we were ushered into the combination living room-bedroom. Cecília lit a white candle for her guardian angel, the *orixá*, Nanã. She did not bother to change into any special ritual garb, but did put on the *guias* (beads) of her various spirits. She sat on a straight chair facing a sofa on which the

couple, their oldest daughter, and myself were seated. There were no opening
songs or special ritual except a brief opening prayer. Cecília did not look at us
as she prepared for possession. Instead, she looked upward and at the various
walls. Then she put her hand over her eyes, drawing it down over her mouth,
yawning. It seemed as if she were attempting to shut out her surroundings in
order to concentrate on receiving her *caboclo*. She drew in two sharp and deep
breaths, holding each one for a few seconds. Her head rapidly fell forward,
and when she straightened up in the chair, Sete Forquilha was possessing her.
There was no perspiration before or during possession.

The *caboclo* greeted the group with a *"boa noite"* ("good evening") and
then asked each person how he was. The husband and two of the girls replied
that they had colds. The rest of us were able to say, "Well, thanks to God."
Next, Sete asked the husband to draw up a chair beside him. The man seemed
to be quite nervous. He frequently moved his position in the chair and fingered
a cushion he was holding. As Sete slowly got into the problem of the house,
the man in frequent outbursts interrupted the *caboclo*. Sete reprimanded him,
telling him that he should first say "I beg your pardon" before interrupting
with a point of disagreement. His wife tried to smooth over the awkward
situation by explaining that her husband was not too familiar with this religion, that he was upset over the problem, and that he had a cold and was not
feeling well. The oldest girl listened intently to everything, but her two
younger sisters silently giggled whenever Sete was not looking in their direction. Nothing new came of the conversation between the *caboclo* and the
man. Sete suggested that the man ask his sisters to allow him to keep the house
while he paid them off in installments. The man did not want to do this, and
Cecília later told me that he had too much pride to ask his sisters this favor.

After the consultation, the *caboclo* asked for a glass of *pinga* (Brazilian
sugar-cane alcohol) and for some leaves of a special plant growing outside the
house. When the oldest girl brought the leaves, Sete Forquilha crushed them
into the *pinga*. He separately called each of those present to his chair to
remove any bad spiritual fluids. He offered each person a drink of the mixture,
which he claimed would deter evil fluids and keep one well. After a closing
prayer, the *caboclo* left Cecília, who remained seated in her chair. She looked
around the room and at the small group of people. For about five seconds
Cecília seemed like a person who has just awakened and is putting the environment into some mental order before proceeding to get up. Having closely
observed Cecília's possessions for nearly a year, I tend to think that this behavior was well acted out by her to make the possession more convincing to
the male head of the household, who might have had some personal doubts
about the validity of spirits. Deep trance is regarded as a good sign that a medium is not faking possession. Cecília recalled and discussed the entire session

with me as we rode home together after the session. She was not in a deep trance.

After the session, the seven of us present went to the kitchen for a light snack and conversation. Cecília asked for and received a photograph of the man's dead mother. She said she would take it home to the small altar filled with statues of the *orixás-santos*. There she would try to make mental contact with the dead woman and ask for her help. Cecília made a tentative appointment for a future session with the family, but as far as I know, the second session did not take place. However, the wife did visit Cecília several times subsequently. The house was not sold immediately, and there was still some hope that the man would swallow his pride and work out an arrangement with his sisters.

ANALYSIS

At the particular time Cecília was trying to decide about developing her mediumship, a number of stressful events occurred. Two of her children died, which probably led Cecília to question her performance as a mother. Her husband behaved in a peculiar manner, firing his employees and losing his bar. This may have made Cecília feel financially insecure. Moreover, she was aware that her husband had a mistress, and this no doubt brought questions to Cecília's mind regarding her role as a wife. For a year or two she attended spiritualist sessions. Then, within several days, six spirits came to her.

The *caboclo* who appeared in a dream was apparently an indication that she was desirable to him, if not to her husband. It is also interesting that an old boyfriend possessed her. He reassured her that she had made the right choice in marrying her husband. If spirits may be regarded as projections of the inner personality, the Japanese spirit tells us a great deal about Cecília. Like Cecília, he was concerned with keeping children from dying. The war in which this spirit was involved seemed to be something like the personal war Cecília found herself in. He was a prisoner, perhaps as Cecília felt herself to be—confined in her apartment and in a marriage that had temporarily gone sour. Finally, the Japanese kept all his secrets to himself until forced under the pressure of hot water on his head to tell all he knew. This was quite similar to Cecília's keeping everything bottled up inside until, with the heat of anger that sometimes leads into the trance state, she (the Japanese) exploded with all she (he) knew.

All of the six spirits that came within this brief interval were male. In addition, Cecília had sometimes earlier been possessed by a male *prêto velho* and by her dead mother's spirit. The preponderance of males here was probably a reversal of sex roles to gain the power that Cecília felt she needed. During the period of my field work, Cecília came across as a strong personality, but as one who handled power in a very indirect way. It contrasted with Nair's more direct and open use of power. Cecília was strong in a nurturant manner. The others in the clique observed that she was like a "mother" to them, and they would sometimes jokingly refer to her as the *mãe de santo* of their private sessions. On visiting Cecília in her home, I frequently encountered some person seeking aid from her or one of her spirits.

Cecília once observed that her religion had made her a "free woman." By this, she explained, she meant that she could go out without her husband to private spirit sessions and afterward to restaurants with Umbandists. Of course, her husband required that she tell him her plans for the evening in advance, but this was a small issue considering that he allowed her to spend nights out until 2:00 and 3:00 A.M. in the presence of other men! I especially recall one night spent with Cecília in the company of three middle-aged married men who shared the expenses of a special apartment *"para brincar"* ("for playing around"), as Cecília put it. The men normally brought their girlfriends to this place, but recently it had become filled with bad fluids. As a result, one of the men had had a bad auto accident, and his wife had become very ill. Believing that a rejected girlfriend had sent an evil *exu* spirit against her former lover, they had asked Cecília to hold a sedate and very proper private spirit session to counteract the black magic of this *exu*. It was not difficult to understand why Cecília felt that her religion made her a relatively free woman.

Cecília very strongly believed that, once a person has developed his or her mediumship, a certain degree of control is expected to be exercised over the spirits. She would tell younger mediums that they could ask their unruly spirits not to possess them until a regular spirit session. One example was a young man who claimed that his spirit wanted to throw him in front of moving buses. Another case involved a young woman who said that her *pombagira* made her behave in an unladylike, sexy manner in front of men. Cecília also said that a medium could ask his spirit not to behave inappropriately at public sessions. This particular outlook, I believe, was what made Cecília shift on the occasion of stress periods from her regular *caboclo*, Sete Forquilha, to another *caboclo*, Pena Branca. It would not have been right for Sete Forquilha to deliver hostile words about Nair or to be jealous of Nair's Pena Verde. On the other hand, it was alright for the more elevated and less controlled Pena Branca, who wanted to head a *centro* with Cecília as his medium, to be annoyed with Nair. I found that it was only after Cecília had been able to work through, and openly admit, her desire to be a cult leader that she gained a measure of control over Pena Branca. Enjoying her husband as she did,

Cecília was able to rationalize away her inner wishes by saying that he would not want a *mãe de santo* (and no sex) for a wife.

Cecília and her spirits were greatly respected by her many friends and acquaintances, who came from all walks of life for personal help. She had a special insight that enabled her to understand in unsophisticated ways the complexities of human life. This ability seemed to come from her own personal experiences and spiritual development over the past 20 years. During that period she had learned to control her spirits and to use them effectively in solving her own difficulties as well as those of others.

NOTES

1. *Incorporar* is a term frequently used in São Paulo to describe spirit possession. Another term used to refer to possession is *receber* (to receive) a spirit. I never heard the Portuguese word *possessão* (possession) used in referring to spirits.

2. Cecília apparently had entered a trance state at this point.

3. This possession occurred sometime during World War II.

4. The spirit she had seen in her kitchen several days earlier.

5. I use the word "she," but it should be noted that Cecília is possessed at this point by a male spirit.

6. I thought perhaps that her spirit wished to speak to me—something not permitted by Nair. This incident occurred near the beginning of my field work, when I was perhaps, overly concerned with the possibility of unwittingly creating disturbances in the field and perhaps being asked to leave the center. As I look back on this affair now, I doubt that Cecília was even aware of my presence. The spirit's strange behavior was probably more related to troubling circumstances in Cecília's life at the time.

7. Technically, a *linha* is headed by an *orixá*. This comment is indicative of the general absence of codification of Umbanda beliefs.

7

The Clique: Two Children of Mamãe Oxum

Mamãe Oxum, linked with the Virgin Mary by some Umbandists, is without doubt the most feminine of all the *orixás*. As goddess of the fresh waters, Mamãe Oxum is quiet, suave, delicate. It is sometimes said she loves rich things. Whenever Oxum possesses one of her *filhos* (children), her behavior contrasts with that of the great undulating Iemanjá, whose domain is the ocean waters.

As the guardian spirit of two members of the clique, João and Maria, Oxum was believed to exert a direct influence over their everyday behavior. Both João and Maria believed that their other, lesser, spirits also played important roles in their lives, and both experienced spontaneous possessions outside the formal context of public and private spirit sessions. Most of the material in this chapter covers their experiences with spirits that occurred during my field work.

JOÃO

It was João who first took me to Nair's center, where I met the clique. At that time he was a waiter in the *pensão* (boarding house) in which I briefly lived. On the surface, João was a mild person. Physically, he was small and delicate, with almost feminine mannerisms and speech. To all his friends it was clear that he was protected and influenced by Mamãe Oxum.

I found it extremely difficult to learn much about João's background. There were great gaps in his life history. Friends of a specific individual under study were usually able to verify for me the data collected from that person or to fill in new material. None of the clique members were able to do this for João's background. I know only that he was born in 1934 in the northern state of Alagoas; that in João's Catholic family one of his brothers was a spiritualist

171

medium; that João had had two years of primary school; and that he later had attended a religious school (Catholic) for three years. João's family moved to São Paulo in 1950, when he was sixteen. His father worked as a carpenter, and João had been unsteadily employed at various jobs. More recently, he had worked as a waiter.

When João was 23 years old, his friends suggested that he begin developing his mediumship. He said that at that time he was suffering both at home and at work. He was not willing, however, to explain the particular details. João remained in Umbanda for about one and a half years. When he was 25 years old, half of his family joined the Pentecostal church. João was also baptized into this Protestant church. Five years later João had more personal difficulties of an unspecified nature, and friends directed him to Nair's center. João's life history, then, does not shed much light on his reasons for being a medium. To understand João's participation in spiritualism, it is necessary to consider some observations of his behavior I made during my field work.

The shy and mild-mannered person I first met was apparently a superficial João. What his friends regarded as his more gross feminine characteristics erupted in the form of Margarida, a female *exu* spirit known as a *pombagira*. João, and everyone who knew him, recognized his homosexual tendencies. Everyone agreed that this behavior was due to the overwhelming influence of Margarida. The first time I saw Margarida was on a sidewalk beside the main throughfare in a middle-class *bairro* at about 12:30 A.M. It was early in the year of field work and that evening I had attended my third session at Nair's center. Afterward, Cecília, João, Juvenir, and myself had gone to a local restaurant for pizza, beer, and *pinga*. João discussed his current problems at the *pensão* where he was working. Most of the help had left that day, and João had had to cook the large meal by himself. As he continued to talk, Cecília was leafing through the pages of a book Nair had lent me. It was filled with pictures of people dressed in the elaborate costumes of the *orixás*. Cecília gave particular attention to a photograph of a man dressed as Oxum Maré (Oxum of the tides, different from Mamãe Oxum). She read aloud the caption, which described the bisexual nature of Oxum Maré. Everybody laughed.

Continuing the conversation, Cecília brought up a male homosexual who for a short time had been a medium at Nair's center. She then moved on to discuss what she believed to be the great masculinity of Brazilian men. Cecília claimed that they were all *quente* (hot) and looked at women only from the waist down. She speculated that what gave Brazilian men this great aspect of their temperament must be *feijão* (beans). The laughter continued as we consumed more *pinga,* and after some more coversation all of us, except João, shared in paying the bill. Abruptly, João jumped out of his chair and ran to the door. Juvenir followed close behind. When Cecília and myself came outside a minute or two later, João was sitting on a retaining wall beside the sidewalk. Margarida had spontaneously possessed him.[1] Margarida, in "her" high-pitched voice, was cursing quite a bit. She said that her horse was a *filho de puta* (son of a whore) and sexually wanted two men who were walking by. Cecília replied that Margarida's horse should put such things out of his mind or things would be black. There was a bit more conversation in which Margarida spoke with agitation and Cecília with deliberate calmness. Cecília suggested to Margarida that her horse should come to Cecília's home to discuss his problems. She told the spirit to leave, and with a few jerks of head and chest, João was again normal.

The four of us then walked about half a block to Cecília's apartment building where she bid us goodnight. A taxi picked up João, Juvenir, and myself. During the short ride to the *pensão* João began to jerk his head in the manner of initiating possession and reached for Juvenir, who held his hand for a few seconds and then asked if he were alright. João replied that he felt better. As the driver stopped a block from the *pensão,* João took out some money to pay the fare. Suddenly, his facial expression changed, and he began to giggle in a high-pitched voice. Margarida had returned, and since women do not usually pay taxi fares, "she" began to fold up the money and put it back into João's pocket. Margarida stuck out her tongue at the driver, who by this time had turned around to look at the scene. He asked João if he were *louco* (crazy, masculine). With a flirtatious nod of the head Margarida responded, "*Não! Estou louca*" ("No! I'm crazy," feminine). Then João became normal again, although still somewhat inebriated. With some difficulty he walked to the *pensão,* taking each step carefully and biting his lower lip. Later in the year I came to know João better. He told me that when he finally reached his room that night, his *prêto velho,* Pai Joaquim, was annoyed by his behavior with Margarida. The *prêto velho* proceeded to castigate João by violently throwing him under the bed.

João's difficulties at the *pensão* continued to grow worse. The servants at the *pensão* had not been paid and began to leave, one by one. João was not only working without pay; he was working harder and longer hours as the others left. Between the time of Margarida's sidewalk appearance on January 5, 1967, and the day he quit his job on January 16, 1967, João's behavior changed. He appeared to become more aggressive, sometimes flailing his arms about. He talked in louder tones of voice and laughed at a high ptich. This behavior was attributed to Margarida.

At times João became extremely nervous. This was especially apparent on Saturday, January 7, 1967, when João, Cecília, Juvenir, Renato (Juvenir' apartment mate), and myself had gathered for an evening of conversation at the apartment of Juvenir and Renato. João's arms, hands, and legs trembled.

He drew attention to himself by teasing and shouting *"cheguei!"* ("I arrived!"). This is a phrase some spirits use to announce their act of possessing a medium. The others in the room knew that João was planning to quit his job, but had no prospect for a new one. Renato and Juvenir told me that João had rarely held a job for more than three months. They felt that he needed a stable job in a large firm like they had, but João lacked the necessary education. The small group had gathered to provide some spiritual help for the afflicted João. As João's cries became louder, Renato calmly looked on; Juvenir attempted to engage me in irrelevant conversation so as to distract me from João's behavior,[2] and Cecília quietly tried to talk with João. Eventually, Cecília was able to calm João sufficiently to initiate a spirit session. *Caboclo* spirits possessed João and Cecília. João's *caboclo* wanted to speak with Juvenir privately, and the two retired to another room for about fifteen minutes. Soon after, both *caboclos* left. Cecília received her *caipoeiro* (hick) spirit, who entertained the group. Finally, the child spirits possessed Cecília, João, and Juvenir. After the spirits left, João appeared to be less tense and had, to some degree, returned to a more subdued state.

The group met once more the following Monday, January 9, 1967, at the same place. There was no spirit session this time. João was less tense. He complained a great deal about Nair, their cult leader, and said he was planning to leave her center. The general gist of the conversation had to do with the way Nair tended to cater to white people who had money. Renato pointed out that Nair usually wanted nothing to do with black people who had little money. No one disagreed.

On Monday, January 16, 1967, João quit working at the *pensão* and found a temporary job in a barbershop. Within a month he had another job as cook and waiter in an exclusive beauty salon. Soon after, João's friends visited his combination living room-bedroom at the beauty salon one Sunday afternoon. They held a special spiritual session to signal an auspicious beginning for João. He liked his new occupation and was still working there as of December 1969.

Another instance of João's spirits playing a role in his everyday affairs occurred on Sunday, March 12, 1967. Juvenir and Renato had invited Cecília, João, and myself for tea and sandwiches. Juvenir was wearing very short shorts, and João continuously made cracks about them. I perceived that João was perhaps stimulated by Juvenir's sensuality. His general behavior suggested to the others that Margarida was nearby, influencing his actions. Someone teased João about this, and he pretended to be annoyed while thoroughly enjoying the attention.

That afternoon the group wanted to listen to the tape-recorded version of the private spirit session they had held the night before at Maria's home. My notes follow:

We go into the living room to listen to the tape of the night before. The *prêtos velhos* are first. Cecília and João get up to dance to the taped *prêto velho* music several times, then sit down. During the music, João is suddenly and violently seized by one of his spirits. Seated on the sofa, he suddenly curls up in what is almost a fetal position. He squirms in this position for about 30 seconds while we watch with some alarm. When João returns to normal, his face is very red and he utters a long sigh, for he has been holding his breath. A few minutes later he gets up to dance again to the *prêto velho* music. While he is dancing, his *prêto velho* comes to him in a normal manner It is Pai Joaquim de Angola.

A stool is brought out for Pai Joaquim to sit on. Someone lights a pipe for him, and a newspaper is laid on the floor for him to spit on. I turn off the tape recorder, but Juvenir and Cecília tell me to record Pai Joaquim. João's body continuously trembles, especially his feet, hands, and head. As the session progresses, the trembling alternately stops and starts.[3] Pai Joaquim tells Juvenir to go change from his shorts into long pants. Juvenir complies. Pai Joaquim calms down somewhat, and Cecília receives her *prêto velho*.

These events were especially interesting for several reasons. It seems apparent that João was sexually stimulated by Juvenir, which was interpreted, half seriously and half jokingly, by the others present as Margarida's influence over João. However, it is more difficult to say that João's initial *choque* (shock) on the sofa was linked to sexual behavior. Finally, it is interesting that Pai Joaquim told Juvenir to change into long pants. This spontaneous possession was part of a series of events during my field work that lent credibility to the beliefs of the clique about João's homosexuality and about his spirits both causing his more feminine behavior (Margarida) and controlling it (Pai Joaquim).

MARIA

The second "child of Oxum" in the clique was Maria. She was born in the interior of the state of São Paulo in 1929. Maria said that she was a "true" Brazilian, being of mixed Italian, *bahiano* (Afro-Brazilian), and Indian ancestry. As a child she had worked in the fields, planting rice, corn, and greens, and helping to hoe out the weeds. There had been time for four years of primary school. Her mother had been a *curandeiro* (healer) who had worked with herbs, but had known little or nothing about spiritualism.

When Maria was 25 years old, she moved to the city of São Paulo. At first she worked as a servant in a private home. Two years later Maria began to study acting while working as a part-time servant. She says that she acted in several theaters. On one occasion she performed in a Macumba production. Maria did not discuss in detail her activities between 1956, when she began to try her luck in the theater, and 1964, when she began to develop her mediumship. Lucinda, a friend of Maria's, told me that during this period Maria had lived with a man for several years and had given birth to a boy. The child died before reaching the age of five. Sometime during this period, Maria began to work as a beautician at home. By 1963, several events had occurred that led Maria to begin her spiritual development in Umbanda. Her stated reasons for entering Umbanda are as follows:

In my life I have had much disillusionment. But, as a beautician, I came to know many *mães de santo* and mediums who frequented my salon, and they always would look at me and say:
"Maria, are you familiar with spiritualism?"
"No."
"You never went?"
"Never."
"Which is to say that you don't know spiritualism?"
"I don't know it."
"But you are a medium. I see a *guia* (guide, spirit) at your side. You have a marvelous shining star at your side."
All of the *mediuns videntes* (mediums who see spirits) always told me these things. Even the young blond man who came by to pick up my laundry every Monday told me that I was a medium. I didn't like it. Understand? I didn't like it, and I didn't believe it because I was born a Catholic. I was such a Catholic that I didn't go for any other religion. So then this young man told me that I was a medium. He said that he practiced spiritualism in Umbanda. He had a spiritual insight one day that he would see me practicing Umbanda. I was still critical. I didn't believe any of this would ever happen. One year later a series of problems started happening to me.
In 1963 I was planning to enter a contest of coiffures at the "House of Italy." I had entered a contest there once before and had won. There were many hairdressers who had won before, but I overtook them that time. They weren't happy. They were envious and thought it was impossible for a hairdresser without a name—which was me—to win. I worked at home. Hidden. My salon wasn't even registered. How could such a person win a contest?
So, in 1963 I arranged seven models and entered them in the "House of Italy" contest. And as we were going to the club, I had a horrible car accident. I wasn't hurt too badly, but the most beautiful model had her neck dislocated. I was terrified. So much blood. I screamed, *"Nossa Senhora da*

Aparecida!" How I screamed! The car seemed to be without brakes and without steering. It went up and down the sidewalk. It ran into cars in front of us. Finally it hit a tree and stopped. The car windows were broken, and everyone was covered with blood. People stopped to help us and to take our group to the hospital. Although my dress was wet with the blood of the others, I took a taxi to the club to advise the directors of the contest that I would be unable to enter.

One month later I went to a Japanese who reads the hand quite well. He took my hand and as he looked at it he told me everything that had happened in that car accident as if he had been there himself. And he had never seen me before! He told me that the car wreck had been sent by a person who was envious of my success. It was someone who despised me and thought I shouldn't enter the club because I would defeat her in the contest. This is to say that someone paid an *exu* to do a powerful work so that all this would happen to me—that I could not enter the contest at the club. The Japanese told me that I had to attend sessions of Umbanda. I replied that I would go, although I was not familiar with spiritualism and did not believe in it.

The first time I went to a center, I thought the mediums were just faking. I believed it was something that anyone could imitate.[4] When it came my turn to speak with the spirit of the cult leader, I stood about half a meter from him. He put his hand on my forehead and I became dizzy. I felt as if I had taken an alcoholic drink. I felt strange, and it seemed as if I were going under. Suddenly my vision disappeared. I no longer knew where I was. When I came to, I was bathed in perspiration from dancing with the other spirits. That is how I began to develop my mediumship. From then on I believed in spiritualism. They told me that I was a good medium and that I should make the ritual clothing for the center and "work." When I don't "work" at a center, nothing goes right for me. I am a medium who needs to practice charity for others.

Maria attended sessions at this Umbanda center for two years. She stopped attending sessions when a close friend, also a medium, was expelled from the center by the *mãe de santo*. The friend had fallen in love with another medium at the center who already had a girlfriend. Malicious gossip about the affair disrupted the smooth running of the center, and the cult leader dealt with the situation by expelling Maria's friend. Maria rarely got along well with persons in authority, and I suspect that it is highly probable that she also did not get along too well with the cult leader, although she did not discuss this with me.

Much of the data I collected on Maria seem to suggest that she was achievement oriented in terms of money and status. Her story about her reasons for becoming a medium indicate this. The remainder of this chapter deals with instances of her concern with, and her use of spirits in relation to, money. The first instance concerns Maria's introduction to Nair's center. After quitting the first center, Maria did not participate in sessions for three months. She said that during this time nothing went right for her and business at her beauty salon dropped off. One Saturday, not one customer came. Maria went to talk with Nair about her problems at the other center and about her lack of business in the salon. She wanted to know if the first cult leader had sent an *exu* to turn her customers against her. Nair, according to Maria responded as follows:

> The other *mãe de santo* did nothing. The only thing holding you back in the salon is your nonparticipation in sessions. You are a medium and you need to "work." Your spirits want to do charitable works. The hour you begin to "work," business will liven up again in your salon.

Maria entered Nair's center as a medium on a Monday, and by the following day her customers had returned. She continued to practice as a medium in Nair's center. Whenever business became slow, Maria dispelled the evil fluids in her salon by exploding gunpowder, lighting a candle, and saying prayers. She confessed to having sometimes wondered whether these things actually helped, but since business frequently improved, she continued to perform the ritual.

The relationship between Maria and Nair was interesting because it seemed to be partly based on money. Nair perceived Maria as a somewhat vain person who was too interested in money. However, since Maria did small favors for her, such as going to Nair's home to do her hair free of charge at least once a week, Nair was willing to overlook Maria's faults. Maria frequently sent her friends to Nair for spiritual help and believed that Nair profited financially in this way. Maria thought that Nair should appreciate her efforts on her behalf more openly. This, however, was difficult for a proud cult leader like Nair. The covert conflict between these two women would erupt to the surface from time to time. The following accout illustrates the use of spirits in this relationship. The first part of the account demonstrates some jealousy between Maria and Cecília.

On December 29, 1966, the major part of the public session at Nair's center had been completed. Nair then asked Cecília to join her in a special dance that would ritually help the center. Although Cecília was not able to aid the center financially, she quietly went about giving a great deal of spiritual assistance to Nair in private sessions. Nair's selection of Cecília for this special dance was perhaps a way of showing her appreciation. Before they could complete the dance, Maria was spontaneously possessed by her *criança* (child) spirit,

Rozinha. My notes follow:

Suddenly, Rozinha springs forward, with a big smile, lifting her skirt slightly, skipping in and out of the dance Cecília and Nair are performing. The dancing stops, and Cecília walks to the wall. Rozinha skips to the railing separating the audience from the sacred area, smiles, says something to the audience, and then continues to skip about. Nair calls a halt to the drumming and tells Rozinha to leave. She smiles and replies, "No!" Nair then tries to humor Rozinha, telling her to leave again. "No! I want to stay here," says Rozinha. She continues her antics while Nair comes to the railing to talk with the audience, keeping her composure but appearing to be a little annoyed. She returns to talk with Rozinha, who is still in no mood to leave and begins to pout. Nair signals the drummers to begin again, and the mediums make their formal exit. Nair is still trying to talk Rozinha into leaving, motioning her to follow the others into the dressing rooms. Rozinha skips to the opposite wall, laughing continuously. The drumming stops. Nair sits on her chair and calls Rozinha to her. She comes, sits on the floor, and Nair talks with her, putting a blue taffeta cloth over the child spirit's head, now resting on Nair's lap. She tells Rozinha to leave and rips the cloth off her head, but it is Rozinha who leaps up, laughing silently, as Nair comes to the railing, smiling herself and talking with the audience. Nair returns to Rozinha, but appears not to know what to do. Rozinha skips a few steps, but now no one in the sacred area is paying any attention to her. Maria, possessed by Rozinha, bobs her head up and down slightly and throws herself across the room, ramming her back into the wall. As Maria appears to be stunned by Rozinha's violent departure, one of the drummers and an assistant go to help her. The drumming stops, and Maria is assisted through the exit.

That night, after the public session, the clique held a special session for their child spirits in Maria's home. Juvenir justified their private session outside the center by claiming it was necessary for the child spirits to come more frequently than Nair would permit. He explained that their mãe de santo did not care for the child spirits because, like live children, they tended to dirty the center. Maria later told me that Rozinha had felt sorry for Nair and had come to bring her happiness, but Nair had not appreciated it. She added that Rozinha, on leaving the center that night, had promised Nair to bring money.

A few weeks later, on January 26, 1967, Nair held a special ritual celebration for Oxóce (St. Sebastian). Umbandists believe that many of the Indian spirits belong to the Linha de Oxóce. That night Maria presented a bouquet of red roses to Pena Verde, who was possessing Nair. The Indian warmly embraced Maria. After the mediums completed the special ritual for Oxóce, which included an elaborate spread of Indian food, Nair called the *criança* spirits to come to earth. Rozinha was the first to arrive and the last to leave. As Rozinha prepared to go, she pushed her face in front of Nair's. Projecting a giant smile, her eyes wide open, Rozinha seemed almost to leer at Nair, who smiled tolerantly. After making two more rounds in the sacred area, Rozinha left Maria.

Several months later Nair presented two "folkloric demonstrations" of Candomblé at her center. The production was elaborate, and the costumes for certain *orixás* were quite expensive. Most of Nair's *filhos* danced for their particular *orixá*. Whenever possible, the *filhos* paid for their costumes, but in a few instances of poverty, Nair did. Several *filhos* were asked to dance for *orixás* other than their own. Nair wanted Maria to dance for Obaluaê and to pay for the expensive straw costume. The members of the center laughed behind Maria's back because she would obviously have preferred dancing for her own beautiful and somewhat vain *orixá*, Mamãe Oxum. Instead, Nair had asked Maria to cover her entire body, from head to toe, with the straw of Obaluaê. Maria, however, agreed to Nair's request without complaint.

When preparation was under way for the second presentation of the "folkloric demonstration," Nair asked Maria to dance also for Iansã. Payment for the second costume evidently was not clearly specified, and a conflict between Nair and Maria ensued one week after Nair's second public demonstration of Candomblé. At the next regular session at the center, Nair's *caboclo,* Pena Verde, burst into a diatribe in which he castigated half of Nair's *filhos*. He said that his horse was especially provoked with Maria, who had refused to pay for the *rabo* (a swordlike instrument) of Iansã. After the session Maria expressed her annoyance, and other members of the clique found reasons to dislike Nair.

The night following Pena Verde's outburst, Maria dreamed of Rozinha, who was feeling sorry for Nair. The child spirit had a vase on her head and was skipping out of the center toward Nair's house. At Nair's front door Rozinha poured out the contents of the vase—glittering gold dust. Maria awoke at this point in her dream. During our conversation about her dream, Maria spoke of her belief that Nair was jealous of the applause occasioned by her dance for Iansã. She explained that many of her friends who frequented her salon had been there and that it was only natural that they should want to offer loud applause for her dance. I did not note that Maria received more applause than any of the other dancers. Maria also observed that she had sold more tickets to the production than any other *filhos* had.

On the morning after her dream, Maria encountered Virgínia (see Chapter 5) on her way to the salon. As she began to relate her dream to Virgínia, Maria was possessed by Rozinha in the street. Her one leg was bent at the knee, as if hopping upward, and Virgínia had to assist Maria upstairs to her salon. Rozinha evidently cried while she was talking with Virgínia, for as the child spirit left her, Maria found herself in tears. Maria said that she felt like crying the remainder of that day while working in her salon.

At the following week's session in Nair's center, Pena Verde once again publicly complained that Maria had not paid for the *rabo*. This time, Maria spoke back to the *caboclo*, telling him that she would purchase the *rabo* if she were permitted to buy the dress of Iansã and to dance for Iansã in the future. Pena Verde replied that Maria could not dance for Iansã in the future because Iansã was not Maria's *orixd*. Maria then declared that she would not buy the *rabo*. Outside the center, Maria began to talk more about leaving Nair. If Nair's *guias* (beads) broke, she said, she would steal one of them because this would protect her against any evil magic Nair might send against her if she were to leave the center. For several weeks Maria did not participate as a medium, although she did sometimes attend as a member of the audience. She explained to Nair that she was not "feeling well" and could not actively take part. Eventually, however, she returned as a medium and once again began to introduce prospective mediums to Nair.

Another instance of the relation of money to Maria's spiritual life concerned Cecília's son-in-law. Maria had lent him a considerable sum of money sometime before my field work had begun. Cecília's daughter disliked Maria and claimed that her husband and Maria must have been on "intimate" terms for Maria to have lent him so much money. At the private session the clique held for a friend of theirs, Maria's *caboclo* Ubiratán called Juvenir aside for a private conversation. Juvenir later told me that Ubiratán had asked him to tell his horse (i.e., Maria) that she should not visit Cecília's home in the future. Juvenir added that this had been the second time Ubiratán had given him this particular message. He believed it was associated with the son-in-law's failure to repay the loan.

Later in the year, the clique held a private session for a man who operated a spaghetti factory. After the major spiritual business for the man had been concluded, various lesser spirits of the clique began to possess the participants, evidently for their own enjoyment as well as for the entertainment of the non-mediums. A *bahiano* (inhabitant of Bahia) spirit possessed Maria and began to converse with Cecília, who was not possessed at the time. The *bahiano* asked for a small sum of money Cecília owed Maria. Cecília requested more time, explaining that her husband was in the process of making payments on his taxi. She added that it would mean so much to her family when the taxi was paid for. In the end no money was returned. It is interesting to note that Maria was in the process of getting money together to make a down payment on an apartment at this time. Later, other members of the clique complained among themselves about the behavior of the *bahiano,* even to the point of questioning the authenticity of Maria's possession. They believed that a spirit would not go so far as to request money on behalf of his medium.

ANALYSIS

Once again we can observe that certain points of stress seem to precipitate trance states and spirit possession. What is unusual is that these states may occur somewhat spontaneously, in the sense of happening outside the ritual context of a public or private session. Trance and possession tended to occur, however, in the presence of other persons, thus raising the question of their spontaneity. A medium may want other persons to be present for two possible reasons: (1) an altered state of awareness could possibly be dangerous, and it is advisable to have someone look after the medium in a trance state; (2) it would be a rather wasted effort for a spirit to speak its medium's inner personal wishes in the absence of other persons, who can then gossip about the matter. This seemed to fit with the image I had of both João and Maria as exhibitionists—in the nicer sense of the term.

João's two experiences of a sort of "double possession," first by Margarida and then by Pai Joaquim, are noteworthy. João was apparently so unsure of his own power, or else had no interest whatever in such matters, that he could not personally control Margarida. It was his old and wise *prêto velho* who would either castigate João or see to it that an environmental element was changed. This happened when Pai Joaquim directed Juvenir to change into less stimulating clothing. I was not aware of any other mediums utilizing this type of double possession. It illustrates one more way that spirit-possession behavior can be adapted to particular individual needs.

Juvenir and Thales, the two young men in the clique whom I discuss in the next chapter, regarded João and Maria as "religious fanatics." They believed that these two children of Mamãe Oxum tended to mix religion and personal life too much. Thales even went so far as to suggest that Maria used her religion not only for financial benefit but also to seduce the men she wanted. Maria was certainly interested in advancing herself financially. However, I was not able to document the latter claim.

NOTES

1. I observed this event during the fifth week after arriving in Brazil. I still had difficulty in understanding Portuguese and was able to pick up only a small amount of what was occurring. Juvenir filled in some details two days later.

2. This incident occurred near the beginning of my year of field work. I would guess that Juvenir, a more educated person, was concerned with the image of Umbanda I would take away. He later became less concerned with concealing what he personally regarded as the more coarse aspects of Umbanda.

3. A certain amount of trembling is usual for the *prêtos velhos*, who died at an old age.

4. Maria, of course, had feigned possession as an actress in commercial Macumba productions.

8

The Clique: Two Young Men

Men do not actively participate as mediums to the extent that women do. In the centers I visited, men accounted for 25 to 40 percent of the total number of mediums. However, the male drummers and directors of centers increase the total number of men participating in a center to approximately 50 percent. The majority of men who do participate as mediums are in their twenties and early thirties. After this age span men tend either to drop out or to assume the role of director, looking after the financial affairs and other more mundane aspects of running an Umbanda center. The relative lack of male participation as mediums is perhaps linked to the strong Brazilian masculinity complex and to the fact that men were not supposed to be possessed by the *orixá* deities in traditional Candomblé rituals (Landes, 1940). A widespread notion in the larger Brazilian population that most males in many of the spiritualist religions are homosexuals continues to exist. However, I did not find this to be true. Umbandists themselves say that many male cult leaders are homosexuals. This claim remains undocumented in my field notes.

Juvenir and Thales, two clique members who were in their early twenties, gave several reasons for the predominance of female mediums. Both pointed out that men work at jobs with regular hours. They are unable to spend several nights per week at late Umbanda sessions and to get up feeling refreshed for their daily work. The same might be said for many female mediums; however, their domestic, secretarial or other duties are not as strenuous as the work men do. Both informants believed that the wearing of ritual costumes, the dancing, and the singing are activities that are more "feminine." Thales noted that women, being more confined to their homes than men, find in the sessions an acceptable opportunity for socializing outside their homes. Men, on the other hand, can come together for an evening of conversation at the local bars. Juvenir was especially fearful that the predominantly middle-class young men he worked with would learn that he was a *"macumbeiro"* (a term sometimes used in a derogatory manner by non-umbandists to refer to Umbanda mediums). Thales thought that homosexuals like

João tended to give outsiders the wrong impression about male mediums. For this reason he seemed to be hesitant about his association with spiritualism. Finally, it should be noted that Brazilians generally regard religion in any form as a feminine activity. Even the Catholic church is unable to recruit a sufficient number of priests. A large percentage of the priests in the country are missionaries from Europe and North America (Wagley, 1971: 217).

Neither of these two young men regarded spiritualism as a major part of their lives. This contrasted sharply with the attitudes and behavior of Nair, Cecília, Maria, and João. Juvenir and Thales differed also in that neither had developed his mediumship as much as the others had.

JUVENIR

Juvenir frequently commented that in recent years Cecília had come to be like a mother to him. His own mother had died when Juvenir, the youngest of nine children, was seventeen. When his Portuguese-born father died, Juvenir left his small hometown in the interior of São Paulo and went to live with his oldest sister in the city of São Paulo. She was 23 years older, and Juvenir felt that she tried to dominate him too much.

Back home, Juvenir had worked as a radio announcer for the small town's station. He had enjoyed this occupation since it brought him a certain amount of prestige and "fan mail." After moving to metropolitan São Paulo, he had tried to obtain a similar job, but was not able to compete successfully. For several years he worked as an accounting clerk in an import firm.

Since Juvenir and his oldest sister did not get along together, Renato took him into his apartment as a favor to Juvenir's sister. They had lived together for five years. The year before my arrival, Renato had helped Juvenir obtain his present job in the accounting department of a major Brazilian airline. Renato worked for the same firm as a university graduate in economics. Juvenir's sister, who was evidently a bit jealous of Renato's assistance, argued that he was a bad influence on Juvenir, for she believed that Juvenir now had less respect for her. It was a complicated triangle, one I never fully understood. However, it did seem possible that the bickering among these three might have been psychologically stressful for Juvenir between the ages of 20 and 25.

When Juvenir was about 20 years old, he had briefly participated as a medium in Umbanda sessions a male friend had held at home. However, his friend was also young and apparently lacked the maturity and sophistication necessary to help other mediums develop spiritually. Juvenir dropped out of this circle of friends, and he felt that for four or five years nothing had gone well for him. He was insecure and nervous for no apparent reason that he could understand.

Sometime during the year before I began field work, Cecília had held a private session for Juvenir's oldest sister. That evening a *criança* spirit possessed Juvenir. For the first time he felt secure about a spirit incorporating him. Cecília told him that he should develop his mediumship and that he might enjoy Nair's center. Juvenir accompanied Cecília the following week and found that he liked Nair "because she is educated." Juvenir himself was the most educated member of the clique. He had graduated from the *gindsia* and was thinking about attending a *colégio* at night. The following week a *caboclo* possessed Juvenir at Nair's center. He explained that at first his *caboclo* did not know what to do, but gradually learned to dance with the others. Juvenir's *caboclo* spoke only once during the year, and with great difficulty then. I believe this was related to the fact that Juvenir was usually in a deep trance and unconscious while possessed. In this state, he rolled up his eyes until only the whites were showing. The exception to very deep trance for Juvenir might have been possession by Joãozinho, his child spirit, when the extreme eye movement did not occur.

Joãozinho was Juvenir's favorite spirit. The boy spirit would roll on his back and pedal an imaginary bicycle in the air, ask for candy and cakes, and blow a spray of carbonated soft drink onto anyone who had the misfortune to be too close. Even when not possessed by Joãozinho, Juvenir would make childish faces at Renato to annoy him. Renato did not think it proper to "play around" with something serious like religion. Whenever he felt like it, Juvenir would pray to Joãozinho. His prayers were "like talking, but I don't hear any words from my child. I just know he is there listening to me. I ask for help in my work, in my studies, in my happiness."

A medium may know the personal history of his various spirits. The spirit itself may tell his own life history while possessing a person. Sometimes another spirit may be able to tell an individual about his spirits. The latter was the case for Joãozinho. At a private session Juvenir asked Maria's Rozinha if she knew anything about his *criança*. Rozinha provided the following account:

> Joãozinho was the son of a *fazendeiro* (large farm owner) in the interior of São Paulo. He was only three years old. A school teacher came to the area. The children in the community attended the school. The three-year-old Joãozinho also attended because he was the son of the wealthy *fazendeiro*. But he was too young to learn. So he ran around and created a great deal of disturbance in the classroom. The teacher didn't correct the child because of his father's status. But one day the teacher got fed up with Joãozinho and put him in the unfinished cellar under the schoolhouse. There a snake bit Joãozinho and killed him. And that is why you are afraid of snakes today.

Juvenir said that he tended to believe Rozinha's account because he was indeed quite fearful of snakes.

The *criança* spirits and the *exus* differ sharply in behavior. The former are playful, joyful, and innocent. The latter are base, crude, and sometimes violent. Juvenir loved his *criança* and made special offerings to him. On the other hand, he did not especially like *exu* spirits and made no offerings to his *exu*. Failing to fulfill the *obrigações* (obligations) to a particular spirit may bring personal difficulties and illnesses to the medium. For some time, Juvenir had been constantly and inexplicably bumping into furniture at work and at home, seriously bruising his arms and legs. He believed this resulted from failure to perform duties for his *exu*. It was highly probably that his *exu* would demand the *obrigação* to be made in a cemetery at midnight; as this was something he greatly feared, Juvenir avoided learning more about the specific details of this duty by restraining his *exu* from possessing him.

However, his personal control over the situation weakened considerably throughout the year. At *exu* sessions it is customary to explode small amounts of gunpowder as a means of driving away evil fluids. When this occurred in the clique's private sessions, Juvenir's *exu* would attempt to possess him, jerking his head up and back, and drawing him backward from the waist until his face became terribly contorted with pain. His knees would bend, causing his body to be drawn downward until his back was only a few inches from the floor. At the same time his hands would stiffen into the hooklike forms of an *exu*. The shock was only momentary, and his rigid body would immediately collapse on the floor. Juvenir would get up on his feet, obviously somewhat stunned and very sore. He reported neck and back aches on the days following these sessions. Members of the clique and their spirits continued to remind Juvenir that the bruises resulting from apparently unexplained bumping into furniture were a sign from his *exu* that an *obrigação* should be offered. They added that neck and back pains resulting from attempted possession by his *exu* would also continue.

Sometime later in the year possession did occur at a private session. At that session, Cecília was possessed by the *exu* Mulambo, an alcoholic derelict. Mulambo was sitting on the floor, where he had made quite a mess with the seven cooked fish used and partially eaten earlier during this *exu* session. Mulambo had asked for a small piece of white cloth and had torn it into small strips. My field notes follow:

Mulambo instructs us to roll up the small pieces of white cloth into balls. He tells us to make circles on the floor with the cloth balls, making our wishes. Then we are to put the balls into the trash—fish bones, fish, intestines, and cigar butts and ashes—accumulating in front of Mulambo. The exu then pours rum over the trash, mashing it together, kneading it. He pours nearly half a cup of rum over his concoction. Mulambo next asks for *pólvera* (gunpowder) and sprinkles five times the normal amount over the mixture in front of him. Juvenir watches the proceedings with glazed eyes, as if terrified. He occasionally stands up; balances himself with one foot flat on the floor and the other foot loose so that the toes are touching the floor; loses his balance temporarily; and supports himself on the wall. This occurs a number of times. He does not interact with the others as he usually does. I begin to wonder if he might not be possessed by an exu fairly soon. His strange behavior is noted by Mulambo, who says nothing.

Mulambo resumes kneading the magical concoction and simultaneously talks with Roberto, for whom the session is being held. Then the exu turns to another man Cecília had invited to the session and asks him to write down on a piece of paper all the names of people he wishes to influence in his business. Mulambo looks at the names, tears the paper into strips, and mashes the strips into the mixture. He pours additional gunpowder on top of it. Juvenir continues to watch with glazed eyes.

Mulambo ignites his magical concoction with sparks from his cigar. An explosion ensues, and João, sitting beside Mulambo, begins to laugh hysterically in a high-pitched voice as Margarida possesses him. Juvenir falls backward to the floor, but he is not possessed. Mulambo calls Juvenir to sit beside him. Juvenir joins the exu on the floor and sits on his own feet. Mulambo holds Juvenir's right hand, quivering slightly. Juvenir leans backward, groaning, but regains his balance. Mulambo takes Juvenir's hand again and after about fifteen seconds succeeds in inducing an exu into Juvenir. Juvenir leans back again, groaning, screaming, but the exu is not entirely incorporated into him. Suddenly Juvenir begins turning around and around in his seated position. The turning is the general pattern Juvenir uses to induce trance and possession by his other spirit.

Juvenir's hands begin to assume the hooklike appearance of an exu. Others, not possessed, help him to his feet. His exu speaks a round of curse words. The other spirits in the room try to get Juvenir's exu to tell his name, but he refuses. He says that his horse is a son-of-a-bitch who did not want to be possessed by him. He adds that his horse does not want to make the necessary *obrigações* and that the people in the room must tell his horse to make the appropriate offerings. When the exu leaves, Juvenir has some difficulty coming out of trance. Juvenir moves into the next room during the final stages of trance termination. He then rushes to the bathroom, where he vomits. He returns to sit in a chair. Mulambo calls Juvenir to him and is very gentle. Juvenir seems more or less resigned to his exu for the time being.

I am not aware that the *obrigação* was made during the year of my field work. This was the last *exu* session the clique held while I was in São Paulo.

THALES

Thales had recently been discharged from the army when I first met him on May 7, 1967. On that day he accompanied the clique on a Sunday outing to Maria's small farm in the country. There the mediums went into the forest to be possessed by their *caboclo* spirits and to leave small offerings for them.

Thales differed somewhat from the others in his general outlook on life and in his everyday behavior. Perhaps this was idiosyncratic, or it may have been related to his background in southern Brazil. Thales had been born and reared in the southernmost state of Rio Grande do Sul. The southern states are more heavily populated by persons of northern European descent, especially German. Thales had some Danish-born ancesters among his grandparents and a northern European surname. He had completed four years of primary school, but regarded himself as a self-taught person. He read widely and could converse to some extent on such esoteric subjects as the Neanderthal man.

Thales did not like to work at one job for more than six months. He preferred to learn what he could at one job and then move on to another one where he could learn something new and different. On first coming to São Paulo, Thales had worked as an electrician. After his discharge from the army he had been employed as a servant in a very wealthy home. Although his salary was nearly equal to that of Juvenir and he had no expenses for room and board, his position was regarded as being somewhat lower in status than that of Juvenir. Thales, however, saw the financial advantage to his job and, according to Cecília, was saving money to open a small shop specializing in men's clothing. Whenever Thales became restless he talked about leaving São Paulo for the Brazilian frontier of Matto Grosso or for the United States, where he could get employment as a servant for a wealthy family. Since he was 21 years old, the specter of the U.S. military draft and Vietnam restrained the latter ambition.

After being introduced by Maria, Thales had participated as a medium in Nair's center before serving his year in the army. Nair had held a special ritual to separate Thales and his spirit to prevent possession during his military service. After returning, Thales no longer wished to participate as a medium. However, during the six and half months I observed him, he was possessed twelve times.

The first possession occurred at a private session one and a half months after I met Thales. Later he began to participate at Nair's center on an irregular basis. His attendance seemed to be regularly tied to the lack of success he had in courting women. As Cecília observed, "When Thales has a girlfriend, he doesn't go to the center. When he doesn't have a woman, he goes." Thales announced that he was ready to get married and settle down, but his difficulties in finding an acceptable (and accepting) woman may have put him under stress. At one point when he was having difficulty with a woman, he did not go to the center, but reportedly was observed to have been drunk.

Thales was under stress in another way. A spirit would possess him during *caboclo* sessions and would behave more or less as if it were a *caboclo*. However, in ten out of twelve possessions, the clique agreed that Thales was possessed by an *exu* who pretended to be a *caboclo*. They pointed out that the spirit did not possess Thales properly. Usually, a *caboclo* is supposed to possess a medium with a few head and chest jerks while the medium is in an upright position. When his spirit possessed him, Thales would make the usual head and chest movements. Then he would bend forward from the waist, with his head and arms dangling downward in front of his legs for a few seconds. With a loud shout or sigh he would straighten himself into an upright position. Sometimes another person would have to help him move into the upright position. During possession his facial expression differed from the forceful countenance of other *caboclos*. His facial muscles would seem to relax, and he would have a small smile. His eyelids would droop slightly, giving him a somewhat dreamy appearance. His spirit never projected the image of fierce aloofness that some *caboclos* do.

In private sessions, Thales never had any difficulty in terminating a trance. However, when he was in Nair's center, his spirit frequently left in a violent manner, sometimes bruising him. Nair and her spirits told Thales to make a special *obrigação* for his *exu*, but he did not wish to comply. One night Nair held a special session during which her *filhos* were possessed first by an *orixá* and then a child spirit. Thales supposedly was possessed by Iemanjá and then by a *criança*. My notes follow:

> Pena Verde calls the *crianças* together to tell them that it is time to leave. In an unorganized fashion they prostrate themselves at the appropriate places in the sacred area. Thale's *criança* prostrates himself in the center of the sacred area, striking his forehead very hard on the floor three times. (This should be done lightly.) His face begins to lose the expression of a child; a grimace replaces it. As he begins to stand up, his spirit forces him backward. He is caught by two large male assistants, who firmly grasp his upper arms. His head is thrown backward and his body is arched. His eyes are tightly squeezed shut. Pena Verde looks sharply at what is happening. As Thales is terminating possession, Pena Verde shouts, "This one is suspended for four weeks!"

After the session Thales said that the other mediums told him of his suspension. He felt it wrong for Nair to do this since he believed the disruption to have been the spirit's fault, not his own. He admitted that it had been an *exu* pretending to be Iemanjá and the *criança*. Thales said that the *exu* had something to tell Nair. According to Thales, since Nair did not want to hear what the *exu* had to say, the spirit struck his head on the floor with such severity. He was not willing to explain the conflict. Thales added that when his body was arched backward, his *exu* made him feel as if his head and chest would be thrown off the lower part of his body. The session just described occurred toward the end of my year of field work. This was the first time Thales openly admitted that an *exu* was possessing him.

The members of the clique reacted to Thales and his spiritual difficulties in various ways. Cecília was always patient and understanding. Maria and João frequently teased Thales and told him that his "*caboclo*" was really an *exu*. João greatly annoyed Thales by suggesting that it was a *pombagira* (female *exu*). Publicly, Juvenir remained aloof, but he and his apartment mate, Renato, discussed Thale's behavior behind his back. They argued that Thales tended to exaggerate his masculinity. The two men at one point said that Thale's grossly masculine behavior was being influenced by an *exu*. At the end of my year of field work, Juvenir suggested that Thales's supermasculine behavior might be a psychological compensation for impotence.

Cecília told me that before going into the army, Thales had liked a mulatto girl who at the time was a *filha* of Nair's. He had paid for various medical expenses when she was sick. Cecília went no further. Juvenir, however, told me the rest of the story which Cecília had once related to him. The girl had had an argument with Nair and had left the center. Nair's *caboclo*, Pena Verde, had told Thales in a public session that he should not see the girl again. Thales had responded that he would look after his own affairs and had told Pena Verde not to meddle. Sometimes later, Thales supposedly had told Cecília that he was impotent. Since he had stopped seeing the girl he believed that she had paid an *exu* to bring him this particular misfortune.

Juvenir was convinced that Thales was impotent and alleged that an *exu* cannot bring impotence. He argued, instead, that Thales's problems were more "psychological" than spiritual in origin. Whether Thales would agree with this third-hand version of his spiritual difficulties is seriously open to question. I was unable to obtain a validation of these stories from either Thales or Cecília. The data are nevertheless useful because they illustrate the nature of some interpersonal relations within the clique.

ANALYSIS

Each medium tends to have his or her favorite spirit. For Juvenir, it was the child spirit Joãozinho. I am not aware that anyone has ever attempted to analyze this phenomenon. Only a tentative suggestion is offered here. The favorite spirit seems to be the one that the medium feels the most comfortable with and can most openly and easily express his needs. Since Juvenir has been the "baby" of his large family, it is tempting to speculate that Joãozinho enabled him to act out this role even as a grown man.

Altered states of awareness appear in many forms. In this chapter we find that Thales did not always have successful experiences with his girlfriends and was therefore experiencing stress. At these times he would attend spirit sessions. However, altered states of awareness are not limited to possession-trance behavior. It is interesting to note that on one occasion Thales utilized the alternative of alcoholic trance to achieve a somewhat similar end.

9

Trance and Spirit Possession at the Individual Level

Altered states of consciousness (ASC) represent complex and not very well understood forms of behavior. To account for a variety of phenomena that may be associated with them, definitions of ASC tend to be somewhat general. Ludwig (1966: 225) considers them to be

> ... any mental state(s), induced by various physiological, psychological, or pharmacological maneuvers or agents, which can be recognized subjectively by the individual himself (or by an objective observer of the individual) as representing a sufficient deviation in subjective experience or psychological functioning from certain general norms for that individual during alert, waking consciousness. This sufficient deviation may be represented by a greater preoccupation than usual with internal sensations or mental processes, changes in the formal characteristics of thought, and impairment of reality testing to various degrees.

In the most general sense of the term, all human beings experience ASC when they are asleep or when they are daydreaming. Some other examples are meditational states, ecstatic trance, hypnotic phenomena, biochemically induced states like those produced by alcohol or hallucinogenic drugs, and states during which glossolalia behavior is observed. Not only are biological ASC varied, but their cultural interpretations and uses are quite diverse. Beliefs about ASC etiology range from naturalistic explanations (e.g., hypnosis, fevers, or biochemical agents) to supernatural folk theories, such as soul loss, shaman's voyage, or spirit possession (Bourguignon, 1968b: 5). Although the cultural interpretation of ASC as spirit possession or the nearby presence of spirits is uniform throughout this particular study of Umbanda, the ASC and the psychobiological and sociopsychological factors related to ASC are varied and rather complicated. These aspects of ASC in Umbanda will be discussed in this chapter in terms of (1) cultural structuring of trance and spirit possession into the individual, (2) trance behavior, (3) pretrance behavior, (4) posttrance behavior, (5) spirit possession in interpersonal relations, and (6) extended participation in Umbanda.

CULTURAL STRUCTURING OF TRANCE AND SPIRIT POSSESSION INTO THE INDIVIDUAL

Possession behavior, like any other form of cultural behavior, is learned. I observed Cecília's grandchildren and their young friends imitating in play the back and forth jerking of the head and chest that is used for inducing and terminating spirit possession. Having visited Umbanda centers on occasion with Cecília, they were imitating the adult behavior they had observed for their own amusement. Their playacting was not discouraged and provided entertainment for their elders. Neither adults nor children considered this behavior to be true spirit possession, for it lacked the usual spiritual disorders that sometimes accompany possession. Moreover, there was no intent of being possessed for the purpose of helping others solve personal problems. Besides learning the stereotyped motor patterns, the children had learned from their family the cultural concept of spirits that possess.

Children do not usually participate in Umbanda centers in any significant way. There are a few exceptions, such as the two sons of Virgínia (see Chapter 5), but they made no attempt to act as spirit mediums and only danced and sang with the other mediums. There was one child medium, about twelve years old, in Badia's Umbanda center. This girl was possessed by spirits that held consultations with clients; however, I was never aware that her spirits dealt with especially serious problems. Usually an individual does not begin to find the concept of spirits meaningful to his personal life until reaching adulthood when family problems and employment difficulties begin to arise.

An individual who decides to develop his mediumship is given special training. Some Umbanda centers hold regular training sessions once a week. This meeting is in addition to the two regularly scheduled public sessions held each week. Those Umbanda centers that lean toward Kardecismo emphasize dome doctrinal learning in addition to the more usual training for trance and possession. Some cult leaders do not hold a special closed session for novices; instead, the training is given during each regular public session. Both Nair and Badia followed the latter practice.

Various techniques are utilized to help a person learn how to dissociate himself from his surroundings. Some of the techniques I observed were similar to those used in hypnosis, such as having the person focus his attention on a lighted candle. Another technique involved turning the person around about five times in front of a cult leader, who then induced trance by passing his hand across the face of the novice and at the same time snapping the fingers. Trance was induced in yet another way when a cult leader held the two hands of a novice, relaxing him, rocking him back and forth on his heels. This technique produced a feeling of weightlessness, and the rocking motion initiated a general motor pattern that easily led into the more specific head and chest jerks that signaled possession by a spirit.

The most frequently used means of inducing ASC in a novice that I saw was having the person turn himself around dozens of times until he became dizzy and lost some mental contact with his environment. Since the individual could easily fall, other mediums gathered in a circle about him to prevent any serious accident. Having gone through this sort of activity over a period of several weeks, the novice usually began to pivot on one foot, which prevented falling; when he stopped turning, he put his body weight on one foot and balanced his body with the opposite foot and leg. The pivot maneuver and the body-balancing technique were never explained to a novice. They seemed to be unconsciously learned by the individual himself. Finally, the head and chest jerks were added.

Once a novice was experiencing an ASC, the cult leader often told or showed the "spirit" how it should behave. If *prêto velho* spirits were in order for a session, the cult leader would push the novice forward so that his body was bent over and head was hung low. Just the opposite effect was desired for a *caboclo* spirit, whose display of strength is achieved through an erect and virile stance. I observed some problems Nair was having one evening when a rather large middle-aged man was bent over in the manner of a *prêto velho*. Since *caboclos* were to be present, Nair asked two male assistants to pull the man's body up, but each time they took their hands away, he again fell into the slumping position. She finally gave up and so did the man. Thereafter he came to the sessions as a client rather than a medium. In summary, the cultural structuring of ASC and spirit possession into the personality of an individual is an imitative process as well as a process of directed learning.

TRANCE BEHAVIOR

The terms "trance" and "altered state of consciousness" are sometimes misunderstood by those who think of these types of behavior as being unconscious and/or uncontrolled activity. Both unconsciousness and a lack of behavioral control were certainly present in some, but not in the majority, of ASC that I observed. We may perhaps better understand ASC by considering the categories used by Umbandists to describe the ASC of spirit mediums.

They recognize unconscious, semiconscious, and conscious mediums. Consciousness in this instance refers to the ability to later remember events that occurred during the ASC.

Most Umbandists say that they prefer to be unconscious since it enables them to be certain that it is a spirit that is really speaking, and not they themselves. This is especially confusing for novices, and Cecília used to assure younger mediums that they would eventually learn to separate what a spirit would say from what the medium himself would normally talk about. By way of contrast, Kardecismo mediums value consciousness during spirit possession (Camargo, 1961: 52). This seems to be tied in with their emphasis on the intellectual abilities of their spirits. My informants found it difficult to explain the semiconscious type of ASC. They could describe it only in terms of passing back and forth between consciousness and unconsciousness.

Although Umbandists expressed preference for unconscious ASC, they estimated that only 15 to 35 percent of their mediums experienced it. My own estimate was considerably lower, or about 5 percent under the following criteria: eyes that were glazed for two or three hours; profuse perspiring for that length of time, even when not physically active; salivating more than normal, but no frothing; some difficulty with motor coordination (i.e., jerky movements some difficulty with speech, and, occasionally, the lack of ability to correctly judge distance when putting a glass on a table or reaching for a cigar); and the need to be supported for about 30 seconds after coming out of the trance. Only Juvenir displayed the upward eye movement with only the whites of the eyes showing during deep trance; however, I do not regard this as entirely idiosyncratic since the same eye pattern occurs in Haitian Voodoo, as illustrated in Lewis's *Ecstatic Religions* (1971, Plate 4a).

In contrast, conscious mediums did not exhibit, or did so to a much lesser extent, the external physiological changes noted for unconscious mediums. Some persons who were conscious reported changes in body image. They said that their body felt larger and their muscles more powerful when possessed by a *caboclo* spirit. A child spirit made them feel lighter and smaller, and a few mediums claimed that the lightness in weight enabled them to spring upward like a child. One conscious medium reported that when her spirits possessed her, people and objects appeared to be small and far away. Facial expressions, gestures, and voices, were modified in all mediums. Nearly all mediums displayed glazed eyes. However, approximately 20 minutes to an hour after spirit possession had occurred, facial expressions, voices, eyes, and gestures returned to a more normal state in most conscious mediums, although they were said to be possessed over a longer period of two or three hours.

Whether an ASC is present in the conscious medium whose behavior soon returns to normal is debatable. The behavior is apparently something like that of an actor who loses awareness of his own self in playing a role. It represents more automatic behavior that requires less forethought or evaluation than is usual. To a certain degree these two functions are normally present in ordinary social interaction. Lacking forethought and evaluation, a person would act out entirely what he immediately felt, rather than basing his next action on prior experiences. The return to a more normal state in most conscious Umbanda mediums seemed to occur while their spirits were holding consultations with clients. A good consultation requires forethought and evaluation, and cannot be based entirely on what the medium immediately feels. It is therefore possible that the conscious medium may be experiencing two general stages of behavior. The first stage is a period of 20 minutes to an hour during which attention is narrowed as the medium focuses on the highly stereotyped spirit role he is playing; this stage may extend into the first part of the consultation period. The second stage is a longer period of extended consultations during which the medium frequently seems more like himself than like his possessing spirit; this stage tends to require evaluative processes to be operative. It is also possible that during the first stage, the past and future are melded to some degree into the narrowed attention of the present. Unfortunately, I was not aware of this possibility at the time I examined Umbanda and therefore did not question my informants about this matter. In a fascinating article contributed by an anonymous author[1] in Tart's *Altered States of Consciousness*, a comparison is made of various ASC: emotion-filled psychotherapy sessions, meditation, daydreaming, ecstasy, anger, lovemaking, and certain kinds of states produced by marihuana. All share the common denominator of an absence, or alteration, of time experienced (Anonymous, 1972: 349):

> The experiences and states I have described are not states which are socially conscious; they are not internally subordinated to social time or schedules. Anger cannot be paced with conscious control, nor can ecstasy. Feelings, fantasies, dreams, and awareness do not incorporate the sense of time which is built up by and maintained in the consciousness.[2] Thus when one is experiencing such content there is no marking of the passage of time, and to the extent this material is the content of awareness, the less social time is noted. Immediate experience is always timeless; time is perceived in relation to the uses of experience in controlling or predicting the future or interpreting the past, the present being perceived in relation to past or future. This is one of the major functions of consciousness. In a normal conscious state when the internal or external input is to be changed or manipulated the time required is automatically projected, based on past experience. This imposes the knowledge of time on the consciousness.

In view of these observations on other types of ASC that are conscious in the sense of being remembered, it seems to me that the actor who loses himself in a rôle, as well as the Umbanda medium in the first stage and also playing a role, is experiencing a light trance, or ASC. The conscious medium, then, is one who is able to move back and forth between normal consciousness in which evaluative processes are present and a conscious ASC in which attention is narrowed and evaluative activity may be diminished.

PRETRANCE BEHAVIOR

The kinds of behavior that precede ASC in Umbanda mediums can perhaps be put into two general categories, according to whether the ASC was purposefully induced or whether it occurred spontaneously (i.e., without the intention and deliberate preparation to enter a trance state). Purposefully induced trances nearly always take place within the ritual context of a public or a private session. They are the most frequently utilized form of ASC. Lewis (1971: 55) refers to such states as "controlled" or "solicited" possession.

Preparation for a public Umbanda session includes a fairly common, but not universal, practice of avoiding heavy meals and alcohol on the day of the session. Field (1960: 59), in her discussion of ASC among rural Ghanaians, places a great deal of emphasis on fasting as a cause of hypoglycemia, which aids the induction of dissociative states. Since Umbanda mediums rarely totally abstain from food, it is not likely that hypoglycemia is a significant factor in inducing trance. A very limited degree of hypoglycemia, however, may be present in some individuals and should not be ruled out all together.

The induction of trance is usually accompanied by polyrhythmic drumming, singing, hand clapping, and sometimes by the ringing of a bell. In most centers, the mediums are dancing and spinning up to the point of the head and chest jerks that signal possession by a spirit. Mediums report that they concentrate on receiving their spirit, sometimes asking it to come. In those Umbanda centers that are closer to Kardecismo, as well as in most private Umbanda sessions, the mediums tend to rely more on quietly concentrating on the arrival of their spirit. There is no drumming; the hand clapping, singing, and dancing are less enthusiastic, if not entirely absent.

In observing several hundred mediums during the year of field work, I saw only one case of hyperventilation being used to induce trance. This woman breathed very deeply for a few minutes while bending her body from the waist at an angle of about 60 degrees to the floor. No hallucinogenic drugs of any sort were used by Umbandists to induce trance.

Trances that occur spontaneously are far less frequent than the purposefully induced ones. As I explained in Chapter 7, the term "spontaneous" may be questioned, since possession does not usually occur when the medium is alone. The spontaneous ASC does indeed serve a purpose, but one of an unconscious nature. The medium does not make advanced plans to switch over to an ASC. The trance state just "happens." Spontaneous trance is almost always preceded by psychological stress of one sort of another. Cecília, under the stress of two of her children dying, and a husband with a mistress, experienced an ASC during which she saw the image of a cowboy spirit in her kitchen. A few days later, when she was feeling bad, she hurried over to the house of her cult leader. When the *mãe de santo* refused to see her immediately, Cecília was probably further frustrated and entered a spontaneous ASC, thus making it difficult for the *mãe* to leave her.

João, required to work harder and without pay in the *pensão* kitchen, went into spontaneous ASC three times in one evening. His anxiety level was probably raised by the prospect of losing his job and having to look for another one, while the triggering device was his inability to help pay for the restaurant tab and taxi fare. The fact that Margarida, instead of another spirit, possessed him was possibly due to the nature of the earlier conversation about sex, as well as to the custom of women not normally paying bills. A third ASC occurred that same evening when João was thrown under his bed by his *prêto velho*, Pai Joaquim. These three examples of ASC should be viewed in the general context of another type of ASC, namely, the alcoholic state João was in that evening. Since alcohol is not usually an important part of the Umbanda setting for ASC, one might be tempted to regard these three ASC as simply inebriated behavior. Whatever the case may be, alcohol was not involved sometime later in the year when a double possession by Margarida and Pai Joaquim again occurred in Juvenir's apartment. I am not aware that João was at that time under any particular stress other than the probable psychological conflict stemming from his homosexual nature.

In Maria's case, the uncalled for appearance of her child spirit, Rozinha, at Nair's center was apparently the result of jealousy over Cecília's special dance for the cult leader. Frustrations of not being appreciated by Nair seemed also to be behind the second spontaneous possession by Rozinha that occurred as Maria went into her beauty salon one day. Maria believed that by bringing clients to Nair and by selling many tickets to Nair's Candomblé productions she had helped her cult leader financially. She was probably disappointed when Nair did not specially recognize her achievements, and Rozinha was an expression of this feeling.

A special variant of the spontaneous ASC resulting from stresses of an emotional nature can be seen in Cecília's first and second experiences with Pena Branca, who was not her regular *caboclo* spirit. Cecília, a normally conscious medium who always emphasized that mediums can exercise a certain degree of control over spirits, spontaneously shifted from a conscious into an unconscious possession trance. During the unconscious state, Pena Branca said that he would cut each year of her life in half if she did not become a cult leader with him as her chief spirit. In this instance, special and elevated familial and financial pressures had preceded the qualitative change in ASC. In addition, the spirit was saying some rather violent and unacceptable things about her, and Cecília may have moved into the unconscious state to avoid hearing this.

Another variant of spontaneous ASC twice reported to me was that of fugue states in two men. In these cases, anger had preceded the ASC. One of the men had broken dishes and furniture in his home before running away for several days. When he finally returned home, he could not remember where he had been or what he had done. He came to Nair's center for help, but during the first several sessions that he attended, his possessing spirit rolled on the floor in a fetal position. At first, the disturbed spirit was fearful of being touched by Nair, thrashing about on the floor and striking and kicking anyone who came near. Considering his body movements, some of the mediums believed that an *exu* was possessing him. Nair, however, worked with the spirit on the assumption that it was a *caboclo* who needed to be enlightened as to proper behavior. After several weeks, the man's spirit was dancing along with the other spirits in a normal fashion.

The common denominator in all of these cases of spontaneous possession trance is psychological conflict, frustration, and anger. Depression may also be present, but this is regarded by many psychologists as anger turned inward on the self. Similar types of ASC precipitated by psychological stress have been reported by Paul (1967) for Guatemala and by Freed and Freed (1964) for India. It seems to me that this type of trance state may be related to what Festinger calls cognitive dissonance, or conflict, at the cerebral level. According to Festinger (1957: 18), cognitive dissonance acts in the same way as a state of drive or need or tension. Just as the presence of hunger will lead to activity to reduce the hunger, so the presence of cognitive dissonance leads to action to lessen it. As psychological stress and dissonance occur, the symptoms of depression, agression, or possibly the conscious suppression of aggression will appear. As already noted in this chapter, strong emotional states, such as aggression, may be regarded as an ASC in that the individual tends to lose the cognitive dimension of time. Since anger is not always an appropriate or culturally acceptable form of behavior, the individual then shifts into a trance state interpreted as possession. The strong feelings can then be acted out in a socially accepted spirit role, and the cognitive conflict is reduced.

POSTTRANCE BEHAVIOR

Umbanda mediums terminate their trances when the cult leader announces that it is time for the spirits to return to their heavenly dwelling places. In some centers, an assistant may quietly go around to the mediums, telling their spirits that it is time to leave. A special song may be sung. Some spinning by the mediums may occur, followed by the head and chest jerks indicating that the spirits have left. The medium frequently drops back into the arms of someone waiting to break the fall. In a private session, one of the spirits may suggest that it is time to leave, and in these sessions less spinning accompanies the termination of trance. Some mediums clutch their abdomen, and a few may hold their hands over their eyes as if avoiding bright light.

Some difficulty may occassionally be encountered in coming out of trance. In Chapter 5, I described the instance of Nair, who had some difficulty in returning to normal after her *caboclo* publicly announced that Nair no longer had sexual relations with her husband. In Chapter 6, I wrote about a private session in which Cecília's *caboclo* had said that he was going to cut her life in half if she did not become a cult leader. The *caboclo* sent a glass of beer crashing to the floor, and Cecília went into a state resembling catatonia for several minutes. Both of these women were normally conscious mediums. It would seem that in these instances, their spirits had said something that was not entirely acceptable to them. Perhaps for this reason, unconsciousness and subsequent difficulty in terminating trance occurred.

Mediums reported feeling very relaxed after possession trance. Personal tensions they may have had before trance were no longer present. Many mediums said that they were hungry, and went home or elsewhere to eat after a session.

SPIRIT POSSESSION IN INTERPERSONAL RELATIONS

Strictly speaking, the term "interpersonal" refers to interaction between two or more individuals. In this discussion of Umbanda, however, I use the term to describe the activity between a spirit and a person. Two major types of interpersonal relations between spirits and people seem to emerge from my material on Umbanda. The first has to do with the relation between a spirit and a client who comes to public or private sessions for supernatural aid. The second is the relation between a spirit and an individual who is not acting in the role of client.

The first type, or the spirit–client relation, within the context of a spirit session depends on how psychologically stable the client appears to be. The term "psychologically stable" is mine. As noted in Chapter 4, Umbandists talk instead about "spiritual disorders" that must be controlled by supernatural means. They also are aware of psychological difficulties, but they confine the use of this term to behavior that an individual can learn to control without supernatural aid. The Umbandist definition of "spiritual," as opposed to "psychological," seems to depend on personal inclination as well as ability to establish a supernatural cause and to perform a supernatural cure.

If the client's behavior appears to be reasonably functional, the spirit makes suggestions that will help to solve the problem. For example, a spirit may tell a client how to manage a difficult spouse or make suggestions on handling his or her children. Problems related to employment, business, and money in general are also prominent in spirit consultations. Not infrequently, headaches, nervousness, and feelings of depression accompany such difficulties. During the consultation the spirit may or may not single out a specific supernatural cause for a problem, but in all cases it will offer some advice. The spirit blows smoke from his cigar or pipe to purify and soothe the client as well as passes the medium's hands over the body of the client to remove bad fluids. He may turn the client around several times to help reduce bad fluids. The spirit may also instruct the person to light a candle and pray to a specific *orixá* for guidance, or to fill a glass full with water to draw bad spiritual fluids away from the client's environment.

In a very limited number of cases, a client may appear to be unstable and not functioning very well at all in situations involving his family or employment. He may have already experienced an altered state of consciousness before coming to the Umbanda center, he may have been induced into a trance by obeying the medium's command to turn around many times, or he may have experienced a spontaneous trance while in the audience at the center. Frequently, such spontaneous trances are uncontrolled because the client has not yet developed his mediumship. The spirit has not yet learned how it should behave. A case discussed in the preceding section, where a man had experienced a fugue state before coming to Nair's center for help, illustrates uncontrolled behavior of brief duration in the center. Usually, in such cases, one of the six causes of spiritual disorders is singled out, and the cult leader suggests that the client develop his mediumship.

Usually, a person who is experiencing spiritual difficulties—whether of the sort that will eventually lead him in the direction of becoming a medium or of the sort that brings him to Umbanda sessions simply to obtain spiritual advice—will also suffer from headaches, nervousness, tension, and a variety of other illnesses. To a large extent, these are psychosomatic in origin, or, as Umbandists put it, they represent "spiritual illnesses." According to Alexander (1950), when the sympathetic nervous system is blocked, such illnesses as migraine, hypertension, hyperthyroidism, cardiac neuroses, arthritis, vasodepressor syncope, and possibly diabetes may occur. When the parasympathetic nervous system is blocked, peptic ulcers, constipation, diarrhea, colitis, fatigue states, and asthma may appear. Since the block is psychological in origin, personal problems and illnesses occur together as part of the same stress syndrome. The Umbanda belief system links personal problems and illnesses to a common etiology—spiritual causes. Consequently, the spirits treat the two problems together, and for this reason they are fairly successful in their therapy.

The second major type of interpersonal relation that I found in Umbanda was that occurring between a spirit and an individual who was not in the role of client. This kind of relation usually, but not always, happened outside the context of a public session. In this type of situation, the medium appeared to use his spirit to represent his normally hidden, or inner, desires *vis-à-vis* other individuals.

A number of cases from my data illustrate this point. For example, Nair's spirits explained that they had caused her husband to leave her so that Nair might develop her mediumship in peace. João's Margarida possessed him in a taxi when he was unable to afford the fare. Later in the year, João's *prêto velho*, Pai Joaquim, told Juvenir to exchange his shorts for longer pants. Juvenir's child spirit would stick out his tongue and make childish faces at Renato, who had frequently admonished Juvenir on the proper behavior for a 25-year-old man. Maria's child spirit, Rozinha, once leered into Nair's face while Nair tolerantly watched. Nair's *caboclo*, Pena Verde, told Maria to pay for the *rabo* of the *orixá*, Iansã. At a private session, I observed Maria's *bahiano* spirit demanding that Cecília repay a small loan. All of these examples illustrate the interaction of a medium and his spirits with persons other than clients. The cases indicate that spirits may be used by the mediums as alternate roles in their personal lives (Bourguignon, 1965: 57).

The spirit roles are normally accepted as valid by the medium's friends and family. However, in five instances I found people questioning their validity. Two cases involved a spirit directly asking for money on behalf of his medium. In the third instance, Nair's *caboclo* announced to the entire center that his medium no longer had sexual relations with her husband. In the fourth case, Nair's spirit asked Ildicir to turn the deed of the center over to Nair, and Ildicir put the *caboclo* to the test described in Chapter 5. Somehow, these four forms of behavior were not socially acceptable, even for spirits. Finally, in the fifth case, João pinched a medium in a public session to find out whether she was possessed. The medium responded, and João, the "tester," decided that she was faking possession!

EXTENDED PARTICIPATION IN UMBANDA

Although large numbers of people come to Umbanda sessions seeking spiritual aid, comparatively few of them actually become mediums. Moreover, not all of those who do develop their mediumship to some extent continue to practice as spirit mediums over an extended period of time. Certain negative sanctions are present and reinforce an individual's decision not to participate as an Umbanda medium. For one thing, men do not participate quite as much as women because of the stigma of homosexuality that is sometimes attached to male mediums. Men have other outlets for built-up tension, such as drinking and conversing in bars. Some of the negative sanctions described by Mischel and Mischel (1958: 258) for Trinidad are also present to some degree in Brazil. First, Umbanda is regarded as more "African" than Kardecismo. In the minds of some Brazilians, (e.g., Nair's husband) this puts Umbanda into a lower intellectual category than Kardecismo. Second, an aversion to complete abandonment and a fear that a spirit may say something bad through its medium help to reinforce the decision of some people to remain either outside spiritualist religions altogether or to participate only as clients seeking spiritual advice.

In contrast, those persons who decide to develop their mediumship do so because of the rewards obtained. For example, they are frequently experiencing some sort of personal problems at the time they decide to become a medium. The data in this study clearly suggest that possession-trance states in the early stages of Umbanda mediumship are usually due to some inability of the individual to operate successfully in his specific sociocultural enviornment. Generally, the personal difficulty of the novice does not make him totally dysfunctional and is one that can be successfully treated over a period of several weeks up to possibly a year. If the disorder extends much beyond this period of time, it is likely that the disturbance is "psychological" or "physical," instead of "spiritual." What is being emphasized here is that Umbanda is not a repository for psychologically disturbed people unable to operate in their social environment. The case histories described in Chapters 5 through 8 can be used as examples of personal problems that novices hope to master by developing their mediumship in Umbanda.

In Nair's case, we have a woman who had given up her teaching career to marry a man who had difficulty providing for his wife. During the early years of her marriage, Nair had lost four children. She had difficulty in coping with family illnesses and familial altercations, and probably questioned why she, an aggressive and independent individual, could not handle such problems.

In Cecília's case, a number of events occurred that might have led her to seriously question the efficacy of her roles as wife and mother. Her husband behaved in a peculiar way, ruining the business he had built up, and was later involved with another woman. Two of Cecília's children died. If spirits may be regarded as projections of the inner personality, it is evident that Cecília was troubled by the events in her daily life. The Japanese spirit seemed to be a projection of her own personal warfare, while her dead-boyfriend's spirit and the *caboclo* in her dream who wanted her sexually were unconscious attempts to reassure herself that she was still a highly desirable woman.

João is yet another example of a person who decided to develop his mediumship when personal difficulties arose, although these remained unspecified to me.

Maria had experienced various problems that may have been significant over a period of years: inability to become an actress; difficulty with a love affair; the death of a child; and a major automobile accident. Any or all of these incidents could have lowered her self-esteem and raised doubts about her ability to adequately function in her social enviornment.

Juvenir was apparently having difficulties with his oldest sister and his apartment mate, Renato, when he entered Umbanda. His inability to secure a job as a radio announcer in São Paulo certainly would have been a blow to his self-image.

Finally, Thales's problems seemed to revolve about his desire to get married and inability to find a woman. Cecília's observation of Thales's behavior is quite interesting: "When Thales has a girlfriend, he doesn't go to the center. When he doesn't have a woman, he goes." Evidently, when Thales had a girlfriend, he was not experiencing psychological stress and felt no need for spirit sessions. The week that Thales did not have a girl and did not attend a session, but got drunk, helps confirm the theory of ASC being utilized by novices to relieve stress.

The mastery of these personal difficulties is a type of self-reward. Most Umbanda mediums, once they have overcome the major problem that led them to develop their spiritual qualities, are just as able as any other person to interact with their families, friends, and co-workers. Of course, there are individuals, such as João and Maria, who, according to their friends, tended to mix their religion and their personal life too much. In this respect, they were like many novices; but the point is that these two persons were sufficiently functional to be contributing in a productive manner to the larger society. The fact that they exhibited their ASC and possession behavior in what was sometimes regarded as bad taste is no more unusual in this cultural context than the flagrant behavior occasionally displayed by the more ordinary person who is not a medium.

For a very few individuals—specifically, cult leaders—being a medium over an extended period of time can be a financially rewarding role. Cult leaders are not usually rich, but they can support themselves. For most Umbanda mediums, however, the rewards of long-term participation are more personal. For Cecília, being a medium meant that she could spend a great deal of time outside her home and in the presence of other men with her husband's approval. Moreover, a large amount of respect is awarded to a medium, such as Cecília, who uses her spiritual capacities in unselfish ways to help others. A large number of mediums probably attend Umbanda centers for the social life it offers. Special *festas* (parties, celebrations) are held for the *orixás*, with food and drink. There are outings to the seashore to celebrate the goddess Iemanjá and to the forests to pay respects to the *caboclo* spirits. There are also special visits that the members of one Umbanda center make to other centers. Furthermore, there is always the possibility of making new friends among the mediums when a person joins a center. Then there are the more theatrical and aesthetic aspects of Umbanda: the special ritual garb, the public dancing and singing, and the attention one gets while possessed. While the character of most spirits in public Umbanda sessions is usually somewhat formal and to some degree subdued, the spirits at private sessions can be extremely entertaining to both their intimate audience and themselves.

Finally, it should be noted that personal difficulties may occur throughout the life span of an individual. There may be ongoing problems like those João was experiencing, (e.g., his homosexual tendencies, which were interpreted as being the behavior of his *pombagira*, Margarida). Other mediums may not experience chronic problems, but temporary difficulties may arise (e.g., the events that seemed to lead up to Cecília's being possessed by Pena Branca, who was not the *caboclo* she usually worked with). It should be emphasized that problems such as João's and Cecília's are not sufficient to make us conclude that long-term mediumship and the use of ASC are indicators of severe psychological disturbances. The same types of individual problems and alternative forms of ASC can be found in the wider Brazilian society, and the rewards for continuing mediumship in Umbanda are far more extensive than salving personal wounds.

NOTES

1. The author preferred to remain anonymous because he, a professional psychologist, was discussing his personal experiences with marihuana.
2. The anonymous author is referring here to *normal* consciousness, as opposed to an ASC. Thus use of this term is a bit confusing since I earlier defined consciousness as the ability to remember what had happened, whether for ASC or for normal consciousness.

10

Umbanda in the Brazilian Sociocultural Setting

Although my research was conducted almost entirely at the level of the individual, it is impossible to ignore the larger sociocultural context of possession-trance states in Umbanda. Most anthropological studies of these phenomena have been in tradition-oriented, non-Western societies. What makes Umbanda so interesting is its existence in a socially complex and developing modern industrial country.

The reasons for the widespread acceptance of the cultural concept of possessing spirits in a modern country like Brazil is related to three things that I discuss in this chapter. First, in Brazil, as in much of Latin America, there exists a cultural premise that man has a highly individuated spiritual self that is at least as important as his social self. The spiritual self involves the more idiosyncratic aspects of personality, whereas the social self refers to those aspects of role behavior that are defined by social rights and duties. The presence of the concept of a spiritual self perhaps enables Brazilians, as a whole, to accept more readily the related cultural concept of possessing spirits than do their North American counterparts.

Second, in contrast to modern possession religions in the United States, which seem to arise from small peripheral segments of the population, Umbanda developed out of a very strong historical base of spirit-possession religions in Brazil. Therefore, the concept of possessing spirits in Umbanda enjoys a solid precedent that extends into recent history, including the period of Umbanda's emergence.

Third, the growth of Umbanda was parallel to rather rapid and extensive economic, political, and social changes in Brazil. During this period, the Catholic Church remained somewhat elitist and tradition oriented, failing to meet the needs of the larger Brazilian population. Futhermore, medical facilities have not kept pace with developments in other spheres of Brazilian society and cannot adequately meet the needs of the masses. In this environment of change in some areas of Brazilian life, together with the relative lack of development in the Catholic Church and medical facilities, Umbanda can be viewed as a religious innovation in a developing society.

I first became aware of the individuality of the spiritual self in attending public Umbanda meetings, where I was struck by the first line of a ritual song frequently used to open spirit sessions. In *unison*, the mediums and those who had come for spiritual aid would sing, "I open my session with God and Our Lady." This song focused on the individual and separate units of "I" and "my," rather than on the team effort of "we" and "our" that are so prominent in North American culture. The song, nonetheless, fits very well into the larger framework of Umbanda cultural behavior: a highly individuated and therefore quite variable belief and ritual system; control of the center by a single cult leader instead of the mediums and/or the congregation; and the frequent existence of jealousy and animosity between mediums as well as cult leaders, which precludes very much in the way of cooperative activity. The limited cooperation that is present seems to occur in the vertical plane, linking inferiors and superiors. The vertical patron–client relationship in Umbanda has been discussed by Brown (1971).

Much of this individuated character can perhaps be related to the cultural premise that "man has a spiritual self." There is a tendency among many North Americans to relegate this sort of premise to the narrow confines of religion. In Brazil, as in much of Latin America, the concept of a spiritual self extends far beyond the boundaries of the religious context. To better understand the Latin notion of the spiritual self, it is useful to consider what constitutes the self-image of an individual. According to Goodenough (1963: 178), the self-image may be divided into two parts: social identity and personal identity. Social identity refers to those aspects of a person that are defined in terms of his social rights and duties. In contrast, personal identity refers to individual and very personal qualities. It includes those features of an individual to which no formal rights and duties are socially ascribed.

In Brazilian culture, person identity is symbolized as the spiritual self. It involves a person's inner worth or dignity and the manner of its expression in virtually all spheres of living. These personal, or spiritual, qualities are sharply distinguished from an individual's social value. It is entirely possible for a Brazilian to be poor in terms of money, but rich in terms of his spiritual self. In contrast, many North Americans tend to emphasize their social identity and social worth to the near exclusion of personal, or spiritual, worth. However, the "expansion of consciousness" movements during the past decade (e.g., the so-called drug movement, women's liberation, and various religious revivals) seem to represent attempts by North Americans to emphasize the worth of the individual self. In that Brazilians widely regard the spiritual self as being extremely important, as well as immortal, it is perhaps less difficult for them to accept the related cultural concept of spirits that can possess an individual.

Also related to the premise that man has a spiritual self is the Brazilian idea that it is difficult for a person to know and understand the spiritual self of another individual unless there is a very close personal relationship between the two. For this reason, only a few people, such as one's family and a small circle of friends, can come to know the spiritual self of an individual. Consequently, Brazilians tend to put people into two very distinct categories, which Santos (1966: 240) refers to as the "I–you, we–they" attitude of Brazilians. "They" are the people outside one's intimate circle, and "they" do not relate to one's spiritual self. Indeed, there are very few means for communicating between "us" and "them." The North American notion of casual friendship, as a type of "in-between" relationship, is not commonly found in Brazil.

These attitudes can help us understand why Umbanda spirits are so popular. A client may have difficulties in his relations with someone in his family or circle of close friends—difficulties he feels he cannot discuss with them directly. The concept of spirits seems to be a very convenient way of extricating oneself from this dilemma. The individual who comes to Umbanda as a client believes that he is speaking with a *spirit*, and not with the *medium*, who just may happen to be his brother, his close friend, or even one of "them." Finally, in ending their public sessions, Umbandists may sing together, "I close my session. . . ." Apparently, the "we-ness" that Santos refers to does not extend beyond one's limited circle of family and intimate friends, and out into the realm of Umbanda structure.

A second factor that perhaps predisposed Brazilians to accept Umbanda spirits was the historical presence of spirit-possession religions throughout Brazil: Batuque in Belém, Casa das Minas in São Luís, Candomblé in Bahia, Xangô in Recife, and Macumba in the more southern areas of Rio de Janeiro and São Paulo. Without doubt, these religions provided a reservoir of preexisting forms, including the concept of possessing spirits, that Umbandists could use as partial cultural models. Syncretic cults like the Umbanda of today were not at all unusual in Brazil, where Africans, Amerindians, and Europeans intermingled to an extent not found in the United States. These earlier religions, however, were practiced almost entirely by the traditional lower class of Brazilian society. The very tiny middle class and the elite subscribed to the Catholic faith; if a few defections occurred, they were in the direction of Kardecismo, introduced in the nineteenth century.

According to McGregor (1967: 168–169), Umbanda emerged during the

1920s. Umbanda seems to be strongest in Rio de Janeiro and São Paulo, but is also found in the large cities of Pôrto Alegre and Belo Horizonte. Leacock and Leacock (1972: 319) note that Umbanda is now moving into Belém as well. Moreover, it is present in the smaller towns in the interior of the state of São Paulo. The period during which Umbanda first appeared in São Paulo and Rio de Janeiro roughly coincided with the initial phases of widespread economic and political changes in the industrial areas of Brazil. As industrialization speeded up, what had once been powerful regional political blocks were reoriented toward a stronger federal government. My general impression is that Umbanda is very much linked with modernization and that its spread accompanies the gradual integration of the more remote areas, such as Belém, into the national socioeconomic structure.

As already mentioned, Umbanda may be regarded as a religious innovation in a developing society. To this end it is useful to consider four major changes that accompanied the development of Umbanda from earlier syncretic religions into a new and distinctive sociocultural entity:

1.   The traditional lower class identity associated with the earlier Afro-Brazilian cults, such as Candomblé, has shifted to an upper-lower and middle class identity in Umbanda.

2.   The conceptualization of what constitutes a personal problem that spirits can deal with has changed somewhat from traditional concerns to those related to an industrial society.

3.   Members of the earlier religions tended to see themselves more in terms of their ethnic and regional identities, whereas Umbandists view themselves first as Brazilian nationals and second as members of a particular ethnic and/or regional group.

4.   A new configuration of spirit types was developed in Umbanda.

Since these innovations are part of the larger societal changes, a brief review of Brazilian development will be helpful.

Prior to the twentieth century, most Brazilians were still engaged in agricultural activities, either as small farmers or as laborers on large farms owned by the aristocracy. Even in the urban areas, the generalized two-part class structure rigidly separated the domestic workers and day laborers from the very tiny middle class and the elite. During this period nearly all manufactured, and especially luxury, goods were imported, and only the better off members of Brazilian society could afford them. Gradually, industries were established in the southern part of Brazil during the latter part of the nineteenth century and the beginning of the twentieth. This shifted political power from the old-plantation northeast to the economically developing areas in the south.

When Vargas assumed the presidency in 1930, political power became more centralized. To aid the development of southern industries, the federal government began to control the selection of imports by heavily taxing luxury items and by providing incentives for the importation of machines to make machines (Poppino, 1968: 243). During the period when Umbanda emerged and then expanded—between 1920 and 1960—the number of factories increased more than eightfold and the industrial labor force grew nearly sevenfold (Poppino, 1968: 239). The federal government during and since the time of Vargas has intensified economic nationalism. It has either directly or indirectly backed large-scale projects, such as the Volta Redonda steel mill, up to the present important project to open up and develop the Amazon region. The thrust of development has been in terms of what former President Kubitschek referred to as "fifty years of progress in five" (Dulles, 1966: 38).

If nationalist sentiment is present, so is currency inflation. During the regime of President Goulart, the cost of living increased 340 percent between 1961 and 1963, while the international exchange rate of the cruzeiro decreased from 300 to 1200 to the U.S. dollar (Dulles, 1966: 48). Population pressures have compounded economic difficulties. According to Chardon (1966: 162), urban growth has accounted to 70 percent of the national population increase between 1950 and 1960. Most of this growth occurred in the industrial south and represented a rural-to-urban migration.

In this milieu of economic modernization, spiraling inflation, and rural-to-urban migration we find Umbanda. Under the impact of industrialization, the traditional social structure is gradually giving way to the emergence of a larger middle class and a developing industrial proletariat that are very much aware of available consumer goods. The content of advertising in Umbanda magazines and newspapers is instructive. The January–February 1967 issue of *Orixá*, a magazine that is published in Pôrto Alegre and calls itself "the Umbandist voíce," carried 32 advertisements devoted to the following goods: television sets, flowers, jewelry and watches, Umbanda ritual paraphernalia, clothing, mechanized agricultural equipment, artificial leather goods, patent medicines, and furniture. The following services were included: dental work, photography, money orders, and secondary education. A radio station also advertised its programming. As noted in Chapter 3, most Umbandists in São Paulo are in the upper-lower and middle classes, and tend to view themselves as upwardly mobile. They do not achieve perhaps as much mobility as they would like, and many go into debt buying on the installment plan. There is always the question of whether there will be enough money, since inflation never seems to end. Nonetheless, a large number of Umbandists in São Paulo have very real middle-class aspirations, and this differentiates them from the membership of the more tradition-oriented spirit religions.

If industrialization and education are moving Umbandists into the middle class, they are also creating new kinds of problems. It is highly doubtful that the spirits in earlier possession religions would have handled such problems as getting into medical school or reducing the rent of a spaghetti factory. As people move into the upper-lower and middle classes, they meet new problems and are faced with the need to make decisions about situations for which they have no previous models. The conceptualization of what constitutes a problem has to some extent changed as people face new situations, and for this reason Umbanda may be regarded as an innovation in a developing society.

As already noted, economic changes influenced the political arena. Prior to the Vargas era, political power lay in the hands of oligarchic regional and/or state groups, whose power was locally based in the economic power of the large landowners (Lopez, 1966: 60). Lopez believes that the Brazilian political structure has undergone profound transformation since 1930. Power has shifted away from the state governments to the urban masses, who are considerably more aware of national political maneuvers than the old rural peasants were.

According to Lopez (1966: 59–77), the basis of the limited democracy Brazil has experienced lies in the concept of *populismo* (populism). Politicians appeal to the urban masses composed of industrial workers and the middle class. Political parties, however, do not reach the masses. For this reason, local leaders known as *cabos eleitorais* act as "intermediaries between the large impersonal institutional framework of the city and the people of a neighborhood, a *favela* or a recreational club" (Lopez, 1966: 64). If their political candidate wins an election, the *cabos eleitorais* can obtain favors for their clients in the form of jobs, public utility installations, and provisions for public transportation (Lopez, 1966: 65). This system of middlemen has evidently penetrated Umbanda, with cult leaders sometimes serving in the capacity of *cabo eleitoral* (Singer, 1965: 74). Brown's study of Umbanda structure in Rio de Janeiro indicates that politicians, along with cult leaders, journalists, and other members of the middle class, run the Umbanda federations in that city and that politicians use Umbanda federations and cult centers to gain wider political support (Brown, 1971: 6).

These data indicate that Umbanda is apparently far more involved with national political affairs than were the earlier regional possession religions. The apparent lack of national political participation by these earlier syncretic cults was probably related to the general lack of power in the former traditional lower class. Economic change seemed to turn not only regional power but also regional identity toward a national orientation. The isolation that formerly separated regional groupings as well as regionally based spirit-possession religions was broken through as improved communication and transportation networks began to link various parts of Brazil into a national structure and identity. This was reflected in the emphasis Umbandists placed on national identity and political activity as they began to see themselves as part of a national culture.

In viewing Umbanda as a religious innovation it is also necessary to consider the configuration of cult spirits. The *orixás* of Candomblé have changed in that they now send spirits of the dead to possess Umbanda mediums. In a sense, these spirits have been "moved upstairs" and are more removed from the everyday ritual activities in Umbanda. The fact that they were retained signifies the great importance Umbandists attach to their African cultural heritage, even though today Umbandists view themselves as Brazilian, not as Afro-Brazilian. Indeed, a large number of Umbandists in São Paulo are of European descent. The shift is somewhat reminiscent of the development of Christianity out of Judaism. As Christianity was accepted by a broader population than had accepted the earlier tribal religion of Judaism, the Old Testament characters became farther removed from the everyday Christian rituals based on New Testament doctrine. Similarly, as Umbanda was accepted by Brazilians other than those of African descent, the *orixá* characters became further removed from the everyday doctrine and rituals of Umbanda. The sequence of evolution is reflected in both Christian and Umbanda rituals. Just as in many Christian churches it is customary to read Old Testament scriptures before proceeding to the New Testament, so Umbandists frequently begin their rituals with *orixá* songs before moving on to songs for the more ordinary Umbanda spirits.

The *exus* and *crianças* are also retentions from Candomblé. Like the *orixás*, they were transformed into spirits of the dead in Umbanda. In contrast to the *orixás*, these two spirits became a part of the more everyday Umbanda spirit world. According to Bascom (1969: 79), Exu is the youngest and cleverest of the Yoruba deities. Acting as a messenger, he delivers sacrifices prescribed by a diviner to the high god Olorun. Being a trickster deity, Exu can start fights or cause "accidents" to occur. In Brazil, Exu is often associated with Satan, although there is some disagreement on this point. In the Afro-Brazilian religious life described by Bastide (1958: 148–172), Exu's activities are not confined to the Candomblé cult of the *orixás*. They extend into three other major areas: the cult of Ifa, related to divination; the cult of Ossaim, having to do with sacred herbs; and the cult of the Eguns, that is, spirits of the dead. It would seem that this quadripartite nature of Exu separated him from the *orixás* and made him a more ordinary spirit in the evolutionary processes leading to Umbanda.

The Umbanda *crianças* are apparently a survival of the childlike *ere* deities of Candomblé. After a medium comes out of a deep trance and possession by an *orixá*, she is possessed by a playful *ere* while in a light trance. This occurs in the more secluded part of the Candomblé cult house and is not normally observed by the public. Landes (1947: 57) writes that the *ere* were usually hungry. They would be put to sleep as children are and sometimes would be in a dead sleep for 24 hours. The *ere*, although a part of Candomblé, do not have the same characteristics as the *orixás*. Again, as in the case of Exu, this was an important factor in separating the *crianças* from the *orixás* in Umbanda.

The origins of the *caboclos* and *prêtos velhos* are not as clear; however, these spirits were present in Macumba ceremonies in Rio de Janeiro and Espírito Santo (Bastide, 1960: 409–421). Whether these two spirits antedate Macumba, I am unable to say.

Umbandists are possessed by spirits other than *caboclos, prêtos velhos, crianças,* and *exus,* but do not attribute to them the same importance. I did not directly investigate this difference; however, as my informants discussed the significance of spirits in their lives, it became evident that the four principal spirit types related to certain kinds of symbolic meanings. The various meanings attached to the spirits were not always shared by all informants, and there may be other sets of referents in addition to the four that I discuss here.

First, the major ethnic heritages in Brazil are represented by three of the four spirits. The *caboclos* symbolize the Brazilian Indian origins, while the *prêtos velhos* represent the African contribution to modern Brazilian culture. As pointed out in Chapter 4, the *exu* is frequently foreign and often European. Sometimes, however, *exus* were special regional characters from Brazil, and further research is needed to clarify this problem of the ethnicity of *exu* spirits. Interestingly, there is a parallel between the way first- and second-generation European and Japanese businessmen in São Paulo are perceived and how *exus* are viewed: both can be relied on to accomplish a difficult job, and both frequently ask for some advance payment! Some of my informants noted that the *criança* was "just like us," that is, the child spirit has the outgoing personality of the Brazilian and lacks a specific racial identity. Wagley (1971: 262–263) tells us that during the 1920s Brazilian writers began to recognize the importance of Indian and African cultures in their national life styles. During this period, the effects of industrialization were beginning to be felt, the traditional class structure dominated by Euro-Brazilians started to erode, and regional identities assumed less importance. Umbanda, emerging at this time, may be thought of as a "national folk religion." Each medium, so to speak, "incorporates" his national heritage as four spiritual symbols.

The four spirit types may also represent the evolutionary stages of spiritualist religions leading up to Umbanda. The African cultural elements in Umbanda are the oldest. Later, Indian and European beliefs were added. The relative ages of the spirits symbolize the way Umbandists view the historical origins of their religion. The *prêto velho* is the oldest, while the *caboclo* and the *exu* are middle-aged. The *criança*, which perhaps symbolizes the new Brazilian, is the youngest.

Some of my informants expressed the idea that the spirits were like the generations found in a family: "The indulgent *prêto velho* is like a grandfather; the stern *caboclo* is more like a father; and the child spirit is like a brother or sister." The *exu*, in contrast, is without spiritual light and perhaps may be regarded as being a stranger outside this family unit. It is not difficult to understand how this third conceptualization of the spirits would be meaningful to those Umbandists who have left their homes and find themselves in the impersonal environment of São Paulo.

Furthermore, the four spirits, when considered as a combined unit, seem to me to represent a well-balanced personality: the calm and indulgent *prêtos velhos*, the stern and aloof *caboclos*, the playful and innocent *crianças*, and the aggressive and base *exus*. The personality traits of the *prêto velho* and *caboclo* are perhaps the most useful to a healthy adult personality, and it is interesting that these two spirits appear in Umbanda centers once each week. Furthermore, each of us needs a bit of the innocence and playfulness of the child, as well as just a small amount of the *exu's* character. Correspondingly, the latter two spirits possess mediums only once each month. Umbanda mediums must learn to play the roles of each of the four spirits. Should one of the four aspects of personality be weakly developed in an Umbanda novice, the mode of behavior is learned within the religious context. The behavioral characteristics learned may then be transferred to the wider social life of the individual; for example, one young and impatient medium said that she had learned to be more patient and calm from her *prêta velha* spirit.

It seems to me that the particular configuration of spirits that emerged in Umbanda is an innovation that is especially adapted to a complex society. Since individuals in a complex society come from a variety of personal backgrounds, a configuration of symbols with multiple referents will be selected by a greater number of people than a set of symbols to which only one meaning may be attached. If the Umbanda spirit symbols had only one set of referents, fewer persons would find Umbanda significant to their lives. If they were to find that one set of referents meaningless, it is quite likely that they would reject the whole of Umbanda. Since there is a choice of referents, however, more people can find the spirit symbols appropriate to their various ways of thinking. Furthermore, a specific individual may find two or more referents meaningful for himself. This would tend to strengthen the importance that person might assign to Umbanda in his life, thus increasing the possibility of his decision to participate in Umbanda activities. Historically, the four spirit symbols apparently emerged and came together as a unit primarily on the unconscious level in response to the changing Brazilian sociocultural environment.

Up to this point, I have been focusing on the sociocultural changes in modern Brazil. There are two social institutions, however, that have not developed to meet present-day needs to any great extent. One of these is medical services. The services of private physicians are often too expensive for most Brazilians. The limited public medical facilities are overcrowded, necessitating delays and long waiting periods. In either case, the patient does not obtain the attention on a variety of personal difficulties usually associated with physical illnesses that he can get during "spiritual consultations" at Umbanda centers.

The second Brazilian institution that has changed relatively little is the Catholic Church. Although some hints of change are present, this institution remains rather closely associated with the elite in Brazil. Moreover, the Church has difficulty in recruiting Brazilian priests, and many of today's clerics are missionaries from foreign countries (Wagley, 1971: 217). The Catholic Church does not seem to be equipping itself to minister to the needs of the Brazilian masses.

As observed in Chapter 2, three possession religions—Umbanda, Kardecismo, and Pentacostalism—seem to thrive in the modern, but ambiguous, Brazilian environment of social change and conservative Catholicism. The presence of such spirit-possession religions in a society that embraces the Catholic Church leads to the question of whether Umbanda can possibly be regarded as an "amoral peripheral possession cult" or as a "central (main) morality possession cult," to use the terms of Lewis (1971).

Peripheral cults typically cater to the socially deprived, that is, women and weaker men in a subordinate social status. The spirits are used to indirectly press home for claims on superiors. A woman's spirit may make extravagant economic demands on the medium's husband and family. For this reason, Lewis views these cults as a part of the "sex war" of traditional societies. Typically, the spirits originate outside the societies they attack, and they are amoral in that they do not serve to uphold the central moral code of the society. Indeed, they serve as a mechanism of protest that is both accepted and contained by the power structure. Any member of a society is open to attack by the spirits and may be initiated into the cult. Cult membership is therefore theoretically unlimited; it is generally the socially impotent, however, who participate.

In contrast, main morality possession cults limit their membership to the politically strong individuals of a society. The spirits involved are ancestral spirits or deities that belong to the society. Therefore, the spirits may be used to directly support the central power of a society. Members of a central morality cult are in the superordinate social position. They are typically men.

How well does Umbanda fit these criteria of Lewis for peripheral and main morality cults? It is my impression that Umbanda is in a somewhat ambiguous position. Umbanda, vis-à-vis Quimbanda, could perhaps be categorized as a central morality religion; but from the vantage point of the Catholic hierarchy, Umbanda—lumped together with Quimbanda—is something more like a peripheral cult. An examination of Umbanda, as well as Quimbanda and Catholicism, in terms of the criteria outlined by Lewis will help bring into focus the problems of attempting to apply these categories to Umbanda.

Catholicism originated as an ecstatic religion of the downtrodden. It moved from its original peripheral position to become a main morality religion. During the historical process of its transformation, Catholicism lost its ecstatic qualities, focusing more on prescribed rituals than on possessed inspiration. Brazilian Catholicism, of course, is not a possession religion, but it is a central morality religion. As such, it embodies all of the major characteristics of a main morality cult, except the belief in possessing spirits. Its male priesthood is limited and is in a superordinate social position. The central morality is directly preached to the people. Linked more to the old order of Brazilian social structure, the morality is of a traditional sort that emphasizes obedience.

In Umbanda, the role of religious specialist is not limited. Everyone is thought to have an innate capacity for mediumship that can be developed in Umbanda sessions. Women outnumber the men. (As already mentioned, 60 to 75 percent of the mediums in the centers I visited were women.) The relatively large numbers of men in Umbanda, however, support Lewis's claim that, as societies become more stratified, more men will participate in peripheral possession cults (Lewis, 1971: 107). This is because in stratified societies it becomes more difficult for men to hold positions of power on the sole ascribed basis of maleness. Umbanda, then, would seem to fit Lewis's criterion of unlimited membership for peripheral cults.

Peripheral possession cults differ from main morality possession religions in that their members usually have low social status and are politically unimportant in terms of decision-making processes in the larger society. Since Umbanda is not restricted to the lower class, it would not seem to be a peripheral religion. On the other hand, one could argue that achieving middle-class status does not abolish inferiority: the subordinate status is merely moved up a notch. Although a few Umbandists have been elected deputies to state governments (See Chapter 3), Umbanda is certainly not a significant part of the central Brazilian political structure. Therefore, Umbanda cannot be regarded as a strong central morality cult in the political sense.

In attempting to determine whether Umbanda supports a central Brazilian moral code we find that the data are somewhat ambiguous. The morality that permeates Umbanda is summed up in the term *caridade* (charity). It is directly preached at Umbanda sessions and very obviously practiced by the mediums, whose spirits provide spiritual support and advice to the large numbers of Brazilians who regularly attend public sessions. Umbandists very definitely see themselves as upholding a central morality, which they feel the Catholic Church has, by and large, ignored in Brazil. The Catholic hierarchy, for its part, views Umbanda as "Macumba: Brazil's Devil Worshippers."[1] The Catholic Church continues to preach its version of a central morality, which is obedience to the traditional social hierarchy. The ambiguity of Umbanda with respect to a central moral code, I believe, stems from the Brazilian milieu of social change. To some extent, two social structures are present in Brazil: the traditional, in which obedience is the central morality; and the modern, in which charity and equality are the central themes. Willems (1966: 221–230) has observed that Umbanda, Kardecismo, and Pentacostalism are similar in that all reject the paternalistic tutelage of the upper class, emphasizing a certain amount of social equality among their members. Umbanda does not uphold the traditional social order, but is this a sufficient reason to call it a peripheral cult? Lewis (1971: 127) argues that peripheral possession cults are able to serve as mechanisms of protest for the downtrodden primarily because the demands of the amoral peripheral spirits are both accepted and contained by the power structure of a society. In that the Catholic Church has neither accepted nor contained Umbanda, it is difficult to categorize it entirely as a peripheral possession cult.

A final criterion separating peripheral possession cults from the main morality ones is the nature of the spirits. Peripheral cult spirits are typically amoral and capricious, for they are often foreign spirits having no interest in upholding the moral code of the society. In contrast, the spirits of central morality cults are ancestors or deities that belong to the society in question. They support the central morality of the politically powerful in a society. Again, keeping in mind the duality of Brazilian social structure, it is immediately apparent that the Umbanda spirits do not represent the traditional upper class, which was almost entirely Euro-Brazilian. On the other hand, Umbanda seems to be a part of an evolving modern structure of classes, in which the upper-lower and middle classes include Afro-Brazilian and Amerindian admixtures, and view themselves as having some measure of political power. Within this context, then, the Umbanda spirits may be regarded as "representative," to use the term of Lerch (1972: 90), of the modern Brazilian social structure. The new social structure, however, is not fully developed. Perhaps the *criança* spirit, youthful and lacking racial identity, best symbolizes Umbanda's present emergent position as a central morality religion.

If Umbanda shows indications of being a peripheral cult when viewed from the Catholic position, it assumes the attributes of a central morality cult when compared to Quimbanda. Since I attended only one private session held in a Quimbanda center, my data for Quimbanda are severely limited. The information I have is primarily Umbandist opinion, as well as data from Umbanda sessions designed to counteract Quimbanda's evil magic. First, the nature of the *exu* spirits in Quimbanda seems to be foreign, although some regional characters exist as *exus*. If Quimbanda mediums are ever possessed by spirits other than *exus*, it certainly never came to my attention. All Umbanda publications, as well as the more general Brazilian news media, very definitely emphasize the role of *exus* in Quimbanda. Second, my data from Umbandists indicate that the people who claim to be bewitched by Quimbanda *exus*, and who subsequently go to Umbanda *exus* for countermagical assistance, are socially either equal or superior to the individual *accused* of initiating and paying for a Quimbanda spiritual work. For example, in matters having to do with love affairs, men accused women of having Quimbanda black magic delivered to them (Pressel, 1972). I have less data on *exu* services related to business affairs, but it is my impression that accusations may occur between men of equal status or women of equal status. This would tend to put Quimbanda in the role of a peripheral cult, with protests by inferior and/or equals being accepted, but contained, by Umbanda acting in the role of a central morality cult. Obviously, more research is needed to help clarify the activities and social position of Quimbandists.

One other point needs to be raised. Lewis (1971: 34) has observed that, as they become more firmly entrenched in the power structure of a society, ecstatic religions lose their tolerance for enthusiasm generated by spirit possession. Prescribed rituals *not* involving possession assume greater importance in an established religion. Why, then, do main morality possession religions continue to exist if they are part of the established hierarchy? According to Lewis, the answer lies in "acute and constantly recurring social and environmental pressures" (Lewis, 1971: 35). Examples are (1) central shamanistic possession in small fluid societies like the Eskimo, who are subject to harsh environmental stress, or (2) conquered communities dominated by alien oppressors.

Superficially, Brazil does not seem to fit either of these conditions. The modern complexity of Brazilian society tends to obscure similarities with Eskimos and/or oppressed people under a foreign yoke. Nonetheless, there are certain parallels. Although the Brazilian masses—including the rising middle class—are not directly combating the forces of nature, they are caught up in the battle against monetary inflation, and employment security is relatively low. There is the ever-present struggle to find sufficient *cruzeiros* to pay next month's installments. Furthermore, Brazil is not directly controlled by a foreign power, but two possible parallels may relate to this issue. First, as social mobility becomes a theoretical possibility, the traditional social order, epitomized by the conservative Catholic Church, may be thought of as a "foreign power" that the industrialized Brazilian masses are attempting to restructure. A second type of "foreign power" that modern Brazilians fear is the economic control of their country by other nations. As already noted, economic development is really economic nationalism. Umbandists in São Paulo proudly point out their home appliances and other products as having been manufactured in their country. In more recent years, a military regime that is comparatively friendly to the United States has assumed control of the central government. In attempting to stabilize the fluctuating economic growth of Brazil, it has resorted to measures that seem repressive to large numbers of Brazilians. The military, as a whole, has never fully supported the Brazilian elite, and Brown, in her study of Umbanda structure in Rio de Janeiro, found that the current political struggle has led to some movement of military officers (presumably, lower echelon) into Umbanda federations, with "some interest expressed in utilizing them for counterinsurgency" (Brown, 1971: 6).

I frankly find it difficult to assign Umbanda to either the peripheral or the main morality cult categories of Lewis. Part of the problem lies in the complexity of Brazilian society, which does not accommodate the generalizations made by Lewis, which were derived from the relatively simple societies anthropologists have traditionally studied. The fact that Umbanda structure extends from some very limited participation in state governments through federations and down to the individual medium means that motivations for participating in Umbanda may vary at differing levels of structure. A second factor that makes it difficult to assign Umbanda to one of Lewis's categories is the presence of sociocultural change in Brazilian society, as a result of which there is a lack of a single agreed-on social structure as well as a single moral code enshrining the power of those in the superordinate status. In contrast, the peripheral and main morality cults discussed by Lewis share an accepted and relatively stable structure, with the former protesting, and the latter supporting, the status quo.

The changes in Brazilian social structure put Umbanda into an ambiguous position. The combination of change and conservatism in Brazilian society creates a situation wherein two social structures coexist. Within the context of the old social order, Umbanda is something like a peripheral cult or possibly what Lewis (1971: 128) refers to as a separatist religious movement. However, within the milieu of an evolving modern social structure, Umbanda becomes a central morality possession religion of *caridade* for the masses afflicted with bad fluids from Quimbanda *exus*.

NOTE

1. Title of a pictorial article in *Our Sunday Visitor*, pp. 8–9, March 12, 1972.

11

Conclusions

In this study, I have attempted to examine some of the features of trance and possession states that are related more to individual behavior than to sociocultural systems. The structural aspects of Umbanda, of course, cannot be disregarded, for they represent the cognitive framework in which the action takes place; for example, the learning of possession trance is guided by socially shared beliefs. Furthermore, since possession trance is so widely accepted in Brazilian society, such behavior cannot be regarded as psychotic in nature. However, the use of these states, even by Umbandists, is thought of as being "different" behavior, in the sense of being an altered state of functioning. Altered states of consciousness of any form can be abused, and should this occur in Umbanda, the individual is ultimately held responsible. If a person's abnormal spiritual behavior extends beyond socially accepted limits and for an indefinite period of time, he is regarded as dysfunctional and "crazy." I did not encounter such persons, perhaps because Umbanda does not include them.

We also saw that Umbanda mediums can project their socially unacceptable feelings onto the spirits. There is less hostility generated toward other people or, for that matter, contained within the medium. Consequently, there is no positive feedback system that could overburden an individual with guilt, thus making therapy more difficult. The novice is able to focus his attention on controlling the behavior of an outside spiritual force, rather than on changing his own behavior.

In the long run, however, by learning to control the alien spiritual force, the medium may transfer the behavior learned in association with a spirit role to his own everyday behavior. Similarly, psychoanalysis may focus on an outside force affecting the patient's behavior (e.g., a parent). The individual may possibly project his own inadequacies onto the parental image. Because it is difficult, if not impossible, for the patient to change the behavior of his parent, it also becomes difficult for him to alter his feelings about the parental image and, ultimately, about his own behavior.

Psychodrama techniques seem to be closer to spirit therapy than psychoanalysis. The patient in a psychodrama session, however, is aware that he is only playacting, whereas the spirit roles in Umbanda are for real. Although the general impression I have is that Umbandists find it fairly easy to incorporate spirit roles into their personalities, mediums will occasionally refuse to be possessed by certain spirits; for example, Juvenir did not want an *exu* to possess him. This is similar to patients who find it impossible or difficult to play certain roles in psychodrama sessions.

The long-term use of altered states of consciousness in their possession-trance form is not viewed here as a sign of abnormal behavior, any more than the long-term socially controlled use of alcohol can be regarded as abnormal. As noted in Chapter 9, participation in Umbanda provides a variety of personal and social pleasures that reinforce an individual's decision to continue his mediumship for as long as 20 years in the case of Cecília and 25 years in the case of Nair. Ribeiro (1956) used the Rorschach test to obtain data on Xangô mediums in Recife and concluded that personality problems were within a range of normalcy and that the women were fairly well adjusted. Stainbrook (1952) has suggested that some Candomblé mediums had "hysterical" characters, but that a schizophrenic personality could not function within the controlled structure of Candomblé rituals.

The distinction I made between spontaneous and controlled possession-trance states in Umbanda mediums appears to be similar to two phases of possession discussed by Lewis (1971). His "primary phase" involves a possession illness that is involuntary and uncontrolled. A "secondary phase" that is voluntary and controlled occurs after a supernatural cure has taken place. Although the data on Umbandists do not contradict Lewis's stages, spontaneous possession that is uncontrolled and involuntary continues in a developed (i.e., cured) Umbanda medium whenever she or he is experiencing psychological stress. The reason for this oversight by Lewis is perhaps related to the emphasis that anthropologists have placed on ideal sociocultural behavior. They have, therefore, tended to overlook the real aspects of individual human behavior.

The anthropological literature provides very little information concerning the various levels of trance behavior. We are aware that, on a gross level, a distinction can be made between unconscious and conscious states, in terms of whether a person is able to remember events that occurred during the trance. I have suggested that conscious possession trance, the events of which are remembered, can be characterized by a narrowing of the attention into the present that entails diminution of forethought and evaluation based on the past and future. Obviously, more research is needed on this subject, and further efforts should be made to determine whether there are different types of conscious and unconscious altered states of consciousness. Although it is still very difficult to provide physiological proof of differences, more indirect means, such as observations of alterations in language and/or outward motor patterns, are certainly at our disposal.

It is important not to neglect the fact that possession-trance states in Umbanda are part of the larger Brazilian sociocultural context. The historical concept of spirit possession and the possible relation of the concept of possessing spirits to the premise of a spiritual self were offered as reasons for widespread belief in spirit possession. The lack of adequate medical facilities and the traditional orientation of the Catholic Church were also cited as contributing to the growth of Umbanda. The hypothesis that Umbanda represents a religious innovation in a developing society was developed in terms of the national and middle-class orientations of Umbandists, as well as in terms of new problems spirits today are called on to handle. Umbanda is also an innovation with respect to its configuration of spirits. It is for these reasons that Umbanda is rapidly expanding as more Brazilian towns become integrated into the developing national framework. It is my impression that Umbanda has become something of a "national folk religion," in the sense of being the religious part of a modern mass culture associated with a technical world.

I also used Lewis's criteria to determine whether Umbanda should be regarded as a peripheral cult or as a central morality cult. The ambiguous results, I believe, are due to the nature of Brazilian society, in which two social orders—the old and the new—coexist. There is no single social order in Brazil as in other more traditional and simple societies. Additional studies of possession trance in complex and changing societies would be useful for constructing theories of these phenomena in nontraditional societies.

It is perhaps appropriate to ask why Umbanda—instead of any one of a number of other possession religions in Brazil—expanded so tremendously. In closing, I suggest some possible answers. First, the literature indicates that the consultation process was more developed in Umbanda than in religions like Candomblé. In a milieu of cultural change where answers to ever-present new problems must be found, the consultation process was a useful adaptation for Umbanda's growth. Second, Umbanda had a broader conceptualization of Brazilian national identity than did earlier religions like Candomblé, which was more securely tied to Afro-Brazilian populations. Third, Umbanda had a definite link with Kardecismo, which was noted for having a middle-class appeal. This made Umbanda more prestigious and hence more acceptable than lower class possession religions. Fourth, although Kardecismo had an aura of middle-class prestige, its emphasis on intellectual qualities did not allow it to appeal to the masses in the way that Umbanda, with its emphasis on the "heart," was able. Fifth, Umbanda's syncretism of the *orixás* with the saints enabled it to adapt better than Kardecismo or Pentacostalism in a country where people continue to think of themselves as officially Catholic.

Whether Umbanda has the potential to eventually establish itself as a fully centralized religion, in which ecstacy in its possession-trance form becomes a heresy, remains to be seen. Alternatively, Brazilians could discard Umbanda sometime in the future. Such changes usually happen when social disruption subsides. We can only hope that there will be continued research on Umbanda to inform us of the outcome.

Part Three: Felicitas D. Goodman

Disturbances in the Apostolic Church: A Trance-Based Upheaval in Yucatán

PREFACE

The field work on which this study of a violent, trance-related societal upheaval is based extends from 1969 to the present. However, my preparation
for observing and understanding such processes goes back much further. It
began with my participation in a project entitled Cross-Cultural Study of
Dissociational States under the direction of Dr. Erika Bourguignon, of the Department of Anthropology, the Ohio State University. To Professor
Bourguignon, under whose guidance I thus began working on the subject of
trance states and developing some initial insights into vocalization while in
trance (the "speaking in tongues" of Christian denominations) I should like to
express my most grateful appreciation. I also want to thank all of my many in-

formants, especially those in Yucatán, for their help and their friendship. The Denison University Research Foundation supported my work in 1969 with a generous summer grant. Denison University also gave financial aid for further field work, making it possible for me to gather information on the development of the cult in the time after the upheaval.

This upheaval took place in an Apostolic congregation in Yucatán during the late summer of 1970. For most of its duration, the people participating in it were in a more or less pronounced condition of trance, in an altered state of consciousness as the term is used by Ludwig (1968).[1] When people are in this manner "dissociated," they engage in a variety of behaviors, such as special types of motions, visions, and also speaking. My initial interest in altered mental states concerned this latter aspect. Analyzing recorded glossolalia (from the Greek *glōssa*, "tongue," and *lalia*, "speech") deriving from a number of linguistically and culturally diverse groups, I noted that some important aspects of these utterances were remarkably similar. These features were specifically the intonation pattern, but also the regularity of the rhythm, the modification of certain sounds according to their position in the utterance, as well as others. I proposed the working hypothesis that the agreements were produced due to the fact that the speakers were in trance during speaking; the agreements thus were a product of the physical parameters of the altered mental state. In order to test this hypothesis and to obtain material for a cross-linguistic comparison, I went to a Mexico City Apostolic congregation, to a similar congregation in the United States, and later to Yucatán to record glossolalia from persons normally speaking Spanish, English, and Mayan. In this way I hoped to examine the similarities between the glossolalia of persons who speak an Indo-European language (English and Spanish) and the agreements or differences that might exist between it and the glossolalia of persons whose native tongue belongs to an entirely different family of languages.

During the field work in Mexico City and in the United States, I had been able to confine my interests to the linguistic and trance-related aspects of glossolalia. In Yucatán, however, societal concomitants increasingly intruded into my field of inquiry. Ethnopsychiatric aspects of certain trance behaviors, the psychological substratum for the arising of crisis cults, and, more generally, peasant society in culture change, became important issues. As a result, the work that I had done to clarify the trance-based features of glossolalia behavior, its acquisition, linguistic peculiarities and attenuation, seemed no more than a prologue. Eventually, it became necessary to bracket out the cross-cultural study of glossolalia for special treatment (Goodman, 1972b) and to concentrate in the present discussion on the societal process. The inquiry into glossolalia had opened the door for me to a perception of trance behavior and had furnished me with a scale for estimating its shifting levels. For the understanding of a trance-based group event, the intimate knowledge of glossolalia proved to be a signally important analytical tool.

NOTE

1. Ludwig (1968: 69–70) states: "For the purpose of discussion, I shall regard "altered states of consciousness" . . . as those mental states, induced by various physiological, psychological, or pharmacological maneuvers or agents, which can be recognized subjectively by the individual himself (or by an objective observer of the individual) as representing a sufficient deviation, in terms of subjective experience or psychological functioning, from certain general norms as determined by the subjective experience and psychological functioning of that individual during alert, waking consciousness." The subject will be taken up in detail in Chapter 4.

1

Introduction

In August 1970, an upheaval took place with a small Apostolic congregation on the Peninsula of Yucatán. At first, the members believed that the events were due to the direct action of the Holy Spirit, signaling the imminent end of the world and the Second Coming of Christ. Subsequently, they came to accept the interpretation that they had been the victims of demonic possession. This "attack by the Adversary" eventually involved at least four congregations: three in various villages and one in an urban center. In the course of this upheaval, no regular services could be held, for whenever the parishioners knelt down to pray, many of them were seized by violent fits manifested by unintelligible speech, trembling, kicking, sobbing, and choking. Women became hysterical and fell to the ground, screaming. The people threw their Bibles out into the churchyard, burned their colored clothes, their shoes, radios, and television sets. They washed each other's feet and then drank the dirty, muddy water. Some members had visions; others walked about restlessly in the village or traveled continuously from congregation to congregation.

The disorders lasted until the beginning of September of that year. They faded away even before an elder arrived from the district office of the southeastern section of the Apostolic Church of Mexico, located in Villahermosa, Tabasco. He explained to the congregations that it had been Satan who had been trying them, not the Holy Spirit giving them instructions as they had initially supposed. Such instances, he said, were well known from the Bible. The simple fact that during possession they had thrown out their Bibles should have told them that their attacker had been the Adversary, who wanted them to get rid of the single most important weapon they could have used to defeat him.

Accounts of similar occurrences are numerous in the annals of recorded history, as Mooney (1896) points out in the preface to his discussion of the Ghost Dance. They have multiplied in the anthropological literature, especially since the upheaval dubbed the *Vailala Madness* (F. E. Williams, 1923) became more widely known. In fact, the similarity between certain elements of this Melanesian "cargo cult" and those of the Yucatecan upheaval is quite striking.

This famous cult developed in the Gulf District of Papua (New Guinea) and was first reported in 1919, some years after the start of the similar Baigona and Taro movements. The excitement started in the villages of Nomu and Arihava. Eventually all the villages from Vailala as far east as Keuru became infected. In the various communities, the people were seen trembling, twitching, swaying, bending, and gesticulating erratically, while muttering unintelligible exclamations. Those affected believed that they were being possessed by some supernatural entity. Soon, others maintained, the ancestral spirits would come and bring the natives all manner of trade goods, unjustly kept from them by the white man. Some people had visions. Women became hysterical, threw off their garments, and fell to the ground. There were bonfires of sacred objects. By 1923, the wild, early phase of the movement had passed.

Similar occurrences—involving seemingly "irrational" behavior, expectations, and prophecies, and then attenuating without any identifiable reason—have continued to surface to this day. Reports of them, usually fragmentary, regularly appear in the news media. Thus UPI (August 7, 1972) distributed a news item from the Isle of Rhodes (Greece) about a violent argument between two women, which landed one in the hospital and the other in jail. They had disagreed on whether Christ would come again on August 15, 1972, or not until three years hence. *Newsweek* (October 18, 1971, p. 61) reported on a Chicago-based sect, calling itself the Black Israelites; its members were convinced that they, rather than the Jews, were the true children of God. Even though expelled from Israel soon after their arrival in that country, they remained certain that they would return to the Promised Land. "We are Israelites," they said, "claiming our land to establish a kingdom of God." It is my contention that even a large number of the student uprisings of the recent past were events of this order. In the case of one, I attempted to show this in detail (Goodman, 1973c).

Despite the fact that crisis cults have been and still are such frequent occurrences, reports about them tend to be sketchy. They are also, as Thrupp (1970: 13) points out, discouragingly unreliable:

> Most direct written evidence about a movement comes from advocates or from hostile witnesses, rarely from a wavering convert and almost never from a quite disinterested onlooker. . . . [Even field workers] cannot identify the first stirring of a movement nor describe its surreptitious phases. . . . We lack any figures as to turnover in the membership of movements, and biographical data.

Conceptualizations or models proposed in the literature for such societal events need therefore be treated with some skepticism. All of them were formulated without the benefit of a constant, step-by-step check for adequacy as against the complete record of a reliably observed field experience. This is precisely where the significance of the research lies that is being reported here. It offers a detailed account of a millenary movement from its initial "surreptitious phases" to its peak and eventual dissolution and fragmentation. This in turn will serve as a basis for a critique of some of the thinking about such cults in the literature and the formulation of a model of crisis cults.

The account of this millenary movement is based on my field work, which was started, as already mentioned, as research on the speaking-in-tongues phenomenon, beginning in Mexico City and then continuing in Yucatán. Because of my teaching schedule, I had to do my field work with interruptions, leaving Yucatán in the fall of 1969. I returned in June 1970, stayed till August, then saw the congregation again in January 1971, and in the summers of 1971, 1972, and 1973. It may be of interest to give some details of the field work at this point.

BUDGET[1]

For the first summer, my budget requirements (and available funds) were minimal. I lived with friends and used the inexpensive public transportation of Mexico City. My equipment consisted of a cheap portable tape recorder, a notebook, and a supply of tapes. Although the research yielded an important initial set of data, this first part of my field work was exploratory, and also a much needed period of apprenticeship concerning the belief system of these congregations, approach to individual informants, and the use of equipment under the rather special circumstances of the worship services.

The support I received from the Society of the Sigma Xi for the second summer provided me with films, tapes, money to pay informants, and minimal medical supplies. Transportation and living costs were financed by a federally guaranteed student loan.

The finances for the third year, now on the basis of a detailed budget, were provided by the Denison University Research Foundation. This made possible the acquisition of better equipment. As other anthropologists before me, I found that some of the "better" equipment was also more difficult to handle; for example, the expensive movie light and power pack never functioned at all, and the excellent tape recorder, although it gave high-fidelity sound tracks for a number of services, was too heavy and bulky to carry to the individual person in trance during the altar calls. The great advantage of the generous funding lay in the larger supply of film footage it made possible, the better pay for informants, and the feasibility of travel to a number of congregations in

Yucatán, facilitating a comparison between them and an understanding of the network relations operative on this level. The later follow-up study was supported by Denison University.

PREPARATION FOR STUDY

Due to the nature of my field work, the preparation could be staggered which I felt was an advantage. Aside from extensive reading, my preparation for the first field trip included an analysis of the glossolalia tapes available at the Cross-Cultural Study on Dissociational States and improving my Spanish, mostly by reading contemporary Mexican authors. Realizing the possibilities for filming in the work with the Mexico City congregation, I took a course in the making of documentary films at the Ohio State University Department of Photography during the following academic year. In prepartion for going into rural areas, I also attended a seminar on field methods offered by the Department of Anthroplogy, added reading material about Yucatán, and started learning Maya.The dominant society, with which I was identified, as an affluent, white outsider, speaks only Spanish. Out of habit, therefore, my informants spoke Spanish with me. It was often instructive to compare what they had said to Eusebia[3] in Mayan and then to me in Spanish. For instance, when Francisca described the Branhamist service to us (see Chapter 7), she spoke only of the importance of the tracts published by the sect. In Spanish, she emphasized that the basis of their faith was still the Bible. The preparation for the third and subsequent stays involved editing the film footage I had brought from the field, analyzing the sound tapes, and making plans for retakes, as well as improving my knowledge of Maya.

EQUIPMENT

Understandably, the equipment taken for a short stay in a village on the paved highway of a modern state has nothing of the complexity of materials needed by anthropologists going into isolated areas for a year or more. My principal enemies were heat and the moisture of the Yucatecan rainy season. For my own comfort I took exclusively cotton clothing, which absorbs moisture and does not burn the skin as does clothing made of synthetic fibers. My typhoid–paratyphoid inoculation proved to be sufficient protection, but the sulfa drugs were no match for the locally rampant dysentery, which responded better to Mexican streptomycin products. Antidiarrhea preparations brought from home were equally useless, but helped my hosts and their friends—

perhaps because of their belief in the superiority of drugs from across the border. I had no need for the broad-spectrum antibiotic ointment I had taken along, but it proved totally effective against a skin infection causing open sores in some children of the congregation, who possibly picked it up from playing on the ground.

CONTACT

After arriving in Mexico City, I looked for a church belonging to the Pentecostal movement and located an Apostolic one (a branch of the Pentecostals) through the telephone directory. The pastor of the congregation, *Hermano* Domingo Torres A., gave me permission to attend the services as an observer, to take notes, to use a tape recorder, and later, to film. He also introduced me to the then bishop of the central district. After returning to the States, I sent them both reprints of articles in which their congregations are mentioned. Pastor Torres was kind enough to recommend me to his fellow pastors in Yucatán, with whom I then exchanged letters preparatory to the work there.

ENTERING THE COMMUNITY

Although we had corresponded about this matter and the minister of the Mérida congregation met me at the bus station, there were no living quarters for me in the village of Utzpak.[2] This was due not to negligence on anybody's part, but simply to the shifting conditions in the village. A house for rent today might be reoccupied by its owner again tomorrow because the family could not find employment in Mérida or for some other reason. The Utzpak hotel had no vacant rooms either: all available space had been rented to engineers working on the nearby highway. This was fortunate for me, because a hotel-room occupancy would not only have separated me from the congregation spatially but would also have been detrimental to my reputation: this is what prostitutes do who come to the village from Mérida on weekends. Renting a vacant house was only slightly better for the same reason. This, however, I did not discover until much later. As luck would have it, my rented house became too moist to live in after an early hurricane, and I moved in with a family associated with the Apostolic congregation. From then on, avoidance patterns, acceptance by the group, and ostracism by the larger society, that is, the village, were integrated into the proper and correct image of a woman belonging to the Utzpak Apostolic church.

The village contains several small grocery stores as well as some bakeries, dry-goods stores, and a market for meat and vegetables. Butchering is done in the village, and the meat butchered at dawn is sold immediately, so that by sunup it is quite often gone. I cooked for myself on a small kerosene stove; as I became more familiar with my surroundings, my work load increased, and I found it more convenient to have Eusebia, my principal informant, cook for me. This arrangement yielded the additional bonus of relaxed and fruitful gossip sessions.

I always boiled the water for drinking and for brushing my teeth. This put me on the level of the infants—adults drink crude well water—and was occasion for some mild ribbing. I bathed as the family did from a bucket of water behind a small curtain in the one-room house and slept in a hammock. I found these living conditions difficult, but not unmanageable. The heat and the humidity, the monotonous food, and particularly the insect pests, foremost among them the enormous tropical cockroaches, were harder to bear. Culture shock was experienced mostly with regard to the lack of privacy, the impossibility ever to "withdraw" anywhere, but was alleviated by the friendship of the women who were my principal informants. It was especially acute on reentry into a totally secular environment, both in Mexico City and later in this country, where particularly after the first summer in Yucatán I had intense feelings of being exposed, unprotected, and distorted.

ROUTINE OF FIELD WORK

In the mornings I usually typed up the field notes from the previous day, at regular intervals mailing the original to my advisor, Professor Bourguignon, and keeping the carbon copies. These field notes, actually a detailed diary, became very important later in reconstructing the "surreptitious phases" of the upheaval, to borrow S. L. Thrupp's phrase.

At about nine o'clock, when it became too hot to work in the house of my landlady, with its stone-and-cement walls and tar-paper roof, I would go over to Eusebia's. Her traditional mud-and-wattle home with its high-rising palm-frond thatch stayed relatively pleasant even during the hottest part of the day. Here I would practice conversational Mayan, learn about the members of the congregation (e.g., about kin relationships) and about the village generally. This was also the time for filming such activities as the women's work or children's play. Often we went to visit other women belonging to the congregation in their homes. In the afternoons, there was more typing to do, then the daily bath, and, at sunset, chats with the neighborhood women—and four times a week church service.

During the church services, I used, with the permission of the minister, both a tape recorder and a Super8 film camera. I recorded the greater part of each service and took notes on every activity, in case of trances writing a description of the accompanying behavior, tape recording, and, whenever possible, also filming. Other activities in the congregation included the recording of conversion stories and the taking of a survey of the congregation. The latter included questions concerning place of birth, age, marital status, years of residence in the community, kin relationships, trade or occupation, date of Apostolic baptism, and first trance experience. For the understanding of the trance-based upheaval, these data later provided the all-important base line.

Sundays were spent almost entirely in the church. The morning service began at 6:00 A.M. (with prayers for the baptism of the Holy Spirit, often extending over several hours); this was followed by Sunday school, then the meetings of the various church organizations, called sections. The day was concluded with the evening service, continuing until ten or eleven o'clock at night. (All these conditions changed after the upheaval.)

INFORMANTS

Accidental encounter and personal attraction initially played a major part in the selection of informants. After becoming better acquainted with the internal structure of the congregation, I was able to choose representatives both of the core group and of the peripheral members, of those recently converted and some others belonging to the congregation from the very beginning. Conversations were usually carried on in Spanish, with Maya becoming increasingly important as my own proficiency improved.

STATUS AND ROLE

As far as the village society was concerned, my explantion that I was a teacher on vacation and wanted to write a book about the Apostolic congregation was quite acceptable, especially after I moved in with a family, thereby clarifying my moral posture. However, despite repeated careful explanation, my role as an observer was not understood by the congregation. My principal informants accepted it out of affection for me, but without complete comprehension. There are still those in the congregation who at this writing, more than four years after my first entry into the group, are convinced that my motivation is commercial. After all, they say, what else could it be? Obviously, I do not want to be converted, receive the Holy Spirit, and go out to do the work of the Lord.

Luckily this view, which I finally countered by saying that my husband was not yet converted and I did not want to be baptized alone, has not interfered with my work as a participant observer. Unfriendly things are said all the time about various members of the congregation without either prompting the persons concerned to withdraw from the congregation or causing anyone to be expelled. Such an action occurred only during the exceptional conditions of the upheaval described below.

During the peak outburst of the upheaval, at the service of July 30 (see p. 300), the minister attacked me by name from the pulpit, threatening me with imminent death if I did not become converted. It was quite a frightening scene, and I thought with apprehension that it would only take a single suggestion after this attack for the entire congregation to descend on the house where I lived—only a few steps away from the temple—and destroy my films, notes, and tapes. Fortunately, the suggestion never came. I was worried, though, whether I would still be welcome at the services. Rather than risking another scene, I decided to ask the minister directly because, knowing the circumstances, I felt that I was in a position to predict his behavior. He would, I hypothesized, be relaxed and friendly because, in the first place, he had been in a state of considerable dissociation the night before and thus probably remembered very little of what he had said. Second, in the terms of the belief system that he and the congregation shared, it had been not he who had spoken against me but rather the Holy Spirit through his mouth. No animosity on his part has been involved. I found the minister in the church, sorting pamphlets with the help of another *hermano*. They received me exactly as expected. When I told them that I would not be present at the baptism planned for the beginning of August, the minister said that he regretted that— they had hoped I would be able to stay. But I should not forget that there was a service that evening.

Being a woman in the enviroment of this Maya fundamentalist church proved no handicap to the gathering of data. The women always had access through their husbands to information classified "male." In fact, I think, a woman field worker has some advantages over her male counterpart, to judge from respective items in the literature.[4] Women share some very elemental experiences: in my case, at least, we had in common the bearing and nursing of children; providing food for our infants in times of famine; nursing the sick; cooking, washing, and sewing, to name the most important ones. Thus a relationship of considerable intimacy was quickly established. One area, however, has until now eluded me: I am very much interested in the physiology of trance behavior, and I hold that glossolalia is a product of neurophysiological processes in a number of ways, as mentioned before. I have found relations between physical exertion and trance, but as yet I have been unable to uncover data on the repercussions of trance activity on sexual behavior. (For a comparison of the two responses see Goodman, 1972b.) In part this may be due to accident. At the time such questions could have been asked—that is, when there was a great deal of trance behavior in the congregation—the composition of my group of informants was not suitable. Perhaps, also, this sort of information is more accessible to a male anthropologist.

As to roles within the group, mine became more and more diversified as time went on. My landlady and I shared equipment (she had no scissors or frying pan, for instance, and I no bucket). Eventually, I became *comadre* (sponsor) at her new baby daughter's *heȼmek* ceremony, when the infant is carried straddled on the hip for the first time. I was the source of small loans as well as gifts to the congregation for improving the church building and for helping in defraying the expenses of trips taken by the various members on church business. My informants used their pay for informant services to replenish their livestock (turkeys and piglets) and in two instances to buy seeds for planting a corn field, making them less dependent on wage labor.

My stay with the congregation was never really terminated, and I go back periodically to be brought up to date on the evolution of their societal structure and trance behavior. Between visits, we are in contact by letters, which, though not very detailed, provide a running account and some firm dates about various events. This contact proved to be of crucial importance with respect to the upheaval. The letters from my two principal informants provided the first hints about what was going on. In addition, Nina, one of these two informants, eighteen years old at the time, kept a kind of field record, even including dates and direct quotations. I had in no way instructed her, and her accomplishment was all the more remarkable since she had had only two years of elementary school.

The detailed report of the upheaval that emerged from all these efforts seems to me to suggest a model different from those proposed in the literature. A detailed discussion of these matters will be presented in Chapter 8, but I should like to anticipate here its schematic outline. What the data admit concerning a crisis cult, as W. La Barre terms it, is that traits of a large-scale movement, in this case Pentecostalism, diffuse to the local level. These traits are principally cultural-change elements, supernatural premises, and especially trance behavior. Locally, then, under specific circumstances determined by the conditions of a particular situation, a violent outbreak may be triggered, utilizing these traits. Such an outbreak will then proceed on three levels: those of culture change, of the trance behavior, and of the supernatural premise. As a result of the upheaval, the culture changes already diffused apparently tend to become less stringent than they were before, the trance behavior may largely disappear, and the supernatural premise emerges considerably strengthened and confirmed. In a wider application, it is entirely possible that some part of these traits is already available locally, and the substratum for a crisis cult becomes complete by the addition of only a few outside features. It is equally possible that the upheaval, rather than dissolving as it did in the present case, will become the starting point for a new large-scale movement.

To show in detail how the upheaval I observed provided the basis for this model, I want first to place the Maya congregation into its historical, geographic, and social environment on the Yucatán Peninsula, as a necessary elucidation of the background of the crisis cult. Next, I need to go into the nature of the Apostolic Church, an offshoot of the Pentecostal movement, and its spread into the area, showing also what distinguishes this movement from other Protestant groups. Since one of the most important traits of the Pentecostal movement generally is the speaking-in-tongues behavior, this will be discussed in detail on the basis of my research done in this field. We shall then narrow our focus and consider the congregation within the Maya village and the Apostolic church there—its organizational structure and ceremonial life, its history and membership.

With this preparation, we should now be ready for a detailed account of the events leading up to the upheaval, the outbreak of the crisis, its eventual dissolution, and its aftereffects.

The adequacy of the model will then be tested against the body of the data provided in the preceding chapter. In this manner I hope to demonstrate that it does in fact show a satisfactory fit with the violent crisis process I had occasion to record in its entirety as a participant observer. On a more general level, it is my hope that model can be used by others to help in the reconstruction of similar, but incompletely described, crisis cults and thus further our understanding of the role and the nature of this important adaptive mechanism of human societies in stress.

NOTES

1. The following discussion is structured on the basis of the field manual by T. R. Williams (1967).

2. Utzpak is not the real name of the village.

3. All names have been changed.

4. Margaret Mead a generation ago called attention to the possibility that women anthropologists may enjoy some advantages in field work not available to their male counterparts. See *The Changing Culture of an Indian Tribe* (New York: Columbia University Press, 1963).

2

Yucatán

Mexico is the largest of the Mesoamerican states, covering 758,259 square miles. It became independent of the Spanish Crown in 1821. As to cultural heritage, it is both Spanish and Indian. Its territory is occupied by a profusion of Indian groups belonging to a large number of different tribes, making this a multiracial and multicultural body politic. Yet the dominant Spanish society ignores the separateness of the Indians, aiming at assimilating them, while proclaiming national pride in the country's aboriginal roots.

The patchwork quilt of the Mexican heartland assumes a strictly homogeneous hue on the Yucatán Peninsula. This is the country of the Maya Indian. An important part of the classical Maya civilization flourished here; and although that structure collapsed before the Spaniards, driven by a violent storm, landed on the northeast corner of the peninsula on March 5, 1517, the Maya peasant persisted. He became the serf on the Spanish haciendas. Later, he was the peon, changing his bonds in name, though not in substance. Through history, he resisted with one bloody uprising after another. The memory of each earlier revolt fed the succeeding one. In the beginning of the Caste War in the 1840s, the name of Jacinto Canek, leader of the 1761 revolt, was written on the walls of houses as a revolutionary slogan (Reed, 1964: 44). In the second decade of this century, the Maya peasants, once more fighting for land in the Mexican revolution, sang in turn a song from the Caste War, the chorus of which is remembered by my informants today:

Yucatecos libres
Marchan al oriente

Allí quitar los malos
Estos como blanca gente.
. . . .
Chícochin . . .
Free Yucantecans

Are marching to the east,
There to expell the bad ones,
Those white people.

The present political division of the peninsula into the states of Yucatán, Campeche, and the Federal Territory of Quintana Roo is the result of the Caste War. Even today Yucatecans feel allegiance not to *la República* (i.e., Mexico), but to *la Península,* or *Yucatán*—that is, to the larger and historically older unit of the entire peninsula.

Yucatecan Mayan is the language that is spoken all over this territory by the villagers. The urbanites speak Spanish, although many of them also have Mayan as their mother tongue. However, they usually hide this fact, for Spanish is the language of prestige. It is used in all official business and public transactions, including church services. Street and radio advertising does use Mayan also, in competition for the peasants' cash. However, instruction is the Mayan language, a few years ago still compulsory in the teachers' training school, has been abolished. The tourist industry is today restoring some prestige to the Mayan language in the urban environment: Mayan courses are offered to foreigners in Mérida, and some of the fashionable hotels near the classical ruins put native costumes on their waitresses and encourage them to speak Mayan for local color.

Because of its cultural and historical separateness from the rest of Mexico, historical Yucatán (i.e., the present states of Yucatán and Campeche, and the Federal Territory of Quintana Roo) will be considered the larger society of which the village of Utzpak and its congregation form a part.

Yucatán is a well-known territory in American anthropology as a result of the work of archeologists, such as Sylvanus Morley; linguists, such as A. M. Tozzer and N. A. McQuown; and cultural anthropologists, foremost among them Robert Redfield. The peninsula covers 139,810 square miles and had, at the 1960 census, a population of 832,437 inhabitants. Its political system is determined by the liberal Mexican constitution, but its political reality differs somewhat from that of the rest of Mexico. In the latter the two-party system is more or less a matter of form. It is viewed by many Mexicans as a pacifier for the powerful neighbor to the north. The PRI (Partido Revolucionario Institucional) has been in power since the Revolution (1910–1920), and PAN (Partido de Acción Nacional) never wins the election. However, the contest is very real in Yucatán, and the PAN candidates have so much popular support that the rumor could come up after the presidential election that it was really PAN that had won, not PRI, at least not in Yucatán.

CLASS STRUCTURE

Yucatán harbors two societies: *los ricos,* the very rich; and *los demás,* the others. The very rich are historically the heirs of the Spanish conquerors. They have ascribed status and, due to their economic strength, possess a disproportionately high concentration of political power. In this study we shall do no more than recognize their separateness, concerning ourselves with *the others.*

Redfield (1941, 1950), in his studies on Yucatán a generation ago, saw a folk–urban continuum in the image that the communities of the peninsula presented to him: the tribal village out in the bush, with its inward-directed lifeways; the peasant village with its ties to the urban centers; the small town with its mixture of urban and peasant inhabitants; and finally the city, epitomized in the only metropolitan center of the peninsula, Mérida. Modern anthropological analysis confirms Redfield's judgment that the Mayan cultivator—outside the rain forest—is indeed a peasant. Using Wolf's (1966, 1969) criteria, we find that he is subject to the dictates of a superordinate state and that he is "existentially involved in cultivation and makes autonomous decisions regarding the process of cultivation" (Wolf, 1969: xiv). He is also first a householder, rather than a producer for a market. He sells only his surplus in order to buy the commodities he himself does not produce.

The picture of Redfield's continuum is also still substantially correct today. The contours, however, have become sharper, the conflicts more clearly perceived, the attendant stress harrowing, the distortion magnified. Some of this Redfield saw emerging in the late 1940s.

> In 1933, this man [who had written an account of his early life for Redfield] was all for progress; he had led his people in their effort to get roads, schools, and all modern advantages for the village. But in 1948 he was thinking mostly of the evils that were soon to come to the village as a result of this same road. . . . Now he saw that the road would bring problems and vices; that new standards of living would result in discontent; that his children would want the pleasures of the town; and that the old way of life, which after all he thought good, was threatened. (Redfield, 1960: 60.)

In other words, there are breaks in the continuum, not so much in the way in which the communities are constituted, but psychologically. Not that these breaks cannot be crossed. The peasant's son can and does become on occasion a trader (a well-developed role before the conquest) or a university student and thus a teacher, doctor, or lawyer. He can become a minister or a priest—or he can find a job in the (very limited) industrial complex, which is based mainly on the tourist business. However, the passage into the urban sphere is impeded by any indication of peasant origin: a Mayan surname, peasant manners and dress, illiteracy, and insufficient knowledge of Spanish, each more serious than the last. The two classes are poised against each other, with discrimination, condescension, and paternalism on the part of the urban dweller—and defensiveness, suspicion, withdrawal, and the ambivalence of both attraction to, and hatred of, the urban world on the part of the peasant.

ECONOMICS

Much of the pressure on the Maya peasant is economic. Traditionally, he grows corn and beans; he also keeps bees for honey and wax. The cultivation of henequen, an indigenous fiber-producing plant, was greatly expanded and taken into hacienda production in the middle of the nineteenth century. The plant needs less rain than does corn, but this type of export-oriented monoculture, sensitive to price fluctuations on the world market, makes Yucatán's economy extremely unstable. Henequen has not been able to compete successfully against synthetic fibers. Because of chronic crisis in the henequen industry, the Maya peasant is deprived of an important opportunity to earn cash wages for augmenting his income and decreasing his risks. Cattle breeding is increasing in importance, but few have the capital to start. The women keep chickens, turkeys, and pigs in the *sembrado* or *solar*, the enclosed area around the house. However, since there is no effort either on the community or the state level to combat the diseases attacking such livestock, this undertaking is most of the time unprofitable.

Arable land is also becoming scarcer, and land is being exhausted. More land is being used by the large haciendas for cattle breeding, partly in reaction to government pressure for a minimum wage for farmhands: cattle breeding requires less labor. Since many Maya peasants own no land except for the plot around the house, this development further decreases the acreage available for *milpas* (corn fields).

On the other hand, when land is available—for instance, in the form of *ejido*[1] land—the peasant cannot work it because he has no money for seed; he is usually not able to create, in Wolf's terms (1966: 6), a replacement fund. The Banco Agrario de Yucatán offers credit at 4 percent interest, but the peasants, unfamiliar with Euroamerican money-management usages, want neither to borrow nor pay back debts. These attitudes are reinforced by recurrent charges of mismanagement against the branch offices of the Bank in the villages; for example, according to newspaper reports, in January 1971 five employees of the branch offices in two Maya villages were savagely beaten with henequen ropes and then forced to leave the communities barefoot over paths strewn with stones and thorns.

Lalive d'Epinay (1968: 63) points out for Chile that in this century there has been very rapid urban development not accompanied by industrial growth, pushing the masses into marginality and maintaining them there. The same situation obtains in Yucatán. The only industry showing any growth worth noting is the tourist industry. Young girls from the villages go to Mérida or even further to work as housemaids; young men labor on the roads and in the forests or try their hand at house-to-house selling of cheap merchandise, especially plastic articles. A large number of them have to find employment outside the peninsula.

WORLD VIEW

The personal stress and, on the group level, the cultural distortion have their roots partly in economics. Since the 1940s, goods of considerable attractiveness and prestige value have become available on the peninsular markets and in the stores of the villages and towns. Their appearance has produced a change in the felt needs of the peasant. Yet his opportunities for earning cash have actually shrunk during the same period. This has led to a *perception of poverty*, despite the fact that the Maya peasant is neither deracinated nor destitute.

Factors other than economic ones seem to contribute even more importantly to the perceived stresses. We might subsume them under the heading of contact with the world view of Western society, producing a discontinuity in the value systems of the Maya peasant. Thus, work for him means growing corn. The *milpa*, the corn field, is not only a place of work but also one of worship (Redfield, 1941: 147). The production of honey and beeswax is equally involved with sacred concerns (Redfield, 1941: 136). This is true as much of the Catholic as of the fundamentalist Protestant peasant. Many of the latter are still known to bring offerings to the spirits of the *milpa*, although they shun the more public ceremonies in honor of the rain gods. Yet from all sides the peasant is being made aware of a different way of life in which work is divested of its sacred elements. This process, which Redfield identified in the 1930s, is continuing, especially with increasing contact with the ways of Mérida, where work is only secular and one kind of job is just like another. One of the older *hermanos* of the Utzpak congregation had broken some ribs in the spring of 1970, and his wife complained that he could no longer work, but kept on trying, each time suffering renewed pain. When I discussed this with the minister Lorenzo,[2] a city man, he said very impatiently, "What does he mean, he can't work? There are all sorts of jobs he can do. Besides, he is a skilled tailor. But these people think that *milpa* work is the only work worth doing, and if they can't do that, they are convinced this is the end."

Finally, and most devastatingly, the Maya peasant is dominated by a society that does not conceptualize social reality in the same way he does. In speaking about another Maya society, that of Zinacantan (Chiapas), Vogt (1969: 571) says:

> The patterned aspect of Zinacanteco culture that impresses me the most is the systematic manner in which structural forms and ritual behavior are replicated at various levels in the society. . . . It is as if the Zinacantecos had constructed a model for their social structure, their ritual behavior, and their conceptualization of the natural and cultural world. . . .

In other words, the natural and cultural world of the Maya is arranged hierarchically. We need not go to Maya antiquity and the tiering of the social order then or to the piling up of the pyramids. There is, even today, a curious linguistic expression of this kind of world view. A Maya peasant will say, "I would come home with twenty pesos, or maybe with fifteen, or ten." Or then again, "I'll invite five friends, or four, or three." There is always this structuring from the base, as if of a pyramid, up toward the sky.[3] Yet modern Mexican society, of which he is part, is constituted on the liberal ideals of the nineteenth century. It denies the validity of this hierarchical image of society and proclaims, instead, one of equality. Everyone is equal before the law, equally called on to vote; everyone has equal access to schools, medical facilities, material goods. When the Maya peasant has dealings with the larger society, however, the equality is nowhere in evidence. The law bows to power, and power is in the hands of the upper class. The schools above the elementary level are in the cities, out of reach for his children. Access to most medical services and to merchandise is predicated on a cash income. The promises the society makes are not kept. Here then is the source of a painful ambivalence: the peasant is placed in a position where he wants those promises to be fulfilled—promises that yet are contrary to his most basic concepts about what kind of world is right. He is made to desire what he hates and dreads, an egalitarian, a nonhierarchical, a disordered world.

During the preparatory phase of the upheaval, in the early summer of 1970, these stresses broke to the surface, grossly magnified. For example, two of the most cherished pieces of equipment in the church were the public address system, entirely unnecessary since the church was so small, and a record player. Both were gifts from congregations in the United States. They were even carried around to the various private homes where services were held on various occasions, such as birthdays. Often, to get electricity, they were rigged

with a spider's web of extension cords to other houses half a block away. "The world" that these objects represented, rich, powerful, alluring, was in this sense hugged very close, fervently desired.

Yet, no matter how much courted, the world would yield pitifully little of its favors. In the glare of insight given to the congregation as the upheaval progressed, this became increasingly clear. As response, the doom of the world was ever more shrilly proclaimed. "The world will be destroyed," *Hermano* Lorenzo shouted from the pulpit, "how wonderful that will be." As we saw, this "world" was a composite of many things. It was the results of the conquest, remembered often in conversation as "the days of slavery"; the shrinking economic base of peasant subsistence and too few paths to satisfactory wage labor; the urban lure and yet a lack of upward mobility; and the consequence of all of this, the peasants' perception of themselves as the poor. To this must be added the increased understanding that if they did make a transition to the city's way of life, this would mean the loss of the cherished, sacred, secret world of the *milpa*. The Pentecostal movement in its entrance into the peninsula, to be sketched next, must be seen in this perspective.

NOTES

1. *Ejido* is a federally administered program providing land for the rural population from haciendas, the large land holdings divided in the 1920s.

2. All names have been changed to protect the identities of the persons involved.

3. As another example, in the Apostolic church in Mexico City, the congregation is aware of the two ranks of ministerial officials: the deacon and the minister. The terms "pastor" and "minister" are used synonymously. By contrast, in Yucatán, the congregation sees itself involved in a complex system of ordering: there is the group of people attending church, but not as yet baptized. Then there are the baptized members of the church. Above them are those baptized members who are working closely with the pastor. Above them comes the (only male) *obrero*, an assistant to the pastor who will on occasion also preach. Above him is the minister, who is fully qualified for pastoral duty, except that he may not baptize. Finally, there is the pastor.

3

The Pentecostal Movement

The majority of Yucatecans is Catholic. However, the Catholic Church has kept aloof from the everyday life of the people to a considerable extent since the Mexican Revolution, so much so that in the fall of 1969, a "pastoral action" meeting was convened in Mexico City to "acquaint the Catholic Church with the social realities of Mexican life."[1] American missionaries have in recent decades come in to supplement the Mexican clergy, and in addition to assuming regular clerical duties, they are working to purge Catholicism of the syncretic patterns of folk religion on the village level, seeking to remove its Indian elements; they are thus making their own contribution to the pressures mounting on Maya peasantry. Despite this increase in Catholic activity, the field is still wide open for Protestant efforts. In addition, state and church are separated according to the Mexican constitution. Thus there is no legal basis for the state authorities to interfere with Protestant proselytizing. (Occasionally this did happen, though, for instance, in the early history of the Presbyterian Church in Yucatán, when the first such congregations were started there shortly after World War I.)

Crossovers from one Protestant denomination to another are frequent in the cities, with the women often taking the lead. Besides the Baptists, Jehovah's Witnesses, and Methodists, the Mormons and lately also the Bahá'í are represented on the peninsula. In recognition of the crisis situation of the Maya peasant, most mission activity is directed at him rather than at the urbanite, with even the Bahá'í mounting regular campaigns in the villages close to Mérida.

THE ADVENT OF PENTECOSTALISM

In the twentieth century, Pentecostalism emerged as the single most important Protestant movement in Latin America. Lalive d'Epinay calls it the refuge of the masses (1968) and speaks of its spread as the Pentecostal explosion.[2]

248

Various churches represent the movement in Mexico, foremost among them the Church of God, the Pentecostals, and the Apostolics. The latter two differ mainly by their greater emphasis on the unitary aspect of the Trinity, a subject made much of by the clergy. The laity, however, seems to see the agreements more than the differences, and movement between the Pentecostals and the Apostolics is quite frequent.

The Apostolic Church of Mexico was started in 1914 by Mexicans who had become acquainted with the movement in the United States (Gaxiola, 1964). According to Gaxiola, the Church is organized into twelve districts, with its headquarters, under a bishop president, in Mexico City. In 1964, it had over 1000 ministers, and the movement was represented in all sections of the country.

In 1949, proselytizing was begun in what was at that time termed the southeastern district: in the states of Tabasco, Yucatán, Oaxaca, Chiapas, and the southern part of Veracruz. Although in this manner Yucatán was nominally included, actual work there did not begin until 1959, when an evangelist named Oscar Gill (or Hill, he signs his name either way) from the Guadalajara congregation started evangelizing there. In the present southeastern district (Yucatán, Campeche, Quintana Roo, a part of Veracruz, and the eastern section of Tabasco), there were eighteen established congregations in 1970, fourteen in villages and four in urban areas.

This district, as all the others, is headed by a bishop. (The present bishop is the cousin of the man who held this office in 1969.) The central offices are in Villahermosa, Tabasco. Half the offerings collected on the local level go there. In turn, the elders representing the bishop's office make regular visits to the various sections. There are three sections: (1) Quintana Roo, Campeche, and Yucatán; (2) Tabasco (consisting of five subsections); and (3) part of Veracruz. Each section is headed by a representative or supervisor, appointed by the bishop.

The bishop's office convenes a yearly meeting of ministers. It is also in charge of holding a yearly biblical institute, at which new candidates for the ministry are trained and those already in office given advanced instruction. Training on the most advanced level takes place in the permanent Biblical Institute at Tepic, Nayarit, which is run by the national organization.

The sections also have their own meetings at regular yearly intervals. At these meetings, new ministers are inducted into office and decisions are made concerning the placement of ministers and the reassignment of others to different congregations. Members of the local congregations are free to attend these meetings, and often do. Evangelizing campaigns may also be organized at the meetings, but more often such efforts are left to the initiative of the congregations.

MECHANISM OF PROPAGATION

It will be recalled how Redfield's informant worried about the road he had fought so hard to get built to his village because vice and the new ways of life would be traveling along it. The insight was certainly prophetic. And it is perhaps significant that the Apostolic Church is spreading along that same highway, as part of the distortion and a way of escaping from its stresses. All the villages that in the summer of 1970 had active congregations were along the highway: Temax, Dzuiché, Limones, Cafetal, Bacalar, Nicolas Bravo, Jesús Gonzales Ortega, Cenotillo, Calkiní, San Antonio Sakachén, Tizimin, Cuarenta-y-Dos, and Campos, as well as the congregation where I worked and which I am calling Utzpak. Efforts at missionizing in Tibolón, accessible only by jungle path, are consistently warded off. Holkah, the neighboring community, is on the paved highway and has a Pentecostal congregation, but when its minister, with some of the members of his church, wanted to hold a service in Tibolón, they were driven off with violence. The Apostolics also tried to get a toehold on Tibolón. In September of 1970, three ministers and several *hermanos* went there to hold a service. They were met and evicted by a spectacular show of force, church bells ringing, fireworks popping, knives and guns openly displayed. However, one of the ministers in the group was a native of Tibolón. After his sister, who lived there, threatened to knife anyone who might touch her younger brother, an agreement was reached that he would be tolerated, but no one else. To make sure of his position, this minister, Felipe, also secured official permission from the authorities in the provincial center of Sotuta. In January 1971, however, the villagers once more prevented him from holding services. His sister was threatened with arson. In 1973 electricity was introduced and the bus company extended its services to the village. Simultaneously, there was a sudden increase in the membership of the Apostolic congregation. All services, however, are still held in Mayan.

The persons that make the first, more or less accidental contact with the evangelist are usually innovators, in the sense that they are searching for religious satisfaction outside the Catholic Church. The ones I have come to know in the Utzpak congregation and elsewhere have without exception a history of prior contact with other Protestant groups. Some of this contact was informal. In other cases, there was conversion and baptism. Their kin, who joined later, do not have such a history. The innovators are also those who, when speaking of their conversion, in contrast to others in the congregation, are very much aware of their anxieties. "Before, I always had this *temor*—terror," one said; or another: "Before, I often wanted to die."

If the innovator is from the city, he will probably start attracting members of his own nuclear family. In Mexico City as well as in Mérida, much "testimony" given at a designated time within the service consists of requests to the congregation to pray for the conversion of members of the nuclear family. After they have been attracted, the propagation tends to travel predominantly via a neighborhood pattern. This is shown by data from all the urban congregations I have come to know, even from such small towns as Chetumal.

If, on the other hand, the family still has viable kinship ties with a village, these ties will be the path by which the innovation will spread almost exclu-

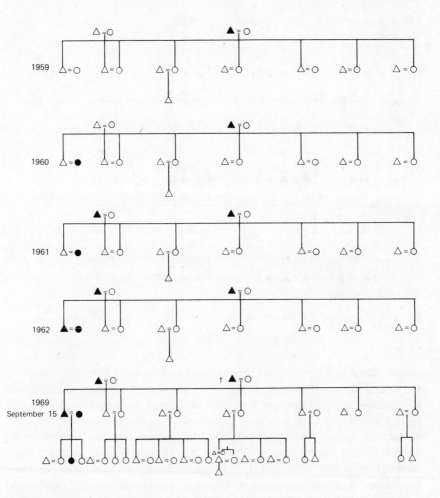

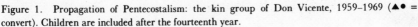

Figure 1. Propagation of Pentecostalism: the kin group of Don Vicente, 1959–1969 (▲● = convert). Children are included after the fourteenth year.

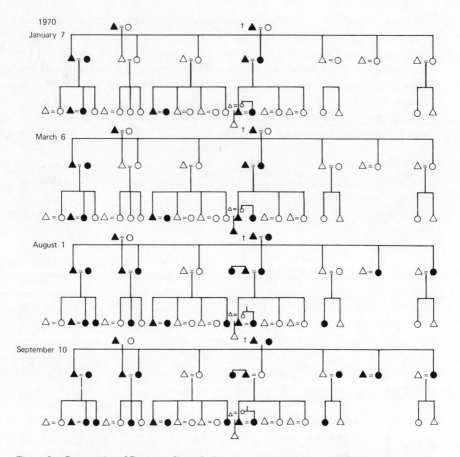

Figure 2. Propagation of Pentecostalism: the kin group of Don Vicente, 1970 (▲● = convert).

sively. We may take Utzpak as an instance. A woman born and raised in
Utzpak came in contact with Oscar Gill in Mérida, where she was living with
her husband. She invited her brother from Utzpak to hear him. He in turn
told a friend about Gill, who then invited the evangelist to preach at his wife's
birthday in Utzpak. Both this man and the woman's brother are among the
hermanos who formed kin "clusters" in the church. In August 1969, there
were 25 members belonging to nine such family clusters. Five of these
represented separate family groups centering around four men and one woman
converted in 1959 and 1960 by Oscar Gill.

Figures 1 and 2 show the growth of one such family cluster over several years. Don Vicente was among the very first converts of Oscar Gill in Utzpak. He was baptized in 1959. His wife Porfiria was sympathetic to the movement, but refused to be baptized for many years. However, she interested her daughter-in-law Ermela, who was converted the following year (1960). The father-in-law of one of Don Vicente's daughters joins in 1961, and in 1962, one of Don Vicente's sons, the husband of Ermela, is also baptized. The stagnation of the congregation is reflected in the fact that in the summer of 1969 the cluster was still at the same stage. Don Vicente had died some time before I came to know the congregation. In September of that year Ermela's oldest daughter, Luisa, joins. From then on, reflecting the tremendous spurt in growth experienced by the congregation, the cluster increases horizontally within the generation of Don Vicente's children and vertically extending to the grandchildren's generation as these beome old enough (see Fig. 2). An almost identical pattern is seen in the local Presbyterian congregation, where nearly half the membership is descended from a couple who joined 35 years ago.[3]

Of the 24 persons baptized in Utzpak between September 15, 1969, and June 15, 1970, only one did not belong to the kinship groups represented in the congregation. In the large baptism of sixteen members on August 1, 1970, again only one, a young girl, had no kin in the congregation; she stopped coming to the services soon after the baptism.

Redfield (1941: 211) argues that the "great family" is no longer a viable social structure among the Maya peasantry and that there is "a disappearance of institutions expressing cohesion in the great family." Wolf also maintains, concerning peasants generally, that relations outside the kin group—dyadic or polyadic relations on a personal basis—are more important than the relations to the kin group beyond the nuclear family.

The manner in which the Apostolic Church has propagated in Yucatán seems to argue that here is, in fact, a new institution expressing cohesion in the "great family," with dyadic contracts, such as *compadrazgo* (godparenthood), explicitly eliminated. There is an interesting reversal operating here: a godfather is not needed, it is said, *because in the church*, "we are all one family." Although from the outside this seems to be a new type of fictive kinship, in reality it is a reassertion of true kinship, for indeed the whole congregation belongs to a limited number of kin groups.

It is almost as if we were seeing in this Maya peasant congregation a new type of kin-based, polyadic, horizontal, many-stranded coalition (Wolf, 1966: 86) with a tendency to endogamy. It is polyadic in that it involves many persons and several kin groups or extended families; horizontal, involving only peasants; and many-stranded by sharing many interests. These include economic exchange (e.g., use of *milpa* land), kinship ties (including preference for marriage partners from within the congregation), as well as recognition of social sanctions, (besides those of the larger society, special ones within the congregation, derived from its belief system). The new social sanctions are reinforced in turn by certain symbols, such as the temple as a spatial and temporal gathering point. "A coalition built up in terms of such a variety of relations," Wolf says (1966: 81), "gives men security in many different contexts."

The perception of the congregation as a kin group is extended to the membership concept. Should conflict between a minister and a particular member arise, the latter will simply stay away from the services or go to the Pentecostals, with everybody understanding that, after the minister has been transferred, which happens periodically, he will come back. As occurred in Utzpak, the minister even pronounced the expulsion formula of "once an *hermano*, now no longer an *hermano*" against a particular member, yet the congregation is still saying under its breath, but with quiet persistence, "once an *hermano*, always an *hermano*"—and expects him to return some day.

We should emphasize, however, that by no means all members of an extended family will join the Apostolic congregation (see Fig. 2). A mechanism of choice may be operative here, as Foster detects in Tzintzuntzan. Speaking of the many roles with which the individual is, so to speak, invested from birth, he writes:

> Ego's only real choice is in the degree to which he will . . . honor the obligations inherent in his several roles . . . and in the selection of the individuals with whom he will honor them. Thus, through selecting relatively few kinsmen from his total family toward whom he lives up to the behavior forms expected of him by virtue of his roles vis-à-vis theirs, ego establishes dyadic contracts which determine his actual behavior. His family provides him with a panel of candidates. He selects (and is selected by) relatively few with whom the significant working relationships are developed. (1963: 1181)

That the selective process may in fact be considerably less arbitrary is demonstrated by the example from the much older Presbyterian congregation quoted above.

A PEASANT MOVEMENT

The success of the Apostolic Church in the cities of Yucatán has been minimal. There is a small congregation in Mérida, another somewhat larger one in Chetumal. In Campeche, there are some services held in private homes because there is no church. This may be related to the absence of industrial development on the peninsula. Lalive d'Epinay attributes the success of Pentecostalism in Chile to the appeal it has for the rootless, migrant population. Willems (1967: 248) speaks of a similar causation in Brazil. But there are no large numbers of deracinated peasants in the cities of Yucatán. Interestingly, not a single one of the provincial towns of Yucatán such as Motul, Valladolid, and so on has been touched by the Apostolics. Perhaps the compromise between urban and peasant ways achieved in these small towns is sufficient to eliminate the distortion felt by the peasants out in the villages.

The urban congregations were all started by men born and raised in the city. Peasant missionizing in the cities is singularly unsuccessful. For instance, Lorenzo, the minister of the Utzpak congregation, was born and raised in Campeche. He was largely responsible for keeping the city's small congregation going and dreamed of a large-scale evangelizing campaign there. Evangelists coming from outside the peninsula, he pointed out, are not successful in Yucatán because they cannot cope with the poverty there. You cannot earn a living evangelizing in Yucatán. However, Lorenzo was training a number of men in Utzpak to evangelize in Campeche. In the daytime, they would wash cars, repair shoes, simple jobs that took no particular training. Working only enough to subsist, they would use the rest of their time to evangelize.

Yet, when the upheaval came and nine *hermanos* did now leave their home village to evangelize, not a single one went to Campeche, or to any other city for that matter. They preached either in other villages where some evangelizing had already been done or, "on instructions from the Holy Spirit," in those villages where they had kin (see p. 313).

Although the success of Apostolic evangelizing in the urban areas has been modest, the small urban congregations are still of great importance to the peasant. In fact, the institution of the urban congregation has been incorporated by the peasant into his arsenal of strategies for adjusting to the urban contact. The home of the pastor and the church in Mérida, for example, represent a friendly haven for the peasant going to market or on some other errand in the city. He can rest there and hang his hammock to stay overnight. The pastor helps in contacts with the bureaucracy. He is there for other emergencies also. When one of the young women from the Utzpak congregation had a delivery requiring surgery, this was performed in the office of a physician in Mérida, who then put her out in the early morning hours to fend for herself. Her husband took her and the newborn infant to the home of the pastor, where the latter's mother nursed her until she was able to go back home. In another instance, a girl from the Utzpak congregation spent four months in the same pastor's house. This came about because during the upheaval in Utzpak there were allegations of sexual misconduct. One of the mothers in exasperation told her daughter she could not come home unless she brought along a physician attesting to her virginity. The girl went to Mérida until a reconciliation with her mother could be worked out.

THE DOGMA

The Apostolics of Yucatán are fundamentalists; they believe verbatim in the Bible, in the Spanish version. However, theirs is a very restrictive dogma. Large stretches of biblical teaching are never touched on. If the Sunday school lesson contained in the leaflets published by the central administration of the church cites passages of little interest to them, these are dutifully read, but hardly discussed, and the biblical text chosen for the attendant church service once more concerns certain pivotal themes. These themes are the following:

1. A hierarchical ordering of reality: Christ is the head of the church, the head rules the body, man is the head of the woman; or a tiering of the supernatural realm: God—angels—man.
2. Proof of the unitary aspect of the Trinity, both linguistic and formal; linguistic, in such arguments as "the text says 'baptize in the name of,' not 'in the *names* of,' so there can only be one God," and formal, in elaborate exegesis of the pertinent passages.
3. Prophesies about the coming of the Messiah in the Old Testament.
4. Stories amplifying the expectation of the Second Coming, such as the one about the wise and the foolish virgins.
5. Texts promising the Second Coming.
6. In particular any and all passages dealing with speaking in tongues: specifically the first Pentecost in the Acts and Paul's experiences.

Admonitions about loving one's neighbor are of little import in a society based so strongly on patterns of reciprocity within the kin group and never appear in the sermons. Sin, however, is a subject of considerable interest (more so than in Mexico City), but again is modified by the special traits of the society. The Mayan Apostolics have, we might say, their own particular sin syndrome. Some of this seems to be linguistically based. There is no word for sin,[4] and the word used today, *pécado*, is a loan-word from Spanish. This fact is reflected in the Spanish usage of the Mayan Apostolics. Sin is most often paraphrased as *cine, baile, tomar, fumar* (picture shows, dances, drinking, smoking), as if in a compulsion of redundancy it were necessary over and over again to recall the semantic content of this alien term.

The formula also serves to set the Apostolics off from the rest of the Christian community, both Catholic and Protestant, for this constellation does not connote sin to them.

Apostolics "leave the world." This is another interpretation of the formula. In the world, people see picture shows, dance, drink, smoke. It is a dangerous place, full of unsuspected pitfalls, just as the city, whence *cine, baile, tomar, fumar* come. The world is where Satan rules. The saintlier a person, the more Satan will try to win him over. Since the world is soon to come to an end with the dawning of the Kingdom of God, Satan has to work doubly hard if he still intends to foil these divine plans. Beyond this, however, Satan is a rather shadowy figure. His entrance on the scene in Utzpak as a sharply drawn personage of visionary reality directly precedes the onset of the upheaval there.

Another one of the attributes of the world is the ever-present temptation of adultery. This leads inevitably to eternal damnation. It has many faces for the Apostolic, all of them equally heinous. Adultery is coveting another man's wife, but also living in consensual union or courting and marrying a Catholic.

Heaven, or the Kingdom of God instituted with the Second Coming, has streets paved with precious stones. Everyone possesses a homestead there, all prepared. To be able to enter, however, one needs to fulfill two conditions:

1. One needs to be baptized with fresh, running water. The ocean will do or a river. (It cannot be water in a tank.) The water washes away the sins of the world, and it is for this reason that infants are not baptized—they have not yet sinned.

2. One needs to speak in tongues. This is the baptism by the Holy Spirit, showing that indeed the supplicant has been *sealed* by the seal of the Lord, has been given the promise of salvation. As far as the congregation is concerned, this is the sign of ultimate commitment.

A person may, and sometimes does, speak in tongues before being baptized with water. This puts him ritually into a dangerous situation, because he is "as an old wine pouch with new wine in it," but the matter can be easily and quickly remedied. Being baptized with water and then not speaking in tongues is infinitely more serious, for the person's entering into heaven is seriously jeopardized. A person in this position is admonished, cajoled, and scolded. "You are an old man," Lorenzo in Utzpak would say to an elderly, highly respected *hermano*. "You are tired and you may die soon. You must try harder to receive the blessing of the Holy Spirit! Fast, pray, think of nothing else."

CULTURE CHANGE

The appearance of the Pentecostal Movement produced considerable culture change, at least for a small part of the society of Yucatán. In various ways, the members of the congregations set themselves off from the larger community. Their greeting is *Paz de Cristo*—Peace in Christ. They call each other *hermanos* and *hermanas*—brothers and sisters. The men do not smoke, drink, gamble, dance, curse or fight; the women wear no jewelry and do not go to any dances. The families do not attend the Catholic church services, the *novenas* in private homes (such as are celebrated on the anniversary of the death of a family member), or the *fiestas* honoring some saint. Movies are forbidden, as is the reading of the *cuentos*, that whole class of popular publications from comic books to girlie magazines. Even for the ministers, the Bible is the only contact with the world of thought: the Bible institutes stress, in addition to devotional matters, such skills as reading, writing, and oratory.

The congregations believe in the faith healing of any ailment, from polio to snake bite and depression. However, Western-type medical strategies and the ministrations of folk healers are not excluded and are often sought simultaneously with treatment by prayer. For instance, one Utzpak child suffering from recurring abdominal swelling was treated by the local physician, bathed in herbal decoctions prescribed by the neighborhood healer, and prayed over in church. One of the former Utzpak ministers was criticized for having "too much faith" and thus causing the death of his infant daughter, who had been afflicted with severe dysentery; instead of taking the child to the local clinic or a physician, he and the congregation continued praying over her.

In the economic range, the professed ideal is for the *hermanos* to work only enough to earn a subsistence for themselves and their families. One of the *hermanos* in the Utzpak congregation gave up a steady job on a ranch and came into the village to live, doing occasional labor, in order to be closer to the church and to be able to attend services regularly.

The most upsetting aspect of the comportment of the Apostolics, as far as the larger society of Yucatán is concerned, is their trance behavior, which is thought to be either "madness" or sorcery. There is some indication that ritualized trance behavior may have been practiced in Yucatán at the time of the Spanish conquest, but if so, its role must have been minor. Bishop Landa, writing in 1560, remarks (1959: 49), "El oficio de los *chilanes* era dar al pueblo las respuestas de los demonios—It was the office of the shamans to give to the people the answers of the demons." This may have been possession trance, since he contrasts (1959: 49) with this activity that of the priests: "El oficio de los sacerdotes era tratar y enseñar sus ciencias y declarar las necesidades y sus remedios, predicar y hechar las fiestas, hacer sacrificios y administrar sus sacramentos—The office of the priests was to promote and teach their sciences, to proclaim emergencies and measures to remove them, to preach and officiate at feasts, to bring sacrifices, and to administer their sacraments."

Trance behavior may also have been involved in a feast celebrated in those years when the god Hozanek reigned and when "había algunos que se ponían a pasar descalzos y desnudos, como ellos andaban, por encima de aquella brasa, de una parte a otra; y pasaban algunos sin lesión—There were people who, naked and without being shod, as they were wont to appear, went on the red-hot coals, from one side to the other; and some passed over the embers without being hurt" (Landa, 1959: 69).

Trance behavior has been reported as part of the Maya shaman's experience, either in the course of recruitment (in Zinacantan, Chiapas, Mexico; see Silver, 1966: 28) or during initiation (in Todos Santos Chuchumatán, Guatemala; see Oakes, 1951: 141, 147). Whether this is the case also in Yucatán, I have had no occasion to investigate. My informants there were certainly unaware of any such behavior. The term *"bobat"* mentioned by Pacheco Cruz (1963: 102) as meaning "prophet," "visionary," and "diviner" occurred locally as *boobah* and translated as "ignorant," "foolish," "silly."

Speaking in trance may have been involved in the early history of the crisis cult of the Talking Cross, which arose in the middle of the last century, during the darkest days of the Caste War (Villa Rojas, 1937, 1945). However, the reports about the beginnings of the movement are inconclusive (Reed, 1964: 137), and again, the details of these events are not remembered in northern Yucatán.

There is, in the area of present-day Yucatán, extensive folklore about transforming witches (nagualism, Saler, 1967), in Mayan called *wai*. There is also some belief in spirit possession in the context of divination and healing, an importation from the spiritualist churches in the Mexican heartland. Importantly, in the villages, the peasants worry about sorcery, such as the strategy called "thirty-three," which, it is thought, can bring paralysis and death to the person so attacked. It is the allegation of sorcery and witchcraft that is most damaging to the Apostolics, producing fear, distrust, and ostracism within the village environment.

In the summer of 1972, an accusation of witchcraft came about in the following way. As already mentioned, the Apostolics were repeatedly rebuffed when they tried to preach in Tibolón, a large village accessible at the time only over jungle paths. One man in particular often disrupted the services and also threatened the participants, among them the family of the sister of Pastor Felipe, with physical violence. Thereupon Don Venancio prayed that the man be punished. Shortly afterward, two of his children became ill with the measles.

One died at home, the other on the way to Sotuta, where his parents were taking him for medical treatment. The distraught father suspected witchcraft and demanded that Don Venancio be questioned. Before the municipal president of Sotuta, Don Venancio admitted to the prayer and said that he had asked for God's wrath to fall on the parents of the children because they were evil and deserved punishment. The official ruled that Don Venancio should go free since prosecuting him would go against the principle that religious practices may not be forbidden.

The spread of Pentecostalism, then, the most popular of the Protestant denominations to touch Latin America, into Yucatán was initially made possible by the aloofness and indifference of the Catholic clergy to social problems on the one hand and constitutional guarantees of the freedom of worship on the other. Its fundamentalism and simple rules of conduct, together with its millenial expectations, appealed more to the peasants than to the urbanites. Usually by accident, the new faith caught the attention of the most restless of the peasants, the seekers, in that sense "innovators," coming, logically, from villages on the new paved highways, along which disturbing culture traits were being carried. In these villages, in turn, Pentecostalism (we are dealing in this report exclusively with its Apostolic form) spread predominantly, although selectively, along the arteries of the kinship network. The propagation, as we saw, did not, however, proceed without obstacles, foremost among them the allegations of witchcraft. We have reason to assume that the larger society perceived the out-of-the-ordinary behavior of the sectarians under this label, exemplified by that sine qua non of salvation, the "baptism of the Holy Spirit." Its external expression, the speaking in tongues, thus needs to be examined in some detail.

NOTES

1. Newspaper report
2. A *New York Times* article (December 10, 1972) estimated that at the present rate of growth, one in every five Brazilians will be Pentecostal by the end of the century.
3. This extended family shows a remarkable regularity with respect to joining the congregation: of the six children of Ego (the present grandmother and first convert), the three daughters brought in their children, but *not* their husbands, the two married sons brought in their children *and* their wives.
4. K'eban, "sin," used by the Bible translators can no longer be elicited.

4

Speaking in Tongues

The central behavior of the Pentecostal congregations, as already pointed out, is speaking in tongues (glossolalia), the utterance of unintelligible vocalization while in an altered mental state, a trance. Although the phenomenon is often mentioned in the ethnographic literature and is important in the history of the primitive Christian church, the literature on it is relatively sparse. Cutten's work (1927) is often quoted as one of the early attempts at describing the behavior in the Christian churches psychologically and historically. May (1956) wrote a review of its occurrence in the non-Christian context, and Pattison (1968) has summarized the research concerning it in the behavioral sciences. Sherrill (1964) has given a recent journalistic account, and Spoerri (1968) considers the behavior from a psychiatrist's vantage point. As mentioned before, some interest in glossolalia has been evinced by linguists (Wolfram, 1966; Jaquith, 1967; Samarin, 1968).

Much of the approach to glossolalia follows the pathology model: persons engaging in glossolalia are described as schizophrenics, hysterics, or epileptics (Sargant, 1959). Research results published since 1960, however, have shown this view to be largely untenable. Alland (1961), working in Negro Pentecostal churches, found glossolalists to be clinically normal. Vivier van Etfeldt (1968), in an investigation carried out in South Africa, showed that the mental health of persons engaging in glossolalia was the same as, or even better than, that of a control group from a conservative church. Hine (1969) has reported very similar findings from the United States, Mexico, Haiti, and Colombia, as has Garrison (1973) from Puerto Rico.

My initial interest, as already pointed out, was predominantly linguistic. In this chapter, I should like to summarize some research results that I obtained since 1968. The details have been reported elsewhere (Goodman, 1969a, 1971a, 1972a).

Glossolalia is an act of vocalization, of uttering sounds while the person is in a particular mental state commonly called trance. Actually, it is not one single behavior, but a behavioral complex. First of all, a subject learns to dissociate;[1]

261

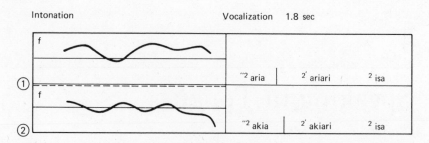

Figure 3.   Utzpak, Yucatán: glossolalia of Lorenzo, 1969.

as far as his sensory perception goes, he is removed from the awareness of ordinary reality. When this has occurred—that is, when he has actually gone
into trance—the subject no longer reacts to strong light (the flashbulb of a
camera), heat (from a 1000-watt movie light I used at very close range in the
small church in Utzpak), manipulation (a woman in the Utzpak congregation
did not feel that her small daughter was unzipping her dress in the back), or
discourse directed at him. (Persons praying in glossolalia are spoken to only
under exceptional circumstances—for example, if they are unable to wake up
from the trance.) None of these stimuli reach the subject's consciousness. The
trance experience does not, however, represent vacuity. It is only that what the
subject experiences is not perceivable to the observer. The subject feels fe-
verish; he may experience a sensation of pressure on his chest or of floating.
Very early in the experience, some report seeing a bright light. On the other
hand, the observer can detect that the subject is physically agitated. In many
instances, he manifests exaggerated perspiration and salivation. Tears may
flow, and the face is flushed; the subject is rigid—or he shivers, shakes,
twitches, or jumps. Many other motion patterns can also be observed. The
term "hyperaroused" can be properly employed to describe this agitated state,
and thus the trance may be referred to as hyperarousal.[2]

   In the second stage of the evolution of the glossolalia behavior, the subject
learns to utter sounds: there is vocalization. Some people, especially those who
acquire the behavior spontaneously, learn both the trance and the vocalization
almost simultaneously. The trance, already instituted beforehand, acts as a
substratum to this vocalization, generating[3] a number of its features. This
generative model is one way of representing the fact that this type of vocalization is not language in the sense of constituting a specific linguistic code[4] (see
also Wolfram, 1966).

   One of the trance-generated features is a strongly rhythmical quality, an
extremely regular alternation of accented and unaccented syllables, as well as
consonants and vowels, resulting from, and being the audible expression of, an

equally regular tightening and relaxation of the muscles of the vocal apparatus (see Figs. 3 and 4). Another one is perceivable as a very special intonation pattern. A unit utterance of glossolalia—that is, a vocalization pattern uttered in one stretch without a prolonged pause between its parts—is heard by the listener as follows: There is an onset in the medium range with respect to the usual range of the particular person's speech. It then rises to a peak which is perceivable as louder, sometimes more intense, or simply much faster. Quite frequently one hears vowels necessitating greater effort in their production (such as [i:] in "shriek" versus [ə], that is, the short and rather dull sound of the first syllable of "accompany") than do the sounds heard in the utterance preceding this position. Finally, the voice of the speaker drops, but this drop is usually much lower than that at the end of a declarative sentence in English, so much so that quite often the respective sounds can hardly be heard.

Neither the regularity of the rhythm (i.e., the alternation of consonants and vowels) nor even this particular intonation pattern, which I have represented in the form of waves, varies with the mother tongue of the speaker. An analysis of the glossolalia of persons speaking different English dialects, Portuguese, Spanish, Niasian (Indonesia), Ga (Subsaharan Africa) or Mayan shows no changes in this pattern (Goodman, 1969a).[5]

In the third stage, after having uttered the glossolalia, most subjects do not immediately wake up; they do not instantly become aware of ordinary reality. They remain somewhat dissociated—not as agitated, as hyperaroused as before, but still not quite collected. In this phase, some appear confused; their speech may show certain anomalies, such as abnormal slowness, and their re-

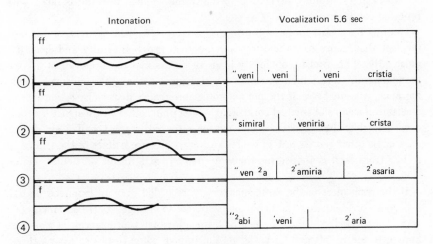

Figure 4.   Utzpak, Yucatán: glossolalia of Lorenzo, 1970.

call of quite ordinary memory content seems lagging. They are on something like a platform, which may last from a few moments to hours or even days. During this period, some inhibitions seem less in evidence than they are in the awake state (e.g., those dictating the "normal" distance during conversation). To be sure, in many cases, the trance state generally brings with it some suppression of inhibitions. In teaching glossolalia, this relinguishing of inhibitions is emphasized, at least in the linguistic range. "If you feel that your language changes," Lorenzo kept telling his congregation, "don't resist it, let it happen" (see p. 282). In the platform phase, however, this loosening of inhibition is especially evident, since people speak intelligibly, but are not quite conscious.

In a final phase, the platform hyperarousal, or residual trance, dissolves. The person returns fully to ordinary reality. He remembers very little of his actions while in trance. Particularly, he cannot judge how long the episode lasted. He may or may not remember that he uttered anything, and he cannot repeat what he said, except if he once more goes into hyperarousal; he remembers none of his movements.

As already mentioned, the Apostolics believe that the behavior represents the baptism of the Holy Spirit and that the Holy Spirit is perceivably present, speaking with their tongues, through their mouths. In other words, the event is interpreted as possession trance.[6] The speaker is thought to be possessed by the Holy Spirit. The first occurrence of the behavior is greeted with joy by the congregation, since it means that another person has joined the group and has been saved from perdition. With this cultural conditioning, the person engaging in glossolalia reports experiencing great joy, relaxation, and hope. Troubles are forgotten, according to many informants, and life is faced with renewed confidence.

Coming back now to the unit utterance I have described, we cannot overlook the fact that many of its features are identical cross-culturally and cross-linguistically. This finding obviously leads us to assume the presence of a common denominator, which must be physiological rather than cultural. What happens, it seems, is that the person going into trance does so by relinquishing a certain measure of cortical control, at which point other brain structures take over, and it is their processes that we see reflected in the vocalization during trance. In other words, the glossolalia utterance is an artifact of the trance: it results from, and is shaped by, the way the body acts in this particular mental state.

If the utterances of the same speaker are recorded over an extended period, it becomes evident that the behavior is subject to change. This fact emerged—very unexpectedly—when I recorded the glossolalia utterances of speakers known to me in Mexico City and in Yucatán in some instances over a three-year period. In his first attempts to acquire the capability, a person achieves only the trance. This we might conceptualize, in analogy to the pattern of the unit utterance, as the medium onset of the behavior complex. To learn to speak while in this mental state requires the expenditure of considerable energy, and when the vocalization is finally achieved, it shows evidence of this effort: it is usually very loud, fast, of high intensity (the person seems to be pressing out the sounds).

For a while, the glossolalist can maintain this high level, this crest of the wave, which seems to be connected with great joy and capable of dissolving even extreme anxiety. Then a drop in the level is experienced. The glossolalia utterance becomes stereotyped: for months on end it is repeated in the same form over and over again, every time the glossolalist goes into trance. Still later, the utterance gives evidence of yet another alteration. The sounds constituting the utterance require less energy to form; for instance, [h] will replace [ʔ], the glottal stop, in the same position. The individual consonant-vowel groups follow each other more slowly. Often, at this stage the pattern becomes very varied, whereas at the height of the experience it is quite simple, consisting only of a few often repeated syllables. The individual utterance becomes longer, but there are fewer utterances in an episode. Occasionally some subjects, especially ministers, acquire the capability of "freezing," or stabilizing, their behavior somewhere along the line of evolution,[7] usually either at this low-intensity level or even further on, when the glossolalia becomes very brief, just a phrase or two. Even at this stage, however, the presence of the altered state is still evident: the eyes are tightly shut and some characteristic movements—a twitch, shrug, or jerk—may accompany the utterance. Often, in this final stage, only the dissociation can be achieved, and eventually the behavior may become extinguished altogether, in the same manner as the individual utterance decays and fades away.

EMOTIONAL CORRELATES OF ATTENUATION

The trance experience, as already pointed out, produces emotional aftereffects of great joy and resolution of anxiety for the Apostolics. According to the informants, sadness, problems, stress are forgotten, and there is renewed hope. However, the attenuation of glossolalia behavior also has its emotional correlates, and these will depend to a considerable extent on what function the trance behavior has assumed in the individual's life.

For a considerable part of the congregation, speaking in tongues, beyond being a prerequisite for entering Heaven, serves the function of identifying them with the group and expressing their commitment to a new way of life.

For them, there is no particular need to repeat the experience. Despite this fact, as shown by the observational data, they will continue the glossolalia behavior. The eventual attenuation and perhaps total disappearance of the trance experience are of no serious consequence, however.

The emphasis for others soon shifts from glossolalia to other experiences within the same behavioral complex. Perhaps, since the glossolalia is remembered only dimly or not at all, such perceptions as "the heat of the Lord rose within me," with all its directness of body processes, assume major significance and represent the true contact with the godhead. As the attenuation proceeds, an "inward prayer" takes the place of the former recordable glossolalia and there seems to be no feeling of loss.

Then there are those for whom the trance experience with its attendant glossolalia is the only bond connecting them with the church. "Man is weak," Lorenzo explains. "He wants that pleasure over and over again." As it pales, they become disinterested and leave, often drifting to other movements. The lore of all the groups that I have come in contact with contains references to such lost members. With puzzlement, the congregation registers that this or that person used to speak in tongues so beautifully, but after a while he got tired of it and no longer came to the services. He went back to a worldly way of life or developed a preference for some other preacher around the corner. Sometimes there is the suspicion that perhaps it had not been divine inspiration that made him speak in tongues.

Finally, there are those who keenly perceive the attenuation of the trance experience and blame themselves for the loss of divine grace. There were reputed to be several of these in the Mexico City congregation, and I came to know one of them, a man I shall call Salvador. He interpreted his loss of the capacity for speaking in tongues (which he later regained) as signifying that *perhaps* the Holy Spirit disapproved of his living in consensual union with his wife at the time, not in a legally sanctioned marriage. He said that "the Holy Spirit is *muy delicado*—easily offended" and felt that this loss of the tongues had been visited on him as a divine punishment. His experience suggests, I think, that he must have been subject to diffuse anxiety before acquiring the capacity for glossolalia; otherwise he would not have been at a loss to say why in his mind he was punished by being deprived of it. Hence we may further assume that he in some way depended on the trance experience to alleviate his condition and thus was also more conscious of its attenuation than others in the congregation who did not depend on it for comfort in this manner. For nine years, off and on, Salvador struggled to regain the capacity for glossolalia (for details, see Goodman, 1972a). Then, after a great deal of prayer and under very special circumstances, he regained it a year before I met him during my field work. The attendant relief he experienced was very obvious: over and over again he spoke about his gratefulness to the Holy Spirit, about the joy of speaking in tongues, and about the changes for the better that had since occurred in his life.

Salvador's case may perhaps furnish a predictive model. In cases where trance behavior with glossolalia is established in the presence of higher than normal anxiety, its attenuation brings a return of the anxiety. The subject will then explore strategies in order to reestablish the glossolalia, which seems to be very difficult, but possible under certain circumstances. In other words, a number of phases emerge here:

1. Glossolalia behavior is acquired in the presence of heightened anxiety.
2. It attenuates.
3. Anxiety reemerges.
4. Efforts are made to reestablish the glossolalia behavior by various strategies.
5. Under special circumstances, the behavior can be recovered.

Glossolalia, as we have seen, is cross-culturally and cross-linguistically similar in a number of features, most importantly in its intonation pattern, which is the audible expression of the neurophysiological trance process. It is, however, far from being only a vocalization pattern. As a behavioral complex, it is not over when the speaker falls silent, but rather lingers on in the form of an attenuated trance. Later aftereffects include changes in memory and the perception of time, and, most of all, a generalized relaxation of tensions and an often intense euphoria. Extremely important in our present context are two observations. The first one concerns the fact that the underlying trance behavior and with it the glossolalia undergo a weakening with time, often leading to a complete extinction of the phenomenon. The other is that, in some instances, those experiencing this waning of the capacity have great difficulty in coping with the loss of a tension-reducing device on which they had learned to depend for the easing of painful stresses. The model developed on the basis of one such case, that of Salvador's, will serve later on to help us analyze the similar experiences of some of the men of the Utzpak congregation. It is to this congregation, the site of the upheaval—its setting, history, and position within the larger society—that we now need to turn.

NOTES

1. There is an extensive literature on dissociation. Field (1960: 19) defines it as "mental mechanism whereby a split-off part of the personality temporarily possesses the entire field of consciousness and behavior."

2. Fischer (1970: 1) represents normal, creative, psychotic, and ecstatic states along a continuum of gradually increasing central nervous system (ergotropic) excitation. "These hy-

peraroused states are experienced in terms of increasing data content and increasing rate of data processing. . . . At the peak of the ecstatic states, interpretive activity ceases or . . . there is no data content from without and thus no rate of data processing within" (1971: 7).

3. The term "generate" is used here in the sense Chomsky (1964) employs it in speaking of the deep structure generating the surface structure in language behavior.

4. Glossolalia is called speaking in tongues in the Christian churches because in some denominations it is thought that the vocalization represents a natural language that could be understood if someone were present who happened to know it. This inference is termed *xenoglossia,* from the Greek *xenox,* "stranger", and *glōssa,* "tongue".

5. In many congregations in the United States, Protestant and especially Catholic ones, glossolalia seems to be uttered at the lowest possible level of dissociation. That we are still dealing with speech automatism is evinced by the frequently heard description, "I opened my mouth and the sounds *just flowed out.*" When a peak discharge does occur, the vocalization is interrupted, and the "ecstasy" is converted into a private experience. In this manner it is not expressed in the characteristic intonation rise.

6. Possession trance is defined in the Cross-Cultural Study of Dissociational States as "physical states or behavior of human beings being attributed to an agency other than the person himself, but not caused by external action on the person" (Bourguignon, 1968a: 2).

7. At least this is my assumption to date to account for the performance of some ministers whose date of conversion and first trance experience is known to me and who in no way indicated that there had been any break in their behavior from then on. Another mechanism may well be operative: the behavior may be lost and then reestablished in a new cycle. This is what I recorded in the case of Lorenzo, the minister of the Utzpak congregation.

5

Community and Congregation

In passing from a characterization of Yucatán to a discussion of the Pentecostal movement, an outline emerged of the culture of the larger society within which the Pentecostalists represent a subgroup with a subculture. They share a considerable number of traits with the dominant society, but also have some of their own, most importantly their fundamentalist Protestantism and their trance behavior.

On proceeding to the local level we discern added complexities. In the terminology of the linguist, there is considerable "embedding" of structure within structure (see Fig. 5a.). There is the all-embracing Yucatecan society with its culture. Though a part of it, the village of Utzpak has traits of its own that distinguish it from some of the other similar communities. The same may be said of the congregation. It is a congregation of Yucatecan Maya Indians belonging to the organization of the Apostolic Church of Mexico and possessing in a large measure traits derived from this national structure. In addition, it shows some special characteristics arising from its being within the confines of the Yucatecan section of this church. Finally, a number of its features originate at the local level. The congregation thus might be thought of as being suspended within a system of concentrical circles. The innermost of these is the community of Utzpak (see Fig. 5b).

A MAYAN VILLAGE

Ethnographic Data. The community of Utzpak lies at the end of one of the paved highways that radiate outward into the peninsula from Mérida, the capital of the state of Yucatán. Its population of 5232[1] is predominantly peasant, in the sense in which the term was defined earlier. The people speak Mayan at home and in public, with much communication, such as business transactions in the stores, being carried on in this language. The men have a better command of Spanish than the women. Generally, however, everybody hesitates to display his Mayan language capability in front of strangers.

269

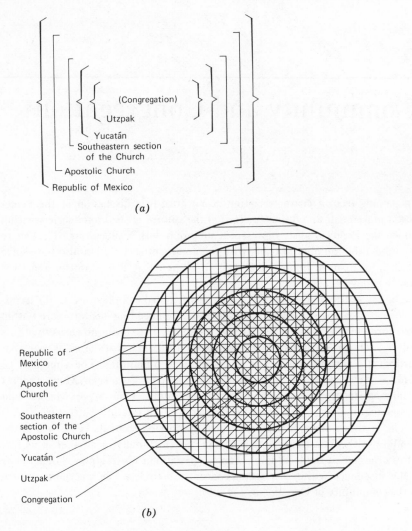

Figure 5. Structural embedding of the congregation.

The peasant character of the village is accentuated by the dress of the people. Most of the women and about half the men still wear the native costume. This consists for the men of white cotton pants and jacket, with *alpargatas* (sandals); for the women of an embroidered, loosely fitting dress, the *ʔipil,* and an obligatory shawl, the *rebozo*. However, though some of the younger men alternate between the informal peasant dress and the more formal city garb of dark pants, white shirt, and dark tie, the women are consistent in their dress without a single exception. A woman either *anda de vestido,* that is, wears (walks in) a dress, or *anda de ʔipil*—wears a folk costume; there is no occasion for which this pattern would be broken. Both groups, however, are equally interested in embroidery. A pattern for a *ʔipil* brought in from another village is immediately examined and usually copied, and the women who wear dresses still embroider *ʔipiles* for sale. Only women embroider, but men and women share equally in the weaving of hammocks, the other generally prevalent handicraft. The fact that city men like Lorenzo, the minister of the Apostolic congregation, did not know how to make a hammock and learned it in the village was a frequent subject for gossip. Hammocks are also made by the households for sale in Mérida.

About 10 percent of the homes of the villages are rectangular, with flat roofs of corrugated tar paper; they are constructed of stones and mortar (*mampostería*) or of cement blocks. These are the houses of the urbanized minority. Most of these homes have electricity; the urbanized women wear dresses, and their children stay in school beyond the second grade. Urbanized men run the stores and the other business enterprises.

The homes of the very rich are not much in evidence in the village, for they are hidden for the most part behind high *mampostería* walls. The owner of the one large cattle ranch has a spacious home near the *plaza,* in the center of town, but he and his family are rarely there.

Of the community's 1080 homes, 90 percent have the traditional oval shape with a thatched roof (apsidal house) and are constructed of mud and wattle, with a dirt floor.

The village has the usual central square, the *plaza,* and a municipal building.

Yet Utzpak also has many-stranded relations with the city, in this case mainly Mérida, and the provincial town of Motul in a very minor, second position. The main factor in this multiple relationship is the paved highway, which was extended to Utzpak in 1961. This makes possible a regular daily bus connection with Mérida. With it come other urban elements. The community now has, in addition to its six corn-grinding mills (grinding the soaked and boiled corn for the daily *tortillas*), a movie theater, a children's clinic, a permanent market hall, eleven stores, and six taverns. It also has a six-grade primary school with nine state and six federally paid teachers. There are two policemen, both part-time employees of the community. Misconduct (mostly fighting) is punished by one to fifteen days of labor for the community. Cases of murder or assault in a home are taken to Mérida. The municipal president acts as judge and mediator in civil disputes. There are twice as many radios as there are homes, about 25 television sets, and 42 motor vehicles.

Economics. The community is outside the henequen belt, and less than 10 percent of the men ever seek work there. Thus the village is only partly subjected to the vagaries of henequen economics, and its poverty is not as overwhelming as that of the communities west of Utzpak. There are some employment opportunities on the large ranches, several of which surround the community. Many of them are cattle ranches, however (240 ranches, one of them very large, the others small with a total of 38,075 head of cattle), and provide for the most part only occasional employment, with no census data about it available. The principal crops are maize (118,000 kg per year) and beans (75,000 kg per year), produced mainly on small holdings for the consumption of the households. *Milpa* (corn field) land can be rented from owners of tracts of varying size. There is also some *ejido* land available, the average plot measuring 4 hectares, for which an application has to be made to the municipal administration, but there is no organized *ejido* program. With a very few exceptions, the peasants own at least the plot on which their home stands; this provides the family with fruit, various chiles, *cilantro* (a popular herb used in cooking), and gourds for many household purposes (from a tree, *Crescentia cujete*, L.). In most instances, the plot is large enough for the poultry and the pigs raised by the housewife.

The majority of the inhabitants of Utzpak is Catholic. There are a mere 300 Protestants in the village, the oldest congregation being that of the Presbyterians. There are also Baptists and Pentecostals, as well as the Apostolic congregation, which in January 1971 claimed to have 80 adult baptized members. The very rich and the few destitute families are Catholic; the Protestants represent a cross section of the lower (i.e., peasant) and upper (urbanized) middle strata.

THE APOSTOLIC CONGREGATION

In 1969, one of the former ministers of the Utzpak congregation gave the following account of its history:[2]

BRIEF HISTORY OF THE APOSTOLIC CHURCH OF THE FAITH IN JESUS CHRIST, UTZPAK, YUCATÁN. WRITTEN BY HERMANO NICOLAS, PASTOR

When the missionary *Hermano* Oscar Hill was in the city of Mérida, he was visited by Señor F. C., who, because he was interested in the things of God, invited *Hermano* Hill to come and visit him in the place of his residence, which is located in the pretty community of Utzpak. *Hermano* Hill accepted this invitation with great pleasure, and after a considerable time, he succeeded with the help of God in having a group of people accept the Word of God. After receiving instruction, these persons were baptized in the name of Jesus Christ on the thirteenth day of July of the year 1960. From that time on, the work kept growing, thanks to our Lord.

The mission time of *Hermano* Hill having been completed, he had to leave the field, and the responsibility passed on to *Hermano* Nicolas, initiated deacon of the Church of Mérida. He stayed in Utzpak only a brief time, for at a convention it was decided to transfer him to the city of Villahermosa, Tabasco, as evangelist. The church in Utzpak was entrusted to *Hermano* Santiago, who stayed with the congregation for the duration of a year.

As a result of the decision of another convention, the small church of Utzpak then passed on to the care of another deacon, *Hermano* Luis, who after a short time had to abandon the work.

After that, care for the church of Utzpak remained in the hands of *Hermano* Nicolas, and the said *hermano* carried this responsibility for a year and a half.

The next person in charge, or rather the pastor, was *Hermano* Felipe, who for about two years came to serve the Lord in this small congregation, which God chose to bless during his stay. The latter on two occasions left for the city of Villahermosa to continue with his theological studies, and during the second stay, he was replaced in Utzpak by *Hermano* Lorenzo.

The church of Utzpak has passed through many struggles, but until now God has supported it with the power of His protection, and in the midst of the storm. He has made it flourish. This church has carried the precious seed on to other communities, such as the city of Temax and the village of Cansahcab, and with the help of God will carry it on to the other communities as well. We are therefore begging those who may come to read these lines to direct their supplication to the Almighty, asking Him to send His bountiful blessings to this church.

This brief history was assembled with good will, and we are giving it as a gift to *Hermana* Felicitas D. Goodman, as a token of our affection, wishing that God may bless her and that one day she may surrender to Him and thus obtain eternal life.

> *Her brother in Christ, Nicolas,*
> *Pastor of the Church in N., Yucatán*

The report is interesting for the constant shift of ministers it depicts. This is a general policy of the Mexican Apostolic Church, although it is not always pursued as consistently as in this case. Some additional data will serve to flesh out the rather sparse presentation.

As pointed out in connection with the manner in which the Apostolic movement is propagated in Yucatán, the initial contact with some innovators in Utzpak came in 1959 via the kinship network. Consuelo lived in Mérida, but was born in Utzpak. Her brother in Utzpak mentioned Oscar Gill (or Hill), the new evangelist from Guadalajara, to some neighbors, one of whom invited him to preach in his home. This was Don F. C., a peasant and former bullfighter, reputed to have had a pact with the Devil, who helped him in vanquishing the bulls. The first members of the future Utzpak congregation were baptized in Mérida.

Oscar Gill left in the fall of 1961, and the Utzpak congregation grew rather fitfully, wracked by factionalism, usually produced by disputes over tithing. The peasants seem to be consistently opposed to the position of the church organization that the congregation owes its pastor a living. Apparently, it is felt that a lay pastor should support his family with the work of his hands, as do other householders. Some *hermanos* hold that it is wrong for the Apostolic minister to want to be "fittingly" maintained by a tax such as tithing, collected from his congregation. If he refuses to live from his own earnings, how is he different from the Catholic clergy, who are getting rich on the backs of the peasantry, charging outrageous fees[3] for masses?

Don F. C. soon became the most vocal proponent of this position. Because of his capacity for disruption, he was thought by many in the congregation to be possessed by Satan. As late as 1969, he built his own čan casita de oración (little house of prayer) and invited the congregation to its consecration. Almost everybody came. However, because the ministers consistently refused to hold services there, the venture eventually failed, and the small building came to be used by some of his numerous family as sleeping quarters. Recently, with the extreme old age of Don F. C., this opposition has lost its leader, but it has never been completely silenced.

As with other rural Apostolic congregations in Yucatán (and, as already mentioned, in Mexico generally), no single minister was permanently in charge of the Utzpak congregation. In the period between 1961 and 1969, five different men held the position. The last of these, Felipe, stayed on the longest, two years altogether. During this time, the congregation dwindled to practically nothing. Many services were attended only by his parents, Nohoč Felipe and Eusebia, and one or the other of the original members.

In June 1969, the church authorities sent Felipe to attend the Bible institute in Villahermosa (Tabasco), and *Hermano* Lorenzo took his place. With his arrival, the membership began picking up at an accelerating rate. By the beginning of August, there was an adult congregation of 25 members, recruited in part from those who had drifted away in the intervening years, in part from new arrivals from the various kin groups already represented. A similarly erratic waxing and waning of membership can be observed in the other Yucatecan Apostolic churches as well. These fluctuations are directly correlated with the type of minister in charge. The successful ones who attract a large following are rousing speakers of some urban sophistication. They are thoroughly convinced that the Second Coming of Christ is close at hand and emphasize the need for baptism by the Holy Spirit, manifested by glossolalia. *Hermano* Lorenzo was this type of minister.

PHYSICAL PLANT AND ECCLESIASTICAL LIFE

The Church. When Lorenzo arrived, the congregation had its own church, located on a side street in the central section of Utzpak. It was built by the *hermanos* on a plot contributed by one of the original members. Constructed of mud and wattle, it has a footing of limestone. It is a long rectangular building, with wooden shutters for windows, a cement floor, and a high, pointed roof of corrugated tar paper over a tied wooden structure. The altar is a raised cement platform in the rear of the church, with a rostrum and a small table on it, both decorated with embroidered covers. The table is placed in front of the rostrum when all or part of a service is conducted by someone who does not have the rank of minister and thus is not allowed on the platform. It then serves as the rostrum. Women are never permitted to ascend to the altar, children are shooed off. Adults sit on wooden folding chairs, and there are some narrow benches for the children. Some biblical scenes drawn by the member of a neighboring congregation, red and white paper streamers, flower vases, and two plastic chandeliers complete the decoration. The church has electricity and the use of a well.

A man-high wall in the back of the altar platform closes off a small section of the building that serves as the *casa pastoral*, the pastor's house. In 1970, the *hermanos* surrounded the entire church property with an *albarrada*, a wall piled from limestone.

The church possesses a number of Bibles, a guitar and a *marimbol* (a native instrument with a wooden resonator and attached metal strips), some rattles, and a high-pitched little bell. The electric guitar, the public address system, and the record player were received in the fall of 1969.

The Services. The services last from two to three hours on Tuesday, Thursday, and Saturday evenings; on Sundays, there is a prayer service for the Holy Spirit from 6:00 to 11:00 A.M., then Sunday school for adults until 1:00 P.M., and another service in the evening. For birthdays, thanksgiving at harvest time, or other special occasions, additional services are held in private homes. All in that, this amounts to fifteen hours or more of church attendance a week.

During services, the women sit on the left side, facing the altar, the men on the right. A typical evening service starts out with a hymn. Standing, the congregation then prays, everyone in his own words. A *corito* follows; this is a short hymn that everyone knows by heart, with a rousing melody and a fast rhythm. All singing is accompanied by guitar and *marimbol*; rattles (in 1969 one made of the lower jaw of a horse with its teeth still in place and painted green) and hand clapping emphasize the rhythm. Clapping tends to become very intense during the *coritos*.

During the subsequent testimony period various members offer a biblical text or praise for some recent blessing set in conventional phrases; they may also request the prayers of those present for some private concern. Another hymn follows and then a *corito* often quite frankly alluding to the trance experience (such as the perception of heat) and asking the Holy Spirit to manifest itself. While this singing is still in progress, the congregation goes to the altar, the men kneeling on the right side, the women on the left. The prayer during this altar call is loud, each person again using his own words. This period may last up to 20 minutes, and usually some speak in tongues. On Sundays it may last much longer. The pastor ends the altar call with a bell signal. The congregation sings another hymn, and then there is an offering of special hymns by individual members or small groups. A reading from the Bible, a *corito*, collection of the offering, and prayer for it are followed by the sermon. After yet another hymn, the congregation engages in a second altar call. The service concludes with a prayer for the sick, who come and kneel at the altar to receive the prayers of the congregation.

DISTINCTIVENESS[4]

Within the village, the fact that the Apostolics emphasize their difference from (and superiority to) everyone else is resented and countered in various ways. There are frequent expressions of dislike from fellow villagers.

> *June 1969. Evening service.* The *hermanos* have been to the *monte* (bush) to cut wood, for the roof of the church is disintegrating. Insect damage and humidity are very hard on the beams. When I get to the church, they are in the processes of cleaning away the saw dust that has fallen in the course of the day. "The repair is urgent," comments Lorenzo. "One strong wind, and the roof falls on our heads. And won't our neighbors enjoy *that*! They don't like the *evangelios* around here." Eusebia says the same thing: "We are not liked here. There is a woman who hardly ever speaks to me. She does not see me in the Catholic church, so she turns up her nose at me."

The Apostolics set themselves off by a different greeting pattern, that is, *Paz de Cristo*; the community in turn does not recognize them in face-to-face encounter:

> I board the bus at the plaza, to go to Mérida. One of the teenagers that used to visit me regularly when I was living in Chucha's house and was thus not yet identified with the Apostolics also boards the bus, and I greet her. She ostentatiously ignores me. I tell Eusebia when she gets on at her corner past the cementary. She shrugs her shoulders. "They know now that you belong to us," she says. Even the bus driver gets into the act of social ostracism. When we get off the bus in the evening, we are not given the "que les vaya bien"—may it go well with you—with which he dispatches the other passengers.

In the economic sphere, discrimination is minimal, surfacing only when personal relations are also involved. This is the case with an old *hermana*, constrained to beg since she has no sons to support her. She often finds the doors closed to her with the comment, "*es evangelia*—she is a Protestant."

The threat of violence is, however, always present, not only against the Apostolics but also against other similar churches, such as the Pentecostals:

> Some months ago a young man came from Cansahcab to work in the little Pentecostal church here. He knew no one in Utzpak. Three men grabbed him near his church, two held him, the third one kept hitting him in the chest and stomach, until he started vomiting blood. They left him lying, and later he crawled to a nearby house and asked for help. He was taken to a sanatorium in Mérida, and he has now recovered, but the Pentecostal church here has practically dissolved. Eusebia thinks that every two weeks somebody comes to hold a service, but there is not much attendance. She worries about her son Felipe, but he tells her that in the first place he knows how to fight, and so can defend himself, in the second place he knows lots of people, and a person who is known is protected, simply by that fact.

As already mentioned, the most extreme form of disapproval is expressed in the allegation of witchcraft, an instance of which was recounted by Eusebia:

> At this corner, we once came by, *Hermana* Valuch, I, and some of the others, and a woman came out of the door, I don't remember her name, and she called us *hechiceras* [witches], and she put her right hand on her left upper arm like this (patting it a little), which means that she was going to beat us. They say that from that time on she has not been able to move her left arm. Well, that's what they say. They even say that the family called the doctor the same evening, but he could do nothing for her. A few months later she died.[5]

The Religious Milieu. The principal accusation leveled by the Apostolics against the Catholics is one of idolatry. There is quite clearly anger in this accusation. The attacks of the Catholics against their Maya adversaries are well remembered.[6] One of the ministers said in a sermon, "The Catholics brought with them a little doll with a pretty face and a well-painted mouth, but all that happened was that people passed from an ugly idol to a pretty one."

The Catholics are the ones called pagans, not the Maya priests who still prepare *hanlicol*, the food for the spirits of the *milpa*. When I asked about the meaning of the term, the answer was, "That is the food *they* prepare for *their gods*." It seemed as though this ceremony were thought of as a realm unto itself, separate and thus not accessible to value judgments so unabashedly hurled against other, Christian, denominations.

The Catholics, the Apostolics hold, are also ignorant: the Catholics, *Hermana* Chela explains, do not know

> that the Bible is the true and exact word of God. Therefore, you have to teach them little by little, and you must not do like *Hermano* Valencio in Temax, who goes up to people and tells them that they must change their ways and be baptized, or they will go straight to hell and eternal damnation. No wonder the men at the plaza beat him up. The people say, "What about the Holy Spirit? Does he walk down the street, do you see him, does he come into your temple?" They don't understand that the Holy Ghost is a spirit and enters the heart.

The Catholics are lost, it is believed, since they do not subscribe to the moral code of the Apostolics. Thus Eusebia mourns the fate of her Catholic sons:

> Many times I feel sad. After all, my sons will not leave the world, they go to dances, to the *cine*, they have several women. So we already know that when Judgment Day comes, they will be on the other side, and that hurts.

The supposed eschatological flippancy of the Catholics is occasion for much amusement.

> When a *hermano* dies," Eusebia remarks, "hardly anybody cries, and there are no candles. After all, we know where he is going, and so there is no reason for tears. Although, of course, no one can be absolutely certain that he has done everything right. Only God knows." Then she laughs. "For the Catholics, it's easier. Remember what *Hermano* Lorenzo said last Sunday? A Catholic can sin all his life, and then, when the final hour comes, he calls the priest to help him. And the *cura* says, "Here, pay me forty pesos for the mass, and off to heaven you go." She shakes her head admiringly, "I wonder where the *Hermano* always gets these things he says."

As far as the Protestant denominations are concerned, the condemnation is less severe. As Emilio, one of the members of the Utzpak congregation puts it, "They go to movies, to dances, so, obviously, their dogma cannot be the truth." Others perceive differences on the emotional and behavioral level:

> What in her mind, I ask *Hermana* Ermela, is the difference between Catholics, Presbyterians, and *Apostolics?* She thinks that the others do not love each other like the Apostolics. Pedro joins the conversation at this point. He agrees with Ermela: "The Presbyterians don't call each other *hermanos*, and those that have money are very proud. There is much pride in the Presbyterian church. Besides," he adds, "their service is very dry. There is no joy there. Mainly, the Apostolics have discipline. I like that. There is much discipline. The Presbyterians have no discipline. People talk to each other, walk in and out. That is not the way it should be."

The ministers, however, hammer away at the level of dogma.

> Nicolas holds a sermon on Hebrews 10: 27. There are thousands or hundreds of Christian movements, but only one teaches the word of Jesus Christ.[7] The other people are merely creatures of God, they are not His children. If somebody were to say to him, here is a baptism that truly saves, he would go there to be baptized. But he will not go unless there is security that it is really so. The baptism of the Holy Spirit is the wings for entering into the Kingdom of God. The baptism of the Holy Spirit is the guarantee of salvation. And the only proper church where this can be obtained in its proper, valid form is the Apostolic one.

As we saw, the village presents the picture of a peasant community of householders engaged in subsistence farming and wage labor. It shares with other Latin-American villages its dual Spanish-Indian character, to which in recent decades the contact with Euro-American market behavior has added its own traits and attendant distoration. In the religious sphere, Catholicism determines the scene in syncretic patterns derived from centuries of interaction with the native heritage. Protestantism, too, has more than 50 years of history in the area. The aggressive missionizing of the various Pentecostal denominations has appeared only recently. The members of these churches find themselves in opposition not only to the Catholics but also to other Protestants. This contributes to a feeling of isolation, but naturally also to one of group centeredness, of *esprit de corps.*

Nothing in this picture, however, lets the particpant observer predict the outbreak of a crisis cult. As we shall see, for that to happen, more is needed than the substratum of a society experiencing novel and distorting pressures—certain other mechanisms also must be set into motion. What these were in the special case of the Utzpak Apostolic congregation should emerge as we trace the multilevel events that led to the crisis, produced its peak, and eventually advanced it into dissolution.

NOTES

1. All figures cited in this chapter are from the 1970 census, unless noted differently.

2. All names have been changed to protect the privacy of the persons involved in the subsequent upheaval in the congregation.

3. In 1970, a nuptial mass cost 400 pesos ($33 in U.S. currency) or more; a farmhand on a ranch earns about 20 pesos a day.

4. Unless stated otherwise, the quotations are taken from my field notes. Some selections from these field notes were published elsewhere (Goodman, 1972b) and are included here with the express permission of the University of Chicago Press. A ballad popular in the Apostolic churches in Yucatán and in the taverns in 1972 had the following stanza: "*Amistades, amigos y parientes/Fueron las gentes que yo relacioné/Me abandonaron por causa de su nombre/Cuando supieron que ya me bautisé/*Acquaintances, friends, and relatives/Were the people who surrounded me/They deserted me for the sake of his name/When they discovered that I was baptized."

5. Although not expressly stated, the understanding here is that the suspicion of sorcery rebounded from those innocently accused, killing, instead the accuser.

6. Making disparaging remarks about the Catholics is traditional not only in Yucatán but all over Mexico. It is the Indian's way of retaliating against the Catholic Church for its universalist claims and intolerance of the Indian's belief system.

7. Here again there is the progression from the large number to the smaller one, as noted before (p. 246).

6

Chronology of Events

Summer of 1969. Lorenzo was a city man, born and raised in Campeche, the second largest city of the peninsula. He was 24 years old when he took over the Utzpak congregation in the late spring of 1969. This was his first appointment to a village congregation and he was enthusiastic and full of ambition. His sermons were fiery, humorous, laced with Mayan expressions—just the right mixture of brimstone and the golden avenues of Heaven. News of such a preacher travels fast. Within weeks, members who had stayed away for years were beginning to drift back, bringing along interested kinsmen.

Lorenzo propped up the sagging organizational fabric of the congregation. He started the "section" of the *Dorcas* (i.e., the married women's) and that of the young people, and instructed them in the parliamentary procedures for running their organizations, pattered after United States usage. He increased the income from the congregation, of which half, as already mentioned, goes to the church district headquarters in Villahermosa, Tabasco, and half toward the expenses of the minister. This he did by insisting on the need for tithing, by inventing all manner of special occasions on which donations had to be made, and by introducing the *talento*. This is an institution, also used by other Apostolic congregations in the Republic, where the church contributes money or material, the members the labor, and the product is sold to benefit the church treasury.

Lorenzo's greatest significance for the congregation of Utzpak lay in his skill in teaching his parishioners how to achieve the trance state and the attendant glossolalia. In the spring of 1969, only two men and none of the women engaged in this behavior. As a result of Lorenzo's activity, this number increased rapidly. The strategy he used may have been his own innovation: I did not see it either in Mexico City or in the four congregations other than Utzpak I came to know in Yucatán, including the one where he himself spoke in tongues for the first time. This strategy did not vary all that summer and became more effective with each succeeding Sunday, because its success added expectation to the already excellent teaching method.

Lorenzo insisted that those desiring to "receive the Holy Spirit" fast on Sunday morning, prior to the prayer service. He then instructed them to kneel close to the altar. Those who had already learned trance behavior and glossolalia were told to kneel behind the candidates. With cultural expectations set up in the preceding sermon and with the rhythmic pattern of the singing, musical accompaniment, and clapping, the congregation and especially the candidates were instructed to pray. The description of one of these prayer services for the Holy Spirit may illustrate the entire process.

July 6, 1969. Lorenzo gives instructions as on the previous Sunday. "If you feel something supernatural," he says, "don't resist it. It is the Holy Spirit. Repeat 'séllame, séllame,' until your tongue gets tired." If the women get tired kneeling, they should stand, but should not go to sit down. Then they should go back to kneeling.

Lorenzo now instructs Floriano and Isaía, who are seeking the manifestation, to kneel directly next to the podium; Nohoč Felipe, Valentin, and Emilio, who haven't already learned the behavior, are to kneel behind them. They should leave enough room between them so that he can pass. (There is a tendency for people to draw closer together in the course of this prayer.)

The congregation sings the hymn "Santo Espíritu descende—Come Down, Holy Spirit." Very soon Floriano, who achieved a trance[1] last Sunday, goes into trance and this time also breaks into glossolalia. Despite his dark complexion, his flush is quite visible. He is totally oblivious of the fact that I have the camera and later the microphone trained on him, the latter often very close to his face. He is kneeling, palms on floor, shaking; there is profuse perspiration, even on the back of his hands, and some small amount of clear salivation. Lorenzo's level is steadily dropping. Finally the session ends.

Lorenzo asks if anybody felt anything, and Floriano comes to the front, facing the congregation, saying that he did. He thinks that he may have had a change of language, but he does not know (after about fifteen minutes of tremendous vocalization). Lorenzo, who had been passing from one supplicant to the other, confirms that indeed Floriano has spoken in tongues. So has Francisca, his wife. She herself is not sure; she claims to have felt something ("gozo—joy," I heard her say later in a bemused fashion to the other women), but she does not know for certain whether her language changed. Again, Lorenzo confirms the fact.

After the pause, Lorenzo repeats his usual instructions. Only Isaía is now without the baptism of the Holy Spirit. Lorenzo orders him to the podium; the four others who are already glossolalists are to kneel in a semicircle behind him.

The congregation now begins the corito. Its text, "Fuego, fuego, fuego es que quiero, dámelo, dámelo, Señor—Fire, fire, fire is what I want, give it to me, give it to me, Lord," is a clear reference to hyperarousal and the accompanying sensation of heat. Lorenzo concentrates every effort on Isaía, a straight-backed dignified man, more Spanish than Indian in appearance, "driving" him by shouting at him both the formula "séllalo, séllalo" and his own glossolalia. By "driving" I mean an effect on a subject similar to the one produced on, for example, a football team by the cheers of an audience, except that here the desired result is not simply greater efforts, but the induction of trance. Emilio goes into glossolalia, but he is exhausted and his pitch is lower than before. Floriano is also back in glossolalia, with a lower pitch. Emilio then recovers, goes very high, drops fast, and returns to "séllalos, séllalos," a sign that he is no longer in trance. In front of him there is a little puddle of clear saliva on the cement floor. The general level drops, and soon everybody is back to ordinary language; people are wiping their faces. A group of neighbor children who had crowded into the side door to watch the goings-on begins to melt away. The people return to their seats.

Lorenzo calls on Isaía to come to the front. Yes, he did feel something, he felt as if he were being compressed inside, but in his language he felt only a small change. This is all that Francisca reported, but apparently Lorenzo has higher requirements for the men. He tells Isaía that he should pray more, and when the Holy Spirit wants to speak, he should let it say what it wants to.

By the end of August 1969, Lorenzo had taught the glossolalia behavior to 22 of his 24 adult members. Much of the glossolalia was very loud at this time, fast, and, as I had recorded elsewhere from beginning speakers, it consisted in most instances of a high-pitched [bububububububububu] or [ʔuʔuʔuʔuʔuʔuʔuʔu]. For the first time in the congregation's history, women as well as men went into hyperarousal. This success was interpreted as indicating that the Second Coming was now much closer at hand than before.

GATHERING MOMENTUM[2]

The feeling of exaltation, of something special going on, was further reinforced by the baptism on August 4, 1969. On this occasion, seven persons were baptized, four women and three men, more than on any previous occasion in the congregation.

Baptism, August 4, 1969. The congregation has been assembled at the church at dawn. Soon Lorenzo and Felipe come around the corner, a panel truck inches across the outcroppings of limestone, tilting this way and that, and stops before the church. Some benches and collapsible chairs are loaded on, the children begin scrambling on board. The women with their babies are helped on next. Eusebia gets to sit on a chair. Beside her is Estela, Francisca's sister, her face taut with fear and doubt: her husband has threatened to beat her if she gets baptized. For the men there is standing room only; they pull their sombreros down over their faces to keep them from blowing off. The sun is burning hot now—it is 7:30 A.M. when we finally pull out. We put towels on our heads for protection, trying to shield the children, who are squealing and squirming. One *hermano* has the guitar of the church, but soon gives up on playing it for lack of space. He starts hymn after hymn after *corito*, everybody singing joyously along.

In Temax, we halt for a little while. There had been talk that somebody from the Temax congregation would also be baptized, but no one shows up. As we pull out, some of the men in front of the tavern shout obscenities in Mayan, and Eusebia, who is my language instructor, looks at me to see if I had understood. We both laugh. The laurel trees along the highway sometimes hang so low that we are brushed by the branches. More laughter. We pass through Cansahcab. When the truck stops at a *tortilleria*, some of the fathers get off to buy tortillas; among them is Chela's husband, who apparently has decided to come along anyway, even if not to be baptized.

Chela and Pedrito, her paralyzed infant, are in the cabin with the driver. We drive on. Soon we bump along a narrow, unfinished country road. As we draw nearer to the coast, there are small, dead trees and tall cacti. Then the coconut trees appear, there are a few houses, and the truck stops. We have arrived at Santa Clara. With baskets, bags, and babies, we walk toward the shore and soon are ankle-deep in sand. The sky is clouded over, there is an occasional drop of rain. We come to a shelter on the shore, a palm-leaf roof on poles, where we stop and deposit our loads. From her big round basket, Eusebia pulls some sheets and with Francisca she makes walls for the shelter, tying the corners of the sheets to the poles.

Now some of the people are beginning to crowd around Felipe, Lorenzo, and Estela. The latter stands, her dark face drawn inward, her eyes big with terror, perfectly still. Felipe is talking as I get there. "Salvation is a personal thing," he says. It concerns no one but her alone. If she has confessed her sins to God, "we are disposed to baptize you." She just stands there, mute, her baby sucking at her breast. The women go to the shelter to change, and when they emerge in old clothes, kerchiefs on their heads, the men go in to change into old pants and shirts: Floriano, Paulino, whose eye healed in time, and, to our surprise, Chela's husband. They all stand before Felipe, who tells them that the baptism represents death. After it comes the new life, a service to God. The baptism would be carried out the same way the Apostles did it, by immersion, first the women, then the men. He reads from Matthew. After being baptized, the person becomes a member of the church. He will sin no more. Neither will he eat the meat of animals choked to death or blood (reference to Mayan ceremonies.) If then he does not keep the promises he has made to God, there will be no pardon, only judgment. Felipe then makes them kneel and repeats the same warnings as before. Everybody joins in the subsequent prayer.

The women join hands. Now Felipe takes the hand of Francisca, who is first, and slowly they begin walking out into the water, while on the shore the rest of the congregation is singing a hymn, with Lorenzo playing the guitar. The words are lost in the rushing of the wind on the water, with which the melody joins into a single pulsing chorus. I walk after them, fully clothed. Luckily, the water is very warm. Some raindrops fall on the lens of my camera. Soon I am in the water up to my belt. Felipe has halted his group further out. They are praying, while only fragments of the hymn still waft by with the wind. I cannot hear him repeating the baptismal formula, but in slow succession, one woman after another is submerged, backward, her hands folded in prayer. Then begins the measured walk back toward the shore, with Lorenzo entoning a different hymn: "*Soy bautisado*—I am baptized."

The women go into the shelter of sheets to change into dry clothes. I have lost sight of Estela in the crowd, but now she comes out from behind the sheets in the wet clothes of her sister Francisca, her face rigid with tension. Somewhere in the back of the crowd, her baby is crying, but she does not turn her head. Elsa, a woman from the congregation in N., also to be baptized today, holds her hand. They are going into the water with Felipe when Estela turns back: she strips the ring from her finger, the only piece of jewelry she is wearing, and hands it to Francisca, who is close behind her, on the shore. Her face relaxes, and with measured steps she wades into the waves with Felipe and Elsa.

The baptism proceeds as before, and then comes the turn of the men. Intermittently, there is a light shower. My arm is getting tired from holding the camera in all sorts of awkward position. I have gone to the shelter to change film. When I get back to the shore, Eusebia touches my arm, "Look, Chela is crying." Chela is standing up to her knees in water, tears running down her face, head bent, intoning a high-pitched [ʔuʔuʔu] glossolalia. Over in front of the tight group of *hermanos,* her husband Artemio kneels, his head bent so low that it touches the sand. Slowly, he gets up, takes his paralyzed son Pedrito from the arms of Violeta, his oldest daughter, and wades into the water to Chela. Eusebia follows them.

Chela immerses the baby in the sea, and she and her husband pray in loud and urgent supplication, while Eusebia keeps wiping the water from the pale little face of the child with the corner of her ʔipil. On the shore, the men are in glossolalia now. At one point, just as Nicolas's powerful voice rises above that of the others and he lifts his hands high in supplication, the sun comes out, as if man's primordial, ecstatic plea were rending the very clouds of the sky and hammering against the locked gates of heaven.

All prayers said and all hymns sung, we finally do get to the *čan almuerzo,* the small lunch, under the palm-leaf roof. Food is shared freely all around, as customary on such ceremonial occasions. Chela goes around to everybody, telling glowingly of how Pedrito moved his feet in the water. Estela suckles her baby, and Floriano scolds his wife because she did not come immediately after the baptism to let her youngest have her čučuʔ—her milk. There is another, stronger, shower, and we wait until it is over before getting into the truck.

Everybody is in high excitement on the way home, except Francisca, who is still complaining about her husband's criticism to anyone who will listen. Soon her voice is drowned out by the singing. Felipe has the guitar, and he starts one hymn on the heels of another. When he gets tired, Nicolas asks for the instrument. He sits high above us, on the roof of the driver's cabin, and shouts down at us, "Sing, *hermanos,* this is how the children of God are known!" He sings and sings, strumming the guitar over the noise of the engine, white teeth, flashing, black eyes above aquiline nose brilliant in his dark face, wiry hair standing straight up in the wind—an Indian prophet in the glory of intoxication. When he finally hands the guitar back down, two strings are broken. Singing, clapping, laughing, we finally stop once more at the door of church.

Afternoon Service. Estela always used to sit in the rear of the church somewhere. Today she sits down beside Eusebia in the first row, hugging her baby, her face serene and relaxed. Lorenzo opens the service. He calls for the hymn *"Soy bautisado"* and then prays for the strength to continue in God's path. He goes into a brief glossolalia.

"Just think," Lorenzo says, "it is Monday afternoon and here we are, in the church, praising God. The time of slavery is no more." He then calls for testimonies. First Anselmo offers a text. Then Chela comes to the front. For ten days, she says, her son Pedrito had not eaten and had a fever; today he started eating again and his temperature is normal. Her husband was baptized with her. God has granted everything she asked. She offers a song, *"Yo tengo una corona en el cielo*—I have a crown in heaven." Then she continues: walking from the shore toward the truck she heard many hymns, but they were not sung by the *hermanos.* Rather, it seemed to her, they were being sung in a very great temple.[3] The service then passes on to Nicolas.

"Gozaos—enjoy yourselves," he quotes the Apostles. Today, God is happy. Although he lives thousands of miles away, he sends his greetings to the congregation in Utzpak. "I am very content with God," Nicolas says.

For some time afterward the congregation marveled at the miracles that had been witnessed at this baptism. Pedrito's fever had broken and he had moved his legs in the water; Paulino's eye had healed in time; Estela and Chela's husband had unexpectedly decided to be baptized; and Chela had heard the voices of an invisible choir. Under these circumstances, the assertions of *Hermano* Nicolas that the Lord was very specially directing his attention toward the Utzpak congregation, fell on fertile ground.

If the increase in membership can be taken as an indicator, this mood of excitement must have continued through the ensuing months, for between August 1969 and June 1970, 24 new members were baptized.

When I saw the congregation again early in July 1970, a number of changes were evident. For instance, the time spent in church activity had notably increased. Nearly every day, there was a service in some private home, often in addition to the regularly scheduled evening service in the church. Sunday afternoons were now taken up entirely by meetings of the three organizations of the church: the men's, the women's, and the young people's. No such increase in activity was evident in any of the other congregations I visited during that summer.

Two features of the service, the taking of the offering and the prayer for the sick, had become more formalized. The people no longer came to the front casually to put their coins into the plastic dish on the table; rather, two members of the church organization sponsoring the particular service passed from row to row, then knelt with the dishes in their hands on either side of the table in front of the altar until the prayer for the offering was completed. This may have been an innovation taken over from *Hermano* Gilberto's congregation, where the offering was taken up in a similar fashion, or perhaps a borrowing from Catholic ritual.

The new manner in which the prayer for the sick was conducted, however, was an Utzpak innovation. During the preceding year, people crowded around the altar informally for this ritual and everyone prayed, the sick and the well together. Now, however, the congregation stayed in their seats; only those who were sick came to the altar, where Emilio alone prayed for them, with the congregation giving only minimal support.

This Emilio was a Maya peasant,[4] born in 1945, gentle and shy. He was one of the innovators[5] in the congregation who had gone from Catholicism to Presbyterianism to Baptism, and from early sex to gambling and heavy drinking, always fleeing from *"ese temor,"* this fear, anxiety. Its resolution did not come until, after undergoing the baptism by water, he also experienced hyperarousal with glossolalia (December 1968).

In 1969, his glossolalia episodes were very long, his kinetic behavior sparing. His glossolalia utterances showed occasional high arousal, but also a rich syllable inventory, indicating that his trance experience might already have been weakening,[6] mingling of meaningful phrases with his glossolalia, and he had evolved a very impressive configuration of motions. His strategy seemed directed at attempting to recreate glossolalia by manipulation: his movements were in part reminiscent of those of the preceding years, but greatly magnified, and the new ones he had added, such as pressing his arms against his rib cage, might be interpreted as efforts to simulate conditions perceived in trance. He justified his behavior, which included extremely prolonged prayers in ordinary language, by saying that he had received the gift of healing by prayer, manifested by an overwhelming urge to pray for the sick. However, no cures were reported of him.[7]

Simultaneously with the changes in church services a breakdown seemed to have occurred in respect to the glossolalia. This apparently resulted from a withdrawal by Lorenzo from the congregation. Spatially, this was expressed by the special use to which Lorenzo put two small tables placed on the altar platform. (Only one table had been there the preceding year. A second one had now been added to serve as a stand for the new record player and the amplifier.) When not in use, Lorenzo placed these two tables on either side of the rostrum in such a way that together with the rostrum they completely separated him from the congregation. They, in fact, formed a barricade along the entire edge of the podium. Behind this wall he stayed nearly all the time, sitting on a chair, or, with his back to the congregation, he prayed at a box that contained the documents of the congregation and was placed against the rear wall. There was no more formal prayer for the Holy Spirit with its effective kneeling arrangement. New members of the congregation were left to themselves, to try and achieve the behavior as best they could. Neither did Lorenzo come down among the supplicants any more to ascertain whether anyone new was being possessed by the Holy Spirit and spoke in tongues. I clearly heard a teenager go into the initial ʔuʔuʔu of glossolalia, and although he also sobbed and choked, his behavior went unnoticed, at least by Lorenzo. No one proclaimed joyously, as had been the custom before, that "so and so, on this day of the Lord such and such, has been baptized by the Holy Spirit."

Lorenzo's withdrawal was also evidenced by a change of tone in his sermons. There was no trace any more of the good humor of the previous year, the jocular use of Mayan phrases. Instead, the torments of hell were painted in more and more vidid colors, and the "filth of the world" was everywhere.

More directly still, he was rude to the men who sought his help, even in such little matters as asking which hymn was to be sung. Toward the women Lorenzo behaved as a city husband who had absolute power over his wife's income. He used the money of the Dorcas, whether collected as dues or earned by talento, at his own discretion, neither asking them for it or accounting for how it was spent. The women bitterly resented this, since Maya peasant women are masters over the income they earn. He ran counter to the sentiments of the men also, as when, for instance, a conflict over the size of the plot arose between him and the old hermano who had donated the land to the church. To the consternation of the members, Lorenzo "read him" out of the congregation.

Lorenzo's glossolalia behavior had also changed from the preceding year. Whereas in the summer of 1969 (he had acquired the behavior in August 1968) his utterances had been so fast that I could hardly transcribe them, and his episodes lengthy and frequent, his utterances now were slower and occurred less often.

Within the realm of the trance behavior of the congregation, there was still another development. In August 1969, a young woman, Anita, the wife of Isaía, had spoken in tongues for the first time. She was in the process of learning how to pick up the bell signal for a return to ordinary reality (a difficulty often seen in this type of trance behavior), with her glossolalia often continuing into the next hymn or other activity, when the pastor's wife returned. The latter had been to her mother's house in Campeche to be delivered of her second child. This young woman, Cilia, had acquired the glossolalia behavior in Campeche some months previously. Whether a delayed return was a practice in the Campeche congregation, which I had no chance to visit or whether for some other reason she had similar difficulties as Anita I could not determine, but her pattern was very similar to that of Anita's. Four other *hermanas*, fourteen to sixteen years old, who had learned to go into glossolalia shortly afterward (one on August 31, two on September 7, and one on October 5) thereupon shaped their behavior in this way, making a practice of the delayed return. This interfered with the structure of the service, where previously the various parts, such as testimony time, singing, sermons, had been strictly separated.

Curiously, during July, Lorenzo also added to this blurring of the ritual structure by making the congregation stand for longer and longer periods during the services, instead of asking them, as customary, to sit during such procedings as lengthy Bible readings. "Dont't sit down," he would command. On a particularly hot day, when everyone was perspiring and swaying on their feet, he said sharply, "We already have rheumatism; it won't go away from sitting, so we might as well stand for the glory of God."

Finally, the congregation was greatly disturbed by the content of some visions that Anselmo had had in May 1970.[8] Anselmo, a Maya peasant and barber, was born in 1944 in a neighboring village. He was also an innovator, the most restless one in this respect in the congregation. He had passed from Catholicism to the Presbyterians, and thence to the Pentecostals, the Baptists, and Jehovah's Witnesses before encountering the Apostolics, among whom he had acquired the glossolalia behavior in July 1969. His wife had a history of prostitution, which she continued after her marriage to him. To remove her from her "friends," he took the family to Utzpak, her home, only to see her take up the same way of life there also. Perhaps in order to prove that her income was not needed or simply to be able to compete better with her men friends, he opened a barbershop in the summer of 1969. This meant that he also had to work on Sundays, which he decided to do, although Lorenzo warned him that decreased attendance in church made people "cold," in other words, indifferent in religious matters and unable to pray with fervor, that is, in tongues. Anselmo's visions were reported to me by Lorenzo as follows:

In early May, Anselmo told the *hermanos* that he did not know what was happening to him, but unless he prayed eight to ten times a day, he did not feel well. These prayers concerned "the conversion of his family," which we need to take here as meaning his wife. Suddenly, during a prayer for the sick, God took his head away, that is, he could not feel his head for several minutes, although touching it, pressing it, stroking it. He thought this strange, stopped praying, and went outside. About 20 meters from the house where he was praying at the time, he fell down, as if pushed, in a dead faint. From then on, he felt that evil forces were pursuing him. A few days later he was in his home, and at about four o'clock in the morning he woke up and, with his eyes wide open, saw demons surrounding him, trying to destroy him. He started off for the church, but two blocks from home he fell down in a dead faint, flakes of foam coming from his mouth. The family called the minister, who came with several *hermanos* and started to pray for him. After several hours Anselmo was freed of this sickness and asked for continued prayers since he had to suffer in this manner because God wanted to give him something very precious.

On the following Sunday, May 17, Anselmo fasted, as was the custom in the church, prayed, and after several periods of prayer got up and said in a loud voice, "*Hermanos,* be watchful, for it is important that we prepare ourselves." He then told about a vision he just had, where God showed him several candles,[9] as if in the process of being extinguished, and a voice, that of the Holy Spirit, told him that this was the condition of the Apostolic Church. It was urgent that the *hermanos* go out and evangelize, for Christ's coming was close at hand.

After that, every time he prayed, God gave him this warning: What was he waiting for? Why did he not leave yet to go and preach to the people?

On June 3, there was a meeting of pastors and their aides in Villahermosa, Tabasco, and at that meeting God gave Anselmo a miraculous gift, that of "distinguishing between the souls." The bishop of the Southeastern Section of the Apostolic Church was present and showed the *hermanos* that such a gift was indeed mentioned in the Bible.[10] This meant that Anselmo saw on the foreheads of truly believing *hermanos* a brilliantly glowing shield, other *hermanos'* faces appeared natural, and still others had frighteningly black foreheads. Later, in various Catholic churches in Mérida, where he went with Lorenzo to distribute Apostolic leaflets, Anselmo saw the priests appearing in diabolical shapes or having the head of a devil. When he had such a vision, he felt that something exceedingly hot entered his body, be began shivering and trembling, his heart started beating at a tremendous rate, and perspiration poured from his body. Afterward it appeared as if nothing at all had happened to him, except that he was very thirsty.

Anselmo was sent to evangelize in San Antonio Sacahchen, which was the only community available at the time within the church organization. From there he was to go on to Calkiní. However, once more he quarreled with his wife about her activities as a prostitute and therefore, before moving to Calkiní, on June 20 he came to consult with Lorenzo in Utzpak, bringing his family with him. His family spent the night in the *casa pastoral,* the pastor's home, and he and Lorenzo hung their hammocks in the church. At about three o'clock in the morning he woke up Lorenzo because he felt a terrifying force surrounding him. He maintained that this force came because he had not been sleeping. Rather, he had gone out to relieve himself and after coming back and lain awake—and then he saw a vision. God showed him a ribbon with a woman on it, an empty ribbon, and a pair of scissors. Lorenzo later helped him interpret this vision as meaning that there were two ways in which God was going to have the *hermanos* work for the church. One was the material plane, but it contained the trap of the woman, that is, of adultery, which is a mortal sin. The other ribbon represented the spiritual plane, such as preaching, evangelizing, which brought no material rewards. The scissors could be used to cut off either ribbon.

This last of Anselmo's visions was never mentioned in the congregation. News of his other visionary experiences, however, quickly spread far and wide. They were the paramount topic of conversation when I arrived in Mérida that summer, on July 2, 1970.

> Eusebia and I go to *Hermano* Nicolas's house, where we encounter his mother Gregoria and his brother's sister-in-law. The work of the Lord is progressing well in Yucatán, Gregoria says. An *hermano* from Utzpak, of all places, had a vision of the Devil and is now preaching in all the cogregations. *Hermano* Anselmo is his name. The women joke about how big might have been the horns of the demons that he saw, without, of course, doubting their reality.
>
> During the bus ride on the way to Utzpak, Eusebia elaborates on Anselmo's visions. One day Anselmo saw many devils with horns who wanted to get him. He fled and collapsed outside. The *hermanos* found him and prayed over him. Since then he has the capacity to see who is truly saved. A person who only pretends appears to him with a completely black face. Another time he again saw the Devil landing on the roof of the Catholic church.

In the Utzpak congregation, in addition to this interest in Anselmo's vision, earlier experiences not formerly so conceptualized were interpreted as due to Satan's presence. For instance, a familiar experience of many subjects learning glossolalia is the fact that initially they enter only into hyperarousal: they feel hot, there is a sensation of floating or pressure on the rib cage, and so on. It was now maintained in the congregation that if this happened—namely, if there was a perception of "something supernatural" without speaking in tongues ensuing promptly—it meant that Satan was trying to enter that person's body, that there was, in other words, immediate danger of demoniacal possession.

Crying children were thought to be possessed by Satan also; thus, Nina reported,

> Vicente's child kept crying in church, but only in church, not outside. When they took the child home, he slept. It was obvious that the Devil possessed the body of the child. The same thing happened also with Lorenzo's younger son. On their way home from Temax, he cried and would not stop, although there was absolutely nothing wrong with him. They prayed over him for an hour, the child stopped crying and was fine. Isaía's youngest child kept crying as soon as the service began. When Anita took him home, there was nothing wrong, and the boy went to sleep. Next day, the same thing happened. In that case also, prayer helped, and the problem did not return. What you have to say in that case is, "*Satands, en el nombre de Jesucristo, yo te reprendo*— Satan, in the name of the Lord I banish you." The Devil will then leave the body of the child, the child starts sleeping, and all is well. He may, however, come back: with Lorenzo's son, for instance, it took seven months before the Devil finally gave up.

In retrospect, the Devil was seen at the deathbed also. Don Vicente, one of the earliest converts of Oscar Gill in Utzpak and represented in the congregation by the largest kin cluster (see Figs. 1 and 2), had died in 1966. His death was remembered in the congregation because, by the instructions he gave on his deathbed, he flouted the burial customs of the community. It was reported in 1969 that

> he said that there should be no food served after he died, for the dead do not eat. He cried, saying that he would die at two o'clock. They stopped praying at two, and he died. His Catholic daughter came to light candles for him, but his son Valentin put them out; she became so angry that she did not come to the funeral. There was not even a wake for Don Vicente: the *hermanos* who were with him slept till morning.

The following elaboration was added in 1970 to this account:

> People that are about to die often are afraid that the Devil might come for
> them. This happened to Don Vicente. When he was on his deathbed, he kept
> begging Felipe, the minister, to stay with him and pray, for he was afraid of
> the Devil.

Anselmo saw Satan in May 1970. Nina, an eighteen-year-old girl, was attacked in June. She was to be baptized on June 15. The night before she had a
vision in which she saw a man in ordinary working clothes floating above the
ground. When she said, *"Gloria a Dios*—Glory to God," he answered in
Mayan, "Not to God, but to me, to me." She understood this to mean that
Satan had come to tempt her and possibly to win her over so she would not
want to be baptized.

On July 11, Lorenzo returned from a visit to various congregations and
reported that in one, that of *Hermano* Gilberto, four people had received the
baptism of the Holy Spirit, and in another one, five.

> All this shows that Christ will soon come. Also, a week ago a bright light ap-
> peared in the sky over Chetumal, many people saw it. In other words, this is
> a time of miracles. The question is whether many people will still be saved
> before He finally comes. Many will go to eternal perdition, and in hell the
> sulfur causes terrible burns and pain.

However, Lorenzo also took cognizance of the increasing role Satan was
playing in the congregation. In his sermon of July 12, he told the congregation:

> The Devil has very little time left to do his work, so he will try everything to
> achieve his goal. Of course he knows what people are close to God, and he
> will concentrate his efforts on them. This is why he will try to rise within the
> Apostolic churches. In Veracruz there is a man who has the same gift as
> Anselmo: he can see what others cannot see, namely, whether a person
> coming into the congregation is a true believer or not. A visitor came to this
> congregation in Veracruz, greeting everybody with *Paz de Cristo,* but the
> *hermano* with this gift immediately recognized him to be the Devil and told
> him, "What do you want here? Why are you trying to deceive us? Get out of
> here!" The man became very angry and started cursing in the vilest way,
> showing in effect that he was what that *hermano* had taken him for.

On the level of the congregation, Satan was now seen also in the secular range. Thus, one of the *hermanas* reported on July 24:

> Last weekend, it is said, the Devil appeared in the prison of Utzpak. There
> was a prisoner there, and the Devil appeared to him and said, *"Buenos dias,
> caballero,* would you like me to get you out of here?" The man started
> shouting, but when the poeple got there, he had already taken off most of his
> clothes. The Devil vanished, they saw only his tail, it looked like the tail of a
> steer.

Among the group of *hermanas,* it was recalled in the conversation ensuing
from this story that the Devil was also seen three years ago in the prison. At
that time a man committed suicide by hanging himself with a belt. The
following year, *Hermano* Peregrino's brother died in the same way. He had
beaten his wife over the head with kindling wood, and when he saw her on the
floor bleeding, he thought he had killed her. In prison after being arrested he
saw the Devil and hung himself by using his pants as a rope.

THE PEAK

In the days from July 26 to July 31, the behavior of the congregation pushed
toward a peak of arousal, rising to its climax on the July 30, with a slight decline already perceivable on July 31. My principal informants, Eusebia and
Nina, in retrospect also pinpointed the night preceding July 30 and the service
of that day as the time "when the attack of Satan really began."

On July 26, Emilio attained a level of arousal similar to that of the preceding year: his labored kinetic pattern disappeared and his glossolalia was
back to a pattern similar to the one recorded the preceding year, although the
episodes were now shorter. Simultaneously, he no longer played any significant role in the prayer for the sick. Two other *hermanos,* Martin and Alfredo,
started praying with him for the healing of the sick. (Eventually, they assumed
the dominant position in this ritual.) During the same service in July 26, Lorenzo announced that Anselmo was weak (spiritually) and alone, the *hermano*
who had been his companion and felllow evangelist had left, and so he, Lorenzo, would go to visit him.

On July 27, Lorenzo left to take his wife Cilia for a visit to her mother in
Campeche; from there, he wanted to go on to see Anselmo. Later on the same
day, however, Anselmo arrived in Utzpak with his wife and took part in that
evening's service.

Lorenzo, not having encountered Anselmo, returned the following day. In
the evening service, he forbade my using the movie camera, saying that it
disturbed him during prayer. This was later interpreted by some of the con-

gregation as showing that he "was not praying right," for if you prayed in the right way, you did not notice such things. No such conflict had arisen before between the minister and myself, and the congregation was hushed and disturbed.

The service takes its usual course. The *Dorcas* offer a hymn, and Joaquina passes to Teresa, who calls for the offering. This time, two women collect, Joaquina and Ermela, already in the completely ritualized new pattern.

Teresa then passes to Lorenzo. He is very imperious. Looking up from his Bible during the reading of the text, he tells the congregation, "Don't sleep and do as I say; those that can, have to stand." He then informs the congregation: "I had to go on a brief trip for a necessity, but God has already brought me back to glorify his name." Adding to the tension already present at this point in the congregation, Lorenzo then announces that tomorrow (i.e., Wednesday) there would be a meeting of all the men of the church; later he limits this to all the men who have been baptized. The women will be informed by their men about what was discussed.

In his sermon, he talks about the parable of the watchman: the watchman is the man responsible for what happens to the people in the city; the same is true today—we all have the responsibility for what happens to the other people when Christ comes again.

Keeping in mind the psychological condition of the congregation at this time, we can appreciate the impact of the remainder of Lorenzo's sermon:

> Now, I want you to pay very close attention. Recently, this past Sunday that is, the Holy Spirit manifested its power to an *hermano* in C., to Peregrino. You all know Peregrino. He is a native of Utzpak. This Sunday, then, he started praying, and the power of the Holy Spirit manifested itself and showed him many churches. These churches, however, were terribly dirty. The people who entered them found themselves surrounded by spider webs; well, the churches were in complete disarray, dirty, and worm-eaten, and that is where the people were. And the *hermano* asked the same power that gave him the vision, and he asked, "What manner of things is this?" And the answer came, "These poor people think that they are truly in a well-ordered church, but just look, all around them they have only disorder." And in truth, there was not a bit of purity around them, much less an immaculate church. And immediately the same voice told him, "They are expecting you to talk to them, and give them the message. Why don't you enter into these homes, into these synagogues, in order to make them all clean? Christ will soon come and you people, what are you doing?"
>
> And this *hermano*, this *Hermano* Peregrino, as he rose, felt something like an attack of trembling in his body, and he started talking to *Hermano* Gilberto and the other *hermanos* who were in that place, and immediately

our *Hermano* Gilberto went to T. to talk to our *Hermano* Gideon there, because he has this wish that we all have, to do something for the honor of Jesus Christ.

Lorenzo then reminds the congregation that Anselmo's vision was also an announcement by the Lord that the Second Coming was imminent. "Everybody is our neighbor," he said, "and we need to help all to be saved before it is too late."

Peregrino was indeed known to everyone in the congregation. He came from a family of some means and was generally respected in Utzpak, where he was born and raised. He was one of the innovators in the sense in which we have defined this term. He visited the services of other Protestant groups, mainly the Baptists and the Latter-Day Saints. He was even baptized by the Baptist minister, but only after the Apostolic baptism and the trance experience did he feel like a different man: previously he had often wanted to die, but the baptism of the Holy Spirit freed him of his death wish. In the summer of 1969, when Peregrino visited the congregation of Utzpak, his glossolalia was very rapid, his kinetic pattern strong, and his trance so deep that during it an apparently psychosomatic condition of not being able to use his right arm disappeared. In July 1970, when I visited the congregation of C., of which he was a member, his glossolalia had slowed down, was not nearly so loud as before, and his kinetic pattern had almost disappeared.

The excitement generated by the news about Peregrino's vision was immediately evident in the congregation's glossolalia behavior. Whereas ordinarily the period following the sermon was one of quiet, of relaxation, there was now a renewed burst of glossolalia, made even more impressive by the fact that one of the men was now also caught in the pattern of delayed return to ordinary reality:

> During the prayer for the sick, there is a great deal of glossolalia. Roberta, a 16-year-old, is rocking and sobbing, Anselmo is very loud. Martin's utterance is still an improbably rapid stutter. He cannot pick up the bell signal and continues with his glossolalia. Finally, he recovers, rubs his hands over his face, presses his fingers against his temples, then sits down, hands before his face.

On the afternoon of July 29, the pastors Gilberto and Nicolas (they were brothers) arrived in Utzpak. They closeted themselves in the church with Lorenzo. Soon the *hermanos* of the Utzpak congregation began assembling, and occasionally very loud prayer and glossolalia were audible from behind the closed doors.

Later in the day, a service was held, dominated by two ideas: the Second Coming was much closer than anyone had thought and might be expected perhaps that night or within days; and to evangelize as widely as possible was now imperative.

Evening Service, July 29. The service takes place in a private home. The only men present are Tacho, Isaía, and the latter's brother Nesto. The service is opened by Nesto, who then passes to Isaía. The latter announces that Gilberto and Nicolas have arrived and that plans are at present being made for the work of the Lord; this is why the *hermanos* are absent. "If you can," Isaía says, "you should pray all night. We don't know when Christ will manifest himself. He is trying to give us some messages, this is what he is at present using the bodies of the *hermanos* in the temple for."

Isaía has chosen for his biblical text that perennial favorite, the first Pentecost in the Acts. In his remarks he refers to Peregrino's vision, and there is a feeling of presence, of urgency that is very catching. Besides, it has rained, it is beastly hot and humid, and this adds to the tension.

Isaía continues: "This night may be like any other night for other people, but for us, it is different. We know that the Second Coming is very close, although the nonbelievers still don't give it credence. The first Pentecost was not a *fiesta* with dances, picture shows, or bullfights, things of the world. It was an invisible *fiesta,* and this is why so many still don't believe. This is not simply a manifestation of the Holy Spirit, as we have all experienced it before, this is the promise we have all been waiting for, for so long. New gifts of the Holy Spirit are being received at this moment in the temple: some *hermanos* are giving an interpretation of the tongues, and many more will begin doing that, now that the Second Coming is so much closer. The same Holy Spirit working on the *hermanos* has also let it be known that not all the people will accept God. However, God does not want the death of a single sinner."

At this point, Isaía, an unusually dignified, quiet man with a great deal of composure, breaks into tears and bends over his Bible; saying, between sobs, "Let us pray," he kneels down. Almost instantly, Violeta, Joaquina, Francisca, then also Anita and Teresa—that is, all the women present who have already received the Holy Spirit—go into glossolalia. Violeta kneels on the dirt floor, rocking on her knees. The others are standing.

Isaía rises and continues his sermon. He admonishes the visitors present (there are always neighbors crowding in the doorways at these services in private homes) not to speak ill about what they have seen; they are not familiar with the manifestations of the Lord, and if they speak ill of what they saw, they might go to eternal perdition. While he speaks, Violeta continues her sobbing, high-intensity glossolalia.

"Messages are now expected from Christ," Isaía says, "about how to go on, how he wants the work to be continued." At this announcement, the women once more go into very loud glossolalia; Violeta still continues (she has been in glossolalia for about seven minutes now) as does Francisca, with the sleeping baby in her arms. Violeta has been in glossolalia for nine minutes and is now upright on her inees; she finally stands up, after a total of about ten minutes. "If some of the *hermanos*," Isia goes on, "want to get together in someone's home to pray through the night, that will be the right thing to do, or people can also pray alone, of course." The service concludes with the usual invitation for a sharing of food: "*Dice la hermana que esperemos un momento*—the *hermana* says we should wait a moment."

While we wait for the food, Isaía announces, "Let us pray for the sick child of this *hermana*," pointing to Chela, who has come in with Pedrito on her arm. "For although we know the Second Coming is now going to be very soon, let us in the meantime pray that this child will get well." Violeta goes into glossolalia again (Pedrito is her brother). Francisca, also in glossolalia, finally goes into the usual "schwa" pattern of exhaustion, "oh səsəsə/oh səsə . . .,"; she then says, "*Obra, ó Jesus*—work your miracle, o Jesus."

Isaía tells Francisca and Teresa, who are giving rapt attention, "Pray, then rest, keep vigil, pray again." The women are wide-eyed and distracted. Then Isaía and the other men leave to join those in the temple. Despite all these events, the women still pass out the sweet rice, emphasizing the ritual character of this food sharing.

For the first time, there was mention in this service of the view that some of the *hermanos* were interpreting what other *hermanos* were saying in tongues. This represented a true innovation for the Utzpak congregation. Although mentioned in the Bible as a gift of the Holy Spirit, interpretation (in this sense) is not a behavior occurring generally in the Apostolic churches in Mexico; neither was it present in any of the Yucatecan churches I had seen. The meaning given the behavior was not strictly biblical, for in the primitive church, though recognized as a "gift of the Spirit," it was not specifically regarded as a capability awarded for translating messages relating to the Second Coming.

The conclusion of the service did not mark the end of activities for the night. If anything, the evolution of events toward the peak became accelerated.

I lived only two houses away from the church, and when I got home, there was still loud prayer coming from it. My impulse was to sneak up and eavesdrop with my tape recorder, but I thought better of it: somebody was sure to see me. During the night I woke up several times with glossolalia in my ears.

On the morning of July 30, the prayer in the church continued. The neighbors were upset because of all the noise and commotion. A young girl from across the street came by to visit and complained that at 12:30 A.M. she still could not sleep because of the noise. Licha, my landlady, wanted to know what all the praying was for; I explained. "It is because so many people still will not believe," she suggested. Then she shook her head. "So Peregrino has the same sort of thing like Anselmo? They say that Anselmo has a power. He can see who is a true believer." Licha was only marginally interested in the congregation, and most of her friends were Catholics. When she said, "The people call the *hermanos* crazy, *locos*," she was probably reporting their reaction accurately.

During the morning, I began to piece together the events of this night, which later was to be remembered by some of my informants as the night when Satan began his attack on the congregation and by the larger community as the time when the madness struck.

Because Nohoč Felipe, the husband of Eusebia, my principal informant, was still at the ranch, working, we had no man to inform us. Tacho, however, had been at the church all night, and Eusebia, out early for shopping, met his wife Valuch. It seems that during the night, the *hermanos* were praying for guidance about who was to go out to evangelize. It was agreed that Emilio, Isaía, Anselmo, Floriano, Nesto, and also Tacho were to go and preach. Tacho, however, did not think he should, since he did not know enough about the Gospel. During the night, Anselmo was listening to Tacho praying in tongues and said, "The Devil is already coming, spreading his wings, you are only for things of this world." Then Tacho started praying again; Anselmo listened and said, "You must go, preach the word of God."

It was further decided that those *hermanos* who do not go to evangelize will give ten pesos to an *hermana* whose husband is in the field. *Hermanas* who are left without husbands will go and stay with the families where the husbands are still present.

From other *hermanas* we heard that, early in the morning, Anselmo tried to hang himself. They commented: "He has the spirit of God, that's why the Devil [*el demonio*] wants to kill him" (i.e., wants to cause him to commit suicide). During this attempt the *hermanos* (we could not find out which ones) saw two angels standing behind Anselmo, one with a sword, the other with a whip.

Some of the women had also prayed through the night, first in Francisca's and then in Teresa's house. In addition to Francisca and Teresa, this "inner" group included Marta, Violeta, Anita, and Joaquina. Eusebia dubbed them "*hač consagradas*—highly consecrated."

At noon, Gilberto and Nicolas left, speeding on their supernatural errand to spread the word about the messages of the Holy Spirit and the imminence of the Second Coming to other congregations.

Later, there was some commotion at the church, and I went over to see what was going on. There were various *hermanas* about, and we chatted a bit about the weather and then saw Anselmo emerging from the church, his face pudgy and his eyes tired. In his appearance there was little of the young peasant of last year who was a barber in his off hours. He had a sparse little mustache now and was wearing dark pants and a buttoned-up white shirt, with a fountain pen in his shirt pocket. He said that he came for three months, since his wife was expecting a baby. At this point, Nesto arrived; when I asked if a service was to be held now, he said it was to be a meeting for married couples only. "Adelante," Anselmo said, and all walked in, while I went back home.

In this service, I heard in the evening, the official announcement was made about the men who are to go "into the field" and about the arrangements for the families to be left behind.

Events surged to the climax in the evening service of that day. The congregation experienced hallucination, demon possession, exorcism, grossly prolonged and unmanageable trance behavior, spontaneous acquisition of glossolalia. In an atmosphere of utter panic, all those uncommitted were exhorted to become baptized, and these passionate pleas were coupled with strident attacks on those who still hung behind.

Evening Service, July 30, 1970. At the outset, there are sixteen men and nineteen women, as well as many children. In the course of the service, many more people crowd in, until the small church fairly bursts at the seams. Somehow, this crowdedness amplifies everything that is to take place this evening. Isaía opens the service, which is to be dedicated to evangelizing. Lorenzo is praying at the box against the rear wall of the church (i.e., the wall of the *casa pastoral*). Isaía begins the service. The first prayer concerns the souls that are approaching (i.e., people who are beginning to show an interest in being converted). After a hymn, Isaía calls for testimonies. Vicente gets up to say a few words; then hyperventilating, literally pumping air, his right hand stretched out stiffly before him, he goes into glossolalia; his face suddenly flushes, the eyes open up wide, he shouts very loudly. Anselmo joins him with the same movement, then Floriano, then almost everybody jumps up, especially in the men's and juvenile sections, where they could hear what Vicente was saying. There is a tremendous burst of prayer, Roberta also goes into glossolalia; Vicente continues with his and is still very tense; he starts shouting again without my being able to distinguish whether he is now speaking in tongues or in ordinary language.

When a modicum of quiet is restored, Isaía says that Vicente just saw Christ, a very rare vision, not given to all. Francisca gets up and, shouting to be heard in the noise, suggests that there should be a prayer for those who will go to evangelize. Nacho joins in this petition, saying that he and Floriano will go to Mérida tomorrow and from there to Cenotillo. Floriano gets up, "Let us all say goodbye in a special prayer." Isaía comments that all these special petitions can be taken care of in front of the altar. He calls for the *corito*

"*Orar sin cesar*—Pray without pause," and the people come forward, crowding around the altar platform, while Lorenzo is still praying at his box. They go into glossolalia with outstretched arms, Floriano perspiring profusely. Violeta[11] is shaking, screaming, and sobbing at the altar, doubled over. Roberta has a similar sobbing pattern. Emilio is shouting out a prayer, still in ordinary language. His little daughter is screaming. Chela has started praying in glossolalia, and now Emilio is in trance too, with a glossolalia very much like the one last year with no kinetics whatever. Violeta continues at the altar; when Isaía rings, she cannot react. Francisca's tears are still flowing profusely, Antia does not react either, Luisa's glossolalia, a very high ʔai ʔai ʔai, also continues. Isaía rings again, still no reaction. A dog wanders in and sniffs at a dead bug on the floor, but no one pays attention to it, though such an occurrence usually produces an instant, indignant reaction.

It is customary to go on with the service and to proceed to the next section, even though someome may still be in glossolalia. Isaía tries to get hold of the situation this way. He calls for special hymns, and the first one to come forward is Alfredo. He begins, but is hardly audible above the very intense glossolalia of Violeta and Luisa, who are both of the same age. Neither reacts to the fact that a special hymn is being offered. Luisa begins alternating between normal language and glossolalia phrases, while Violeta reverts to more varied syllables, showing that in both the intensity of the trance is diminishing. Lorenzo continues with his back to us. His left hand on his hip, he is kneeling and praying. Alfredo's singing still cannot be heard. Anselmo is sitting beside Vicente in the front row of the men, shaking him by the neck; Vicente finally stops shouting. There is much saliva in front of Luisa, who is back in glossolalia. Violeta is still in; Lorenzo throws a glance at her and continues with his prayer. Luisa's dress is soaked with perspiration. Teresa, Francisca, and Joaquina are also back in glossolalia. Violeta and Luisa are rocking back and forth on their knees. Luisa's mantilla slips from her head, but no one makes a motion to adjust it. Finally, *she does* while still in the glossolalia pattern. The children sitting near Luisa on a bench watch her intently.

Vicente has calmed down; he sits with eyes closed, his head slightly leaning back. Luisa has returned to consciousness and is praying in ordinary language, but she continues rocking on her knees and then goes back into glossolalia. Violeta is still in dissociation. This goes on although Alfredo has now completed his hymn, and Nacho and Nesto are offering one. Once more regaining conscious control, Luisa wipes her eyes—as does Violeta also, but only for a brief moment, then she is back in glossolalia. There may be others—I am concentrating on the main actors, and there is a tremendous din accompanying all this. Lorenzo is still kneeling at the box, once more Luisa wipes her eyes, Violeta is sobbing and rocking, her glossolalia now at the -sə-sə-sə-level of near exhaustion. Angela has gotten up and has gone back to her seat, but Violeta continues with sə-sə-sə-sə.

A *corito* is called for and the offering is gathered in, while Violeta has briefly regained consciousness, only to lapse once more, even more strongly, into the glossolalia pattern. Vicente offers a special hymn, and Violeta's kinetic pattern becomes very energetic: her elbows are trembling and she repeatedly throws her body to one side and then another; her rich pulse inventory is audible in the pause before the general prayer is started. Holding her head very rigid, she closes and opens her hands, continuing to rock on her knees. At his box, still kneeling, Lorenzo lifts his arms in supplication. Violeta slips backs into the -sə-sə-sə pattern.

Isaía passes to Lorenzo, while Violeta, having lost most of her vocalization capacity, is sighing rhythmically ʔohhh, ʔohhh. Lorenzo, at the rostrum now, announces the biblical text to be read, from the Acts, but since Violeta continues, he puts his hand on her head, bending down to her. Instead of calming her, this sends her into a brief but very steep recovery of the trance level, after which she has trouble swallowing; shaken by the rhythm of the trance, she struggles with the accumulating saliva, obviously with very rigid throat muscles.

Chela, large with child, is now beside her daughter Violeta, trying to get her to come out of the trance. Lorenzo does not get to read the passage. Over on the men's side, another scene is developing: Martin is holding his arms high with his characteristics weaving pattern and utters his very fast staccato glossolalia, his eyes tightly shut and facing Nacho and Vicente. Anselmo leans over to Martin, as if trying to understand. Violeta still cannot swallow. Chela has her hand on her daughter's shoulder, Violeta is sighing, "Sí, Dios mio, sí, no puedo... —yes, Lord, yes, I cannot...." Nacho is meanwhile "interpreting" Martin's glossolalia to him while Anselmo explains quietly to Vicente. This is in part conjecture about what I see: we cannot hear what is being said over the deafening welter of sounds with everyone praying very loudly, although just minutes ago Lorenzo had asked for silent prayer. Chela has begun to fan Violeta, who is back to a sighing pattern, still in trance. She is handed a glass of water for her daughter, who cannot swallow it. Vicente is asking for a prayer, and to make way for the congregation Violeta is led, or rather taken, away from the altar, to the first chair of the center row in the juvenile section, directly beside Eusebia's chair and mine. She does not sit on it, rather her head rests on its back, her legs stretched out on the front edge of the seat. Both Chela and Eusebia are now fanning her, while another cup of water is being handed toward the front.

Suddenly there is an uproar close to Violeta, on the men's side, where Anselmo has gone down on his knees. Lorenzo is by his side almost instantly, pressing Anselmo's head between his hands and shouting first in glossolalia, then in ordinary speech. From the latter we understand that Anselmo has all of a sudden been possessed by the Devil. He quickly recovers, tells Lorenzo that the Devil has gone out into the street, and leads Lorenzo out through the men's aisle, with most of the adult men behind them. A tremendous upsurge of glossolalia is audible from the outside, sending Violeta back into a recovery of the trance level as she lies diagonally on the chair, her head rigidly back, her hands stiff and hard looking. When she starts speaking in trance, first in real language, then in glossolalia, Francisca sobs out and also goes into dissociation; so do all the other women around. Two small brothers and three sisters of Violeta, sitting on the children's bench beside me, are sobbing in real distress. Isaía comes over to Violeta, in glossolalia, his eyes tightly closed, then he goes back to the table. Nina sinks on her knees beside Violeta, in glossolalia, she collapses on her elbows and stays that way—very rigid, her hands as stiff as a Dresden figurine's—all through the rest of the service, only occasionally rocking slightly. Roberta, another sixteen-year-old, is also in very high glossolalia, getting quite hoarse. Pedro, my landlord, has appeared in the back, a rare guest at the services, attracted by all the commotion (especially by the one in the street, I hear the next day). Chela is crying over Violeta; she tells her children to leave, but none of them—and they are all sobbing—obeys. Some more water is passed down. Violeta is beginning to sob out names—Marta's is one, then that of the husband of Reyes—which are eagerly listened for and passed on down toward the back of the church, as being a revelation of the Holy Spirit about those of deficient devotion. Lorenzo comes in from the outside, goes up to her and, putting his hands on her head, tells her to control herself. When she keeps repeating the same phrases over and over again, he says, "*Ya lo diste*—you've already said that, "*ya lo diste.*" Her chest is heaving. He continues in a soothing but loud voice, "*Sí, hija, sí, hija*— yes, daughter, yes, daughter" while shaking her head lightly. Roberta, two rows back, screams out a glossolalia very much modeled on Violeta's but without names. "God will use you," Lorenzo says to Violeta, "yes, he will. I know (about Reyes's husband, who is considered *muy rebelde*, very obstinate in matters of the Lord, because her prefers *Hermano* Gruber's Baptist services to those of the Apostolics), I know already. Give her water." Then he repeats, "*Sí, hija, sí. . . .*"

This scene is overcut by another, where Vicente, Isaía, Alfredo, and Floriano are bending over Gaspar, an elderly man in a blue shirt. Anselmo tries to hear him, shakes his head, then draws closer to listen in. Chela and Lorenzo take Violeta out, to the rear, into the *casa pastoral*. Nina says next day, "Violeta was sick, because the Spirit (i.e., being possessed by the Holy Spirit) is intoxicating." Chela's children are still crying in front. Lorenzo comes back in, places his hand on the head of Gaspar, in recognition of his glossolalia. Roberta is still in a sobbing glossolalia, and Marta is kneeling in front with Anselmo, who prays over her in a strange, very drawn-out manner, "*Sí, Dios mío, maniféstate*—yes, my Lord, manifest yourself," very different from his usual speaking voice. Roberta is still in glossolalia, and Lorenzo is up at the rostrum, trying to get hold of the congregation, whose attention is being thrown hither and thither by all the different goings-on. He warns the visitors not to think that what they are seeing is anything sad, it is a most joyous occasion, and they should not be confounded by science, which speaks against the manifestation of God and its reality. There is loud glossolalia by Marta, Luisa, and Roberta. Lorenzo continues: he has to say all the words that God is giving him to say. His face is flushed, contorted; off and on there are tears. All of a sudden, he too comes up with names. "And you, Eusebia, and Nina, and the husband of Reyes, and Socorro, wife of Anselmo, you all, you must consecrate yourself to Him or perish. I am pushed by a power to say these things, these are not my words," he shouts into the microphone of the public address system. "The Devil is now defeated, give into God!"

"And you, *Hermana* Felicitas," he continues, his face even more contorted in the mask of crying, his lips trembling, "if you don't surrender to God, you will most certainly die!" Then he goes into glossolalia, confirming my impression that he had been in dissociation all along, and since this has lowered his inhibitions, he has been led to hurl imprecations against those keeping aloof for one reason or another. My old friend Eusebia wipes her eyes with the corner of her *rebozo* (shawl). Her face betrays no emotion.

"Let us pray," commands Lorenzo with a quieter voice. Eusebia and I are side by side, with Nina in deep dissociation at her mother's feet on the floor. Eusebia nods to me, we stand there, the condemned. Over on the men's side, I see Gregorio, the brother-in-law of Nicolas, a very tall and strong man by local standards, surveying the scene with an amused smile.

Gaspar, a small but heavy man, is embracing Anselmo, who can hardly withstand his bear hug. Both are shaking to the rhythm of their glossolalia. Lorenzo has knelt down behind the rostrum. Martin is in front of the rostrum, extending his weaving arms and rubbing his hands together while uttering such rapid glossolalia that on the tape it sounds as if there were a mechanical failure in the recorder. Eusebia has taken off her glasses and is wiping them.

Anselmo, who has begun making the rounds trying to get people to declare that they want to be baptized, is now at my seat. He bends over me, his spittle and sweat dribbling on my notebook page. He exhorts me to get baptized. I say that I am already baptized. "How? By immersion or by a little bit of water on your head?" "By a little water." He is saddened. "But that is not sufficient, my daughter," he says, breathing heavily. There is some rattled-off quotation about Jonah in the stomach of the whale and then the question, "Have you at least already repented?" "Oh, yes." "Then why not get baptized tomorrow?" "I'll have to wait for my husband, and when he also repents, we will be baptized together." He straightens out, his hand still on my head, and ejaculates a joyous "Alleluia." Lorenzo rings his bell. To the back of me, Roberta is in glossolalia; so is Anita, who is hanging on her chair, rather than sitting on it.

Lorenzo is urging: anyone who has not been baptized should do it now, this is the last opportunity, there is no other. People start coming forward to the altar. Floriano is standing close to where I sit, inviting people to come and volunteer to be baptized, "Come one, come all, Christ will promptly arrive, there is not time to lose . . .," like a ticket vendor for the show of the bearded lady. Eight women and nine men come forward to the altar. Lorenzo is crying into the microphone, children are crying, Teresa is crying, Nina is still in dissociation. Floriano, Vicente, and Emilio are kneeling behind those who want to be baptized, praying for them, while Marta is at the altar, shouting glosso-lalia.

Someone, perhaps an irate neighbor, is knocking, Martin sends one of the young men to investigate. There is more knocking. The prayer becomes noticeably more subdued. Marta, however, is still in glossolalia, every bit a copy of Violeta. Anselmo continues hunting for baptismal prospects. He is concentrating on a woman in the back. Lorenzo is on his knees behind the rostrum. I see Eusebia's lips moving in prayer. Nina is in the same posture as before, but no glossolalia is audible. Anselmo is praising the Lord, since another candidate for baptism has been gained. Roberta has lost level in her glossolalia, going into a tə-tə-tə pattern. Anselmo has passed on to still another person, rocking on his heels as he talks and prays. Then he goes to Nicolas's brother-in-law, but soon gives up on him.

Lorenzo rises and rings, but no one pays attention. Anselmo has come to the front, now loudly praying for the conversion of his wife. There is a woman in front of the altar, praying loudly. "So many times I've had the op-portunity to be baptized and never made use of it. O Lord, I want to be baptized now. . . ." She is Ermela's daughter, known to a number of people as a prostitute. Lorenzo points to her, Floriano and Martin kneel down on either side of her; she has gone into dissociation, and now the two men drive her into glossolalia by shouting their own utterances at her in their prayer.

Once more, Lorenzo rings, but cannot get hold of the congregation. Anselmo is now by a girl behind me. Vicente is praying loudly, his baby in his arms. The girl gives her consent to be baptized, and Anselmo shouts out his gratitude. He is very loud. At this point it is he who is really the master of the congregation, not Lorenzo, who is still trying to command attention by ringing his bell. There is a moment's silence, like a breath pause, and then our usually impassive guitarist, Agosto, throws up his arms and, weaving back and forth on his feet, eyes tightly closed, head slightly back, also goes into glossolalia. Martin comes and puts his hand under his head, Emilio is behind him, also Vicente and Alfredo. Lorenzo comes down from the platform and goes into glossolalia. Anselmo on his relentless quest has now approached yet another woman in the rear of the church.

Two more women have come to the front and want to be baptized. They are on their knees, praying loudly, while Martin stands facing them, his eyes tightly closed, in his so easily recognizable rapid glossolalia. Lorenzo has gone back up on the platform and announces that all day tomorrow there will be *doctrina* (instruction about the baptism) for those who have come for-ward to the altar. In the back, there is still some sobbing. Anselmo has gone on to Pedro, while Lorenzo once more whips up the passions for baptism. I catch a glimpse of him as his calculating, shrewd glance sweeps over the con-gregation. It is now 10:30 P.M. Anselmo comes marching down the aisle between the men's and the juvenile sections, his trunk slanting slightly for-

ward, right arm stiffly up in a Roman salute type of gesture, his legs quite stiff
at the knees. With one finger, very rigidly he points to the microcphone,
which Lorenzo relinguishes, and with mounting excitement begins shouting
into it, face flushed, eyes first half closed, then torn open as if by an outside
agency, perspiration dripping from his forehead: "Jehovah is with us. . . .
Jehovah has said, six o'clock tomorrow morning. He who forgets is not with
Jehovah."
Lorenzo takes the microphone: "This is Jehova's message for tomorrow."

This enormous discharge of the peak was remarkable in a number of ways.
It produced first of all a nearly total disintegration of the ritual structure. In
addition, in response to the accumulating tension, to the mounting expectations of the Second Coming—and certainly also to the crowding in the church,
the pulsing noise level, the rhythmic pounding of the many glossolalia utterances—everyone's trance level became boosted. This effect appeared to be
quite uncontrollable for the individual participant, assuming an autonomous
aspect. Yet this magnification appeared to be structured—I would suggest bio-
logically structured. For instance, Nina had first spoken in tongues about four
years before these events. She had converted the behavior more and more into
an internal event, no longer expressed by glossolalia. Now she deepened it into
a state resembling catatonia. Emilio and Lorenzo, both in the attenuating
phase, recovered the degree of dissociation they had possessed a year ago.
Violeta, speaking in tongues for not quite a year, reverted to levels seen in very
recent glossolalia speakers. Finally Vicente, who had acquired the trance behavior the same summer, was thrown into hallucination. Moreover, his
strategy for inducing dissociation represented an—apparently spontaneous—
innovation for the Utzpak congregation. It was not used in this manner in the
Apostolic churches of Mexico or the peninsula. However, though methods for
inducing the trance can apparently be discovered fortuitously, means to end it
need to be developed by experimentation. We saw several manipulations tried:
the person in trance was patted on the back, shaken by the neck or by the
head, or had his head pressed (in trying to expel the Demon from Anselmo).
Violeta was given water to drink and finally placed into a hammock to sleep
off the "intoxication."
The behavior of Anselmo and Lorenzo demonstrates how even at relatively
high trance levels (witness the flushing, tears, saliva, perspiration, stiff leg and
neck muscles) ordinary language remains possible, although it is often
phonetically and grammatically distorted. Occasionally, in this state of trance
a person produces poetic phrases of great lyrical beauty. Thus the woman at
the altar prayed, "So many times I've had the opportunity to be baptized and
never made use of it. O Lord, I want to be baptized now." During the service

of July 31 (see p. 308) Anselmo cried from the rostrum, "My wife's heart is simple, but she loves me to destroy me," which prompted Nina to remark, "I never thought Anselmo could speak with such grandeur."

Finally, and this is important for understanding the ensuing platform phase of the upheaval, there is a general lowering of inhibitions, best expressed by Lorenzo's statement, "I am pushed by a power to say these things, these are not my words."

PLATFORM PHASE

The night after this service, the *hermanos* stayed together, praying in the temple and the *casa pastoral*. At one point Anselmo saw a big wheel of many colors, turning very fast, and a person at a considerable distance from it. Martin interpreted it to him by explaining that the person he saw at a distance was really in the middle of the wheel and was Christ.

Because the night before Anselmo had attempted to commit suicide, this night the *hermanos* kept watch over him. He sat or knelt on a sheet of plastic in the *casa pastoral*, and they tied a cowbell to him so that they would be awakened should he move suspiciously or attempt to leave. In these two days, especially since Cilia and her little children were in Campeche and thus not in the way, the *casa pastoral* assumed the role of an adjunct to the church and its activities.

The service of July 31 was announced as a preparation for those to be baptized the following day. Some of its features marked it as part of the peak, but the level of arousal was somewhat lower, so that we might regard it as the point at which the next phase in the upheaval started.

Evening Service, July 31. Nesto opens the service. He is noticeably hoarse, as is Vicente, to whom he passes later on. During the second altar call, Francisca goes into a lengthy glossolalia, which continues into the special hymns. Violeta, Roberta, Luisa, Nina are all in glossolalia also, but they keep it under considerable control. Lorenzo, in his sermon, tells that fourteen want to be baptized, but that Satan is already working on some of them and has worked this morning and this afternoon. However, we should remember that we may not have another opportunity. "What is easier," he asks, "serve Jesus or burn forever?"

He reads off the names of those who have already indicated their desire to be baptized. If there is anyone else, would he please come forward, so he can be given a brief instruction and can join tomorrow's baptism.

Adela, Martin's wife, holds up her hand. Lorenzo praises her resolve and asks her to come and sit down in the front of the juvenile section, which had been cleared for the baptismal candidates. "He who becomes baptized," Lorenzo tells her, "can forever stay in the presence of Jehovah. In the water, one dies, there are no more dances, no more sin: the dead do not sin." He has her read several biblical passages aloud, which she does with assurance and considerable facility.

At this point, there are loud voices from the *casa pastoral;* we hear the formula of excorcism: "*Yo te reprendo*" and a great shout of various glossolalia utterances. The effect is singularly dramatic and is not lost on the congregation. In the course of the evening, several groups make very impressive use of it. The *hermanos* come back. "Do not be frightened," Lorenzo tells the congregation. "Eventually we will all be tried, every one of us." Anselmo kneels down at the altar. What occurs next is a scene of the Devil possessing Anselmo and with Anselmo's voice demanding Adela. It is a struggle of the inner core of the congregation, under the leadership of Lorenzo, against the Devil, until the latter finally leaves, having been defeated once more.

It goes like this: Isaía comes in, eyes closed, weaving while he walks, in glossolalia. He places his hand on Anselmo's head. Martin follows, places his hand on Anselmo's temple. Lorenzo calls for prayer. Anselmo is shouting his demand for Adela. Violeta and Roberta are in glossolalia, as is Lorenzo, still behind the rostrum; he is very hoarse. Vicente comes in and joins the prayer. Isaía regains consciousness, but Anita and Francisca are now in trance. Anselmo goes to his seat. Lorenzo comes from behind the rostrum, in glossolalia, and goes to Anselmo. The glossolalia as the most powerful kind of prayer and at the same time a manifestation of the Holy Spirit once more becomes a weapon with which to fight Satan. Both Anselmo and Lorenzo then lapse into ordinary speech, but both are visibly in hyperarousal.

The Devil, through Anselmo, says that he wants Adela. Lorenzo shouts that he cannot have her, that this is a good, Christian woman, who wants this baptism, this *alimento* (food). This exchange is repeated with a slight variation, then Lorenzo goes back to the rostrum. Vicente has participated very loudly in glossolalia; Anita, Francisca, Roberta, and Violeta are also in glossolalia. Anselmo has his fists pressed against his forehead, jutting outward, so that they give the impression of being horns. Vicente continues in glossolalia, very loudly; Lorenzo has resumed a quiet prayer at the microphone.

Anselmo gets up from his seat, goes to Lorenzo, and points to the microphone, which Lorenzo hands to him. "Let the service continue," he says, giving us to understand that once more the Devil has left, "Jehovah, Lord of hosts, is with you. My wife's heart is simple, but she loves me to destroy me. However, one must not love father, mother, wife, or son more than God. Jesus loves us, the Holy Spirit is proof of that. My wife is afraid that if she came into the temple, she might receive the Holy Spirit. Her mother knows Satan too. The two of them are surrounded by thousands and thousands of angels. But they cannot enter here, they are out there in the *monte* (bush, jungle), they belong there. If they were to enter here, Jesus would destroy them. For the baptism, people have to be sepulchered, as Jesus was for three days in the earth."

Anselmo's outstretched hand slowly forms a fist, in the very typical motion of light hyperarousal. "All those who still want to be baptized," he says, "should come to the altar, so they can be prayed over." With eyes closed, he points to the front of the altar. Nine women, all young, heed the call, as well as four young men. Anselmo, now with eyes closed, hands the microphone back to Lorenzo. Some baptismal candidates, or would-be-ones rather, go back to their seats. The others are prayed over. Anselmo takes the microphone again, staring wide-eyed, "For the second time, the Lord has used us." He gives the microphone back.

Lorenzo at this point resumes control over the proceedings. He announces that all those who want to be baptized should be at the church tomorrow at six: there will be a truck to take everybody who wants to come out to Santa Clara. He calls for a hymn. While the singing is still going on, Nesto comes in, in the same kind of stiff posture as his brother Isaía before him (at first, in fact, I take him for Isaía), eyes closed, in glossolalia. He is leading two women, who kneel down in front of the altar. Martin walks on behind them, also in dissociation, with his "prayer kinetics" now well stereotyped. He puts his left hand on the head of one of the women, the one on the left. He is followed by Vicente, who remains standing close to me. I watch him. He starts hyperventilating again, actually pumping air through his nose in rapid, deep inhalations, which sends him almost instantly into glossolalia. Francisca goes into glossolalia. Lorenzo comes down from the rostrum and starts praying over the same woman, shaking her head. Emilio joins, praying loudly, "Séllala, séllala . . ."—seal her, seal her!" Finally there is a small movement, and I recognize with a start who it is that has occasioned all this attention: Socorro, the wife of Anselmo!

Violeta goes into intense glossolalia. Even old Valentin, Ermela's husband, usually very quiet, lets go with a loud glossolalia utterance. Nesto gets up, and Lorenzo talks quietly with him and Martin while the glossolalias and prayers are still going on. They leave, and soon there are loud voices in prayer and glossolalia from the casa pastoral. Presently Francisca and some other hermanas join them, so that we have the bright cadences of the glossolalia accompanying the tense events in the church, without the latter being disrupted. Socorro gets up, wipes her eyes, and sits down in the middle section on the chair that is closest to Eusebia's. The other woman, Porfiria (a long-time churchgoer, but never keen on getting baptized), and a young man sit down in the same row in the men's section. Socorro's face is very dark in the shadow of her rebozo (shawl), not a muscle is moving: she is totally frozen still.

Lorenzo's first comment, almost in a hush, is, "Let God have mercy on all of us and on all those who truly repent."

Again there is an upsurge of voices from the casa pastoral, perfectly in tune with, and in counterpoint to, the events in the church.

Lorenzo continues that sometimes it pleases God to surprise people— never for material ends, but so that His name can be glorified. There is a powerful answer in prayer and glossolalia from the congregation. He takes up the subject that in baptism there is a chance to receive the forgiveness of sins. He then addresses Porfiria, saying that she has listened to the Word of God for a long time and this is probably her last opportunity to become baptized, that if she is baptized tomorrow, she will have to resolve to serve Christ from now on until the end of what days she may have left.

Lorenzo then turns to the young man beside Porfiria. Is he already aware of the fact that there is only one God, not three? He nods. Does he realize that if he does go through with the baptism, the things of the world are no longer for him? No smoking, no drinking, no bad company? That from then on, his way leads only from his home to the church? That there is no reading of *cuentos* (popular magazines, including comic books) but only the Bible? The young man assents. Then Lorenzo continues with something that was never mentioned in all the *doctrina* (baptismal instructions) I had heard last year. He says, "God's Word says clearly that those who are truly the children of God possess everything in common. If one has a peso, and it is needed for God's work, he will have to give it. No one may be egoistical, much less avaricious. The Scripture says clearly that if we surrender to Christ, then, both within the phrasing and the spirit of the Word of God, everything we own must also be surrendered if God needs it for his sacred and blessed work." Anselmo goes out. Since the young man voices no objection, he is told that there will be one more *doctrina* in the water tomorrow, and if he still wants it, they will baptize him.

Lorenzo then turns to Socorro, who has her eyes fixed on her lap. "*Hermana* Socorro, you have received much instruction, not to say more than enough instruction," he begins. He points out the significance of the baptismal event and the need for complete repentence. "All old matters have already passed and have now been made new. You must have no thought except to serve Christ faithfully." If she has any other thought, the baptism will not be valid.

"¿Ud. ya entendí, hermana, que nada más Jesucristo es dios?—Did you understand, *hermana*, that only Jesus Christ is God?"

Socorro continues to look down on her lap.

"*Conteste, hermana*—Answer, *hermana*."

Silence.

"¿Ha comprendido que solamente Jesucristo es Dios?—Did you understand that only Christ is God?"

Silence. He switches to Mayan.[12]

"*Letí, wa má?*—That one or not?"

Eusebia leans over to her, put her hand on her arm, and says quietly in Maya, "Answer the *hermano*, Socorro." No reaction.

"*Letí, kiik?*—That one, older sister?"

No answer.

Anselmo comes back from outside and kneels down at the altar to pray.

"Do you want to be baptized, *hermana*, in the name of Jesus Christ? Do you?"

A hardly perceivable nod.

Lorenzo sighs. "*Muy bien.* . . . But remember, from now on, you cannot fight with your husband any more. You will be completely under the commands of God. Under no conditions may you ever oppose your husband again." He outlines the significance of baptism once more. "The pact is between you and God, I will not be responsible for the blood that will fall on your head if you don't fulfill what you will promise. You will have to go wherever God may send you. Remember, none of us is his own master, we are under the order of the Holy Spirit. Everything that It orders must be accepted."

Anselmo rises from his knees before the altar, cleans the dust off his white peasant pants by filliping, and goes back to his seat in the men's section. While Lorenzo announces that there are now all in all eighteen candidates to be baptized tomorrow, the prayer in the *casa pastoral* once more rises high, Violeta's glossolalia and that of one man being clearly audible.

Lorenzo concludes the service and announces a prayer for the sick. Luisa comes to the altar and kneels down. Lorenzo and Martin place their hands on her head; she is in glossolalia, so is Alfredo behind her. Martin begins to pat the nape of her neck rhythmically. Two of Francisca's children have fallen asleep on the floor. Some people begin to leave. Others stay to pray through the night.

As we can see, there were carry-overs in this service from the peak reached the day before—principally the demonic possession and the prolonged glossolalia, which continued to interfere with the ritual structure. However, the trance level was generally lower on this occasion than it had been in the July 30 service. Both the dissociation and the glossolalia were under better control. Vicente hyperventilated once more, but again, as an indication of the decreased energy content of the arousal, this produced only glossolalia, not hallucination. It was within this altered state of lowered intensity that the principal participants played out the magnificent drama of Satan demanding Adela and going down to defeat, and later the coercion of Socorro into baptism.

Weighing the events of the upheaval at this point, I conjectured that what I had witnessed was the start of a revitalization movement. Taking my clue from Wallace's model (see Chapter 8), I felt that I had seen the dissipation of the trance behavior of the group. What would follow now, I expected, would be a movement incorporating the innovations the congregation had elaborated on the ritual level as well as those very important ones in the secular range of communal living and property sharing, possibly with some elements of antiurban, nativistic content.

Since my departure was scheduled for the next day, I could not attend the baptism. I did, however, interrupt my homeward trip to visit *Hermano* Nicolas's congregation in N.; to make a copy of the baptismal record entries there. The impression of having seen the start of a revitalization movement following the Wallace model was reinforced by this visit.

> Before letting me see the baptismal record of his church, Nicolas gives me a little private sermon about the necessity of believing in the eternity of the soul. He himself has already learned how to live without women, and everybody else will have to begin leading a different sort of life. He hopes that I have taken some spiritual values with me from this experience in Utzpak. "Yesterday, sixteen were baptized in Santa Clara, it was a marvellous fiesta of the Spirit. Afterward, when I came back here to hold a service, I really felt the presence of the Lord."

It all seemed rather commonplace, with an emphasis on a changed life style. Of course there was considerable interest in the congregation at N. concerning the events in Utzpak, but nothing more than that.

> *Hermano* Valencio of the Temax congregation is at the temple in N. There develops a conversation between him, one of the *hermanas* of the N. congregation, and myself. The *hermana* says, "Tell what wonders you saw at Utzpak, all those outpourings of the Holy Spirit." When I hesitate, Valencio answers that Violeta said that certain people must surrender to Jesus, such as Nina, and Eusebia, and the husband of Reyes. Why the husband of Reyes? "He is very rebellious in the matters of the Lord." "And how do you know that what Violeta said was something from above?" "Because she was in a faint when she spoke." He tells her of the various gifts of the Holy Spirit that people received, such as the gift of interpretation that Nacho now has.

I certainly had no way of anticipating that the platform phase of the trance would not dissolve promptly, but would rather lead the congregation of Utzpak and also that of N. into events very similar to those reported of the Vailala Madness. Thus I was at a loss on how to interpret a letter I received from Nina, dated September 16, 1970:

> I have many new things to tell you about what happened in the temple in the way of manifestations because of the spirits of the Devil that had entered. All the *hermanos* believed it. Satan our Adversary robbed all of the congregation of its sanity. About the time when you left, this was when the manifestations began. During all of the month of August the most horrible things happened in the church.

Then under the data of October 12, 1970, she wrote:

> I could not check the names of the persons baptized for you because when there were the events of Satan, the book was lost.

In January of 1971 I was able to spend ten days in Yucatán. This was only four months after the end of the upheaval, so that the details were still fresh in the memories of my informants. For the reconstruction to follow below, I used first of all the notes made by Nina, who had recorded the events of August 13, 20, 22, and 23.[13] In January, Nina and her mother (Eusebia, my principal informant in Yucatán) went over the events with me again and again. All this I recorded on tape. Since quite often they also discussed occurrences that I had carefully recorded in my field notes, I could once more verify what I already knew from previous experience, namely, that both of these women had unimpeachable memories. Furthermore, in late January 1971, I had occasion to interview a young *hermana* from the N. congregation who had also been strongly involved in the events. Her narration agreed wit those of Nina and Eusebia in every point. I am therefore confident that the account given here is a reliable and accurate picture of the events of this phase of the upheaval. The report that follows is a composite of my own reconstruction and the accounts given by Nina and Eusebia.

On August 1, there was a baptism at the seaport of Santa Clara, and sixteen men and women were baptized.

> NINA. There were some persons there in bathing suits, and they were disturbing the baptism, standing around, watching and generally being in the way. Lorenzo then called Martin and asked him to pray so that the people who were disturbing the baptism would go away. Martin started praying, and one by one the people that were disturbing, left. And all the *hermanos* were aware of what was happening and it was considered a work of God.

The day after the baptism, nine men went to preach in other villages. They were Isaía, Nesto, Anselmo, Vicente, Alfredo, Iminio, José, Nacho, and Floriano. Lorenzo tried to talk other men into going also, but they refused on the grounds that, if everyone went, there would be none left to earn the money to take care of the children.

The wives of the evangelists went to live at the church; they slept there and cooked there, even for the *hermanos* who stopped in. Isaía, before leaving for his work "in the field," had realized 12,000 pesos, from the sale of twelve steers. Of this he gave 1000 pesos as his tithe. Half of it Lorenzo kept as his share by the rules of the church organization, and half was earmarked for supporting the *hermanas* and their children at the church.

> EUSEBIA. *Hermana* Francisca was in charge of preparing the food. Lorenzo gave her money, and she went out to do the shopping, to buy food, to buy maize, all that. They had of everything, of beans, rice, just everything. But the *hermanas* tell that she went out and bought meat for herself. Then, before

the other *hermanas* came home to eat (from such errands as evangelizing), she would already be done with eating. When the others arrive, there is hardly any food. She has already eaten, she has eaten meat, and to the others she gives beans, that's all she gives them. She is the one in charge, therefore she eats well. She buys soap, a plastic bag of FAB, of those that cost one peso and fifty, and to the *hermanas* she gives a little FAB and a bit of soap, and she has the entire bag and piece of soap. You know who told me all this? Socorro, the wife of Anselmo.

Pues, bit by bit, the *hermanas* began going home. The wife of Vicente went first. Her children are crying, they want cookies, but there is no money to buy any. The last one to stay on was Francisca. She was ashamed to go home because the people were talking about her, saying that she had an affair with Lorenzo. Somebody was said to have come to the *casa pastoral,* found Francisca in the hammock, and there was *Hermano* Lorenzo, with his pants down. There was nothing to it, it was all gossip, but she was ashamed anyway. But finally, she also went home again. By the end of August, none of them was left at the church.

In the second week of August, Socorro had her baby in the shower corner of the *casa pastoral.* It was a little girl. One of the *hermanas* took care of her. When the baby was two days old, she went home.

The *hermanos* in the various villages also had a number of problems. The first one to come back was Nacho, who had gone out as the associate of Floriano. He said that one evening he saw from the outside how Floriano was preaching. He grabbed a stone and wanted to throw it at Floriano. He did not do it, but came back to Utzpak right away. He told Lorenzo that he felt that he had sinned against the Holy Spirit and could not go on evangelizing. Soon after that, Vicente also returned. In the village where he was preaching, a girl fell in love with him. He left and went to T., where Isaía had taken over a congregation that was already a going concern. However, Vicente was unhappy there also and went home.

The others in the field held out a little longer, but they had not learned how to live off a congregation and, receiving no financial support from Utzpak, were near starvation. Floriano lived on 50 centavos worth of tortillas a day and a bit of butter. The other *hermanos* finally joined Floriano in Ct., and they did not even have the bus fare to return. No one knows how they made it home, but they appeared one day, nearly starved, so thin that they could hardly keep their trousers up.

After the baptism, the life of the congregation lost what little structure had still been preserved. There were meetings every evening, but no regular services were held, only prayer sessions. Moreover, as soon as anyone would kneel down, he or she would go into hyperarousal:

NINA. And they would speak, prophesying like Isaiah and saying that
Christ would come soon and everybody should be baptized. At this time, they
said nothing bad against anybody else as yet.

EUSEBIA. They would pray awfully long, sometimes until eleven o'clock at
night. They did not speak in tongues, but just screamed, and then the
hermanos would take the *hermanas* to the hammocks in the *casa pastoral*, for
they could not walk, they were as if drunk. And even in the hammocks, they
would continue screaming. Some, like Marta, would walk around, with wide
open eyes, breathing heavily, saying, "If you don't believe in God, you will
lose your soul."

  And sometimes they would kneel down and they'd start looking around
to see who isn't praying. I can see what they are doing because I don't close
my eyes. When they look at me, I close my eyes, then I look again. And
Violeta would say, "*Hermana* Socorro isn't praying," or "Tola isn't." And
the *hermanos* would come up to us and say, "Pray, *hermanas*, pray."

Nacho lived in the church, and the *hermanas* cooked for him and made him
his bath:

EUSEBIA. He was attacked very strongly, and the evil spirits did not leave
him so soon, it took a whole month before he was free of them again. As soon
as he knelt down to pray, he began to cry, and then his brain began to hurt at
the base of his skull. He would throw himself on the ground and would know
nothing of himself. He said, it felt like *aire* [the air; in Latin-American folk
medicine, the cause of many illnesses], like a pain going through him. During
prayer, he never said anything.

  He was attacked by the evil spirits even in the *monte* [bush], and when he
was this way attacked, he always wanted to go. He would go to Mérida or
just anywhere. And since he couldn't find his way back, some *hermana* would
have to go out and find him again.

  Once Nacho left, and *Hermano* Nicolas, who was in Utzpak at the time,
was angry and said, "He is *hermano* no longer." Nicolas said that also about
the *hermanas*. If an *hermana* left, he would right away say, "She is *hermana*
no longer."

The same restlessness took hold of other members of the congregation. Lorenzo, for one, kept going back and forth between Utzpak and Nicolas's congregation in N. After returning home, he would just sit in the church and

speak to no one, giving no sermons:

> EUSEBIA. His hair was mussy, he was staring around, and seemed angry with us, who knows why? But it was this way all the time. This is why all those bad things happened.

Emilio was similarly afflicted and kept on the move between N. and Utzpak. When in the church, he would pray for extended periods, an hour or more at a stretch, while continually hitting his head with his hands. He was the only one who did that. He seemed to be in a perpetual low-level trance:

> EUSEBIA. Emilio was attacked all the time. He would go back and forth between Utzpak and N., and when he wasn't praying, he would say what everybody should be doing and what was right, what was wrong.
> NINA. Emilio would say to those who were fasting that it was good. And if God forgave someone, Emilio would be the one to tell him that it was so. And the people believed him because they thought that he was possessed by the Spirit of God.

All these goings-on did not, of course, go unnoticed by the village people:

> EUSEBIA. Doña Juana's husband, they say, shot into the church, into the roof, because the congregation made so much noise. I never heard the shot, so I don't know.
> The people also said that the young girls were virgins no longer, that Nicolas took them, and all the *hermanos* did too, because they heard them scream, and they knew that the *hermanos* took them to their hammocks.
> All in all they said that the *hermanos* were mad, shouting and praying all night.
> NINA. When the *Señores Cristianos* and the *Dorcas* would go out to evangelize in the village, the people did not listen to them. They said, "How can you go out and evangelize? You don't even know if you are worshiping God, or whether the devils are possessing you!"

In the second week of August, Cilia, Lorenzo's wife, came back from a visit to her mother. She would pray long and hard, hitting the floor with her hands, although she did not do this every day, having small children to take care of. In the meantime, the church had become very dirty, so dirty that one could kneel no longer:

> EUSEBIA. The children urinated on the floor, and no one wiped it up. Floriano had a cold and spit out everywhere. It was as if the people were blind. They didn't see the dirt. They even put the covers on the tables and on the rostrum backward, and did not turn them right side up until a week later, when *Hermano* Nicolas came from N.

At this time, a new elaboration appeared, perhaps a late response to my incessant note-taking. Since it was thought that everything said by those possessed was the word of the Holy Spirit, those *hermanos* who knew how to write would go from person to person and write down what they were saying. They said that they would send these notes "far away," but no one seemed to know where or even if it was ever done. Later on, an exchange of such notes developed between the Utzpak congregation and that of Nicolas in N.

Then, under August 13, Nina has the following entry:

> Marta said, "Where is Don Tacho? He should be here so he can hear this. If he will not consecrate himself to the Lord, he will die, both in the flesh and in the spirit, and will go to hell with all his riches." Then she said, "I'm not going home, the Devil is there." And this made her mother very angry.

This ushered in a period of mutual recriminations, appearing mostly as an attack on the outsiders, the noncommitted, the doubters. At first it was couched in decrees for extended fasting by these particular members. Again the teenagers took the lead. According to Nina, one of them, Pilar, ordered "10 days of fasting for Nina, 15 days for Socorro, 15 days for Eusebia, and 30 days for Nohoč Felipe, all from six to six. She also mentioned others."

They certainly picked their targets well. Don Tacho, mentioned first in a direct attack, was one of the oldest members in terms of years of belonging to the congregation, one of the first to be baptized by Oscar Gill. He and his wife Valuch kept wavering, sometimes taking the pronouncements by the various young *hermanas* seriously, sometimes not. Nohoč Felipe paid no attention to either the attacks or the fasts decreed. In fact, he hardly even believed that the Holy Spirit was involved in the events at the church. Both Nina and her mother definitely qualify as wavering converts, to borrow a term from S. L. Thrupp. As Nina says, "Sometimes I believed [that it was the Holy Spirit that was possessing the congregation], sometimes I didn't. The more they told me that I had to believe, the less I believed."

As to the fasting, Socorro did not do it at all, and neither did Nohoč Felipe. Nina resorted to eating a hefty meal before six in the morning and then fasted until six at night. Francisca fasted for ten days, got very thin, and eventually became sick. Nacho overdid it so badly that he could not fasten his trousers. Chela and her daughter Violeta were to fast for only three days, and they did; Eusebia persisted for six.

> EUSEBIA. You could see that Francisca fasted, for she was heavy before and now she got very thin. I am thin, so you can't see if I fast or not. I did it for six days and felt that I was dying of hunger. While fasting we stayed in the church all day, because at home you might forget and eat something or take

some water. I became so weak, I could not hear any more, and I could not do my washing, I had no strength. But all our clothes were dirty, so on Saturday I said, "I'll eat." And I did, and then I did my washing.

It is necessary now to switch to the action in the congregation in N. As already mentioned, the events of late July in Utzpak were discussed in this congregation with some interest on August 1, when I visited there. Then, due to the restless peregrinations of such *hermanos* as Emilio, Martin, and Nacho, the congregation of N. soon became totally involved.

In this congregation, probably on August 18, a girl of nineteen, a student at the University of Yucatán here called Olga, proclaimed that the Holy Spirit wanted everything shiny—such as eyeglasses, ballpoint pens, and buttons—to be eliminated. My informants, including the one from N., are in agreement that this was not a vision, just a communication from what Olga thought was the Holy Spirit. She also said that all colors other than white would have to be eliminated; this pertained especially to the Bibles, because of the red edges of the pages. The Bibles were thrown into the yard and other elaborations of this suggestion also appeared. For example, Emilio and Martin from Utzpak, who happened to be present, said that they could see the Devil with his horns in the rose design woven into the red brocade curtain that covered the wall behind the altar. They were in acute distress and suggested that the curtain be burned. There followed other manifestations of considerable hyperarousal: Martin continued in mild hallucination, seeing a white cross on the chest of believers; when a large black moth called *mahanay* in Mayan strayed into the church, Olga cried out that it was Satan, that she could see him, and that the monster should be killed.

Turning everything white and burning offensive objects were the two suggestions taken up most ardently. After this service, Olga and her mother went home and burned the family television set. (This so upset the father of the family, not a member of the congregation, that he beat his wife and three daughters and left them.)

After Lorenzo arrived in N. on August 20, the red curtain of the church was in fact burned. The Bibles were collected from the yard and their edgings were painted black. Then a certain *Hermano* Pedro started giving others.[14] He climbed up on the *albarrada* (limestone garden wall) and shouted, "*Hermanos,* Jesus Christ is already here." From the church, the people answered, "*Gloria a Dios, aleluya.*" Then, conscious of what the neighbors might think, they cautioned him, "Don't shout so loud." He answered, "I give orders here. I am the Father, yes or no?" And they replied, "Yes, we accept it." One *hermano* added, "Father, you have already come!"

He then ordered a tin washtub to be brought and filled with water. The *hermanos* were to bathe each other's feet in that. It had rained and their feet were muddy. Yet no one objected when afterward Pedro ordered them to drink of the water, calling it the water of life. They all drank of it. Then they asked him, "Father, what do you want, purified water or the water of life?" It is told with some amusement today that Pedro asked for purified water for himself.

In Utzpak, these incidents were apparently recounted on the same or the next day, for on August 20, Nina recorded similar patterns there. In addition, Marta engaged in some unimaginably sacrilegious cursing in church (even in a secular context, this would be an entirely unthinkable demeanor for a Mayan peasant woman):

> NINA. Thursday, August 20. Pilar says, "Throw out everything that is red. Throw out the Bibles."
> Marta says, "Nina, take off your [colored] dress, it disturbs us." And she says to Pilar, "Pilar, you take off your [colored] dress, and then you can put on my [white] uniform." And Pilar answered, "Let's do that."
> Pilar then said, "Throw out everything that is red. Throw out everything that has colors in it, throw out the books, the tables, the rostrum." And Marta sat on the altar, her legs aparts, and kept swearing, saying, "*Puta, puta*" [prostitute]. Then they prayed very loud, as if prophesying again."

There is once more great fear of Satan. Marta has a vision. She sees an eagle overhead, and it is shrieking. "That," she says, "is Satan."[15] Later, Marta has another vision, of the tail of Satan:

> NINA. "Here is its tail," she said. "Close the windows and don't allow anyone to open the door. No one should go outside." And she was standing at the door with some others, pushing against it, as if there were someone outside trying to force his way in. And there were noises heard, as if the plastic chandeliers were being moved by the Demon, which, of course, they were. So, the chandeliers were thrown out into the yard. Marta began to cry, "For a long time now he has wanted to fetch me." And she begged that the door be kept closed and also all the windows.
> EUSEBIA. And they threw out everything, even the guitar and the *marimbol*, and the flower vases. The children played with them, and everything stayed out all night.

On August 21, Nina tells us,

> I went into the *casa pastoral*. Marta was there in her hammock. She was thoroughly possessed and was praying and crying. When I came in, she said to me, "Nina, kneel down and pray." "I only pray to God," I answered and knelt down to start praying. Marta said, "The Demon has left you." At that

moment Cilia came in, and Marta said, "Now the Demon will attack Cilia."
Thereupon Cilia fell down, screaming. Lorenzo, Emilio, Nacho, and two
other *hermanos* came rushing in to pray over her, but she lay there on the
ground, kicking them, and she was stronger than five of them. Finally they
put her into her hammock, and there she fell asleep, and that way the condition went by. Then Nicolas came, and Lorenzo went with Cilia to N., and
there the demons attacked her again. She had something like a seizure, and
she moved with tremendous force.

Simultaneously, the assaults on the outsiders were continued. On August
20, Pilar had said to Nina, "Nina, consecrate yourself. Jesus Christ wants
you to consecrate yourself." Whereupon Nina, perceiving that this much
repeated demand discredited her religious integrity, answered, "Yes, I am already doing that, I am consecrating myself. But how about you? Didn't Jesus
Christ tell you to let the hems out of your dresses and to put sleeves into
them?" When Pilar admitted to this, Nina asked, "And didn't he tell you
that you had chosen the wrong boyfriend, because he has not been baptized?"
"Yes," said Pilar, "he did tell me that."

On August 22, these divisive tendencies came to a head. Lorenzo had gone
to the congregation in N., and Nicolas had instead come to visit the one in
Utzpak. Again there was no structure to the meeting in the church. Immediately at the outset, Violeta began to make demands:

NINA.   "Throw out *Hermano* Tacho," "Violeta says, because his laughter
kills me."

"Glory to God," counters Tacho, "but you won't throw me out of here."

"He is laughing," persists Violeta, "throw him out."

Nicolas was at the rostrum [which was too heavy and thus had not been
thrown out] and asked the congregation to pray that *Hermano* Tacho would
leave. He was sitting toward the back, and no matter how much the congregation prayed, he would not leave. Finally, Nicolas came down from the
pulpit and asked Tacho to leave. He did, saying, "The spirit of Satan is in
this church." Eusebia agreed with him. "Yes, *Hermano* Tacho," she said,
"Satan is here."

The wife of Tacho, *Hermana* Valuch, was also in the church, with her
sons. When she saw that her husband was being expelled, she also wanted to
leave. Before going, she called to her son Gabi. But he would not go, he
rather wanted to listen to Violeta. When Violeta heard that they were calling
Gabi, she said, "No, you must not take Gabi with you. His father will go to
perdition with all his wealth, and if *Hermana* Valuch won't consecrate
herself, she will also go to hell, and if Gabi won't consecrate himself, he will
also go to hell. And throw out Angel, too."

This was a young man who had just begun to come to the church. And they did throw him out. Then she demanded, "Throw out Gregorio, he is only coming to laugh at us. And you, Nina," she continued, "consecrate yourself."

Eusebia at this point advised her friend Valuch that she had better leave. "They are stupid and pigheaded," she said.

After this incident, Nicolas officially informed the congregation about the revelation that the Lord wanted everything red or colored to be eliminated and that everything should be white. He then told Eusebia, "*Hermana,* you will have to put seams into your ʔipil so that the flowers will not show, for the Lord wants no colors. And you must go and find a white mantilla to put on your head." "*Hermano,*" Eusebia answered, "if a woman has money, she buys one. It is not found in the street."

The next day, August 23, was a Sunday. The congregation arrived early in the morning, but there was no Sunday school. Instead they were told that, according to the revelation, the Holy Spirit gave them two weeks to burn everything that was not white. They were all sent home to carry out these instructions.

EUSEBIA.   I saw Violeta and Marta talking together, so I went close to listen, and they were saying, "This evening we'll see who did it and who didn't."

We went home, my husband, Nina, and I, and we were not quite sure whether to believe it or not that these were truly the orders of the Holy Spirit. In a way, we believed it. So we took all the calendars with their pictures from the walls, because they had red in them, and we burned them. Nohoč Felipe had a red handkerchief, and I said to him, "I won't burn it, I'll save it." And I hid it away. In the church they had said that nothing red was to remain in the house. So I took my pink dish that has the shape of a shell, put it into a bag, and hid that too, outside. We burned no clothes, but we did take the casing off the radio, because that had colors on it, and burned that.

Other people went home and, being as poor as we are, did not burn anything either, like Ermela, for instance. But Chela went home and burned her radio, and they burned some dresses belonging to herself and Violeta, her daughter. They also burned a good blanket. Now [this was told in January] that it has gotten cold, she had to sell one of her turkeys to buy another blanket. Many others also burned their dresses.

Back at the church in the meantime, they threw out everything—Bibles, the covers for the table and for the rostrum, books, papers, pictures. They burned many papers and also wanted to burn the *marimbol.* Nohoč Felipe had paid 60 pesos for it. They poured gasoline on it, but it escaped. Nobody knows why it did not burn. What could not be burned, they painted white— the rostrum and also the tar paper they had bought for the new *casa pastoral.*

They also threw out the large embroidered covers from the church. I saw the one I had bought, and I had paid 60 pesos for it. When I saw that, I picked it up. Francisca saw me do it and said, "What do you want that for? This has to be burned." I said, "I need it. I'll put it on my table." So I took it home, washed and ironed it, and put it away. Later in the month, Cilia asked me, "Where is the large *mantel,* did you take it to your house?" "Yes, it is in my house." I didn't say I took it, or anything. So I brought it back, and when I prayed, I put it, folded small, into the inside corner of the rostrum, out of sight. Who knows when they found it, but finally they put it up again.

In the afternoon, the *hermanas* borrowed an electric sewing machine and took it to the *casa pastoral.* There they sewed white dresses, even for Socorro. But Socorro refused to wear it, because she does not wear dresses, she wears the ?ipil.

I also refused to buy anything white and I told Nina, "If they want to give you white material for a dress, you won't accept it, not one half meter."

NINA.   When the evening came, most everybody was barefoot and had white dresses on. But there were some who did not come in white, and they were sent home to change. Then the entire congregation formed a prayer circle, and they were once more severely attacked by the Adversary. Especially, this was true of Luisa. "Eusebia is doubting," she said. "She answered *Hermano* Nicolas in an evil way [about the white mantilla]. She should not have answered that way. She is doubting." She was crying, and she was drunk with the spirit. Then Luisa continued, "*Hermanos,* it is not two weeks that we have for burning everything: we have only three days. All shoes should be burned," she said.

Then *Hermano* Floriano, possessed by the same evil spirit, demanded the shoes of those who had come with shoes on, put them into a sack, but since there was no gasoline, he could not burn them. Many *hermanos* went and hid their shoes and the next day painted them white.

EUSEBIA.   Floriano also wanted to burn Felipe's *alpargatas* [sandals]. He said, "Come on, burn them, I'll also burn my new shoes." But I told him, "You are young, you can still get new ones. Felipe is old, where is he going to get new ones? He doesn't make much money." So we put all our shoes into a bag, and Nina took them and watched them.

NINA.   That Sunday when all that was not white was burned I had a blue dress on, and my blue purse was on a chair. When we were in a circle praying, Marta took my purse. Its color made her angry, and she hit a little boy with it. Nicolas took it and threw it out the window. If I had been possessed by the Evil One, I would have gone out, gotten it, and hit them with it, because I was very angry. But I went on praying. Sometime later that evening, I saw a dark shape near the altar. Still later I realized that it was the mother of Marta praying there.

All this time, Nicolas went around in the church crying, saying that it was the Holy Spirit that was doing all of this, that you must believe it. However, he rarely prayed, just helped others who were *agonizando* [in trance], holding them so that they would not fall off the chair, giving them water, supporting them so that they would not suffocate. He also wrote down everything the *hermanos* were saying, telling the congregation that these were things that the Holy Spirit was telling them, and later he took these notes to N., so they would know there also about the messages of the Holy Spirit.

Some other congregations burned things too: Isaía's congregation in T., Peregrino's in B. (there is some doubt about the accuracy of the latter intelligence: the *hermanos* are ashamed now, Eusebia says, and will not talk about what went on in the other congregations), and Gilberto's congregation in C.

In the meantime, Lorenzo had arrived in N. The curtain was burned, and now events took another turn: some of the members of the congregation were married, although they had not yet been baptized in the church. This is forbidden in the Apostolic Church. In the words of the informant from the N. congregation:[16]

> *Hermano* Lorenzo arrived, and he had this of the Evil One. Of course, no one knew it was the Evil One at the time. He told us to pray and to fast. The curtain was burned. Then the Evil One married some of the people in the church, although they were not baptized. He knew all the names, and he called them out. It was the mouth of *Hermano* Pedro that he used. Olga was one that they married with her boyfriend who was not baptized, and then two other couples, by using a text from Genesis about how the world began. They even fetched veils, and they embraced and kissed in church.
>
> Then there were two *hermanas,* one of them the sister-in-law of *Hermano* Gilberto, the brother of Nicolas. They began to pray, and they decided to have a drawing for Nicolas and thus determine by lot which one of them should have him. They asked for guidance on the matter and the Evil One answered, again through Pedro, that this was the way it should be done. When Lorenzo went back to Utzpak, they told him to inform Nicolas that the two girls wanted to marry him. But when he came back, he did not marry. They say that in Utzpak, he laughed about them. Soon afterward, his brother Gilberto came with an *hermano* from the church office in Villahermosa and he told them that it was Satan, not the Holy Spirit, that was making them do all those things.[17]

THE END

The platform phase apparently began to wane right after the burning of colored objects. In retrospect, speaking about the upheaval in January 1971,

Eusebia and Nina agreed that at this point "the evil was beginning to pass." A number of people did not burn their shoes, but painted them white instead. The Bibles were collected from the yard where they had been thrown and merely their edges were colored black. The formal end, however, came with a visit from Villahermosa.

In the week of August 23, in N., *Hermana* Consuelo was accused in the church by her sons of being unfaithful to the Lord and told that she should fast and repent or she would be expelled from the congregation.[18] As already mentioned, Consuelo was one of the very earliest members of the Apostolic Church in Yucatán, one of the first converts of Oscar Gill. She was also an extremely devout woman, one of those who had successfully maintained her glossolalia behavior, occasionally had visions, and often spoke in tongues in church.

Convinced by this personal distress that the events in the church could not have been divinely inspired—being so obviously wrong in her case—Consuelo traveled to Villahermosa, Tabasco, to the offices of the Church. She reported what was going on and spoke to Don Venancio, who was a highly revered *hermano,* one thought to have total knowledge of the Bible as a gift of divine inspiration. He traveled with her to C., to the congregation of Gilberto, which was also involved in the upheaval. He convinced Gilberto that it was not the Holy Spirit that was possessing the congregations, quite the contrary. Together they then traveled to N., whence, in the company of pastor Nicolas, they went on to Utzpak, arriving on September 10. A baptism was scheduled on that day for five new members in the seaport of Santa Clara. There they spoke with Emilio and told him that it had been not the Holy Spirit, but rather Satan, that had possessed the congregation. Emilio wept bitterly, saying, "And that I should have been one of those who thought that it was the Spirit of God!"

After the baptism, there was a service at the church in Utzpak.

> NINA. When *Hermano* Venancio came to Utzpak in the middle of September, all was already quiet. He held a sermon in which he said that the congregation should know the Bible better and that this had not been the Holy Spirit acting in them. They should no longer pray by shouting and screaming, for the Lord was not deaf. He also said that this had to happen to the congregation, because the Adversary knew that theirs was the right religion, and so he was attacking them first of all. And those that had been most active in these things were ashamed, like Violeta and Marta; previously, they had always sat in front, now they went to the back and stayed there, and did not sit in the front any more.

Taking into consideration the heartbreak and frustration that the events in the congregation had brought to Eusebia, one should forgive her, I think, if she availed herself of the presence of *Hermano* Venancio, her friend of many years, to obtain a bit of personal satisfaction.

> EUSEBIA. Floriano was the one who burned the shoes. So when Don Venancio comes, I talk with him, and when Floriano comes by, I say, "Here, *Hermano,* is the *maestro de quemar los zapatos*—the master of shoe burning. So Floriano does not want to let that pass and says to Don Venancio, "*Hermano,* how many masters are there?" And Don Venancio says, "There are only two, the Evil One and the Lord." Floriano was angry at me for a long time, but now he has started talking to me again.

An interesting late repercussion in the larger community might be worth mentioning here because it demonstrates how the vision experience, in the same manner as glossolalia, may on occasion be acquired spontaneously by a soi-disant bystander. In the last days of October a member of the Presbyterian church in Utzpak had a vision which he took to mean that he should speak the truth in his church and preach what was in the Bible. He tried to do that, but the other members of this very conservative group would not listen to him. So he joined the Apostolic congregation and was baptized there with his wife on November 17, 1970.

Interpreting in January 1971 what had happened to the congregation, Eusebia reiterates the official position:

> The *hermanos* say that this had to happen because this is the right religion. In other religions people go to the picture shows, they go to dances, even right after a service. It was not the *hermanos* who did all those things: it was Satan that made them throw out the Bibles. But I think it became possible because the *hermanos* in the church hated each other. Many still do.

Nina adds her version:

> The Evil One had so confused, so emptied the minds of the *hermanos* that they did not recognize that the hour had arrived when God wanted to test them. Because when they started throwing out the Bibles, they should have realized that this was the weapon for defeating the enemy. But they had no such insight.

When the Presbyterians, however, gloat that the Apostolics were attacked by Satan and they were not, the congregation has a favorite reply: "That is because the Devil is already sure of *you!*"

The bewildering panorama of events adding up to the upheaval, or crisis cult, will be analyzed in Chapter 8. What should be clear at this point is that we are dealing with an event that is doubly based in societal and psychobiological processes. Although to all appearances its roots can be traced to the summer of 1969 with the entrance of the new minister into the congregation, its overt, acute phase lasted less than two months, and the cult seemed to be dissolved by the middle of September 1970 at the latest. Tardy effects, however, continued to appear. The longitudinal study of these is still in progress, and the next chapter relates the data I was able to obtain through the summer of 1973.

NOTES

1. For a detailed discussion of trance and attendant behavior see Goodman (1972a).

2. A summary of the events of the upheaval was first published elsewhere (Bourguignon, 1973).

3. This is clearly a reference to auditory hallucination. There was no church within miles, neither was there any radio turned on in any of the huts.

4. Data about the personal life and the experiences of Emilio and the others dicussed here come from conversion stories, of which I collected a total of 28 in the course of my field work, 18 of them in Yucatán. (Details in Goodman, 1972a).

5. "Innovator" is here used to mean that he joined the congregation as a result of a search rather than by being recruited along the kinship network.

6. For a detailed discussion of this phenomenon see Goodman (1972a).

7. Soon after the upheaval, in late September 1970, a faith healer came from the congregation in T. Although several influential *hermanos* doubted his powers, a number of cures were immediately attributed to him.

8. For a detailed discussion of hallucination in these congregations see Goodman (1973b).

9. No candles are used in Apostolic services.

10. A reference to 1 Corinthians 12:10.

11. Fifteen years old, speaking in tongues since September 7, 1969.

12. Lorenzo has only minimal command of Mayan. Correct usage here would be *beyó,* not *letí;* also, *kiik* is used only in a secular context, such as kinship.

13. Initially, Nina jotted her notes down in church, but Lorenzo objected, saying that Nina was not in school, so why was she writing in church? She then wrote her record of the events at home. This was a considerable accomplishment, as she had had only two years of formal schooling. I had never consciously trained her or even asked her to do this. I think she wrote her account out of an interest in intellectual activity (she had for years taken notes on sermons, recorded quotations from the Bible, and made a collection of new hymns), but probably mainly because her mother and I were such good friends, and she felt that she was doing me a favor. She and her mother are very close. She gave direct quotations of what to her were the most striking statements in a given situation, and each time she also gave the dates. Her entries were for the 13th, 20th, 22nd, and 23rd of August. This gave me reliable fixed points for arranging the data.

14. The way it is told today, "the Evil One started giving orders through his mouth."

15. There is a belief in Utzpak that is reminiscent of this vision content. Unexplained deaths of infants are thought to have been caused by a black bird, larger than a buzzard, flying overhead and causing evil things to happen.

16. All through the interview this young woman's body twitched, as if in a grossly magnified nervous tick. As soon as the conversation turned to other matters, the twitch stopped. She is said also to have been possessed during the upheaval.

17. None of the marriages described in this account were consummated.

18. In January 1971, my informant from the N. congregation said about Consuelo's sons that this showed that they were at that time possessed by "the Evil Spirit."

7

The Congregation After the Upheaval

When I saw the congregation again in January 1971, not one of the innovations introduced during the peak and the platform phases of the upheaval was still in force. In some areas, an actual attrition had taken place. Thus, for instance, Nina was no longer president of the juvenile section. Violeta had taken her place, and the section was suffering in its activities because the other members considered her inefficient. Eusebia and Socorro withdrew from the *Dorcas*, although they still attended church. Because of Marta's attack on her mother ("I won't go home, the Devil lives there"), her family had not been to any services since early September. Tacho and his family attended the services of the Pentecostals in Utzpak, saying that they would return when Lorenzo was replaced by another minister.

The members most active in the upheaval stepped into the background and usually did not participate in the altar calls. They were negligent in attendance. At the service of January 19, 1971, which I had an opportunity to attend, not one of them was present. One reason may have been the bean harvest then in progress, but Lorenzo seemed to think otherwise because he asked for a prayer for the *hermanos* who were absent, saying, "Who knows why they attend so little, or what their problems might be?" Only the Sunday services were well attended, but the extensive periods of prayer, though retained, were not dedicated to the purpose of receiving the Holy Spirit.

Services in private homes did on occasion still take place. One was being planned for the end of January, to celebrate the fifteenth birthday of Valentin's daughter. This is an important occasion in the larger society and among the Catholics, especially in the city, where it is celebrated with a private mass and a *fiesta* in the home of the girl. The family had earmarked a pig to be slaughtered for the occasion. Thus, city patterns continued to be viewed as de-

328

sirable. "At the congregation in Mérida," Nina said, "there was such a lovely celebration, with the *hermanas* baking cookies for the children and bringing everyone presents wrapped in colored paper."

Some innovations were introduced since the upheaval. Sometime in October, a separate service for the children was started, "so they would not run around in the street during the services." One of the unmarried young men was in charge first, but he could not stand the children, so Anselmo took over.

The church was clean once more. The plastic chandeliers had not been replaced, but there were some new prints on the wall. The front facing of the rostrum, formerly blue, with the words "*Dios es amor*—God is love" painted on it, was still white, a lingering reminder of the upheaval.[1] Another change in the physical plant was of greater importance: a new *casa pastoral* was completed behind the church, and although of the same traditional mud-and-wattle construction as the church, it was not oval like the village homes, but square. This spatial concession to city ways may have helped Lorenzo to overcome, at least temporarily, his culture shock of the previous year. He was no longer barricaded from his congregation and sat on a small bench beside the men when playing the guitar to accompany the singing. There were no longer any allegations of financial mismanagement against him, but the feeling lingered that he was alienated from the congregation. Thus he was criticized for going to Campeche for Christmas to attend the wedding of his wife's sister instead of staying with the congregation to celebrate.

As to the *trance behavior*, none of it was visible in the congregation. There might have been some anxiety about triggering it, for during the entire service of January 19, 1971, they did not sing a single *corito*, that brief chorus with its gay melody, fast rhythm, and open invitation to trance behavior, so intimately connected in the people's minds with speaking in tongues. Perhaps, also, at least for some, the behavior was lost. As Nina said, "They thought [during the upheaval] that every time you knelt down, the Holy Spirit would come. But now it is not that way." During the above-mentioned service, there was no glossolalia at all, except at the very end, during the prayer for the sick, when Nesto and Lorenzo uttered a very brief phrase each. It seems that the collective and very rapid attenuation of trance behavior which the group underwent and which marked the end of the upheaval involved even those who had only recently acquired the glossolalia, such as Alfredo and Martin; under ordinary circumstances, the behavior can be maintained for several years and, on an attenuated level, much longer by some (see Goodman, 1972a).

The two *supernatural premises* taken into the upheaval—the Second Coming and Satan—passed through unscathed, however. It is tempting to relate their emergent strength to the point in time when they were introduced: the Second Coming, available from the very start, remained the strongest. It was still believed to be due very soon: "Next week, very soon; *má? tu šáantahi*—it will not be long," said Eusebia. Nina added, "Previously, I didn't feel this way about it. But now, it seems, I can think of nothing else. And I remember all those people in the city, and how sad it is that there are not enough workers to convert them." There seemed to be consensus in the congregation on this point.

Satan, having arrived second on the scene, had lost nothing of his reality, but there seemed to be a subtle modification. He appeared somehow less formidable, manageable like a wicked neighbor, for he came, tempted people, and then gave up.

The figure of Christ, the latecomer, which did not appear until the service of July 30 and was then played out by the illusive figure in the turning wheel of colors, remained the weakest. In fact, the latter vision was not remembered as one seen by Anselmo and interpreted by Martin: it was thought that Martin had seen it and that it indeed portended the coming end of the world.

DEVELOPMENT SINCE JANUARY 1971

Despite the fact that he and his family were now somewhat more comfortably off, Lorenzo continued restlessly searching for other possibilities. He was absent from Utzpak much of the time, and in his absence various *hermanos* conducted the services, but these were "very cold."

Don Venancio took over the orphan congregation temporarily, and this caused many people who had drifted away to come back. Unfortunately, he had to leave, and Lorenzo brought in, from the church in C., a young man who was personally loyal to him but had not even been promoted to the lowest rank in the church hierarchy, that of *obrero* (worker). This action caused a great deal of resentment in the congregation, since this *Hermano* Pito insisted on preaching from the rostrum rather than from the small table placed before the altar, thus presuming to a higher rank than he possessed.

The various church orgnizations further deteriorated. The people claimed that they were not doing anything, no money was being saved to construct the masonry temple they had dreamed of. In fact, most of the money that the sections were earning by *talento*, as well as the membership dues, went to pay for Lorenzo's frequent trips. He seems to have used the congregation at this time mainly as a source of income. He would come, "borrow" the money that had accumulated, ask for an offering for his next trip, and leave again. In disgust, Martin resigned as treasurer of the *Señores Cristianos*.

Anselmo had again had problems with his wife. This time, it seems, he suspected her unjustly, but the men on the plaza kept goading him, saying,

"That *hermana* sure is sweet on men." After some violent quarrels, when only the intervention of the *hermanos* prevented him from murdering his wife, he left her and went to Villahermosa to work as a barber. She asked for help from her mother, but was refused. Anselmo's mother gave her some corn and a few handfuls of beans, but she was soon destitute and to feed her four little daughters went back to prostitution.

In the spring of 1971, there seems to have been a slight recovery of the trance behavior, with a number of men and women, almost entirely those who had actively participated in the upheaval, occassionally speaking in tongues. However, the service formerly dedicated solely to praying for the manifestation of the Holy Spirit was not reintroduced.

Satan continued as an important supernatural premise. When the husband of one of the *hermanas* had an accident in the bush, the incident was related in the following manner both by Nina and by Eusebia:

> Juan climbed on the cottonwood tree to cut branches for his horse. He was attacked by devils: one was on his back, the other at his throat, the third pulled him down. He fell from the tree and twisted his neck. Although it was not broken, he was paralyzed, and the *hermanos* went to his house to pray for him. Anselmo had come to see his wife, but he had gone back to dancing, cursing, and drinking. When the *hermanos* went to pray for Juan, he went along. But when Juan saw him, he said, "Don't pray for me, the Devil has already taken you." Anselmo sat down in the back and cried.

On June 28, 1971, when I arrived in Yucatán for the continuation of my field work, there was a pastors' meeting in Mérida. At this meeting, there seems to have been a great deal of dissension on a number of doctrinal matters. There were disputes about the nature of the soul: Was it in the breath or in the blood? Did man have only a soul or also a spirit? Was the latter the spirit of God? Would God destroy the world visibly at the Second Coming? Lorenzo was said to have maintained that the world had already been destroyed, but it had been done invisibly, and the world had emerged cleansed.

Despite these conflicts, which seemed to weigh heavily on the assembled ministers, three *hermanos*, all participants in the upheaval—Lorenzo, Nicolas, and Isaía—showed a curious gaiety, a "luminous happiness" that distinguished them from the others present at the meeting. I felt that this might have been a late aftereffect of the experience of the upheaval. At about the same time, namely, the first half of July, there were reports that various participants in the upheaval had had dreams that I felt might also be directly related to that experience. Thus it was recounted that Consuelo of the congregation in N. dreamt that she saw a minister in a church and thought it was *Hermano* Nicolas, but she was not sure. He had black clothes on and was holding a black Bible with blank, white pages. Another dream was reported of Peregrino (whose vision in 1970 helped trigger the upheaval). He saw his pastor, *Hermano* Gilberto, in a deep well. He tried to get out, but kept slipping back. Then smoke came up from the well.

The church service in Utzpak of June 29, 1971 was rather well attended, but there was no separate children's service any more. Moreover, as Eusebia pointed out,

> There is something wrong with the *hermanos*. They stay for the songs, but during the prayers and especially during the sermons, they leave, they go to the well, or out into the street. I think they are holding their own services there. [She laughs] They continually go back and forth like that. Ermela does it, and Emilio, and Nacho, they all do it.

In the same service, Lorenzo mentioned in his sermon that at the meeting in Mérida there had been a lot of problems. "Many churches hate each other," he said, "but once more, peace has been confirmed." He also announced that he would leave Utzpak and establish a second church in N., while Don Venancio would come to work with *Hermano* Pito in Utzpak. The latter then asked for an offering for Lorenzo's trip to N., but very few came forward to contribute. Perhaps he had finally exhausted their patience.

On July 6, Anselmo took part in the church service. He was tanned, hoarse, sweaty, with nothing of the pudginess of last year nor even of the suave attire. He gave a testimony, saying that he was going to take his family to Isla Arena, Tabasco, where he would work in the sugarcane plantations. Nothing has been heard of him since.

In the sermons of that summer, no mention was made of the gifts of the Holy Spirit, and in reciting Bible quotations everyone carefully stayed away from texts referring to glossolalia. The recovery of the trance behavior did not repeat itself during the brief time that Don Venancio spent with the congregation, and subsequently the congregation was again left to *Hermano* Pito. Attendance continued at about 30 adults for the rest of the summer, but Nina noted some changes in the general behavior of the congregation. In addition to the comings and goings of the *hermanos* during the services that Eusebia had also observed, fewer and fewer members were taking part in the presentation of hymns in front of the altars of the various societies. For instance, on August 1, seven members of the *Señores Cristianos* and seven *Dorcas* presented hymns, as against twelve members of each organization who sat out the presentation. On August 3, eight *Dorcas* sang, six did not; on August 7, eleven sang, twelve did not; and the following Tuesday the ratio was two to six. There was talking in church, and even *Hermano* Pito, who was supposed to be in charge, kept wandering in and out during the services.

In early September 1971, Pito received a letter from Lorenzo, and Nina recorded the following summary of its contents:

The *hermanos* of the congregation in the town of C. had collected money to support evangelizing. Each of them also, over a period of time, had contributed 5 pesos[2] every week toward this purpose. But when *Hermano* Gilberto saw all that money accumulating, which by then amounted to about 12,000 pesos, he asked the treasurer of the congregation to lend it to him for the construction of a masonry temple. Instead of a temple, however, they constructed a *casa pastoral*.[3] Soon all the money was spent. The *casa pastoral* was not completed, there was no masonry temple either, and in disgust, 30 *hermanos* left, and Gilberto had only 8 *hermanos* in his congregation.

It happened that Lorenzo came to C. just as this time with Don Venancio. He made contact with the dissatisfied *hermanos* and with Don Venancio held a service for them in a private house, although Gilberto had warned them not to go, since they were divisionists. When Gilberto realized that he was losing his congregation, he humbled himself before those 30 *hermanos,* he begged their forgiveness, he even cried, saying that Don Venancio was right in what he was teaching and that all should learn the spiritual matters of the Lord. This reconciled the *hermanos.*

On September 21, 1971, there was another pastors' meeting, this time at Villahermosa, and a new minister, a man from Tabasco, was assigned to the Utzpak congregation. He was able to keep the membership stable, but he had problems with discipline in the congregation. The *hermanos* did not care to testify any more, not offering as much as a text "*en la honra y gloria de Dios.*" Not even the visit of Isaía, now a minister, acted as a stimulant. Nina's record for November 13 reads as follows:

Marta kneels down to pray, but she does not pray, she chats with the other girls; then she gets up and goes out into the street. Before the end of the altar call, she comes back in, kneels down once more and says, "Let us pray, *hermanos!*" She closes her eyes to pray, but opens them again, and this is how the altar call ended, and she finished and had not prayed.

By the middle of December a new factor entered the scene: Lorenzo began preaching a new doctrine and with the support of Don Venancio began looking for converts. In part, their doctrine was based on economics. They maintained that tithing had no foundation in the New Testament. No one should demand tithing of the *hermanos,* and the congregations should not be required to send their tithe to the district offices of the church and a share of their offerings to the central offices of the Apostolic Church in Mexico City.

In addition, it was apparently at about this time that in the town of Campeche Lorenzo came in contact with a representative of a group originating in the United States and claiming to preach the doctrines of a "famous evangelist" called William M. Branham.[4] Two factors helped to invest the contact with an aura of importance. One lay in the person of this representative, E. T., who came from Mexico City and was considered "dangerous, a fighter"— a Yucatecan stereotype for men coming from the heartland of Mexico. The other was the report that this E. T. immediately gave Lorenzo a tape recorder and two tapes with William M. Branham's sermons translated into Spanish. Such equipment carried considerable prestige.

On December 23, 1971, Lorenzo and Don Venancio came to Utzpak to speak about their new convictions. There was a heated discussion with the leading men in the *casa pastoral,* where *Hermano* Nicolas was also present. Nina reports about the service on December 25, when the dispute was brought out into the open:

> *Hermano* Lorenzo was also present at this service, but no one mentioned his name. *Hermano* Nicolas said that both Lorenzo and Don Venancio would be expelled from the Apostolic Church because they were preaching an erroneous doctrine. So tonight Lorenzo sang a hymn that was very appropriate to the occasion. It said that "for me, life is in Christ, although I have to suffer. Even if the world wants to hurt me, I can endure it all in Christ who gives me eternal life when I die." There was no end to the *"Gloria a Dios"* from the congregation. *Hermano* Nicolas was very sad, and it was then that when he and Blanca [his wife] sang, the congregation seemed to abhor their voices.

According to members of the Utzpak congregation who heard them on tape, the Brahman sermons proclaim that he who listens to them will learn to walk in the wisdom of the Lord. He who says "Jehovah" is really saying "Satan." Christian churches are bad, the church organizations are bad, and the baptisms given by other churches are invalid and must be renewed by using the formula "I baptize you in the name of the Lord Jesus." In the services, it is reported, the Branham converts use the Apostolic hymnal, and they do not speak in tongues. They no longer use the Apostolic greeting *"Paz de Cristo."*

To clarify matters, a pastors' convention was called for February 15–18, 1972, in Villahermosa. Lorenzo and Don Venancio were invited. Various pastors got up and talked, but when they called on Lorenzo, he had left, and so had Don Venancio. So no church was assigned to them. Lorenzo is said to have remarked, "If you give us no church, we'll go someplace else, even under a tree, but we must preach." Any further activity on their part, the convention decided, would not be considered to be on behalf of the Apostolic Church.

In April of 1972, in the town of T., Lorenzo and Don Venancio held a baptism. The two men baptized each other, then Don Venancio ordained himself bishop and Lorenzo became pastor. Floriano, one of Lorenzo's faithfuls in the Utzpak church, together with Justo, a nephew of Don Venancio's, were declared initiates. They named their church the Invisible Apostolic Church and proceeded to search for converts among the Apostolic congregations with which they were familiar and which had participated in the upheaval, while E. T. went evangelizing to communities where the group did not possess such a bridgehead.

By May 1972, however, Don Venancio had second thoughts about the biblical foundation of what the Branham tapes preached. Sometime in the middle of the month he had a revelation. He described the experience to me in an interview in June 1973:

> I had had some lengthy discussions about matters of faith with the pastor of the church in N. and was in a great deal of doubt. After praying day and night for three weeks and being in mental torment, I could not sleep, and thinking about all these matters, at about one or two in the morning, I saw all of a sudden an enormous abyss opening up under my feet. I trembled for fear, but the Divinity came and began pulling me up. "What are you doing in that abyss?" he asked. Then he spoke to me of many things, and I began to understand how every part of the Scripture was there to give support to the mind so that it might understand what was the nature of the creation and the creator.
>
> Since then, for me, the Bible has become as if transparent. No matter what I read in it, it always has this marvellous clarity about it.

Using this new-found clarity, Don Venancio began expressing some ideas about various theological issues that were at variance with the accepted doctrines of the Apostolic Church. A theologian was sent to Yucatán from the Bible Institute in Tepic, Nayarit to debate these issues with him, but they could come to no agreement and he was expelled from the Church. As he put it, "I did not desert te Apostolics: they separated themselves from me." Simultaneoulsy, he also dissolved his relationship with Lorenzo and the Branhamists.

During the following months and extending into 1973, there was a three-way split in the Apostolic Church on the Peninsula of Yucatán: there were the followers of Lorenzo, the adherents of Don Venancio, and the group that stayed within the established congregations, which I refer to below as the conservatives. Perhaps we should also mention a fourth group—those who divorced themselves entirely. They either ended up with the Pentecostals or went "to the plaza," that is, became completely disinterested in religious affiliation. The latter comprised the larger section of this group.

Considering each one of the groups in a more detailed manner as of the summer of 1973, we note that Lorenzo originally established his headquarters in C. His congregation there consisted of the Branhamist evangelist E. T. with his wife, a family from T. (formerly Apostolics from Isaía's congregation), and Floriano with his wife Francisca and their children. These people salvaged a semblance of the communal life attempted during the upheaval. They live on the same lot in adjoining rented houses, and have put up a sign, saying, "Entrance forbidden, because Christians live here. No man dressed as a woman, and no woman dressed as a man is admitted."

The women wear dresses well below the knee and no mantilla, for according to Branham, that is only for whores. Women are to wear a wedding ring, not customary among the lower class or the peasantry. The reason for this is that ". . . othewise a man might fall in love with a women he meets in church, not knowing that she is married." This obviously Euro-American intrusion is occasion for some amused comment among the conservatives: "Maybe by following this Branham, a man acquires some magic, so that when he shakes hands with a woman, she falls in love with him. That's why she needs the ring. It is for protection."

Conservatives are also skeptical toward other claims of the sect. Branham is said to have performed many healings and miracles. Therefore, the Branhamists claim that praying in his name will, for instance, change the weather. They relate that once a storm came up in C., they prayed, and no rain came.

The Branhamist congregation in C., for which I have data, holds services every night. They use the hymnal of the Apostolic Church. During prayer. there is continual reference to "*nuestro precioso Hermano* William, *nuestro preciosisimo Hermano* William,"—"our precious Brother William, our most precious Brother William." No one speaks in tongues. Preaching is done by everyone, and the sermons are based not on the Bible, but on Branhamist tracts. Branham is considered the Lord's Prophet, the last of a line of prophets including Jesus. His most often cited prophesy concerns the end of the world: These are the last days. Once the final two of a series of seven catastrophies (an earthquake that will destroy San Francisco and World War III) have taken place, the millenium will ensue.

Early in 1973 Lorenzo, still chasing his dream about establishing a congregation in Campeche, moved his family there. As before, when he was still evangelizing for the Apostolics, he remains unsuccessful in this town, but continues gaining converts in the villages.

Don Venancio directs little effort toward proselytizing in the towns and also concentrates on the peasants. He is rigidly fundamentalist. His adherents, who consider themselves Apostolics, emphasize this when they set themselves apart from the Branhamists. They do, however, insist that those joining Don Venancio be rebaptized, which is costing them converts among Apostolics otherwise sympathetic to them. Don Venancio's attraction seems to be chiefly his insistence on the imminent end of the world, deemphasized by the Apostolic Church, although he keeps pointing out that God's time is not man's time, and thus refuses to stipulate an exact date for this hoped-for event.

He travels from village to village, picking up converts not only among the Apostolics, but also among disgruntled Catholics. He preaches in the homes, writing out lengthy Bible quotations in longhand on white cardboard, which are then placed as decorations on the walls. His congregations do not use glossolalia. He himself used to speak in tongues, but he no longer does. "Since I don't understand what I am saying in tongues, I am afraid I might utter a blasphemy," he explained. "So when I feel the urge coming, I suppress it."

Perhaps Don Venancio commands the loyalty of his followers in the villages because even though he is of impressive intellectual stature and has a perfect command of Spanish, he is also "home-grown," intensely Mayan and peasant. He possesses a large plot of land in a village not too far from C. His three sons and four daughters all live on this land in various homesteads with their spouses and children. This family arrangement of patrilocality is often discussed in Yucatán, where aboriginally matrilocal residence patterns were the rule. The latter still occur quite frequently, in addition to the more recent neolocal pattern. As Eusebia says, "They even cook in one kitchen, eat from one pot, and they have not quarreled in years." His entire extended family joined his church, and the feelings of loyalty are so strong that one of his sons wanted to go to C. and kill Gilberto over the religious conflict the latter was having with his father.

The conservative part of the congregation has been stagnating since the end of the upheaval, with its membership hovering at approximately fifteen adults ever since. Few of these come to the weekday services in the temple. Those held in private homes and the Sunday services are somewhat more popular. The record player and the public address system were stored away in a box because they were supposedly broken. No rattles were used to accompany the singing in the services I attended in the summer of 1972 and again in 1973, and no one clapped for the *coritos*. Glossolalia had entirely disappeared. This puzzles visitors who come from other congregations to preach in Utzpak and who do not know anything about the upheaval or at most have heard reference to the time "when some *hermanos* thought they had some special wisdom." Their exhortations to the congregation that they should let the Holy Spirit use them, that "even the young daughter of *Hermano* X was able to speak in tongues" so why not they, fall on deaf ears. The confusion of the outsiders is compounded because on occasion some of the *hermanos* of Utzpak *will* speak in tongues—when they are not in the home temple. Thus Nohoč Felipe reported about a very emotional occasion in Tibolón where he and Valentin were present. At this time eight women were baptized. Unexpectedly, both men spoke in tongues, and indicative of the high arousal. Nohoč Felipe had a vision involving his wife Eusebia, who was not present. He saw hail falling on her, larger than hens' eggs.

During the worship services, the *hermanos* persisted in their behavior of walking in and out of the temple. The prayer for the sick deteriorated into a brief formula, as the following entry for July 11, 1972 shows:

> At the end of the service, during the last prayer spoken by all the congregation, the *hermano* in charge of that part of the proceedings lets his voice rise above the others: "If anybody is sick, please, Lord, heal them." That was all.

Felipe, a mediocre preacher who had been the pastor of the congregation from 1965 to 1969 (with several interruptions), was pastor in 1972, but since the congregation was so small, he commuted to T. to work there as a salesman to supplement his pastoral income and came to Utzpak only on weekends. The minister who took his place in 1973, equally uninspiring, followed the same pattern. Since the end of the upheaval, no one has felt the urge to go out and evangelize.

The dispirited mood of the conservative section is perhaps best characterized by the following conversation I had with Felipe in 1972. I asked, "Why is there no more teaching about the Second Coming?"

"The hermanos are bored with that topic."

"Why don't you talk about the baptism of the Holy Spirit?"

"There are many other topics in the Bible."

"Why is there no longer a society for the young people?"

"They all got married."

"What happened to the prayer for the Holy Spirit on Sunday mornings?"

"The custom just got lost."

Actually, the subject of the Second Coming is still of considerable interest, although it seems to have lost its urgency. "It will happen because the Bible says so," maintains Ermela. Another *hermana* says, "Ever since I've been hearing the Gospel, the *hermanos* kept saying that Christ will come soon. But he did not come." Nohoč Felipe joins in, dreamily, "The stars will fall, the sun and the moon will lose their light." Eusebia comments, "When he comes, I wonder if I'll see him. He may go looking for the souls in the temple, but I may be at home, working, or sleeping." Then she adds, "Felipe says that he knows of a man who predicted that it will happen in 1980. It wasn't an *hermano* from here." To this Nohoč Felipe answers, "How could he have gotten that into his head? Not even the angels know when it is going to happen."

As the congregation stood in 1973, there was little to distinguish it from other small Protestant congregations of a traditional bent, except for the memories of the time "when *those things* happened in the temple."

Interestingly enough, the separations discussed above did not follow the kinship network, as did the propagation of the Apostolic movement on the Yucatán Peninsula originally. In addition, there were apparently no discernable psychological mechanisms involved. Kildahl (1972) found a dependency relationship between the subject and the person guiding him into glossolalia. There is, however, no indication in the present case that all or even the majority of the members of the congregation that were taught to speak in tongues by Lorenzo followed him into his Invisible Apostolic Church. If the above dependency did initially exist, it certainly was dissipated soon after the dissolution of the platform phase of the upheaval. That those participants in the upheaval who could not cope with the fact that the end of the world did not arrive at the appointed time would seek out new prophets who would reassure them on this count does account for some of the development in Utzpak, but not for what happened in the rest of the area, with some congregations going with one prophet, others with the next one.

Instead, certain geographic demarcations seem to emerge. For example, in Utzpak everyone north of the homestead of Eusebia and Nohoč Felipe went to Lorenzo, most important the affluent Martin and his wife. Those south of this line stayed with the temple. Later on, the line was somewhat blurred because a number of people balked at being rebaptized, which both Don Venancio and Lorenzo demanded of their converts. Most of these chose instead to return to the temple. In July 1972, there were at least three villages where the entire congregation went with Lorenzo, while there were others where he could not acquire a single convert. This picture has not changed materially since then. In addition, he also gained the congregation in T. where Isaía became pastor during the upheaval. When Lorenzo became a threat to the Apostolics there, Isaía was sent to a remote congregation, out of his reach, and a pastor loyal to the Church was put in his place. But nearly the entire congregation fell to Lorenzo anyway.

Gilberto, as mentioned before, had a great deal of trouble with his congregation in C., although not on religious but on financial grounds. Although courted by both Lorenzo and Don Venancio, not one of the members of this congregation joined up with either of these men, although Gilberto's wife is the niece of Don Venancio. Finally, the city congregation of N., quite literally a creation of the brothers Gilberto and Nicolas, became small temporarily, but did not side with Lorenzo. The problems in this case arose from a quarrel with Nicolas. He fell in love with a girl who was pregnant by a man she did not want to marry. After her child was born, she and Nicolas were married in the Apostolic church in N., and the *hermanos* were upset that even the papers of the city reported that the Apostolic minister married a woman who wore a white dress and a veil, and carried her baby daughter in her arms. By 1973, however, the congregation had recovered its former size.

The case of Don Venancio too is instructive in this respect. Four members of this very close-knit extended family did not live in the village where his homestead was located, but in C. These four did not join his church.

Also the people who stayed within the Apostolic Church tended to emphasize *locality*. As Valentin quite eloquently put it, "How would I desert my temple? This is where I first came to know the word of God. Here I received the Holy Spirit. I will never leave my temple." In the fall of 1972, the considerably weakened congregation of Utzpak formed a society for the purpose of having the temple written over to them. (It was previously registered in the name of Nicolas.)

The two new sects, as should be obvious from the above discussion, are connected with the congregation, as it were, by an umbilical cord, while the fourth group cut itself off completely. Of the latter, two families joined the Pentecostals. They have a small congregation in the village without a pastor of their own. These were the families of Don E., whom Lorenzo had "read out" of the congregation in the early phase of the upheaval, and that of Tacho, expelled during its height. The experience had apparently been too painful to forget.

Significantly, the young women who were the most important participants in the upheaval, all drifted away "into the world," excepting only Cilia, who of course remained with her husband Lorenzo. Violeta married Nacho in the Apostolic church in Utzpak, and they went on to Mérida to work. Failing in this enterprise, they came back to the village. In 1973 Violeta bore a son but did not present him at the temple, as is customary in the congregation.

Marta did not succeed in making Mérida her permanent home either. Her mother allowed her to return home about eight months after the upheaval, although she did not bring with her a doctor's certificate that she was still a virgin. In 1973, she was working at one of the *tortillerías* in Utzpak.

As to Pilar, she eloped with a young man from Tabasco, working in Utzpak. Such a "traditional" marriage arrangement is considered a mortal sin by the Apostolics. For a year, she did not even write to her mother, who was still a member of the original congregation. In the summer of 1973, she came back to Utzpak with her husband and a 5-month-old daughter. She did not bother to get legally married, and she did not present her child at the temple. None of these young women attends church.

The postupheaval phase, then, was characterized initally by some late and insignificant recovery of the trance behavior. Even that disappeared by the summer of 1971. Satan assumed the aspect of a dangerous neighbor, no more, and the Second Coming was still much on people's minds. There was further deterioration of innovations, shifting the congregation away from Pentecostalism toward the comportment of a more conservative Protestant sect.

In the fall of the year, the trance behavior disappeared entirely. In the further evolution, the ritual was greatly simplified, and Satan appeared as part of the aboriginal world of the jungle. There was no trace left of the innovations that initially marked the congregation as an Apostolic one.

In the flux of change, rents then occurred in the fabric of the congregation, involving also other groups that had participated in the upheaval. These had repercussions on the organizational level of the Apostolic Church of the southeastern section. By December 1971, there was a full-blown fragmentation into three different groups, with some members entirely lost to religious innovation and finding their way into "the world." Subsequently the evolution continued along the same lines during 1972 and 1973.

We are now ready to attempt to produce an overview of the entire evolution and to test the data against modular constructs.

NOTES

1. There was no formalized wearing of the white dresses in the church, although some women do still wear those sewed during the upheaval. The men did not regularly wear the dark trousers and white shirt with tie of the city any more, as was done in August 1970.

2. Equivalent to $0.40 in U.S. currency.

3. Eusebia's comment at this point was, "He saw all the fancy houses of other pastors and wanted one like that himself."

4. William Branham was a prominent "deliverance evangelist," born in 1909 near Berksville, Kentucky. "The cornerstone of 'deliverance evangelism'. . . is the belief that just as God wants everyone to be saved from sin, so also does He desire everyone to be well" (Nichol, 1966: 221–222). Actually, Branham himself never claimed to have the power of healing. Rather, he maintained that he had received two gifts: he could feel it in his left hand what illness a person had and he could discern the thoughts and deeds in the past life of an individual (Lindsay, 1950: 79). When confronted with a sick person, he said he could see if God had already healed him, and he would then proclaim this fact. "She (a small Finnish girl on crutches) looked at me with her baby blue eyes, tears rolling down her cheeks. I saw a vision . . . and I knew the child was healed. I said, 'Honey, you're healed'" (Lindsay n.d.: 43–44). In the evening, Branham allegedly saw the child again, asked that her crutches be removed, and she ran up and down the steps and across the platform.

   In the late 1940s he preached to large "Full Gospel" meetings. He was invited to speak in the Scandinavian countries and in South Africa. A fellow minister, Gordon Linsay, published his biography and also a collection of sermons. Soon after the South African trip, the two men separated. At issue may have been attempts by Branham to form his own church, which Lindsay may have opposed. "The Lord knew that he [Branham] would never attempt to start another organization of his own," Lindsay (1950: 13) says in the biography of the evangelist. Yet in a personal communication to this author, Lindsay speaks of people who tried to put words into the preacher's mouth, and the same statement also appears in essence in the above mentioned book (1950: 11). Sermons by Branham are not included in the tapes issued by the *Christ for the Nations, Inc.* organization, of which Lindsay is president. The Spanish-language tracts and tapes of Branham's sermons mentioned by the informants are distributed by Spoken Word Publications, Jeffersonville, Indiana. William Branham died on December 24, 1965.

8

Analysis

The upheaval described in the preceding chapters can be classed as a millenary movement. Such movements are very frequent occurrences. Thrupp (1970: 11) speaks of them as "religious movements that have been animated by the idea of a perfect age or perfect land." In order to achieve this hoped-for perfection, a new way of life is sought. As Burridge (1969: 165) puts it,

> The phraseology of millenial aspirations always envisages a new set of rules, new kinds of obligations, a new earth in which heaven is more brightly mirrored. Yet heaven and earth are distinct and opposed. And from this basic opposition between no rules and new rules, it would seem, there arises the transition process exemplified in various kinds of millenarian activity.

Linton, in the earliest discussion of "nativistic movements," under which he subsumes messianic, millenary cults, pinpoints the feature of change, arising in his view from culture-contact situations, as a "conscious organized attempt" (1943: 499) at such change. Mühlmann (1968) and Wallace (1966) take up this feature of *conscious* change. This interpretation, however, is criticized by La Barre (1971: 8) as leaving all crisis cults reactionary "and makes them conscious contrivances—whereas many crisis cults are clearly past-discarding, reformative, acculturational, and unconscious in mode." [1]

La Barre (1970: 42) calls these societal events "crisis cults":

> I have adopted the simple term "crisis cult" both for its brevity and its inclusiveness, intending only to imply the insight of Malinowski that there is no cult without crisis. That is to say, there must be an unresolved problem or crisis, chronic or acute, and unresolved by ordinary secular means, before there is a cult response. The term "cult" also implies a distinction from ordinary secular actions or social movements . . . [and points up] the typically dereistic and in some cases the minority aspects of the response.

As to the causes of these cults, La Barre (1971) lists various theories advanced in the literature, implicating political, military, economic, messianic, "Great Man," acculturative, and psychological stress factors.

In regard to the latter, we should mention the often cited approach of Aberle (1970), who points out that relative deprivation is a dominant theme running through the cults. This feature has been discussed very extensively in the literature; it is defined as a negative discrepancy between legitimate expectation and actuality. Aberle suggests, on the societal level, a twelve-way typology based on this stress, which in his mind may be the cause of the crisis cults. He identifies possession, status, behavior, and worth as areas of deprivation. As reference points he suggests past versus present circumstances, present versus future circumstances, and one's own versus someone else's present circumstances.

The problem with Aberle's typology is twofold. In the first place, as with deprivation theory generally, it does not account for the fact that, in situations of deprivation, a millennial movement is only one of many possible reactions (Thrupp, 1970: 26). Second, as Lessa and Vogt (1965: 537) point out in commenting on Aberle's paper, no particular movement can be fitted neatly into any one of the cells resulting from Aberle's scheme.

It might be interesting to recall here that the members of a conference held a decade ago on millennial dreams "showed a strong resistance to 'reductionism,' that is, to any assumption that either the ethos of a movement or the turn it gave to the development of myth or of formal reasoning about the character of the perfect age was necessarily a direct reflection of a social or a political situation" (Thrupp, 1970: 25–26).

This is basically also the objection La Barre advances against the single-cause theories concerning crisis cults—namely, that they are of no predictive value since their approach produces, as it were, a "tunnel vision" and prevents the analyst from perceiving the complexity of these societal processes. In addition, they concentrate too largely, in La Barre's view (1970: 283), on the "outer" stressor realities of history, economics, politics, and war. Instead, he proposes that crisis cults also involve sacred superego-assuaging behaviors that "are often regressive and do not evolve at all, but only change; they adapt not to an outer but to an inner world whose cultural tensions change" (1970: 282–283). He further suggests that culture generally, and religion as one of its components, may be thought of as adaptive mechanisms peculiar "to this kind of animal"—namely, man. Since man's history is an unbroken succession of crisis situations, crisis cults, representing adaptive mechanisms in this sense, he maintains, arise continually and in all parts of the world.[2] But La Barre paints a much wider canvas. Showing the many processes at work, he asserts that acculturation is not the cause but rather the arena where crisis cults arise (1970: 20) and

the innovator's ambivalence toward his culture, his tribes's ambivalence toward either native or alien culture or both, the crisis of cultural faith, and

the psychological relationship between innovator and group are all essential. In both prophet and group, mere cognition of cultural difference must
in some way also involve emotional stress.[3] (La Barre, 1970: 278.)

La Barre further advances the notion that crisis cults tend to offer largely
"autistic" solutions to the problems of the group, and their phrasing is condi-
tioned universally by two specific human traits. One of these is "the articulate
consciousness of an intricate subjective life in consequence of a big brain," the
other "a biological experience of extended early security that is inveterately
sought again when later adaptations go awry" (1970: 197). Thus there is in
crisis cults "the child's fear and awe toward the father, symbolized as his
maleness, generalized, and projected into the supernatural unknown" (1970:
366).

As to possible psychological mechanisms operative in these cults, La Barre
(1970: 51) directs attention to certain contemporary interests:

> Psychologists have been pursuing two trends of research that need only to be
> integrated with the others [i.e., the psychiatrist's study of cults and cultists,
> and the anthropologist's descriptions of crisis cults] for a fresh understanding
> of the human propensity for religion to emerge.[4] These two developments are
> the studies of sensory deprivation, and of the psychophysiology of sleep and
> dreams. To this may be added new psychiatric developments in ego
> psychology and the study of patients suffering from "cultural shock."

La Barre's designation of the movements in question as "crisis cults" is by
far the best generic term yet suggested for the type of societal process we are
interested in. All other usages, such as Linton's "nativistic movements" and
Wallace's "revitalization," seem to fit specific variants only. Also his insight
into the common psychological base of the cults is most illuminating. There
are, however, two points that I should like to take issue with, on the basis of
the findings related to the upheaval reported here.

One point is that due to his overriding interest in psychoanalytic concepts
and approaches, La Barre does not feel the need for coming to grips with the
systematic relationships that apparently exist between the social and
geographic environment, the psychological substratum, and the cultural evolution accompanying the cult. In his encyclopedic presentation, the individual
crisis cults too often emerge as chaotic jumbles, which, no doubt, they were to
the *outside* observer, including the recording chronicler and the analyzing his-
torian. What is clearly needed is a historic and geographic distribution study,
as suggested by Bourguignon (1973b). Beyond this, I would suggest, we require a more satisfying conceptualization of the psychological base and its relationship to the attendant cultural evolution than that offered by La Barre.

La Barre, and this is the second point I want to come to, clings—most unfortunately, to my mind—to terminology heavily freighted with implied pathology. Why, I should like to ask, do we have to speak of disorientation, paranoia, neurosis? Especially since he clearly recognizes the psychological processes that are expressed in crisis cults as adaptive mechanisms? He notes the relationship, on the experiential level, of these processes to sleep, especially to rapid eye-movement (REM) sleep. Are we to call that too a neurotic process? He calls attention to the condition of patients suffering from culture shock and to experiences accompanying sensory deprivation. All of these behaviors may be subsumed under the general heading of "altered mental states." For some reason, not accounted for, the term does not appear in his discussion.

I would propose that the pathology model, inherent in the terminology La Barre uses, is not suitable for describing altered mental states. There is absolutely nothing pathological about adaptive mechanisms, as he himself describes them. To my mind, and there is a great deal of research supporting this view, the adpative mechanisms termed altered mental states or altered states of consciousness have a number of features in common. They occur in clinically healthy subjects. The states are strategies of the organism to resolve certain accumulated stresses, to state it in the most general terms. After a suitable length of time, they dissolve, without any need for treatment of whatever kind. This is true of sleep, where the REM sleep has this kind of function. It is true of the trances in which glossolalia takes place: the individual episode is concluded, usually within a certain portion allotted to the behavior in the service, and after a few years the overall comportment also fades (Goodman, 1972a). Psychologically or religiously induced hallucinations have a strictly structured course and dissolve, usually in little more than a month (Goodman, 1973b). The same may be said of hallucinations produced by sensory deprivation (Henney, 1973). The hyperaroused altered mental state giving rise to crisis cults, as the present case shows, equally attenuates in a relatively short time without external intervention. Interposing the concept of pathology only clouds the issue.

In this sense, I contend, the present case makes it possible for us to carry La Barre's argument a step further toward an understanding of crisis cults. Just one step, perhaps, but I think an important one, because it demonstrates that man's adaptive behavior is not sick, but healthy—and beyond that, normative. It is strictly governed by biological laws that allow him to play out his needs in a culturally structured way, but within stringently circumscribed confines written into his neurophysiological makeup. This, in a general way, is also La Barre's position.

One of the most important discussions of crisis cults in the literature is that presented by Wallace (1961, 1970).[5] According to the model he proposes, societies are in a moving equilibrium, a steady state, in which cultural change occurs slowly, with only minor oscillations in organization level. However, in a subsequent phase, termed the period of increased individual stress, the system is progressively unbalanced by various more or less catastrophic external or internal factors, so that the culture of the society is perceived progressively as being disorganized and inadequate.

During the next phase, that of cultural distortion, various dysfunctional expedients, such as alcoholism or breaches of sexual and kinship mores, are adopted by some members of the society, leading to a continuous decline in organization.

Societies might disintegrate at this point if they cannot return to the steady state by way of a change in the next period, termed that of revitalization. If a revitalization does occur, there is first of all the formulation of a code by an individual or a group, producing a utopian image of a "goal culture," while the existing culture is described as evil or inadequate. The two are connected by a transfer culture, which needs to be carried out in order for the goal culture to become reality.

> Not infrequently in primitive societies the code, or the core of it, is formulated by one idividual in the course of a hallucinatory revelation: such prophetic experiences are apt to launch religiously oriented movements, since the source of the revelation is apt to be regarded as a supernatural being. (Wallace, 1970: 192.)

This phase is followed by an effort at communicating the code and then by the organization of the converts so gained during the period of organization.

Basing his discussion in part on Gerlach and Hine (1968), Wallace then continues (1970: 194), and this is of special interest in this context, as follows:

> In such programs as Pentecostalism, Black Power, and the New Left, there is typically a considerable number of local or special issue groups loosely joined. . . .Each segment may be, in effect, a separate revitalization organization of the simple kind described above.

Subsequently there is an adaptation of the code to various exigencies of the new situation and the increased membership; a cultural transformation when the transfer culture and, in some cases, the goal culture can be put into operation; and finally the routinization, when the movement's function shifts from innovation to that of maintenance. With this process, a new steady state has been achieved.

The revitalization of the society is based, according to Wallace, on a new code. This code has its fountainhead "not infrequently" in a hallucinatory revelation of a leader or a prophet; there is, however, also the possibility of a nonhallucinatory code formulation.

> In either case, the formulation of the code constitutes a reformulation of the author's own mazeway and often brings him renewed confidence in the future and a remission of the complaints he experienced before. It may be suggested that such mazeway resynthesis processes are merely extreme forms of the reorganizing dream processes that seem to be associated with REM (rapid-eye-movement) sleep, which are necessary to normal health. (Wallace, 1970: 192–193.)

We should note how carefully in this statement Wallace stays clear of any implications of pathology. The insights gained from the present study support and amplify this position. In testing his model against the development in Yucatán, however, and against the details of the Utzpak upheaval, we find only a greatly restricted fit.

1. *The steady state.* The relatively slow and chainlike culture change that Wallace visualizes for the steady state has probably not been seen in Yucatán for at least a millennium. The classical Maya collapse in the late ninth century may have been followed by a revitalization movement, but if so, there seems to be no archeological record that has been so interpreted. Since the Spanish conquest, the Mayan peasantry has had a series of crises with hardly any steady state and has periodically reacted with bloody revolts. The last and longest of these (1847–1901) did "in its darkest days" (Reed, 1964: 134) bring forth a revitalization movement as a result of the massive defeat of the Maya at the hand of the Ladinos. The record concerning the "Talking Cross" movement as we read it shows a good agreement with the Wallace model, but then, we only have the sketchiest of data (Villa Rojas, 1937, 1945). For those Maya who did not withdraw into the present Territory of Quintana Roo, the period of stress continued. It did not really let up until the Maya participated in yet another peasant war, the Mexican Revolution. It is a matter of debate whether the period between the Revolution and the present can be classed as a steady state. At least since the 1940s, with increased contact with Western goods and life ways, there is good evidence that the Mayan population has been subject to increased stress. Thus the Mayan peasantry might be viewed at this point as participating in state 2 of the Wallace model.

2. *The period of increased individual stress.* Since the 1940s, in the above sense, there have been new life ways perceived in Yucatán, new roles had to be confronted and learned, new expectations were aroused.

3. *The period of cultural distortion.* The distinction between this state 3 of the Wallace model and the previous one seems somewhat contrived for

Yucatán. "Socially dysfunctional expedients" (Wallace, 1970: 191) such as alcoholism, can be assumed to have been part of what Redfield (1940) terms social disorganization, which he saw especially in the urban sphere. "Veniality in public officials," "breaches of sexual and kinship mores," and similar behavior characterized Mérida in the nineteenth century. These were some of the traits that Redfield's informant, cited earlier, feared would come to Chan Kom along with the new paved highway.

4. *The period of revitalization*

(*a*) Formulation of a code. The code for the Yucatecan Pentecostal (Apostolic) movement, as already mentioned, was not formulated in Yucatán. It was taken over from the Mexican Apostolic Church. There in turn it was derived from the movement in the United States, where it goes back to various millennial movements that arose at about the turn of the century.

(*b*) Communication (of the code) is not applicable to the Yucatecan Apostolics, since they were not in touch with the originators. Rather, they may be thought of as a group of converts.

(*c*) Organization. As converts, they do participate in this phase; however, this state is not conceived of as being a finite one: conversion must go on all the time, and the supply of unconverted is thought of as infinite. In other words, this revitalization movement addresses itself to the whole world rather than to a limited community or society.

(*d*) Adaptation. In this state, changes are supposedly affected in the code. Because of the strict fundamentalist nature of the Pentecostal sects, however, a "hardening of the code" (Wallace, 1970: 195) is built into their belief system, and no adaptation of it takes place, only possibly an elaboration of the ritual.

(*e*) Cultural transformation. The adherents of the movement profess to a change in their life ways. The view of "before a sinner, afterward a changed person, full of the grace of the Lord" is a part of the code and as such has become strongly formulaic.

(*f*) Routinization. Since the number of unconverted people is conceived of as infinite, "the functional reasons for the movement's existence as an innovative force" (Wallace, 1970: 195) cannot disappear by definition. Neither, of course, can the goal culture be achieved, since it is the Kingdom of God, signaled by the Second Coming of Christ. What can, theoretically, be reached is the transfer culture, which according to Wallace (1970: 192) is "a system of operations that, if faithfully carried out, will transform the existing culture into the goal culture." This transfer culture may be thought of as spreading eventually to the entire society. (Wallace foresees this possibility for certain transfer cultures.) The transfer culture is, to the Apostolics, the life of the congregation, both in its ritual and its secular aspects.

5. *The new steady state.* This stage has not been attained in Yucatán. Its theoretical possibility cannot, however, be ruled out.

Yet, despite its overall applicability to the Pentecostal movement, Wallace's model does not seem to account for the upheaval. He does refer to local movements, but considers them simply replications of the large-scale process, using the framework suggested by Gerlach and Hine (1968). Wallace states (1970: 194):

> Each segment may be, in effect, a separate revitalization organization of the simple kind described [in the model]; the individual groups differ in the details of code, in emotional style, in appeal to different social classes.

The complexity of the upheaval at Utzpak does not admit this generalization. This millennial movement did not emerge in the crisis situation. Rather, it was accepted in diffusion. The manner in which the Pentecostals focus on only a very limited segment of the Bible is not original to Yucatán, but was imported from Mexico proper, whither it came from the United States. We thus see a situation in which a cult whose ideas had been available in Latin America since the beginning of the century gained rapid, wide acceptance with the emergence of a particular crisis.

In the Utzpak upheaval, there is an additional compounding of levels. There is the general crisis situation. Then occurs an embracing of the diffusing elements of a crisis cult, specifically a number of new culture traits, the expectation of the Second Coming, and the trance behavior. Subsequently a sudden third, superimposed evolution emerges. The congregation, utilizing the elements provided by the overall Pentecostal movement, engages in a more or less locally restricted upheaval, in response to specific, locally defined stresses. In several important aspects, this cult is qualitatively different from the overall movement of which it is a part. Thus Wallace's model applies in part to the large-scale process, in part to the local segment. It refers, on the one hand, to the initiation of cults and, on the other hand, to diachronic processes. The distinction between the various levels is nowhere clarified in a satisfactory manner.

Because of the limited applicability of the model to the Utzpak upheaval, the question thus arises whether this upheaval might not represent a different class of societal processes than the one Wallace examined. What precludes this objection is the striking agreement between the Utzpak upheaval and the details of the Vailala Madness, which Wallace treats in some detail (1966), as well as of many other cults mentioned by both Wallace and La Barre. In the light of this fact it seems worthwhile to attempt to formulate a more adequate model.

To this end, we need to discuss first of all the traits of the Pentecostal movement that diffused in Yucatán by the way of Apostolic missionizing.

These traits fall roughly into three categories:

1. *The moral code.* The moral code of the Pentecostals may be summarized as demanding a refutation of all "worldly" pleasures and a life style based on what are thought to be biblical ideals.

2. *The supernatural premise.* This is principally the belief in the presence of the Holy Spirit, manifested by the speaking in tongues, and in the Second Coming of Christ "in our lifetime."

3. *The trance behavior.* This is subsumed under the heading of "speaking in tongues." A case could be made, I think, for the supposition that, of the three trait complexes, the trance behavior may have been the most significant for the propagation of the Pentecostal movement. This contention might be based on a number of considerations, which I propose to discuss in some detail.

Since at least the end of the last century (as pointed out by Lalive d'Epinay, 1968, for Chile and by Willems, 1967, for Brazil) several Protestant denominations have made considerable efforts at proselytizing in the Latin-American area. However, in Mexico, as elsewhere, their activities produced minimal results until the period shortly before and after World War II. At this time the combined stresses of industrialization, urban growth, and other economic and psychological factors coincided with the sudden and phenomenal growth of only one of these denominations. This was the Pentecostal movement with its various branches. It might be argued, then, that the Pentecostal movement must contain traits that make it especially attractive to people under severe stress. Both Lalive d'Epinay (1968) and Willems (1967) see the principal attraction of Pentecostalism basically in the enhanced status it offers to the disadvantaged, as well as in its strong group cohesion. My informants, however, are unanimous in their claim that for them the "baptism of the Holy Spirit," that is, the trance behavior, was the deciding factor. Thus, although the social elements stressed by the authors cited are doubtless important, I feel that the availability of the trance behavior needs to be accorded more attention than it has hitherto received.

Trance behavior looms large in the descriptive data of most of the revitalization movements known from the historical and the ethnographic record. Both La Barre and Wallace recognize the presence in their data of psychophysiological factors. To account for them, however, La Barre looks in the direction of culture shock, which he considers a subvariety of social deprivation, and this he classes as an instance of sensory deprivation. In his view, culture shock and social and sensory deprivation "in turn relate to the universal human phenomena of the vision, the hallucination, and the dream" (1970: 55). In the discussion that follows this statement, La Barre equates dream and vision: "Historically, revelation in the crisis cult is often the literal dream-vision of the charismatic founder of the cult." He then devotes, as already mentioned, considerable attention to REM sleep, in which dreaming occurs.

Now, there exists undoubtedly a striking connection between dreams and visions. Bourguignon (1972) discusses this problem in some detail and points out that whether the ethnographic informant reports having had a dream or a vision will to a large extent depend on his cultural dogma. The numerous published reports on crisis cults, however, including the present case, do not speak only of visions. They present voluminous material on glossolalia, "uncontrollable" kinetic behavior, weeping, catatonic states. None of these is sleep-based; but rather, they represent various manifestations of other altered states of consciousness, of trance (Ludwig, 1968).

For his part, Wallace (1970) sees two psychological mechanisms in revitalization movements: (1) mazeway resynthesis and (2) hysterical conversion. The former, he maintains, is exemplified in the career of the prophet, who formulates the code during a "hallucinatory trance." The latter is typical of the mass follower who is repeatedly subjected to suggestion by a charismatic leader and an excited crowd.

> The convert of this type may, during conversion display various dissociative behaviors (rage, speaking in tongues, rolling on the ground, weeping, and so on). But persons can be maintained in this state of hysterical conversion for months or years, if the "trance" is continuously maintained by the symbolic environment . . . and continuous suggestion.[6] (Wallace, 1970: 197.)

The hallucinatory trance, Wallace feels, produces a permanent change (mazeway resynthesis) in the personality structure, while in the case of hysterical conversion, the convert is liable to relapse into his earlier social personality.

Thus Wallace stipulates two qualitatively different trance experiences, having qualitatively different effects. The data presented here admit of no such distinction. Hallucination, rage, speaking in tongues, weeping, the behaviors enumerated by Wallace, appear as parts of a single trance-based behavioral complex, as mentioned also above.

Turning now to the local level, the Utzpak congregation at the time of Lorenzo's arrival represented a true segment of the Pentecostal movement, the Apostolic Church of Yucatán. As such, it mirrored on the local level the culture changes already realized in that movement: the new moral code and life style, a supernatural premise, and, principally, the availability of the trance state.

In June 1969, Lorenzo initiated a period of rapid change, although still almost entirely within the pattern configuration of the Apostolic Church: the congregation experienced a sudden expansion of membership, a proliferation of internal structural elements (organizational), an elaboration of ritual (formalization of the prayer for the Holy Spirit). The method Lorenzo employed for inducing the trance behavior and the glossolalia in the supplicants was at this point the first specifically Utzpak innovation. It resulted in the acquisition of this behavior by nearly the entire group within a relatively short time.

Then, beginning in the late fall of 1969, certain disquieting elements began to intrude into the life of the congregation, generating considerable anxiety. These were the following:

1. The behavior of four leading men in the congregation: (a) Lorenzo, the minister; (b) Anselmo; (c) Emilio; (d) Peregrino (to some extent marginally because he was not physically present).

2. The behavior of seven young women in the congregation, four unmarried teenagers, and three young married women in their early twenties.

It was at this time, according to my informants, that Lorenzo began withdrawing from the congregation, expressing this withdrawal, this rejection of the group, spatially and behaviorally, as described in Chapter 6. Added on to Lorenzo's withdrawal, the congregation heard of Emilio's claim to have received the gift of healing by prayer. His newly evolved, highly visible motion pattern wrought a modification in the routinized prayer for the sick. Within the flow of events, the next factor was then Anselmo's visionary experiences with their powerful anxiety-producing elements; concurrently, the delayed-return trance behavior of the young women began eroding the ritual structure of service, rubbing out the demarcation lines between the parts of the service in which trance behavior was accepted and proper, and those in which it was not.

That this was the evolution of the process leading to the upheaval is a matter of record. Why it should have happened is at this point a conjecture based on some insights gained from the study of the trance behavior of the various groups I have had the opportunity to observe. On the basis of these observations, I want to make the following assumptions:

Lorenzo, Emilio, Anselmo, and Peregrino, the men whose behavior is of interest to us, have two important traits in common: (1) they acquired the trance behavior within the same period of less than a year;[7] (2) their conversion stories, in contrast to those supplied by other members of the congregation, contain the feature of elevated anxiety. It will be recalled here that, on the basis of the conversion story supplied by Salvador (see p. 266), I identified several phases that emerge when the trance behavior with glossolalia is acquired in the presence of heightened anxiety: (1) as the behavior attenuates, the anxiety reemerges; (2) strategies are tried to reestablish the glossolalia behavior; and (3) under special circumstances, the behavior can be recovered. I am assuming then that the behavior of the four men followed these stages and was due to their reaction to the attenuation of their trance experience. It might be noted here in passing that they experienced attenuation in the same sequence in which they acquired the trance behavior: first Lorenzo, then Emilio, then Anselmo—with Peregrino somewhere in between. In the case of Emilio this is most clearly evident. In his kinetic patterns he over and over again mimicked trance-produced effects, such as pressure on his chest and what this observer felt was a groping for vocalization. At the same time, his glossolalia was much "weaker" (showing a lower energy level) than it had been the preceding year.

I am also suggesting that Anselmo's and Peregrino's vision experiences resulted from strategies employed to recover former trance levels, mainly fasting and prolonged prayer. When I saw these two men again in the summer of 1970, their glossolalia showed considerable attenuation. My assumption at this point is that hallucinations of this "naturally" (without the use of drugs) induced type are an alternate manifestation of the same hyperarousal that generates (in the Chomskian sense, as explained earlier) the glossolalia; this can, of course, only be a supposition because as yet we know so little about the physiology of hyperarousal. Alternatively, they might possibly be an expression of an even more intense hyperarousal. Fischer (1969: 171) hypothesizes that hallucination represents the point of highest arousal on the perception–hallucination continuum:

> Symbolic interpretations of one's own central nervous system activity, are experiences along the perception–hallucination (dreaming) continuum and can be characterized . . . by an increase in the level of autonomic arousal.

The fact that so many informants report having had a vision of a bright light before achieving vocalization leads me to think that this is at least a reasonable assumption: observational data show that in many instances a great deal of energy is marshaled in order to achieve glossolalia, and we may thus suggest that the initial experience is the hallucination, which is then followed by the vocalization, when some of the accumulated energy is already spent.

In the case of Lorenzo, I am proposing that two mechanisms were at work. One was the attenuation of the trance behavior. His conversion story shows that the trance experience rescued him, he felt permanently, from succumbing to the temptations of the world, which had happened to him several times previously. By the summer of 1970, his glossolalia had to some extent attenuated, and at the same tim he had become extremely fanatical in his religious posture. These facts seem to me to bear out the interpretation that he was experiencing renewed anxieties concerning his ability to resist temptation. At the same time, he also appears to have been subject to considerable culture shock. The Utzpak congregation was the first rural congregation that he had intimate contact with. He was a city man, as mentioned earlier, and his previous experience with evangelizing was acquired almost exclusively in an urban environment.

The behavior of the young women, as I have pointed out, though highly disruptive for the congregation, represents, in my mind, not an initiated comportment, as that of the men, but a reactive one. In other words, I want to argue that their behavior was part of the reaction of the congregation to Lorenzo's withdrawal, although it incorporated some elements specifically their own.

In support of this contention, I should like to offer the following: Lorenzo represented for the congregation the entrance into, and the protection from, the simultaneously desired, hated, and feared urban reality. His prolonged rejection of the group threatened their security more severely than all the other events that were experienced later. La Barre's view of a group that had exhausted all other modes of adaptation and was now engaged in producing a projected sacred system of a father image does not seem applicable here at all. In fact, it was precisely the person representing the father image, if we want to operate in these terms at all, who was withdrawing, who was betraying them; and they were reacting to this betrayal.

If we want to apply a model to this situation, the one that Mannoni (1956) suggests for the environment of colonialism seems much better suited. He postulates that the revolts that broke out in Madagascar when the French colonial administration withdrew after World War II were the result of extreme anxiety reactions developing from a dependency on the colonial masters and the subsequent abandonment by them. In fact, although Mannoni does not see the Madagascar revolts in this light, an upheaval very similar to the Ghost Dance may have taken place there. Witness the resemblance of the charm described in the following account to the magical protective shirt of the latter movement:

> After the "rebels" had attacked Antelomita . . . there was found among the dead a Protestant minister, a Malagasy, and clenched between his teeth was a bit of wood on a string—the *ody-basy*, a charm which is supposed to protect the wearer against rifle-fire. It is placed in the mouth in the moment of danger.[8] (Mannoni, 1956: 149.)

The following example from the Madagascar account is even closer to the events in Utzpak:

> Fear crystallized in the form of terrifying visions. In Madagascar, a number of people claimed to have seen supernatural beings. Reports of a centaur in Vatomandry [where, the author adds in a footnote, a few months later the revolt was to break out with extreme violence] spread terror among the people and they shut themselves up in their houses. (Mannoni, 1956: 136–137.)

To return to the behavior of the young women in Utzpak, they started going into trance roughly in the fall of 1969 and the winter of 1969–1970. It may even be that their earlier pattern of prolonged, delayed return was already a reaction to Lorenzo's behavior. There was initially an infatuation with the suave and fascinating city man. Within the larger society, that is, the village, rumors of seduction kept cropping up during the upheaval, and gossip in the neighborhood of the temple revolved around the behavior of Lorenzo with respect to the young women. Replacing sex with religion, the young women then displaced this infatuation into the religious realm. As Lorenzo began withdrawing, they felt stress building up. Their delayed wakening from the trance may well have had to do with their inability to achieve a discharge of these accumulated tensions. It is significant here that, of the central group of young women in the congregation, only Nina did not experience the delayed return to consciousness. She had had a number of personal disagreements with Lorenzo and was highly critical of him.

In this context, a scene from the July 30 service comes to mind, where Violeta, already on the descending line of her trance behavior that evening, went into a very steep recovery of her energy level when Lorenzo, with the expressed intent of calming her and helping her to waken, put his hand on her head.

Another factor that should not be overlooked is the element of adolescent rebellion, expressed by attacks against some of the older men. Due to longer school attendance and more extensive contact with the life style of Mérida, Violeta and her companions were more oriented toward the city than were their mothers. The young women thus may have turned on the older men in the congregation—Nohoč Felipe and especially Tacho, a man of better than average income—because they did not provide the guidance needed to break into urban ways. We may recall Marta's comment that she would not go home because Satan (meaning her father) was there. This represents once more a transposition of the experiences of this group into the religious sphere, with the Holy Spirit and Christ taking the place of the good father and Satan that of the bad one. Lorenzo, then, represents the ambivalent figure, seducing and yet rejecting them.[9]

The older women did not assume the delayed-return pattern in their trance behavior, and neither were they involved in these personal attacks. "The older women did not speak this way," Eusebia keeps pointing out. Although Lorenzo's withdrawal produced anxiety in them also, as evinced by many statements in this direction, they were not in the same sense dependent on him. In summary, then, I would argue that, as a crisis cult, the Utzpak upheaval was produced not by the congregation's regression to a father figure and their commitment to its highly authoritarian repressive, but rather by Lorenzo's abdicating this role.[10]

THE UPHEAVAL

The evolution of events that flow from these many different sources cannot be meaningfully united into a single strand, as Wallace suggests. Rather, they seem to be arranged on three more or less interacting levels: (1) culture change (2) supernatural premise,[11] and (3) trance behavior.

Culture Change. During the introductory phase, Lorenzo's manner of inducing trance is the first significant independent invention. It is elaborated within a service of prayer for the Holy Spirit that as a result of this innovation becomes more strongly formalized than elsewhere in the Apostolic congregations. The institution of the sections (organizations) of the juveniles and of the women is a borrowing, but in emphasizing in the latter a different role for women it represents a considerable departure from earlier practices. This is underlined by including the women in the trance behavior.

By the summer of 1970, in a period of gathering momentum, there is an increase in the number of services, a possibly borrowed elaboration of the collection of offerings, and Emilio's innovations in the prayer for the sick. Simultaneously, we see a disintegration of the formal prayer for the Holy Spirit.

During the peak, glossolalia is treated as having a concrete message content and is interpreted; it is also employed in exorcism. The customary bell signal for awaking from the trance is discarded, and new strategies are tried: shaking the person, pressing his head or laying hands on it, fanning him, or making him drink water. Common property is proclaimed.

In the platform phase, the disintegration of the structure of the devotional life of the congregation is complete. The *casa pastoral*, the use of which within the prayer activity was already initiated during the peak, is further integrated. The prayer activity is elaborated late in this phase, with the members, instead of kneeling individually, forming a circle. The message content of the trance utterances is further emphasized. Since these trance utterances are now exclusively in ordinary language, they are written down and treated as actual communications from the divine source. Various members of the congregation are expelled. As the result of what I consider to have been a trance-produced pattern of restless wanderings, the behavior of the platform phase spreads to other congregations, specifically to one in which similar conditions with respect to the acquisition of trance prevailed. Color is eliminated (an innovation initiated at N.), and the wearing of white clothing and shoes is introduced.

Property sharing, communal living, and aggressive missionizing disappear in the course of the platform phase. After the upheaval attenuates, only a single one of the many innovations introduced during the upheaval remains in effect in the congregation: the institution of the section of the Dorcas, started early in the evolution of the cult.

In the late postupheaval period, that is, since early in 1970, in the main two new behaviors begin asserting themselves: a search in the Bible for fresh topics and the tendency of many of the members not to stay put during services, but to wander in and out. The former seems to me to be an attempt to intellectualize the experience, a search for meaning. Perhaps the splintering of the group of congregations involved in the cult can also be viewed within this framework: if the by now "conservative" Pentecostal (Apostolic) observance seems lacking in richness of content, perhaps there are more fascinating approaches elsewhere. Similarly, the "revelation" of Don Venancio as well as the dispute of the ministers over the nature of the soul may come under this heading. These concerns seem now to have assumed the same kind of urgency as the earlier eagerness for the trance behavior. For example, on July 8, 1972, the Utzpak congregation was visited by a minister of one of the groups that had been marginally involved in the events at Utzpak. While waiting for the service to begin, this minister became involved with one of the *hermanos* in a discussion of the nature of the body at resurrection. Their dispute became so heated that the visitor, instead of sitting in front and participating actively in the service, as custom demanded, retired angrily to the back. Neither man attended the next service, and although the minister stayed in Utzpak several days longer (he had come with his family to visit his desperately ill father-in-law), he did not come to any more services.

The latter behavior, namely, the tendency to interrupt the experience of the service by going out into the street, may be just that. Without being able to verbalize their need, the *hermanos* may in fact be protecting themselves: by interrupting the ritual, they break the effect it has on them. That this motivation is certainly subconsciously present is shown in my mind also by the cautious avoidance not only of the biblical topics relevant to speaking in tongues as evidenced by the glossolalia of Nohoč Felipe and Valentin in Tibolón, and other "gifts of the Spirit" but also of much of the clapping and other trappings of an "enthusiastic" church service.

However, its meaning may in fact go beyond all this. It may be a symbolic declaration of the fact that the outside world is no longer felt to be inimical. During the upheaval, the *hermanos* pressed against the door of the church from the inside to "keep Satan out." Now the door is kept open, and temple and street merge into one. From here, there is only one more step to the plaza, that is, to a completely secularized life. For instance, Violeta, such a key figure in the upheaval, married *Hermano* Nacho and, although only temporarily, they moved to Mérida. She no longer attends church services. The other young women acted in a similar fashion. On the other hand, the "world," which apparently has lost its threatening aspect, has also lost some of its earlier attraction. The public address system and the record player are locked away, no one seems interested in finding out whether the equipment could be repaired or at what cost. There is no talk of having the congregation contribute money for this purpose, and no one asks the field worker for help in the matter, as certainly would have happened earlier.

In this sense, then, there seems to be a dissolution of the pain of ambivalence, representing, certainly, an important change in attitudes, but no acquisition of new traits, only less resistance to different life ways. Neither the old nor the new life styles seem so crucially important any more. This is perhaps also illustrated by the geographic rather than the extended-family propagation of the splits among the congregations, representing an inadvertently acquired new trait, a step away from kin-oriented and toward a more regionally oriented thinking. Culture change might, then, be thought of as coming in the guise of slight shifts in the image of the world rather than as an incorporation of new traits. The true adaptive change seems to consist of the newly acquired ability to tolerate formerly painful intrusions into the cultural environment.[12]

Supernatural Premise. The supernatural premise is originally derived from the belief system of the Apostolic Church, mainly in the form of the Second Coming and the actual presence of the Holy Spirit in the person speaking in tongues. Satan, of marginal significance initially, is introduced early in the phase of gathering momentum. During the peak, both premises are continually reinforced. Satan possesses Anselmo and needs to be expelled not only from this temporary abode but also from the street in front of the church where he seeks refuge. His attacks confirm the Second Coming symmetrically: the closer Satan comes, the more intensely he mounts his attack, the more imminent the Second Coming. The Holy Spirit is also invested with greater immediate reality, since it is seen "intoxicating" (in the words of the congregation) the young women. Vicente's vision of Christ is a late addition, not supplied until the peak.

During the platform phase, Satan and the Second Coming once more mutually confirm each other. All actions are directed toward the Second

Coming; this is the rationale behind the urge to carry out all the suggestions perceived as instructions for measures necessary to hasten the arrival of the Kingdom of God. As these are being obeyed, Satan presses against the doors and windows, shows his tail, flies over in the shape of an eagle (large black-moth in N.), and moves the chandeliers in the church.

After the dissolution of the platform phase, the figure of Christ, introduced by a late vision, becomes shadowy and unimportant; the Holy Spirit, the Second Coming, and Satan emerge, not disproved, but rather considerably strengthened. However, already at this point, the symmetrical relationship between Satan and the Second Coming begins to dissolve. Satan's role is no longer to demonstrate the imminence of the Second Coming. Instead, he is thought to have tempted the congregation because they belonged to the true church. As the later postupheaval period developed, the relationship between the two premises disappeared entirely, and each one moved separately. The Second Coming is now deeply embedded in the belief system, it is something "everyone knows will happen," nothing can shake this conviction; but the time of its occurrence is once more nebulous. Those that cannot cope with this uncertainty leave the Apostolic Church and join Lorenzo or Don Venancio.

Satan, on the other side, is totally expelled from the community. His exorcism is complete. He has escaped into the bush, where spirits of many different convictions and functions customarily assemble—and there he lies in wait for the unwary, to attack him, as he (or rather a dissolution of his horror into three entities) did Juan.

The trance experience also, and most decisively, confirmed the reality of the Holy Spirit for the congregation. There is an interesting bit of circumstantial evidence concerning this point. Don Venancio and Lorenzo demanded that their converts submit to another baptism. As early as the summer of 1972, *hermanos* whom they had thought to have safely corralled into their new churches came drifting back to their original congregations because they could not face the new baptism. Over and over again, this was the justification they gave for their defection: they spoke with outrage of the requirement of a new baptism. Why should they be so upset about this? I propose that it is because in the minds of the congregation the Holy Spirit is most intimately connected with the baptismal rite. In fact, despite all claims to the contrary, these congregations do not believe in the Trinity. Rather, the Holy Spirit is *the* experienced divinity. And in the upheaval, they experienced it in the most awesome way, as something sacred and also exceedingly dangerous. Another baptism might be an offense against this divine essence. It follows that mention of the Holy Spirit will be avoided with studied care. When in the summer of the 1972 a visiting minister asked in his sermon the rhetorical question, "And when, *hermanos*, has anyone recently received the Holy Spirit in this congregation?" there was not a single "alleluia" or "*Gloria a Dios*" in reply.[13]

Trance Behavior.   Both men and women learn to speak in tongues early in the preparatory phase. Thus the trance behavior is available for the entire congregation, and all of the members are nearly simultaneously subject to the evolution of this behavior pattern. Due to its high visibility, onlookers acquire it spontaneously. Vicente independently discovers hyperventilation and goes into hallucination rather than glossolalia. In the terms of the model suggested on the basis of Salvador's conversion story, Lorenzo, Emilio, and Anselmo and perhaps Peregrino (on whom I have fewer direct observational data) are acting out their responses to the attenuation of the hyperarousal during the phase of gathering momentum.

During the peak, the delayed return to ordinary reality becomes the most important feature. In the platform phase, as is also observed on the individual level elsewhere, suggestibility (or, expressed in other terms, a lowering of inhibition) becomes very pronounced, making the congregation vulnerable to suggestions supplied either internally or from the outside.[14] How compelling this suggestive pattern is in residual hyperarousal is demonstrated by the incident of Cilia's possession. Marta simply predicts it will happen, and instantly a violent possession ensues.

During the platform phase, the hyperarousal is of rather low intensity. It is triggered simply by kneeling down and is facilitated by prolonged fasting. There is hardly any glossolalia any more, the subjects usually keep their eyes wide open, they act "as if drunk," and breathe heavily. On or about August 20, a renewed peak may have occurred (something that also happens in the individual utterance—see Fig. 4), coinciding with a remarkable sensitivity to visual stimuli, such as color and glare. (At this point, I cannot even speculate on the physiology of this, which to my mind is undoubtedly a trance-produced phenomenon.) Subsequently, there is a very rapid drop in, and dissolution of, the hyperarousal.

In the immediate postupheaval phase, this dissolution seemed to be complete. In January 1971, no one in the congregation spoke in tongues. The spring of that year, however, saw a brief renewal of the glossolalia behavior, and there were sporadic occurences even after that. In addition, in May of that year, another possibly related experience was reported: some persons who had been deeply involved in the upheaval reported some puzzling dreams.

This may be a more frequent late occurrence after the waning of a crisis cult than the available reports indicate and may have gone unrecorded because of its lesser visibility. However, in discussing what amounts to crisis cults in the Aztec empire shortly before the arrival of the Spaniards, Séjourné (1964: 50) reports that Moctezuma II ordered everyone who dreamt anything at all about the end of the empire and the arrival of the "Lord of everything" to be brought before him. Disappointed that their dreams contained no definite answer, he had them all killed.

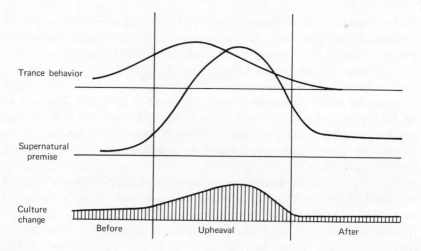

Figure 6. Wave evolution on three levels of the upheaval of the Yucatecan Apostolic congregation.

Another late aftereffect of the trance experience seems to have been that curious gaiety, a "luminous happiness" characterizing the three ministers and
especially also Violeta, whom I saw again in the summer of 1971. The final
dissolution of the last remnants of the group trance experience does not seem
to have occurred before the end of 1971. The diagnostic signal for the com-
pletion of the process may have been the split produced at this time in the congregations by Lorenzo and Don Venancio, representing an attempt at in-
tellectualizing, at conscious integration.

Figure 6 is an attempt to provide a visual representation of the model
contained in the foregoing discussion. Provided a group is subject to certain
very severe stresses and the trance behavior is already available, an upheaval
may ensue, proceeding along three distinct levels. The bottom line on Figure 6
is that of culture change. Certain changes are available to the group and have
already been integrated before the upheaval starts. During the upheaval, there
are many innovations, but these do not persist beyond the attenuation of the
"madness." Rather, the culture-change complex emerges from the chain of
events, not strengthened, not amplified by new elements, but somewhat impoverished, weakened, pallid by comparison with its flow before the upheaval
started.

The supernatural premise, represented in Figure 6 above the level of the
culture change, contains elements originally supplied by the movement of
which the local segment is a part (or possibly by the larger culture, or by inno-

vations developed elsewhere, or within a particular segment of the culture, but always prior to the upheaval). These elements emerge considerably amplified and strengthened by the events of the upheaval. A supernatural premise introduced late (such as in the Christ vision during the peak) does not participate in this confirmation.

The trance behavior, finally, goes through a wave pattern of an onset (in a range above the base line shown in Figure 6 because it apparently needs to be available before the initiation of the upheaval), a rise to a peak, and a gradual attenuation. At one point during the upheaval, the supernatural premises available earlier become strongly enmeshed with the trance behavior, and it is for this reason, I assume, that the supernatural premise emerges confirmed: the trance behavior confirms it.

NOTES

1. This criticism does not quite do justice to Mühlmann, who recognizes the revolutionary (and thus not "contrived") character of the crisis cults: "Die seit einigen Jahrzehnten begonnenen Studien über die nativistischen und messianisch-chiliastischen Bewegungen in diesen Ländern haben deren revolutionäre Grundtendenz eindeutig erwiesen—The studies begun some decades ago of the nativistic and messianic-chiliastic movements in these countries [Sudan, Egypt, Arabia, Iran, and Indonesia] have clearly proven their revolutionary tendencies" (1968: 232).

2. Not, as Ribeiro (1970: 16–17), advances, only in areas where there is a tradition of such cults; rather, the tradition exists everywhere.

3. This runs counter to Festinger's argument (1957) that crisis cults are produced by cognitive dissonance.

4. La Barre, like Wallace (1956) before him, sees religion emerging from crisis cults.

5. In the second edition (1970) of his work *Culture and Personality*, Wallace somewhat expanded the discussion of revitalization movements. The present discussion is based on this version.

6. This view that "hysterical conversion" can be maintained for extended periods contrasts sharply with the hypothesis advanced by Sargant (1959) that conversion experiences represent a temporary but dramatic interruption of normal brain functioning.

7. Lorenzo acquired the trance behavior on August 21, 1968; Emilio, in December 1968; Peregrino, early in 1969 (exact date unknown to me); Anselmo, on July 6, 1969.

8. It is attractive to speculate whether this "Protestant minister" might have been a member of some Pentecostal sect. Pentecostalism was carried to Africa by American-trained Negroes early in this century. "From the 1890's onwards [there was in South Africa] a much larger number of coloured Americans who had come to assist the formation of the independent African churches. Although many of these were from orthodox bodies . . . others, in the new century, came from such millennial and radical groups as the Church of God and the Saints of Christ." (Shepperson, 1970: 152). On the other hand, we must not overlook that Madagascar also has its own possession-trance cults. In either case, with the trance behavior already available in the group, and also with the presence of a dependency–abandonment syndrome, an upheaval similar to the one in Utzpak could easily have arisen.

9. The attacks on Nina and Eusebia were probably derivative, in the sense that they did acquire a coveted guide, a patron in their contact with the urban world, in the person of the anthropologist. "Nina, you will go to perdition because of this diabolical woman," Violeta said on August 20, "ever since she arrived, you became lost."

10. Kildahl (1972), as already mentioned, emphasizes the importance to the glossolalist of the person who guides him into the behavior. He feels that glossolalists, more than other people, have a need to submit to an authority figure. My data, however, show no such agreement in personality structure among the glossolalists.

11. Wallace (1966: 52) defines religion as ritual behavior with a supernatural premise.

12. These findings contradict the views of Wallace when he says, "It is impossible to exaggerate the importance of these two psychological processes (mazeway resynthesis and historical conversion) for culture change, for they make possible the rapid substitution of a new cultural *Gestalt* for an old, and thus the rapid cultural transformation of whole populations" (1970: 198).

13. This is why, I think, the discussion of Festinger et al. (1956) is not relevant here. The group of people who believed that the destruction of the world would take place at a certain date did not go through a confirmatory experience of this type. Only Mrs. Keech, apparently, was in an altered state of consciousness, in which she wrote down her messages. (See Goodman, 1971b for trance and graphic automatisms.)

14. Although not to all such proposals: due perhaps to the much greater social control exerted by the village culture on marriage patterns, the suggestion about indiscriminate marrying in church coming from N., an urban congregation, is not acted on in Utzpak.

Bibliography

ABERLE, DAVID
    1970   A note on relative deprivation theory as applied to millenarian and other cult movements. In *Millennial Dreams in Action*. Sylvia L. Thrupp, Ed. New York: Schocken Books.

ALEXANDER, FRANZ
    1950   *Psychosomatic Medicine: Its Principles and Applications*. New York: W. W. Norton and Company, Inc.

ALLAND, ALEXANDER
    1961   Possession in a revivalist Negro Church. *Journal for the Scientific Study of Religion* **1**, No. 2.

ANONYMOUS
    1967   The Shakers. *Life* **62**: 58–70 (March 17).

ANONYMOUS
    1972   The effects of marijuana on consciousness. In *Altered States of Consciousness*. Charles T. Tart, Ed. Garden City, N.Y.: Doubleday & Company, Inc.

ARNHOFF, FRANKLIN N., HENRY V. LEON, and CHARLES A. BROWNFIELD
    1962   Sensory deprivation: its effects on human learning. *Science* **138**: 899–900.

BARNETT, H. G.
    1957   *Indian Shakers*. Carbondale, Ill.: Southern Illinois University Press.

BASCOM, WILLIAM
    1969   *The Yoruba of Southwestern Nigeria*. New York: Holt, Rinehart and Winston.

BASTIDE, ROGER
    1958   *Le Candomblé de Bahia (rite Nagô)*. Paris: Mouton and Company.
    1960   *Les Religions Africaines au Bresil*. Paris: Presses Universitaires de France.
    1972   *African Civilization in the New World*. New York: Harper Torchbook. (First published as *Les Amériques noires*. Paris: Editions Payot, 1967.)

BELO, JANE
    1960   *Trance in Bali*. New York: Columbia University Press.

BEXTON, W. H., W. HERON, and T. H. SCOTT
    1954   Effects of decreased variation in the sensory environment. *Canadian Journal of Psychology* **8**: 70–76.

BIBLIOGRAFIA GENERAL YUCATANENSE
1944   *Enciclopedia Yucatanese,* Vol. VIII. Ciudad de México: Edición Official de Gobierno de Yucatán.

BOURGUIGON, ERIKA
1954   Reinterpretation and the mechanisms of culture change. *The Ohio Journal of Science* **54:** 329–334.
1965   The theory of spirit possession. In *Context and Meaning in Cultural Anthropology.* Melford E. Spiro, Ed. New York: The Free Press.
1967   Religious syncretism among New World Negroes. Paper presented to the Symposium on the New World Negro, Annual Meeting of the American Anthropological Association.
1968a *Final Report, Cross-Cultural Study of Dissociational States.* Columbus, Ohio: The Ohio State University Research Foundation.
1968b World distribution and patterns of possession states. In *Trance and Possession States.* Raymond Prince, Ed. Montreal: R. M. Bucke Memorial Society.
1972   Dreams and altered states of consciousness in anthropological research. In *Psychological Anthropology.* Francis L. K. Hsu, Ed. Cambridge, Mass.: Schenkman Publishing Company.
1973a Cross-cultural perspectives on the religious uses of altered states of consciousness. In *Religious Responses: Contemporary Movements in America.* Irving I. Zaretsky and Mark P. Leone, Eds. Princeton, N.J.: Princeton University Press.

BOURGUIGNON, ERIKA, EDITOR
1973   *Religion, Altered States of Consciousness and Social Change.* Columbus Ohio: The Ohio State University Press.

BOURGUIGNON, ERIKA, and L. PETTAY
1962   Research Proposal: A Cross-Cultural Study of Dissociational States. Submitted to the National Institute of Mental Health.

BOWEN, MARJORIE
1937   *Wrestling Jacob.* London: William Heinemann, Ltd.

BROWN, DIANA
1971   Umbanda: Patron–client relations in an urban religious movement. Paper presented to the 70th Annual Meeting of the American Anthropological Association, New York, November 17–20.

BURNS, SIR ALAN
1954   *History of the British West Indies.* London: George Allen & Unwin.

BURRIDGE, KENELM (K.O.L.)
1954   Cargo cult activity in Tangu. *Oceania* **24:** 241–253.
1960   *Mambu: A Melanesian Millenium.* London: Methuen & Co., Ltd.
1969   *New Heaven, New Earth: A Study of Millenarian Activities.* New York: Schocken Books.

CAMARGO, CANDIDO PROCOPIO FERREIRA DE
1961 *Kardecismo e Umbanda: Uma Interpretação Sociológica.* São Paulo: Livraria Pioneira Editôra.

CARIBBEAN MONTHLY BULLETIN
1967 February

CARMICHAEL, MRS.
1833 *Domestic Manner and Social Conditions of the White, Coloured, and Negro Population of the West Indies.* 2 vols. London: Whittaker, Treacher, and Co.

CARR, ANDREW T.
1953 A Rada community in Trinidad. *Caribbean Quarterly* 3: 36–54.

CASTANEDA, CARLOS
1968 *The Teachings of Don Juan: A Yaqui Way of Knowledge.* Berkeley and Los Angeles: University of California Press.

CHARDON, ROLAND E.
1966 Changes in the geographic distribution of population in Brazil, 1950–1960. In *New Perspectives of Brazil.* Eric N. Baklanoff, Ed. Nashville, Tenn.: Vanderbilt Unversity Press.

CHOMSKY, NOAM
1964 Current issues in linguistic theory. In *The Structure of Language.* Jerry Fodor and Jerold J. Kats, Eds. Englewood Cliffs, N.J.: Prentice-Hall.

CLARK, ELMER T.
1937 *The Small Sects in America.* Nashville, Tenn.: Cokesbury Press.

COELHO, RUY
1948 The Black Caribs of Central America: A Problem in Three-Way Acculturation. Unpublished manuscript.

COHEN, SANFORD I., ALBERT J. SILVERMAN, BERNARD BRESSLER, and BARRY SHMAVONIAN
1961 Problems in isolation studies. In *Sensory Deprivation.* Philip Solomon, Philip Kubzansky, P. Herbert Leiderman, Jack H. Mendelson, Richard Trumbull, and Donald Wexler, Eds. Cambridge, Mass.: Harvard University Press.

CRUZ, PACHECO
1963 *Compendio del idioma maya.* VI edición. Mérida, Yucatán: Imprenta "Manlio."

CURTIN, PHILIP D.
1955 *Two Jamaicas.* Cambridge, Mass.: Harvard University Press.

CUTTEN, G. B.
1927 *Speaking with Tongues: Historically and Psychologically Considered.* New Haven; Conn.: Yale University Press.

DARMADJI, TJIPTONO, and WOLFGANG PFEIFFER
1969 Kuda Kepang—ein javanisches Trancespiel. *Selecta* No. 41: 3283–3290.

DAVENPORT, FREDERICK M.
   1965   Primitive traits in religious revivals. In *Life in Society*. Thomas E. Lass-
          well, John H. Burma, and Sidney H. Aronson, Eds. Chicago: Scott,
          Foresman and Company.

DEFRADOS, JEAN
   1968   La divination en Grèce. In *La Divination*, Vol. I. André Caquot and
          Marcel Leibovici, Eds. Paris: Presses universitaires de France, pp.
          157–195.

DOANE, B. K., WINSTON MAHATOO, W. HERON, and T. H. SCOTT
   1959   Changes in perceptual function after isolation. *Canadian Journal of
          Psychology* 13: 210–219.

DORSAINVIL, J. C.
   1931   *Vodou et Névrose, Port-au-Prince, Haiti.*

DREW, SAMUEL
   1818   *The Life of the Rev. Thomas Coke, LL.D.* New York: J. Soule and T.
          Mason.

DULLES, JOHN W. F.
   1966   Post-dictatorship Brazil, 1945–1965. In *New Perspectives of Brazil*. Eric
          N. Baklanoff, Ed. Nashville Tenn.: Vanderbilt University Press.

DUNCAN, EBENEZER
   1963   *A Brief History of Saint Vincent with Studies in Citizenship*. Kingstown,
          St. Vincent: Government Printing Office. (First edition, 1941).

FESTINGER, LEON
   1957   *A Theory of Cognitive Dissonance*. Evanston Ill.: Row, Peterson and
          Company.

FESTINGER, LEON, HENRY W., RIECKEN, and STANLEY SCHACHTER
   1956   *When Prophecy Fails*. New York: Harper Torchbook.

FIELD, M. J.
   1960   *Search for Security: An Ethno-psychiatric Study of Rural Ghana*.
          Evanston, Ill.: Northwestern University Press.

FISCHER, ROLAND
   1969   The perception–hallucination continuum. A re-examination. *Diseases of
          the Nervous System* 30: 161:171.
   1970   Uber das Rhythmisch-Ornamentale im Halluzinatorisch-Schöpferischen.
          Confinia Psychiatrica 13: 1–25.
   1972   On separateness and oneness, an I–self dialogue. *Confinia Psychiatrica* (in
          press).

FOSTER, GEORGE M.
   1961   The dyadic contract: a model for the social structure of a Mexican peasant
          Village. *American Anthropologist* 63: 1173–1192.

FREED, STANLEY A., and RUTH S. FREED
   1964   Spirit possession as illness in a North Indian village. *Ethnology* 3: 152–71.

FREEDMAN, SANFORD J., HENRY U. GRUNEBAUM, and MILTON GREENBLATT
1961 Perceptual and cognitive changes in sensory deprivation. In *Sensory Deprivation*. P. Solomon, P. Kubzansky, P. Leiderman, J. Mendelson, R. Trumbull, and D. Wexler, Eds. Cambridge, Mass.: Harvard University Press.

FUCHS, PETER
1960 Der Margai-Kult der Hadjerai. *Mitteilungen der Anthropologischen Gesellschaft in Wien*, No. 90.

GARCIA, A.
1965 *History of the West Indies*. London: George G. Harrap & Co.

GARRISON, VIVIAN
1973 Marginal religion and psychosocial deviancy: a controlled comparison of Puerto Rican Pentecostals and Catholics. in *Religious Responses: Contemporary Movements in America*. Irving I. Zaretsky and Mark P. Leone, Eds. Princeton, N.J.: Princeton University Press.

GAXIOLA, MACLOVIO L.
1964 *Historia de la Iglesia Apóstolica de la fe en Cristo Jesus de México*. México, D.F.: Librería Latinoamericana.

GERLACH, LUTHER P., and VIRGINIA H. HINE
1968 Five factors crucial to the growth and spread of a modern religious movement. *Journal for the Scientific Study of Religion* 7: 23–40.

GILL, M., and M. BRENMAN
1961. *Hypnosis and Related States: Psychoanalytic Studies in Regression*. New York: International Universities Press.

GLUCKMAN, MAX
1954 *Rituals of Rebellion in South-East Africa*. Manchester, England: Manchester University Press.

GOODENOUGH, WARD
1963 *Cooperation in Change*. New York: Russell Sage Foundation.

GOODMAN, FELICITAS D.
1968 Glossolalia: speaking in tongues in four cultural settings. Cross-Cultural Study of Dissociational States, Working Paper No. 24. Department of Anthropology, the Ohio State University.
1969a Glossolalia: speaking in tongues in four cultural settings. *Confinia Psychiatrica* 12: 113–129.
1969b Phonetic analysis of glossolalia in four cultural settings. *Journal for the Scientific Study of Religion* 8: 227–239.
1971a The acquisition of glossolalia behavior. *Semiotica* 3: 77–82.
1971b Glossolalia and single-limb trance: Some parallels. *Psychotherapy and Psychosomatics* 19: 92–103.
1972a *Speaking in Tongues: A Cross-Cultural Study of Glossolalia*. Chicago: Chicago University Press.

1972b Features of glossolalia behavior and human sexual response. Paper presented to the 71st Meeting of the American Anthropological Association, Toronto, December 2.

1973a The Apostolics of Yucatán: a case study of a religious movement. In *Religion, Altered States of Consciousness, and Social Change.* Erika Bourguignon, Ed. Columbus; Ohio: The Ohio State University Press.

1973b Glossolalia and hallucination in Pentecostal congregations. *Psychiatria Clinica* **6**: 97–103.

1973c Prognosis: a new religion? In *Religious Responses: Contemporary Movements in America.* Irving I. Zaretsky and Mark P. Leone, Eds. Princeton, N.J.: Princeton University Press.

GOVEIA, ELSA V.

1965   *Slave Society in the British Leeward Islands at the End of the Eighteenth Century.* New Haven Conn.: Yale University Press.

1966   Comment on "Anglicanism, Catholicism, and the Negro slave." *Comparative Studies in Society and History* **8**: 328–330.

GREAT BRITAIN COLONIAL OFFICE

1966   *St. Vincent: Annual Report for the Years 1962 and 1963.* Colonial Office Colonial Annual Report Series. London: Her Majesty's Stationery Office.

GREENBAUM, LENORA

1973   Societal correlates of possession trance in Sub-Saharan Africa. In *Religion, Altered States of Consciousness, and Social Change.* Erika Bourguignon, Ed. Columbus, Ohio: The Ohio State University Press.

GUSSLER, JUDITH

1973   Social change, ecology, and spirit possession among the South African Nguni. In *Religion, Altered States of Consciousness, and Social Change.* Erika Bourguignon, Ed. Columbus, Ohio: The Ohio State University Press.

HADLEY, C. V. D.

1949   Personality patterns, social class, and aggression in the British West Indies. *Human Relations* **11**: 349–362.

HARRIS, GRACE

1957   Possession 'hysteria' in a Kenya tribe. *American Anthropologist* **59**: 1046–1066.

HARRIS, MARVIN

1970   Referential ambiguity in the calculus of Brazilian racial identity. *Southwestern Journal of Anthropology* **26**: 1–14.

HENNEY, JEANNETTE H.

1966   The Luo and Mr. Gluckman. Paper presented at the 75th Annual Meeting of the Ohio Academy of Science, Columbus, Ohio.

1967   Trance behavior among the shakers of St. Vincent. The Ohio State University Cross-Cultural Study of Dissociational States, Working Paper No. 8.

1968   Spirit Possession Belief and Trance Behavior in a Religious Group in St. Vincent, British West Indies. Unpublished Ph.D. thesis, the Ohio State University, Columbus, Ohio.

1972   The relationship of trance and sex in a West Indies religious group. Paper presented to the Symposium on Trance and Sex at the 71st Annual Meeting of the American Anthropological Association, Toronto.

1973   The Shakers of St. Vincent: a stable religion. In *Religion, Altered States of Consciousness, and Social Change.* Erika Bourguignon, Ed. Columbus, Ohio: The Ohio State University Press.

HERON, WOODBURN

1966   Cognitive and physiological effects of perceptual isolation. In *Sensory Deprivation.* Philip Solomon, Philip Kubzansky, P. Herbert Leiderman, Jack H. Mendelson, Richard Trumbull, and Donald Wexler, Eds. Cambridge, Mass.: Harvard University Press.

HERON, WOODBURN, B. K. DOANE, and T. H. SCOTT

1956   Visual disturbances after prolonged perceptual isolation. *Canadian Journal of Psychology* **10:** 13–18.

HERSKOVITS, M. J.

1937a   *Life in a Haitian Valley.* New York: Alfred A. Knopf.

1937b   African gods and Catholic saints in New World Negro belief. *American Anthropologist* **39:** 635–643.

1943   The southernmost outposts of New World Africanisms. *American Anthropologist* **45:** 495–510.

1947   *Man and His Works.* New York: Alfred A. Knopf.

1948   The contribution of Afroamerican studies to Africanist research. *American Anthropologist* **50:** 1–10.

1958   *The Myth of the Negro Past.* (First published in 1941, Harper.) Boston: Beacon Press.

1959   The Panan: an Afrobahian religious rite of transition. *Caribbean Quarterly* **5:** 276–283.

1966   The social organization of the Candomblé. In *The New World Negro: Selected Papers in Afro-American Studies.* Frances S. Herskovits, Ed. Bloomington: Indiana University Press.

HERSKOVITS, M. J., and FRANCES S. HERSKOVITS

1936   *Suriname Folk-lore.* New York: Columbia University Press.

1947   *Trinidad Village.* New York: Alfred A. Knopf.

HIME, VIRGINIA H.

1969   Pentecostal glossolalia: toward a functional interpretation. *Journal for the Scientific Study of Religion* **8:** 211–226.

HOGG, DONALD

1960   *The Convince Cult in Jamaica.* Yale University Publications in Anthropology, 58.

JACKSON, C. WESLEY, JR., and E. LOWELL KELLY
1962   Influence of suggestion and subjects' prior knowledge in research on sensory deprivation. *Science* **135**: 211–212.

JACKSON, C. WESLEY, JR., and JOHN C. POLLARD
1962   Sensory deprivation and suggestion: a theoretical approach. *Behavioral Science* **7**: 332:342.

JACKSON, THOMAS
1839   *The Century of Wesleyan Methodism: A Brief Sketch of the Rise, Progress, and Present State of the Wesleyan Methodist Societies throughout the World.* New York: T. Mason and G. Lane.

JAQUITH, JAMES R.
1967   Toward a typology of formal communicative behavior: glossolalia. *Anthropological Linguistics* **9**(8): 1–8.

KILDAHL, JOHN P.
1972   *The Psychology of Speaking in Tongues.* New York: Harper and Row.

KLEIN, HERBERT S.
1966   Anglicanism, Catholicism, and the Negro slave. *Comparative Studies in Society and History* **8**: 295–327.

KOPYTOFF, IGOR
1965   The Suku of southwestern Congo. In *Peoples of Africa.* James L. Gibbs. Ed. New York: Holt, Rinehart and Winston, Inc.

KRACKE, WAUD H.
1967   The maintenance of the ego: Implications of sensory deprivation research for psychoanalytic ego psychology. *British Journal of Medical psychology* **40**:17–28.

LA BARRE, WESTON
1962   *They Shall Take up Serpents.* Minneapolis: University of Minnesota Press.
1970   *The Ghost Dance: The Origins of Religion.* Garden City, N.Y.: Doubleday.
1971   Materials for a history of studies of crisis cults: a bibliographic essay. *Current Anthropology* **12**: 3–45.

LALIVE D'EPINAY, CHRISTIAN
1968   *El Refugio de las Masas.* Santiago, Chile: Editorial del Pacífico.

LANDA, FRAY DIEGO DE
1959   *Relación de las Cosas de Yucatán.* Biblioteca Porrua, 13. México D.F.: Editorial Porrua.

LANDES, RUTH
1940   A cult matriarchate and male homosexuality. *Journal of Abnormal and Social Psychology* **35**: 387–397.
1947   *The City of Women.* New York: Macmillan Company.

LAWRENCE, P.
1954 Cargo cult and religious beliefs among the Garia. *International Archives of Anthropology* **47**(1): 1–20.
1955 The Madang District cargo cult. *South Pacific* **8**(1): 6–13.

LEACOCK, SETH, and RUTH LEACOCK
1972 *Spirits of the Deep: A Study of an Afro-Brazilian Cult.* Garden City, N.Y.: Doubleday Natural History Press.

LEIRIS, MICHEL
1958 La possession et ses aspêts théâtraux ches les Ethiopiens de Gondar. *L'Home* **1.** Paris: Plon.

LERCH, PATRICIA
1972 The Role of Women in Possession-Trance Cults in Brazil. Unpublished M.A. thesis, the Ohio State University.

LESSA, WILLIAM A., and EVAN Z. VOGT, EDS.
1965 *Reader in Comparative Religion: An Anthropological Approach.* New York: Harper and Row.

LEVY, MARIA STELLA
1968 The Umbanda Is for All of Us. Unpublished M.A. thesis, the University of Wisconsin.

LEWIS, I. M.
1966 Spirit possession and deprivation cults. *Man,* n.s., **I:** 307–329.
1971 *Ecstatic Religion: An Anthropological Study of Spirit Possession and Shamanism.* Middlesex, England: Penguin Books.

LINDSAY, GORDON, ED.
n.d. *William Branham Sermons: How God Called Me to Africa and Other Sermons.* Dallas, Texas: The Voice of Healing Press.

LINDSAY, GORDON, with WILLIAM BRANHAM
1950 *A Man Sent from God.* Jeffersonville, Ind. William Branham.

LINTON, RALPH
1943 Nativistic movements. *American Anthropologist* **45:** 230–240. Reprinted in *Reader in Comparative Religion: An Anthropological Approach.* Second Edition. William A. Lessa and Evan Z. Vogt, Eds. New York: Harper and Row.

LOPEZ, JUAREZ R. B.
1966 Some basic developments in Brazilian politics and society. In *New Perspectives of Brazil.* Eric N. Baklanoff, Ed. Nashville Tenn.: Vanderbilt University Press.

LOWENTHAL, DAVID
1967 Race and color in the West Indies. *Daedalus* **96:** 580–626.

LUDWIG, ARNOLD M.
1966 Altered states of consciousness. *Archives of General Psychiatry* **15:**

225–234. Reprinted in Trance and Possession States. Raymond Prince, Ed. Montreal: R. M. Bucke Memorial Society, 1968.

1972   Altered states of consciousness. In *Altered States of Consciousness*. Charles T. Tart, Ed. Garden City, N.Y.: Doubleday & Company, Inc.

MANNONI, O.

1956   *Prospero and Caliban: The Psychology of Colonization*. Translated by Pamela Powesland. New York: Frederick A. Praeger.

MATHIESON, WILLIAM LAW

1926   *British Slavery and Its Abolition*. London: Longmans, Green and Co., Ltd.

MAY, L. CARLYLE

1956   A survey of glossolalia and related phenomena in non-Christian religions. *American Anthropologist* 58: 75–96.

MCGREGOR, PEDRO

1967   *Jesus of the Spirits*. New York: Stein and Day.

MEDELSON, JACK H., PHILIP E. KUBZANSKY, P. HERBERT LEIDERMAN, DONALD WEXLER, and PHILIP SOLOMON

1961   Physiological and psychological aspects of sensory deprivation—a case analysis. In *Sensory Deprivation*. P. Solomon, P. Kubzansky, P. Leiderman, J. Mendelson, R. Trumbull, D. Wexler, Eds. Cambridge, Mass.: Harvard University Press.

METRAUX, ALFRED

1959   *Voodoo in Haiti*. New York: Oxford University Press.

MINTZ, SIDNEY

1960   Peasant markets. *Scientific American* 203: 112–118, 120, 122.

1964   The employment of capital by market women in Haiti. In *Capital, Saving and Credit in Peasant Societies*. Raymond Firth and B. S. Yancey, Eds. Chicago: Aldine Publishing Co.

1966   The Caribbean as a socio-cultural area. *Journal of World History* 9: 911–937.

MISCHEL, FRANCES OSTERMAN

1958   A Shango religious group and the problem of prestige in Trinidadian society, Ph.D. dissertation, the Ohio State University, Columbus, Ohio.

MISCHEL, WALTER, and FRANCES MISCHEL

1958   Psychological aspects of spirit possession. *American Anthropologist* 60: 249–260.

MOLINA, FONT GUSTAVO

1965   *Gesta de los Mayas y otros relatos del viejo Yucatán*. México: León Sanchez.

MOONEY, JAMES

1896   *The Ghost Dance Religion and the Sioux Outbreak of 1890*. Fourteenth Annual Report, Bureau of American Ethnology, Part 2.

MOORE, JOSEPH G.
  1965   Religious syncretism in Jamaica. *Practical Anthropology* **12**: 63–70.

MOORE, J. G. and G. E. SIMPSON
  1957–   A comparative study of acculturation in Morant Bay and West Kingston,
  1958   Jamaica. *Zaire* **11**: 979–1019; **12**: 65–87.

MORLEY, SYLVANUS G.
  1956   *The Ancient Maya.* Third Edition. Stanford, Calif.: Stanford University
          Press.

MÜHLMANN, WILHELM E.
  1968   *Geschichte der Anthropologie.* Second Edition. Frankfurt am Main:
          Anthenäum Verlag.

MURDOCK, G. P.
  1967   *Ethnographic Atlas: A Summary.* Pittsburgh: University of Pittsburgh
          Press.

NADEL, S. F.
  1946   A study of shamanism in the Nuba Mountains. *Journal of the Royal
          Anthropological Institute* **76**: 25–37.

NICHOL, JOHN THOMAS
  1966   *Pentecostalism.* New York: Harper & Row.

OAKES, MAUD
  1951   *The Two Crosses of Todos Santos.* Princeton, N.J.: University of
          Princeton Press.

ORNE, MARTIN T., and KARL E. SCHEIBE
  1964   The contribution of nondeprivation factors in the production of sensory
          deprivation effects: the psychology of the "panic button." *Journal of
          Abnormal and Social Psychology* **68**: 3–12.

PALMER, GARY
  1966   Trance and Dissociation: A Cross-Cultural Study in Psychological
          Physiology. Unpublished M.A. thesis, University of Minnesota.

PATTISON, E. MANSELL
  1968   Behavioral science research on the nature of glossolalia. *Journal of the
          American Scientific Affiliation* September: 73–86.

PAUL, BENJAMIN D.
  1967   Mental disorder and self-regulating processes in culture: a Guatemalan
          illustration. In *Personalities and Cultures.* Robert Hunt, Ed. Garden City,
          N.Y.: The Natural History Press.

POPPINO, ROLLIE E.
  1968   *Brazil: The Land and People.* New York: Oxford University Press.

POUILLON, JEAN
  1964   La structure du pouvoir chez les Hadjerai (Tchad). *L'Homme: Revue
          française d'anthropologie* **4**: 17–70.

POWDERMAKER, HORTENSE

1966   *Stranger and Friend: The Way of an Anthropologist*. New York: W. W. Norton & Co.

PRESSEL, ESTHER

1972   Spiritual dichotomy in social relations between men and women. Paper presented to the 71st Annual Meeting of the American Anthropological Association, New York, November 29 to December 3.

RAE, JAMES STANLEY

1927   *The Laws of St. Vincent Containing the Ordinances of the Colony in Force on the 4th Day of May, 1926*. Revised Edition, 2 vols. Millbank, S. W. I.: Crown Agents for the Colonies.

RAGATZ, LOWELL JOSEPH

1928   *The Fall of the Planter Class in the British Caribbean, 1763–1833*. New York: The Century Co.

REDFIELD, ROBERT

1941   *The Folk Culture of Yucatán*. Chicago: The University of Chicago Press.

1950   *A Village That Chose Progress*. Chicago: The Chicago University Press.

1960   *The Little Community: Peasant Society and Culture*. Chicago and London: Chicago University Press.

REED, NELSON

1964   *The Caste War of Yucatán*. Stanford Calif.: Stanford University Press.

RENSHAW, PARKE

1966   A new religion for Brazilians. *Practical Anthropology* **13**: 126–138.

RIBEIRO, RENE

1956   Possessão—Problema de etnopsicologia. *Boletim do Instituto Joaquim Nebuco* **5**: 5–44.

1970   Brazilian messianic cults. In *Millennial Dreams in Action*. Sylvia L. Thrupp, Ed. New York: Schocken Books.

SALER, BENSON

1967   Nagual, witch, and sorcerer in a Quiché village. In *Magic, Witchcraft, and Curing*. John Middleton, Ed. Garden City, N.Y.: The Natural History Press.

SAMARIN, WILLIAM J.

1968   The linguisticality of glossolalia. *The Hartford Quarterly* **8**(4): 49–75.

SANTOS, JOHN F.

1966   A psychologist reflects on Brazil and Brazilians. In *New Perspectives of Brazil*. Eric N. Baklanoff, Ed. Nashville, Tenn.: Vanderbilt University Press.

SARGANT, WILLIAM

1959   *Battle for the Mind*. (First published in 1957 by Wm. Heinemann Ltd. London, Pan Books Ltd.) Garden City, N.Y.: Doubleday.

SCOTT, T. H., W. H. BEXTON, W. HERON, and B. K. DOANE
1959   Cognitive effects of perceptual isolation. *Canadian Journal of Psychology* 13: 200–209.

SEJOURNE, LAURETTE
1964   *Pensamiento y religión en el México antiguo.* México: Fondo de Cultura Económica.

SHEPPERSON, GEORGE
1970   Nyasaland and the millennium. In *Millenial Dreams in Action. Sylvia L. Thrupp, Ed. New York: Schocken Books.*

SHERRILL, JOHN L.
1964   *They Speak with Other Tongues.* New York: McGraw-Hill Book Co., Inc.

SHURLEY, JAY T.
1962   Mental imagery in profound experimental sensory isolation. In *Hallucinations.* Louis Jolyon West, Ed. New York: Grune & Stratton.

SILVER, DANIEL B.
1966   Zinacantan Shamanism. Ph.D. dissertation, Harvard University.

SILVERMAN, A. J., S. I. COHEN, B. BRESSLER, and H. SHMAVONIAN
1962   Hallucinations in sensory deprivation. In *Hallucinations.* Louis Jolyon West, Ed. New York: Grune & Stratton.

SIMEY, T. S.
1947   *Welfare and Planning in the West Indies.* (First edition published in 1946.) London: Oxford University Press.

SIMPSON, GEORGE E.
1956   Jamaican revivalist cults. *Social and Economic Studies* 5: i–xi; 321–442.
1961   *Cult Music of Trinidad.* Folkways Ethnic Album FE 4478. New York: Folkways Records and Service Corp.
1962   Social stratification in the Caribbean. *Phylon* 23: 29–46.
1964   The acculturative process in Trinidadian Shango. *Anthropological Quarterly* 37: 16–27.
1965   *The Shango Cult in Trinidad.* Caribbean Monograph Series, No. 2.
1966   Baptismal, "mourning," and "building" ceremonies of the Shouters in Trinidad. *Journal of American Folklore* 79: 537–550.
1970   *Religious Cults of the Caribbean: Trinidad, Jamaica, and Haiti.* Caribbean Monograph Series, No. 7.

SIMPSON, GEORGE E., and PETER B. HAMMOND
1960   Discussion on "The African Heritage in the Caribbean." In *Caribbean Studies: A Symposium.* Vera Rubin, Ed. Seattle: University of Washington Press.

SINGER, PAULO
1965   A política das classes dominantes. In *Política e Revolução Social no Brasil.* Octávio Ianni, Paulo Singer, Gabriel Singer, and Francisco C. Weffort, Eds. Rio de Janeiro: Editôra Civilização Brasileira S.A.

SMITH, M. G.
  1960   The African heritage in the Caribbean. In *Caribbean Studies: A Symposium*. Vera Rubin, ED. Seattle: University of Washington Press.
  1962   *Kinship and Community in Carriacou*. New Haven, Conn.: Yale University Press.
  1963   *Dark Puritan*. Kingston, Jamaica: Department of Extra-mural Studies, University of the West Indies.
  1965   *The Plural Society In the British West Indies*. Berkeley: University of California Press.

SMYTHIES, J. R.
  1956   A logical and cultural analysis of hallucinatory sense-experience. *Journal of Mental Science* 102: 336–342.

SOLOMON, PHILIP, and JACK MENDELSON
  1962   Hallucinations in sensory deprivation. In *Hallucinations*. Louis Jolyon West, Ed. New York: Grune & Stratton.

SOUTHEY, ROBERT
  1925   *The Life of Wesley and the Rise and Progress of Methodism*. 2 vols. Maurice H. Fitzgerald, Ed. London: Oxford University Press.

SPOERRI, THEODOR
  1963   *Schall und Ton in der Medizin*. München: J. P. Lehmanns Verlag.
  1968   Ekstatische Rede und Glossolalie. In *Beiträge zur Ekstase*. Th. Spoerri, Ed. Bibliotheca Psychiatrica et Neurologica No. 134. Basel: S. Karger.

STAINBROOK, EDWARD
  1952   Some characteristics of the psychopathology of schizophrenic behavior in Bahian society. *American Journal of Psychiatry* 109: 330–334.

THRUPP, SYLVIA L.
  1970   *Millennial Dreams in Action: Studies in Revolutionary Religious Movements*. New York: Schocken Books.

VERNON, JACK A.
  1963   *Inside the Black Room*. New York: Clarkson N. Potter.

VERNON, JACK, and JOHN HOFFMAN
  1956   Effect of sensory deprivation on learning rate in human beings. *Science* 123: 1074–1075.

VERNON, JACK, and THOMAS E. MCGILL
  1957   The effect of sensory deprivation upon rote learning. *American Journal of Psychology* 70: 637–639.

VERNON, JACK, THOMAS E. MCGILL, and HAROLD SCHIFFMAN
  1958   Visual hallucinations during perceptual isolation. *Canadian Journal of Psychology* 12: 31–34.

VILLA ROJAS, ALFONSO
  1937   El culto de la Cruz que Habla entre los mayas del Territorio de Quintana Roo. *Diario del Sureste, 20 de noviembre*. Mérida, Yucatán.

1945 *The Maya of East Central Quintana Roo.* Washington, D.C.: Carnegie Institution.

VIVIER VAN ETFELDT L. M.
1968 The glossolalic and his personality. In *Beiträge zur Ekstase. Theodor Spoerri, Ed. Psychiatrica et Neurologica No. 134.* Basel: S. Karger.

VOGT, EGON Z.
1969 *Zinacantan: A Maya Community in the Highlands of Chiapas.* Cambridge, Mass.: The Belknap Press of Harvard University Press.

WAGLEY, CHARLES
1963 *An Introduction to Brazil.* New York: Columbia University Press.
1971 *An Introduction to Brazil.* Revised Edition. New York: Columbia University Press.

WALLACE, ANTHONY F. C.
1956 Revitalization Movements. *American Anthropologist* **58:** 264–281.
1959 Cultural determinants of response to hallucinatory experience. *AMA Archives of General Psychiatry* **I:** 58–69.
1961 *Cultural and Personality.* New York: Random House.
1966 *Religion: An Anthropological View.* New York: Random House.
1970 *Culture and Personality.* Second Edition. New York: Random House.

WALLACE, ANTHONY F. C., and RAYMOND D. FOGELSON
1965 The identity struggle. In *Intensive Family Therapy.* Ivan Boszormenyi-Nagy and James L. Framo, Eds. New York: Harper & Row.

WEBER, MAX
1958 *The Protestant Ethic and the Spirit of Capitalism.* (First published 1904–1905.) Translated by Talcott Parson. New York: Charles Scribner's Sons.

WEINSTEIN, EDWIN A.
1962 Social aspects of hallucinations. In *Hallucinations.* Louis Jolyon West, Ed. New York: Grun& Stratton.

WILLEMS, EMILIO
1966 Religious mass movements and social change in Brazil. In *New Perspectives of Brazil.* Eric N. Baklanoff, Ed. Nashville, Tenn.: Vanderbilt University Press.
1967 *Followers of the New Faith: Culture Change and the Rise of Protestantism in Brazil and Chile.* Nashville, Tenn.: Vanderbilt University Press.

WILLIAMS, F. E.
1923 *The Vailala Madness.* Port Moresby: Territory of Papua, Anthropology Report No. 4. Bobbs-Merrill Reprints in Anthropology, A-241.

WILLIAMS, THOMAS RHYS
1967 *Field Methods in the Study of Culture.* New York: Holt, Rinehart and Winston.

WINDWARD ISLANDS POPULATION CENSUS
  1960   Trinidad: Central Statistical Office.

WOLF, ERIC R.
  1966   *Peasants.* Englewood Cliffs, N.J.: Prentice Hall.
  1969   *Peasant Wars of the Twentieth Century.* New York: Harper & Row.

WOLFRAM, WALTER A.
  1966   The Sociolinguistics of Glossolalia. Unpublished M.A. thesis, Hartford
          Seminary Foundation.

WORSLEY, PETER
  1968   *The Trumpet Shall Sound.* New York: Schocken Books; London:
          MacGibbon & Kee.

YINGER, J. MILTON
  1946   *Religion in the Struggle for Power.* Durham, N.C.: Duke University
          Press.
  1957   *Religion, Society and the Individual.* New York: Macmillan Co.

ZUBEK, J. P.
  1964   Effects of prolonged sensory and perceptual deprivation. *British Medical
          Bulletin* **20:** 38–42.

ZUBEK, J. P., D. PYSHKAR, W. SANSOM, and J. GOWING
  1961   Perceptual changes after prolonged perceptual isolation. *Canadian Journal
          of Psychology* **15:** 83–100.

ZUBEK, JOHN P., WILMA SANSOM, and A. PRYSIANZNIUK
  1960   Intellectual changes during prolonged perceptual isolation (darkness and
          silence). *Canadian Journal of Psychology* **14:** 233–243.

ZUCKERMAN, MARVIN
  1969a   Hallucinations, reported sensations, and images. In *Sensory Deprivation:
          Fifteen Years of Research.* John P. Zubek, Ed. New York: Appleton-
          Century-Crofts.
  1969b   Theoretical formulations: I. In *Sensory Deprivation: Fifteen Years of Re-
          search.* John P. Zubek, Ed. New York: Appleton-Century-Crofts.

Index

Pronunciation

For the pronunciation of Portuguese words, see p. 114.

Maya vowels have the same quality as Spanish ones, with these exceptions: double vowel indicates length, and an acute accent makes the vowel high-toned. As to consonants, the ? symbol stands for the glottal stop; č is pronounced like ch in child; š is like sh in shoe. In the Spanish transcription of Mayan place names, dz equals ts?, and k is k?.